Facilitating Higher Education Growth through Fundraising and Philanthropy

Henry C. Alphin Jr.
Drexel University, USA

Jennie Lavine
Higher Colleges of Technology, United Arab Emirates

Stormy Stark
Pennsylvania State University, USA

Adam Hocker
Pennsylvania State University, USA

A volume in the Advances in Educational Marketing, Administration, and Leadership (AEMAL) Book Series

Published in the United States of America by
Information Science Reference (an imprint of IGI Global)
701 E. Chocolate Avenue
Hershey PA 17033
Tel: 717-533-8845
Fax: 717-533-8661
E-mail: cust@igi-global.com
Web site: http://www.igi-global.com

Library of Congress Cataloging-in-Publication Data

Names: Alphin, Henry C., Jr., 1977-
Title: Facilitating higher education growth through fundraising and
  philanthropy / Henry C. Alphin Jr., Jennie Lavine, Storny Stark, and Adam
  Hocker, editors.
Description: Hershey, PA : Information Science Reference, 2016. | Includes
  bibliographical references and index.
Identifiers: LCCN 2015037567| ISBN 9781466696648 (hardcover) | ISBN
  9781466696655 (ebook)
Subjects: LCSH: Education, Higher--Finance. | Universities and
  colleges--Finance. | Educational fund raising. | Charitable uses, trusts,
  and foundations.
Classification: LCC LB2341.98 .F34 2016 | DDC 378.1/06--dc23 LC record available at http://lccn.
loc.gov/2015037567

This book is published in the IGI Global book series Advances in Educational Marketing, Administration, and Leadership (AEMAL) (ISSN: 2326-9022; eISSN: 2326-9030)

British Cataloguing in Publication Data
A Cataloguing in Publication record for this book is available from the British Library.

Advances in Educational Marketing, Administration, and Leadership (AEMAL) Book Series

ISSN: 2326-9022
EISSN: 2326-9030

MISSION

With more educational institutions entering into public, higher, and professional education, the educational environment has grown increasingly competitive. With this increase in competitiveness has come the need for a greater focus on leadership within the institutions, on administrative handling of educational matters, and on the marketing of the services offered.

The **Advances in Educational Marketing, Administration, & Leadership (AEMAL) Book Series** strives to provide publications that address all these areas and present trending, current research to assist professionals, administrators, and others involved in the education sector in making their decisions.

COVERAGE

- Technologies and Educational Marketing
- Educational Leadership
- Consumer Behavior
- Academic Pricing
- Enrollment Management
- Governance in P-12 and Higher Education
- Faculty Administration and Management
- Academic Administration
- Direct marketing of educational programs
- Educational Marketing Campaigns

IGI Global is currently accepting manuscripts for publication within this series. To submit a proposal for a volume in this series, please contact our Acquisition Editors at Acquisitions@igi-global.com or visit: http://www.igi-global.com/publish/.

The Advances in Educational Marketing, Administration, and Leadership (AEMAL) Book Series (ISSN 2326-9022) is published by IGI Global, 701 E. Chocolate Avenue, Hershey, PA 17033-1240, USA, www.igi-global.com. This series is composed of titles available for purchase individually; each title is edited to be contextually exclusive from any other title within the series. For pricing and ordering information please visit http://www.igi-global.com/book-series/advances-educational-marketing-administration-leadership/73677. Postmaster: Send all address changes to above address.

Titles in this Series

For a list of additional titles in this series, please visit: www.igi-global.com

Developing Successful Strategies for Global Policies and Cyber Transparency in E-Learning
Gulsun Eby (Anadolu University (College of Open Education), Turkey) T. Volkan Yuzer (Anadolu University (College of Open Education), Turkey) and Simber Atay (Dokuz Eylul University (College of Art), Turkey)
Information Science Reference • copyright 2016 • 356pp • H/C (ISBN: 9781466688445) • US $195.00 (our price)

Impact of Economic Crisis on Education and the Next-Generation Workforce
Patricia Ordóñez de Pablos (University of Oviedo, Spain) and Robert D. Tennyson (University of Minnesota, USA)
Information Science Reference • copyright 2016 • 384pp • H/C (ISBN: 9781466694552) • US $195.00 (our price)

Censorship and Student Communication in Online and Offline Settings
Joseph O. Oluwole (Montclair State University, USA) and Preston C. Green III (University of Connecticut, USA)
Information Science Reference • copyright 2016 • 623pp • H/C (ISBN: 9781466695191) • US $235.00 (our price)

Open Learning and Formal Credentialing in Higher Education Curriculum Models and Institutional Policies
Shirley Reushle (University of Southern Queensland, Australia) Amy Antonio (University of Southern Queensland, Australia) and Mike Keppell (Swinburne University of Technology, Australia)
Information Science Reference • copyright 2016 • 344pp • H/C (ISBN: 9781466688568) • US $195.00 (our price)

Examining the Impact of Community Colleges on the Global Workforce
Stephanie J. Jones (Texas Tech University, USA) and Dimitra Jackson Smith (Texas Tech University, USA)
Information Science Reference • copyright 2015 • 295pp • H/C (ISBN: 9781466684812) • US $185.00 (our price)

www.igi-global.com

701 E. Chocolate Ave., Hershey, PA 17033
Order online at www.igi-global.com or call 717-533-8845 x100
To place a standing order for titles released in this series,
contact: cust@igi-global.com
Mon-Fri 8:00 am - 5:00 pm (est) or fax 24 hours a day 717-533-8661

I dedicate this book to my grandmothers, Ruth Dachiu and Josephine Juliano, and to Tyler Fahringer, a promising future leader.

I'm thankful for the unwavering support of my wife, Kristin H. Wilson-Alphin; our parents, Charlie Brown and Jean Alphin, Tom and Natalie Wilson; and Lauren Wilson.

-Henry C. Alphin Jr.

For Kaiis, who encourages me to be the best I can be.

-Jennie Lavine

For my Mom and Dad "D" and the world's best Godfather, my Uncle Frank, with much love

For Fred Loomis and Gertrude Fraser, amazing mentors and teachers—your wisdom, support, and guidance is priceless

For TLS—Just because

For LLH—unconditional and undying love

-Stormy Stark

For my parents, John and Leslie, who worked so hard to give me a life that would allow me to work on this book, as well as a lifetime of love and support; for my brother Eric and Denise, who have always made a special place for me; for my grandmother, Flossie Sultzaberger, who is always thinking about me and my grandfather David, who always showed me a kind heart and a warm hug; for my great-aunt, Bonnie Patschke, who has always encouraged and supported my career in education and my great-uncle Carl who always smiled when he saw me; for my grandparents, Betty and Clarence, who are no longer with me but showed me love that will be with me forever; and for the rest of my family and friends who have made me what I am today.

-Adam Hocker

Editorial Advisory Board

Table of Contents

Section 2
Community, Culture, and Economic Development in Higher Education Fundraising and Philanthropy

Section 3
Higher Education Fundraising and Philanthropic Support in Action

Detailed Table of Contents

Section 1
Studying Higher Education Philanthropy and Developing a Growth Strategy

Colleges and universities are historic institutions in the U.S. that have sprung up since the founding of Harvard College in 1636. Though their evolution and development is quite simple, the involvement of numerous organizations and groups with philanthropy and higher education is quite complex. Utilizing resource dependency theory and institutional theory, this chapter reviews the historical, sociological, and organizational overview of the practices of philanthropy as it relates to American higher education. Two conceptual frameworks are developed and proposed by the author for teacher-scholars and advanced practitioners seeking to conduct formal research on institutional advancement in higher education. The paper argues that the fundraising professionals (e.g., board of trustees, the president, development officers) role on securing major resources and private gifts within the organization and field level is the result of coercion, imitation, and conformity to institutional rule, institutional isomorphism, and normatively based decision making in higher education.

Chapter 2
Larry Catá Backer, Pennsylvania State University, USA
Nabih Haddad, Michigan State University, USA

Educational scholars have examined the relationship of philanthropy and its
contributions to the public university. Yet, there has been little discussion of the
influence of philanthropy on the governance space of the public research university,
and specifically as conditional philanthropy may affect academic integrity and shared
governance. In this chapter, we consider these larger issues in the context of a study
of a recent case. Drawing on public records, interviews, and university documents,
the chapter examines conditional donation of The Charles G. Koch Foundation
(CKF) to the Florida State University (FSU). We suggest that the Koch Foundation
gift appears to illustrate a new model of governance based philanthropy. It has done
so by tying donations to control or influence of the internal governing mechanics
of an academic unit of a public university. This model has generated controversy.
Though there was substantial faculty and student backlash, the model appears to
be evidence of a new philanthropic relationship between the public university and
substantial donors, one in which donors may change the nature of traditional shared
governance relationships within the university. We maintain that instances of such
"new" strategic philanthropy require greater focus on and sensitivity to shared
governance and faculty input as a way to ensure accountability, especially to preserve
the integrity of the academic enterprise and its public mission where donors seek to
leverage philanthropy into choices relating to faculty hires, courses and programs
traditionally at the center of faculty prerogatives in shared governance.

Chapter 3
Leigh Nanney Hersey, University of Memphis, USA

Universities and colleges are embracing social media as a tool to spread the
message about their institutions. Common uses include recruiting new students,
connecting with current students, and staying connected with alumni. Nonprofit
organizations in the United States also consider social media an important part of
their fundraising toolbox, but use it more for recruiting volunteers, advocacy, and
fundraising. Colleges and universities are also seeing the need to use social media
for development purposes, whether they are private or state-supported institutions.
This chapter explores how universities are using Twitter to promote year-end giving.
Findings from this research suggest that while some universities seem to effectively
use social media, others are inconsistent and even dormant in their messaging.

Funding in higher education continues to be volatile and complex, so senior leaders must focus on fundraising among a host of other key roles (Bornstein, 2003, 2011; Cheng, 2011; Clevenger, 2014; Cohen, 2010; Drezner & Huels, 2014; Essex & Ansbach, 1993; Gould, 2003; Hodson, 2010; Kaufman, 2004; Rhodes, 2001; Tromble, 1998). The goal is creating win-win relationships with a donor and the institution (Bornstein, 2003, 2011; Bruch & Walter, 2005; Carroll & Buchholtz, 2015; Clevenger; Eddy, 2010; Levy, 1999; Prince & File, 2001; Siegel, 2012). There is "a new ecology—a context deeply different from that in which many of today's institutions, assumptions, and habits were formed" (Fulton & Blau, 2005, p. 4). Senior leaders must have a toolbox filled with expertise to be effective fundraisers.

Section 2
Community, Culture, and Economic Development in Higher Education Fundraising and Philanthropy

In this chapter we aim to discuss the opportunities for FDI and venture philanthropy in higher education for the Middle East and North Africa. The MENA region has gathered interest due to the large population and increasing governmental influence on improving higher education in general in the region, and creating partnerships with organizations to better match higher educational options and employment. The GCC plays a large role in the impetus of foreign institutes wanting to invest in the economically developing MENA region. There are many challenges to overcome, some of which are great enough to discourage FDI; but overlooking the initial challenges, there are a wealth of opportunities awaiting exploration.

In 2002, Lake Region State College closed their "Agricultural Farm Business Management" program, due to low enrollment and lack of interest. However considering that agriculture is one of the leading economic developers in North Dakota, Lake Region State College (LRSC) leaders and the community felt this might have been a premature closing, and decided to look at other agriculture workforce initiatives, considering ways to revitalize the agriculture workforce and its needs. This was an ambitious goal considering how rural LRSC is, with roughly 2000 in student matriculation in a given year. Before looking at reinventing, or "rebirthing" the ag program, challenges and steps needed to be addressed and employed. The following chapter will provide a case study on how LRSC leaders, its community, and the alignment of philanthropic support was able to revitalize or "rebirth" the agriculture program to the new cutting edge of Precision Agriculture.

The question of interest in this chapter is the recent project referred to as the Partnership for Higher Education in Africa, and the partner Foundations' goal to contribute to the transformation of a select number of universities in selected African countries. Can public universities in sub-Saharan Africa fully accept the solutions proposed by a private donorship from the West? In exploring the question this chapter draws upon the theoretical frameworks of neo-institutionalism and resource dependency to analyze the related issues. It also reviews, within a neo-institutional perspective, the long-standing debate on U.S. foundations' international activities, and discusses these foundations' perceived influence over Africa's higher education system. Applied to the relationship between U.S. foundations and African universities, this lens seeks to shed new light on the debate about donor funding and its influence on educational reforms.

Chapter 8

By examining philanthropy towards Zaytuna College, the first Muslim liberal arts college in the U.S. and ISNA, and contextualizing it in the discourses of giving among American Muslims, this paper seeks to offer a theoretical framework for contextualizing Islamic philanthropy during 'crisis'. I argue that philanthropy in this context should be seen as a gradually evolving 'discursive tradition,' and not an unchanging one. Given the discourse of Islam in America being one framed in the rubric of 'crisis,' and the attempts by American Muslim organizations to garner philanthropic support using this framework; it is important to understand how certain crisis situations impacted discourses of philanthropy towards this sector. This paper attempts a Foucaldian analysis of how American Muslims negotiate this discursive tension in the realm of giving. I build on the work of various scholars and offer a framework that treats philanthropy towards Islamic schools, cultural and educational institutions as a 'discursive tradition' to understand how the dynamics of philanthropy are changing in this sector. I propose that a discursive approach could also offer us new insights into how philanthropy is being transformed, under certain institutional constraints and relations of power.

Section 3
Higher Education Fundraising and Philanthropic Support in Action

Chapter 9

Effective approaches in higher education development will look at a variety of topics ranging from corporate and foundation relations, to alumni participation, the importance of online giving, campaigns, top advancement trends in higher education, and the ever-critical cultivation of major and mega gifts. The education of a constituency about the importance of private gifts to both public and private institutions cannot be overstated as well given that tuition costs soar yet prospective students, parents, and boards continue to fight for the value proposition. After reading, reviewing, and studying this chapter, faculty, students, and professionals alike will have surveyed knowledge of effective approach in higher education development and will have a greater appreciation for the work that development staff encounter every day. The objective of this book "to explore contemporary and future philanthropy approaches and development theory in international higher education," will certainly be enhanced exponentially by the thorough and useful information presented.

Chapter 10

Wayne P. Webster, Ripon College, USA
Rick C. Jakeman, The George Washington University, USA
Susan Swayze, The George Washington University, USA

This chapter describes how constituencies of a four-year, private liberal arts and science college perceived the effect of philanthropy on the strategic planning process. Due to their reliance upon tuition revenues and private support, liberal arts and science colleges are particularly susceptible to ebbs and flows in the economy. How these institutions plan for the future and the extent to which philanthropy factors into strategic plans provides crucial information about the future of these higher education institutions (Connell, 2006). Gaining a deep understanding of how philanthropy shapes a strategic planning process and the decision-making model that was used during the process provides insight into how philanthropy, strategic planning, and decision-making models intersect to form a new decision-making model, described as feedback and revenue.

Chapter 11

Morgan R. Clevenger, Wilkes University, USA
Cynthia J. MacGregor, Missouri State University, USA

Corporate and foundation relations development officers (CFRs) play a vital role in philanthropy and resource development within higher education. Specifically, these leaders focus time building relationships with individuals who represent corporations and foundations that are able contribute to the needs and programs of an academic institution (Clevenger, 2014; Hunt, 2012; Sanzone, 2000; Saul, 2011; Walton & Gasman, 2008). CFRs must be intimately familiar with their own institution, organizational priorities, and key leaders to be able to create and orchestrate touch-points, engagement and volunteer opportunities, and mutually beneficial inter-organizational partnerships. CFRs manage a complex intersection of internal constituents' programs and interests while simultaneously trying to meet aggressive signature philanthropic platforms for companies or foundation programmatic initiatives.

Chapter 12

Fundraising efforts at institutions of higher education continue to be a top priority, especially as funding from state governments decline. Public institutions have been looking to private institutions, as they are believed to have been leading the way in cultivating alumni donations since their inception. Higher education institutions must understand what determines the greatest alumni giving if the field is to improve their fundraising efforts, and student and alumni engagement is a key indicator of philanthropic gifts. A survey was administered to gather important insight into the giving behavior of alumni of an engineering department at a large research university located in the Midwestern area of the United States. The purpose of this survey is to understand the correlation between alumni giving and engagement while a student and as alumni.

Foreword

Philanthropy and its associated actions toward higher education are understudied around the world. In the United States, where giving towards higher education is well established, voluntary dollars given to support colleges and universities reached new highs in 2014. Individuals, foundations, corporations and other organizations contributed nearly $37.5 billion to American colleges and universities, according to the Council for Aid to Education. While this level of giving is impressive and can have major effects on the institutions, the students, faculty, staff, and communities that received the funds, fundraising success is not evenly distributed across the sector. The top 20 fundraising institutions in 2014—which account of less than one-half of one percent of all U.S. degree-granting institutions—accounted for 28.6% ($10.7 Billion) of the overall total.

Outside of the United States philanthropic giving and the professionalization of the fundraising field for higher education is much more nascent—yet it is increasing. The relative youth of both the field and philanthropic giving is mostly out of only a recent need to find funding beyond government appropriations. As such there is little written about philanthropic giving or fundraising, from an academic or even practitioner perspective, outside of the United States.

Surprisingly, this dearth of literature even extends to the United States, where voluntary giving towards higher education has existed for nearly four centuries. It is simply the case, that while there is a need to understand giving—its effects, donor motivations, organizational operations, etc. both in well-established and more emerging cultures—few pages of academic journals or books are devoted to the study of philanthropic giving.

There is an emerging field of philanthropic scholars in the field of higher education. Beginning with publishing of *The Campus Green: Fund Raising in Higher Education* as part of the Association of the Study of Higher Education (ASHE) research report series in 1990, a handful of scholars, such as myself, Alberto Cabrera, Timothy Caboni, Charles Clotfelter, Amy Wells Dolan, Marybeth Gasman, Frances Huehls, Stanly Katz, James Monks, Eve Proper, Genevieve Shaker, John

Thelin, Richard Trollinger, Andrea Walton, David Weerts, and a growing number of scholar-practitioners have come to establish the field of study. We have looked at the cultivation of prosocial and other philanthropic behaviors, donative motivation, the development of theory and practice in fundraising and marketing, and the effect philanthropy has on governance and organizational effectiveness, just to name a few. We have used the disciplines and fields of anthropology, biology, business, economics, education, history, marketing, political science, public policy, religion, social psychology, and sociology in this interdisciplinary field to do our scholarship. Yet, there are still questions to ask and theories to be developed.

Alphin, Lavine, Stark, and Hocker's *Facilitating Higher Education Growth through Fundraising and Philanthropy* is the next contribution to the field. These relative new-comers to the study of philanthropy and fundraising came together and edited a book full of other new voices that further push the scholarly and practitioner conversations forward. They do this through a number of essays and empirical pieces that update answers to long standing questions and raise new queries regarding the field in the U.S. and abroad.

Within *Facilitating Higher Education* the authors continue to build on an emerging literature that helps expand our conception of philanthropy and its donors. The authors do this through essays and research that look at both donors and solicitation practices that are often overlooked by practitioners and scholars alike. In particular, the work of Sabithulla Khan, that offers a theoretical framework for contextualizing Islamic philanthropy towards higher education, further expands our understanding of cultures of giving in a religious minority that is often misunderstood and certainly under-researched within philanthropic studies. Similarly, the chapter by two of this book's editors, Henry C. Alphin Jr. and Jennie Lavine, that looks at philanthropic potential for institutions of higher education in the Middle East and North Africa—and in particular the Gulf countries, explores the globalization of the philanthropic giving toward higher education through the case of an emerging higher education sector. Fabrice Jaumont, additionally, writes about the globalization of higher education philanthropy as he joins the long standing conversation on donor control. Specifically, he looks at the uneven partnerships of U.S. foundations and universities in sub-Saharan Africa. While others have similar research questions, Jaumont calls for the use of a neo-institutional interpretation when trying to assess a foundation's involvement in a different country and culture.

Along with essays looking at different cultures of giving this book offers two chapters that take a look at new fundraising strategies that are based on social media and the Internet, more specifically through Twitter and crowdfunding. While fundraising tools and mechanisms are continually changing and will continue to evolve as technology progresses, these essays are most compelling to me, not for their particular cases, but as ways to engage new donors—younger alumni and donors from the millennial generation—meeting them where they are in relevant, contemporary mechanisms.

Philanthropy and fundraising is playing an increasingly important role in American higher education and across the globe. As such, there is a need for more research that not only describes best-practices but builds theory and understanding of how philanthropic giving works within the context of higher education. The insights contained in these essays provide us with an opportunity to better understand emerging practices, new cultures of giving, and reflect on more established aspects of our field in new ways. I welcome them into the ongoing and emerging discussion. I hope that these new voices remain a part of the conversation for decades to come.

Noah D. Drezner
Teachers College, Columbia University, USA
August 2015

Preface

Philanthropy, fundraising, and creating a solid donor pool are not easy skills to cultivate. True, some individuals are born with the gift of networking and the ability to always seal the deal, but for the rest of the world, creating a staff who understands the nuances of philanthropy is a process that takes time, dedication, and quite often, trial and error. In addition to the tactical capabilities needed to be a successful fundraiser and development officer for Institutions of Higher Education (IHEs), there are strategic considerations, such as the logistical reality that many students are choosing to travel abroad to study and then return to their home countries to live and work, as well as the fact that technology can be both a strategic tool and a hindrance in the quest to create the greatest endowments, as well as positioning one's own institution as a powerhouse when it comes to financial security.

U.S institutions, such as Harvard, Princeton, and the University of Michigan, possess large endowments that may make the task of fundraising seem monumental to smaller IHEs. In fact Beney (2010) writes, regarding Cheslock and Gianneschi's (2008) article, that the authors "found a significant correlation between the selectivity of the institution (and arguably also its perceived quality) and relative fundraising performance" but yet the "results do not indicate that individual institutions counteract relatively poor state funding with relatively more private gifts". Based on that study, and Beney's perspective, we can surmise that smaller, less prestigious organizations are not stepping up to the plate and fundraising effectively.

Cheslock and Gianneschi's (2008) study opens up some interesting questions that the editors hope to answer in this text. The study is almost ten years old. What has changed? Has technology evolved to the point that smaller colleges can be more competitive fundraisers? Can smaller IHEs use technology and social media, such as Instagram and Twitter, to make their alumni feel more connected to the institution and, therefore, more willing to donate back to their alma maters? Has the economy recovered to the point that alumni have more expendable income that they can donate to these IHEs?

There is a definite argument to be made that size, ranking, and location all provide different advantages when it comes to fundraising. Larger institutions have a large donor pool to draw from because they have more students and more graduates. There is a distinct amount of "low hanging fruit" to retrieve from a larger pool. However, smaller institutions have an ace in their pockets, if they choose to implement a correct strategy. Within a smaller school, there is the ability to build a greater sense of community and of institutional pride. Instilling those values from the moment a student is admitted until the moment they turn their tassels and graduate allows a small institution to fundraise almost as if they are soliciting money from family members to provide upkeep on a beloved family landmark. Using Instagram and Twitter to continually highlight the beauty of a campus and the improvements being made help make graduates feel as though they are connected with their college even when they are far away. More importantly, using technology is a low cost investment that helps alumni recall the wonderful memories of close friends and favorite faculty from their college days, which helps continue the sense of community. When properly leveraged, the sense of community can last a lifetime and really boost the endowments of smaller IHEs.

Ranking is another area where schools can capitalize. An institution does not need to be the top ranked school to garner huge alumni support. A college ranked as a good value, one that has a top ten ranking for a particular program, or is highly ranked for its diversity can capitalize on those numbers and use them as tools to engage donors. Highlighting what your institution does well is a crucial component of a successful marketing and fundraising approach, but even more critical is the strategy an institution uses to communicate those strengths to their alumni base. For example, creating a YouTube channel where the institution posts a variety of items, which could include a wonderful female engineering professor giving a lecture, an engaging guest lecturer visiting campus, or even the commencement speaker, can be a way to get the attention of potential donors. When James Madison University won the NCAA Division 1-AA National Football title in 2004, JMU mailed every alumnus a poster celebrating the win. These methods of connecting to your alumni base are excellent ways to garner financial support without being one of the highest ranked schools in the country.

Regardless of the size, ranking, type, or location of an IHE, development professionals need to keep in mind a few things. First, training donor specialists, which we will discuss in detail in this text, is vitally important to donor relations. In this case, the return on investment is huge because the money invested in cultivating a young development hire into an expert in donor relations will be returned in terms of donor commitment to your institution. Second, explore your resources. Before investing in a huge commercial donor tracking system or outsourcing your social media needs, see what can be done in-house. You'd be surprised how many assets you already have on your staff. Finally, remember that everything old can be made new again. Recycle ideas. Research which campaigns have worked well and which have not. Capture the institutional knowledge of retiring employees. Some campaigns and ideas are timeless and tireless. Just like pop culture recycles ideas (the Muppets are returning to television in 2015), so too can academia. Keeping what has worked well and listening to what your employees believe has brought success in the past. Work smarter by recycling ideas, which will save you money and let your endowment grow.

All of these ideas are a part of a larger theme that is talked about in this book, that colleges, universities, community colleges, and trade schools of any size are facing a financial reality where state funding is dwindling and new funding sources are needed. While studies can tell a development officer what to do and successful IHE campaigns can show a development officer how important philanthropy is, what matters is the "how-to" that can make a difference shift the ledger sheet from red to black ink.

The skeptical international development officer could dismiss these ideas because philanthropy in the United States works differently than it does where their institution is located. But this book offers perspectives from outside the United States as well as from cultures that exist both in the United States and overseas. The editors wanted an international perspective that would focus on dilemmas of IHEs that do not embrace, or cannot specifically utilize, the Western model of higher education and development. This mix of perspectives gives a development officer a bigger fundraising toolbox and can adapt to a range of possibilities and reach a wider community of donors that will be needed to meet the development demands of the future.

IHEs can better utilize their local communities in a reciprocal manner, one where the relationship benefits all parties. This type of approach can be used wherever the IHE is located, from an urban Western institution to an underfunded and rural college, nonprofit and for-profit, small and large endowment. Higher education growth through fundraising combined with economic and community development is an approach that utilizes local and regional communities as an integral part of the growth and development strategy. Examples include workforce development, industry collaboration, research parks, direct community engagement, faculty expertise in solving local problems, community lectures and community association development, and better navigation of the town gown relationship.

This book is timely, relevant, and develops further the relatively nascent field of higher education philanthropy, fundraising, and economic development as scholarly research disciplines. Faculty—for knowledge and as a textbook, researchers, development officers, IHE senior leadership, IHE professional staff, college students, economic development leaders and practitioners, community leaders, industry and entrepreneurial professionals and leadership – as well as those professionals who seek greater involvement and interaction with the wealth of knowledge in IHEs, and government officials will all find the information in this book useful and required knowledge for better understanding the higher education philanthropy and growth collaboration initiative.

ORGANIZATION OF THE BOOK

The book has 3 sections consisting of 12 chapters. A brief description of the chapters follows.

Section 1: Studying Higher Education Philanthropy and Developing a Growth Strategy

Chapter 1: *Interpretive Frameworks for Fundraising Professionals in Higher Education – Applying Resource Dependency and Institutional Theory on Philanthropy Research*
Roy Y. Chan

This chapter highlights the challenges that fundraising professionals to further advance academic knowledge and ultimately contribute to policy making in the hope of facilitating higher education growth through fundraising and philanthropy education. Furthermore the chapter critically examines two major theoretical contributions in organizational theory - resource dependence theory (RDT) and institutional theory - on the organizational structures and resource flows of academic organizations, with special attention to the environments (e.g., isomorphism, knowledge systems, institutional beliefs, rules, and rituals) of institutional advancement at American colleges and universities.

Chapter 2: *Philanthropy and the Character of the Public Research University – The Intersections of Private Giving, Institutional Autonomy, and Shared Governance*
Larry Cata Backer
Nabih Haddad

This chapter examines the influence of philanthropy on the increasingly contested governance space of the public research university, and against the backdrop of academic integrity and shared governance. It is done so by situating the analysis specifically on The Charles G. Koch Foundation's (CKF) and Florida State University's (FSU) economics department.

This chapter states how universities and colleges are embracing social media as a tool to spread the message about their institutions. Common uses include recruiting new students, connecting with current students, and staying connected with alumni. Universities are also using social media to fundraise, but do not know how to take full advantage of it. This chapter explores how American universities are using Twitter to promote individual donations to their institutions and examines 75 university twitter feeds to observe how this platform of raising funds is being utilized.

This chapter discusses the effect senior leaders have as fundraises. Higher education continues to face resource challenges, so creating win-win, long-term relationships are of high importance. Senior leaders such as presidents, advancement officers, community and government relations officers, and corporate and foundation relations officers must spend time building relationships with individuals (e.g., alumni, major donors, philanthropists, and community friends) and other organizations' leaders who can contribute to the needs and programs of the institution. Senior leaders must have a toolbox filled with expertise to be effective fundraisers including: a visionary thinking, an inspirational attitude, optimism, personal commitment and connectivity, excellent communications, ethical integrity, maturity, professionalism, sensitivity, "a systematic perspective to create strong relationships".

Section 2: Community, Culture, and Economic Development in Higher Education Fundraising and Philanthropy

This chapter will attempt to create an overall analysis of opportunities and challenges for foreign direct investment (FDI) and venture philanthropy for institutions of higher education (IHEs) in the Middle East and North Africa (MENA) region. More recently the growth of the focus on higher education in the Arab world has attracted the attention of many private companies wanting to contribute to the rising of the Gulf States. The chapter examines the potential opportunities and not to mention obstacles of higher education funding in the GCC and more specifically the UAE, which is the growing powerhouse of the Gulf.

Chapter 6: *Rebirth of a Program via Community, Industry, and Philanthropic Support*
Cathleen B. Ruch

This chapter focuses on two-year institutions that are recognized as a vital backbone in economic and workforce development especially in rural locations. A push for two-year institutions to work with specific industries and offer content-specific courses or programs continues. Business leaders continue to voice their disapproval regarding higher education not producing the necessary workforce. With this kind of censure, two-year institutions eliminate programs that are not closely related to workforce. This has caused many institutes to cut programs as the state funding went from 70% to 30%.

Chapter 7: *Unequal Partnerships – The Dynamics of Collaboration between U.S. Philanthropic Foundations and African Universities*
Fabrice Jaumont

This chapter reviews the issues around the impact of donor funding on education and hpow its reforms have resurfaced both in the local and global arenas. A 2010 report published by the Partnership for Higher Education in Africa (PHEA)—a consortium of seven U.S. private foundations whose collective goal was to revive higher education in Africa—claims that the PHEA has "directly or indirectly improved conditions for 4.1 million African students enrolled at 379 universities and colleges" during its ten-year existence (2000-2010). Simultaneously, both the Washington Post and the New York Times discussed the negative impact of major private donors' gifts on the United States' secondary school system, particularly during the dire economic climate which left schools facing abysmal budget cuts.

Chapter 8: *Islamic Philanthropy and Higher Education – Re-Imagining Tradition to Meet Contemporary Challenges*
Sabithulla Khan

This paper seeks to offer a theoretical framework for contextualizing Islamic philanthropy during 'crisis' in the U.S. and argues that philanthropy in this context should be seen as a gradually evolving 'discursive tradition'. Given the discourse of Islam in America being one framed in the rubric of crisis and the attempts by

American Muslim organizations to garner philanthropic support using this framework; it is important to understand how certain crisis situations impacted discourses of philanthropy towards this sector. This paper attempts a Foucaldian analysis of how American Muslims negotiate this discursive tension in the realm of giving.

Section 3: Higher Education Fundraising and Philanthropic Support in Action

Chapter 9: *Effective Approaches in Higher Education Development – A Survey in Fundraising Best Practices*
Andrew A. Shafer

Every year new advancement strategies and tactics are presented in books, papers, online, and at conferences around the world. Fundraise this way, engage alumni that way, marketing your mission with this twist. The reality? Advancement, and more specifically, development/fundraising at its core has not changed in hundreds of years. This chapter will look at a variety of topics ranging from corporate and foundation relations, to alumni participation, the importance of online giving, campaigns, top advancement trends in higher education, and the ever-critical cultivation of major and mega gifts. The education of a constituency about the importance of private gifts to both public and private institutions cannot be overstated given that tuition costs soar yet prospective students, parents, and boards continue to fight for the value proposition. After reviewing, faculty, students, and professionals alike will have surveyed knowledge of effective approaches in higher education development and will have a greater appreciation for the work that development staff encounter every day.

Chapter 10: *The Role of Philanthropy on the Strategic Planning Process of a Selective Liberal Arts and Science College*
Wayne P. Webster
Rick C. Jakeman
Susan Swayze

This chapter will describe how constituencies of a four-year, private liberal arts college perceived the effect of philanthropy on the strategic planning process. Liberal arts colleges typically receive little direct state or federal government support and rely predominantly on tuition revenues, endowment earnings, and philanthropic support to balance their budgets

This chapter will detail the strategic planning process and the various decision-making models during the 2010-2012 academic years at one private liberal arts college.

Chapter 11: *The Corporate and Foundation Relations Development Officer*
Morgan Clevenger
Cynthia J. MacGregor

Like other institutional leaders, corporate and foundation relations (CFR) development officers play a vital role in philanthropy and resource development within higher education. Specifically, these leaders focus their time on building relationships with individuals who represent corporations and foundations that are able to contribute to the needs and programs of the academic institution.

Chapter 12: *Alumni Giving and Social Exchange – A Study of Alumni Giving Behavior*
Lauren E. B. Dodge

This book chapter will cover the survey results pertaining to donor attitudes involving donor intent, historical perspectives on donor responsibility and control of donated funds, attempts to reform educational programs through selective or creative philanthropy, and finally, will offer conclusions and recommendations for practitioners.

REFERENCES

Beney, A. (2010, December 16). Giving cause for hope. *Times Higher Education*. Retrieved from https://www.timeshighereducation.com/features/giving-cause-for-hope/414584.article

Cheslock, J., & Gianneschi, M. (2008). Replacing state appropriations with alternative revenue sources: The case of voluntary support. *The Journal of Higher Education*, 79(2), 208–229.

Section 1
Studying Higher Education Philanthropy and Developing a Growth Strategy

Chapter 1
Studying Philanthropy and Fundraising in the Field of Higher Education:
A Proposed Conceptual Model

Roy Y. Chan
Indiana University – Bloomington, USA

ABSTRACT

Colleges and universities are historic institutions in the U.S. that have sprung up since the founding of Harvard College in 1636. Though their evolution and development is quite simple, the involvement of numerous organizations and groups with philanthropy and higher education is quite complex. Utilizing resource dependency theory and institutional theory, this chapter reviews the historical, sociological, and organizational overview of the practices of philanthropy as it relates to American higher education. Two conceptual frameworks are developed and proposed by the author for teacher-scholars and advanced practitioners seeking to conduct formal research on institutional advancement in higher education. The paper argues that the fundraising professionals (e.g., board of trustees, the president, development officers) role on securing major resources and private gifts within the organization and field level is the result of coercion, imitation, and conformity to institutional rule, institutional isomorphism, and normatively based decision making in higher education.

DOI: 10.4018/978-1-4666-9664-8.ch001

INTRODUCTION

In the last 10 years, expectations about the role of philanthropy and fundraising in higher education have increased. Notably, these expectations are based on assumptions and actual behavior that philanthropic organizations can enhance the capacity and performance of postsecondary institutions (Institute for Higher Education Policy, 2011). Today, no institutions of higher education have survived without some form of fundraising or gifts for the institution (Bernstein, 2013). Every public and private institution is grappling with a philanthropic agenda in the 21st century. As financial aid support declines and tuition rates continue to rise, colleges and universities have grown much more dependent on the increased philanthropic involvements of the wealthy to fund academic and professional programs, to raise college participation and completion rates, and to build state-of-the-art facilities for high quality teaching and research in higher education.

Generally, the role of philanthropy and fundraising has played an enormous role in fulfilling individuals' career goals and promises, and the vitality of American society. Payton (1988) once defined philanthropy as the "voluntary action for the public good." These voluntary actions performed by philanthropists and the wealthy are often viewed as heroes of the 21st century, whose gifts have fueled the advancement of lifelong learning in higher education. While the term philanthropy is seen as a broad concept that encompasses the wide range of private giving for larger public purposes, philanthropy research today has not been widely accepted as part of higher education research for very long. As philanthropy research has moved from once being increasingly atheoretical to now university-based scholarship (Drezner & Huehls, 2014), bridging new ideas and theories into university practice is vastly needed to help teacher-scholars and advanced practitioners conceptualize organizational behavior and their effectiveness to organizational performance in higher education (Bastedo, 2012; Dee, 2014; Kelly, 2002).

To clarify, institutions of higher education are under intense pressure to conform to new fundraising policies and procedures (e.g., gift acceptance policy, donor-privacy policy) worldwide against the changing demographics, increased competition, and reduced state and federal funding for postsecondary education (Hendrickson, Lane, Harris, & Dorman, 2012). Specifically, colleges and universities have to compete for students and resources (e.g., financial, physical, natural, human, information, labor) by adopting market-like ideologies or market-oriented mechanisms to stay competitive in the global marketplace (Edwards, 2004). Statistically speaking, state spending on higher education has significantly increased to $10.5 billion from 1990 to 2010 (Quinterno & Orozco, 2012). Although state funding in higher education budgets continues to drop across the United States, private gifts to support the needs of colleges and universities is vastly growing nationwide as a result to globalization and the increasing adoption of neoliberal policies moving away from funding postsecondary education (Giroux, 2014).

Nowadays, many organizations of higher education are value-driven and profit seeking (Pfeffer, 1972; Villalonga & McGahan, 2005; Weitz & Shenhav, 2000), federations of loosely coupled parts (Weick, 1976), and are dependent on a network of interconnectedness with outside individuals and organizations (Pfeffer, 1987). Typically, postsecondary education is predominantly seen as a private commodity in which higher education's commitment to serve the public good in a democratic society is being replaced by "economic rationality" (Atlbach, 2002; Gumport, 2000). Though the study of higher education organizations has expanded significantly with broader organizational theory (Youn & Murphy, 1997), particularly within the disciplines of economics, psychology, and sociology in the nonprofit sector, limited research have yet to explore the academic structures (e.g., norms, rules, routines, schemes) and subcultures (e.g., political, bureaucratic, symbolic, human resource) of university advancement. Furthermore, there is no consensus among scholars about what should be studied, nor the most appropriate disciplinary settings in philanthropy and advancement research (Keidan, Jung, & Pharoah, 2014).

Consequently, this chapter attempts to ignite new excitement from scholars and practitioners for conducting formal research on institutional advancement in higher education. As philanthropy continues to strengthen the U.S. economy and enhance the quality of life for all people, this article seeks to build a coherent theory for higher education fundraising that is consistent with existing theories of organizations. Unlike numerous past research that have solely focused on best practices (Brittingham & Pezullo, 1990; Rowland, 1983; Worth, 2002), this paper investigate on the role of organizational theory – namely resource dependency theory and institutional theory - in explaining the evolving role of fundraising professionals in higher education, with special attention to the environments (e.g., isomorphism, knowledge systems, institutional beliefs, rules, and rituals) of institutional advancement at American colleges and universities. However, given the global nature of the higher education industry, it is expected that this chapter will have applicability and pertinence beyond the United States and to all types of universities (e.g., public, private, for-profit) around the world. The ultimate goal of this chapter is to challenge fundraising professionals, researchers, and senior officials to advance philanthropy research and contribute to public policy (e.g., giving campaigns, tax breaks, match-funding schemes) and legal scholarship (e.g., regulation of charitable giving) through teaching in hopes of advancing fundraising in the evolving field of higher education philanthropy in the coming decades (Bloland, 2002; Caboni, 2010).

PHILANTHROPY AND HIGHER EDUCATION
AS A FIELD OF RESEARCH

The study of philanthropy as a distinct scholarly field of inquiry within higher education administration is a relatively new phenomenon (Proper & Caboni, 2014). Notably, the growing interest in the study of philanthropy has led fundraising professionals to examine the role and function of institutional advancement, a field that includes fundraising, alumni relations, public relations, and marketing. Historically, philanthropists and philanthropy has played an integral part to American higher education since the founding of Harvard College in 1636. Specifically, philanthropy has created educational opportunity for countless young men and women whose lives have been enriched and whose contributions to society have been greater. For example, John Harvard, an English minster and godly gentleman, was recognized as the first private donor to set the foundation for professional fundraising in U.S. higher education. While several philanthropists and humanitarians (e.g., William Hibbens, Hugh Peter, Thomas Weld, Elihu Yale) have played a pivotal role in the creation of Harvard College, philanthropy and fundraising for colleges and universities did not become an organized activity until the turn of the twentieth century when educational fundraising became more professionalized through well-organized advancement and development programs (Thelin & Trollinger, 2014).

To clarify, the term "development" did not come into use until the 1920s when Northwestern University established the nation's first Department of Development during a period that many scholars dubbed the "golden era" of higher education philanthropy. Although the term "development" did not gain widespread recognition until after World War II, the concept of raising money and asking for money would leave many questions about how the alumni relations, public relations, and fundraising functions should be organized in the academy. Historically, the Ford Foundation, Carnegie Foundation, and the U.S. Education Department's Fund for the Improvement of Postsecondary Education typically threw out the general concept of philanthropy. Such issue prompted A. Westley Rowland (1986), editor of the *Handbook of Institutional Advancement*, to establish the phrase "institutional advancement" to expand philanthropy research into the field of higher education administration. Rowland (1986) defined institutional advancement as an all "encompassing activity and program undertaken by an institution to develop understanding and support from all its constituencies in order to achieve its goals in securing such resources as students, faculty, and dollars" (p. xiii). Though the approaches to fundraising for colleges and universities have slightly changed since the intergenerational "great wealth transfer" era (Schervish & Havens, 1998), the current work of educational fundraising still remains vastly the same today across the United States and abroad.

4

Statistically speaking, during the 2014 fiscal year, donors gave more than $37 billion to U.S. colleges and universities the most ever raised in a one-year period and nearly a 10 percent increase over 2012 (*Giving USA*, 2015). Such increase is likely due to the fact that more students and alumni are reporting greater satisfaction with their college experience; a long-serving president; institutional maturity; a strong national ranking; a high percentage of tenured professors; a relatively large endowment; and regional location (Johnson Grossnickle and Associates, 2013). While alumni often serve as the primary fundraising constituency for colleges and universities, private giving from parents, community members, as well as athletic fans have also begun to support institutions of higher education during the era of public austerity and private abundance (Proper & Caboni, 2014). For example, Harvard University alumni John Paulson donated $400 million to the School of Engineering and Applied Sciences in June 2015 to provide endowment for faculty development, research, scholarships, and financial aid. Mr. Paulson's "mega-size" gift became the largest private donation in the history of Harvard, second to Gerard L. Chan, director of the Morningside Foundation, when he donated more than $350 million in 2014 to further scientific research and scholarship at the Harvard University's Gerard L. Chan School of Public Health. Similarly, the William and Flora Hewlett Foundation made a gift of approximately $113 million at UC Berkeley to establish 100 endowed faculty chairs in 2007 (Thelin & Trollinger, 2014). Comparatively, the Rockefeller Foundation gave $45-million in the 1920s to improve medical-school education while the Ford Foundation helped to create the discipline of area studies with $270-million in grants it made during the 1950s and 1960s (Gose, 2013). In other words, large-scale philanthropic organizations and private donors have significantly enhanced the quality of research units (i.e., schools, departments, research centers), improved undergraduate curriculum (i.e., teaching and learning, core curriculum), and reformed professional and graduate education such as completion, productivity, and technology.

Today, approximately 72,000 foundations exist in the United States, of which more than half of community foundations (i.e., Boston Foundation, College for All Texans Foundation) and corporate foundations (i.e., Spencer Foundation, Ford Foundation were formally established to support higher education reforms in the past thirty years (Thelin & Trollinger, 2014). For example, since 2006, the Bill & Melinda Gates Foundation, the country's largest philanthropy with more $36-billion in assets, has spent more than $472-million to remake U.S. higher education in hopes of pushing more students, more quickly, toward graduation (Parry, Field, & Supiano, 2013). Specifically, the Gates Foundation, whose vision is to help re-channel the public dollars that states spent into raising college completion in an effort to lift more Americans out of poverty, has donated nearly $17-million to Jobs for the Future and $65-million to Next Generation Learning Challenges in hopes for streamlining remedial classes in community colleges for needy students. Such push has helped influence higher-education policy at the state level to a degree that is unprecedented for a private foundation. Similar to the Gates Foundation, the Lumina Foundation, the largest private foundation in the United States devoted solely to higher education, has spent more than $250-million to support college-reform movements such as, Complete College America and Achieving the Dream, in hopes of streamlining or eliminating remedial classes and providing colleges with financial incentives to graduate mores students on-time (Mangan, 2013). In a similar fashion, the Carnegie Corporation of New York donated more than $2 million to the Council for the Advancement and Support of Education (CASE) to help non-American universities build an infrastructure for raising funds that aligns with the increasing costs and declining government support for postsecondary education. Likewise, the Alfred P. Sloan Foundation gave millions of dollars to support distance-education projects as well as existing distance-learning opportunities (e.g., Sloan Consortium Online Catalog) while the Mellon Foundation has made several private gifts to support online digital repositories (i.e., JSTOR, Project MUSE) and massive online courses (MOOCs) to disseminate new knowledge or ideas in American society (Bernstein, 2013). In other words, large-scale philanthropic foundations are increasingly supporting new innovation and ideas in higher education while also being the magnet for generous support from alumni, individuals, foundations, and corporations. While large-scale philanthropic foundations have often provided stable and unrestricted funds to support scientific research (i.e., research grants), faculty development (i.e., teaching and research), academic programs (i.e., new curricular) and scholarships (e.g., Gates Millennium Scholars Program) since the great recession of 2008, limited research have yet to examine the public purpose and value of philanthropy research in higher education (Proper & Caboni, 2014). Furthermore, numerous past assessments on the role of philanthropy in shaping U.S. higher education institutions have either been replicated from past research or highly focused on best practice (Worth, 2002). As a result, new formal research that bridge theory and practice is vastly needed to understand the effects of giving on institutional types such as, Minority-Serving Institutions (MSIs), religious institutions and community colleges, as well as specific units within institutions such as, giving to athletic programs, in the emerging field of higher education philanthropy (Drezner & Huehls, 2014).

Just as Merle Curti (1958) first defined philanthropy as the "love of man, charity, benevolence, humanitarianism, social reform," new formal research that investigates the role of philanthropy in academe is crucially needed to understand how private gifts foster systematic change and promote "catalytic" or "strategic" reforms in higher education. Robert Bremmer (1988) once emphasized that "The aim of philanthropy in its broadest sense is improvement in the quality of human life" (p. 3) Similarly,

Ellen Condliffe Lagemann (2002) once stated that American philanthropy represents "a long tradition of…efforts to establish the values, shape the beliefs, and define the behaviors that would join people to one another" (p. 103). Consequently, new formal research that assess the fundraisers ability (or inability) to secure large-scale philanthropic gifts in higher education is vastly needed to understand the role of fundraising professionals (e.g., board of trustees, the president, development officers, treasurers, financial agents) in shaping the evolution of colleges and universities across the United States and abroad.

THEORETICAL CONSTRUCTS: PAST AND PRESENT

Traditionally, the partnership between foundation and higher education has made possible an excellent system of higher learning in the United States (Thelin & Trollinger, 2014). Such tradition has helped board of trustees, the president, and development professionals to bring incredible resources and wealth to higher education organizations across the United States and abroad. Today, fundraising professionals have played an incalculable role in the fundraising efforts for the university as private major donors, and a prominent force in the emergence and transformation of the modern American university (Carbone, 1986; Hall, 1992; Caboni, 2010). In addition to fundraisers, development professionals communicate with many constituents (i.e., gift planning, gifts processing, research prospects) and units (i.e., development, alumni affairs, external relations) within their academic environment to enhance institutional performance and prestige in higher education. Resource dependency theory is based on this notion that institutional effectiveness and efficiency depends on the leaders' (e.g., board members, presidents, provosts, deans, chairs) capacity to secure financial resources needed for higher education (Drezner & Huehls, 2014). As colleges and universities are grappling with a philanthropic agenda, both financially and politically, fundraising professionals are highly dependent on large-scale philanthropic organizations and private donors to sustain and transform American higher education against the growing state disinvestment for postsecondary education.

Resource Dependence Theory (RDT) and Academic Organizations

Generally, the concept of resource dependence theory (RDT) is based on the premise that educational organizations are highly dependent on resources from outside sources (e.g., state, professions, donors) as a result of resource scarcity and conflicts in today's global economy (Pfeffer & Salanicik, 1978; Sherer & Lee, 2002).

Jeffrey Pfeffer and Gerald Salanick (1978) are perhaps the two main theorists who developed the lens of RDT to explain the behavior, structure, stability, and change of academic organizations. They argue that in complex environments, academic organizations are highly dependent upon members of its environment as a result of competition and efficiency. As higher education institution seek to acquire resources that are "self- sustaining" or sustainable, leaders of higher education (e.g., trustees, president, development professionals) are required to maximize their autonomy (e.g., freedom to make decisions) and legitimacy (i.e., influence) from outside groups to ensure short-term and long-term survivability (Scott & Davis, 2007; Thompson, 1967). This is highly evident in many U.S. colleges and universities, whereby boards of institutions seek financial resources from their external partners (e.g., alumni, donors, community partners, corporate partners) and community supporters (e.g., state legislators, governors, mayor) to achieve organizational survival and success. Organizations are in constant interaction with other entities. For example, in March 2014, the Board of Regents for Higher Education at Connecticut State Colleges and Universities (ConSCU) applied for a $500,000 grant from the Kresge Foundation to establish "student success center" programs at several community colleges in Connecticut, with the long-term goal of helping low-income minority students persist and transfer into a four-year bachelor's degree program (ConSCU, 2014). Similarly, in October 2014, the Boston based organization Let's Get Ready received a $1.1 million grant from the Michael & Susan Dell Foundation to continue helping more than 8,700 low-income students enter and complete a college education (Let's Get Ready, 2014). Comparatively, the famous Koch brothers' – Charlie G. and David H. – donated more $12.7 million to colleges and universities in 2012, funding initiatives such as programs as the "moral imperatives of free markets and individual liberty" (Levinthal, 2014). In other words, members who work in academic and/or large-scale philanthropic organizations are expected to build mutual relationships with outside groups in order to secure financial resources or inputs for low-income, ethnic minority, and first-generation college students to complete higher education. These independent actors may consist of suppliers, customers, and human resources.

Figure 1 presents a conceptual model designed by the author to explain the interdependencies between fundraising professionals in higher education organizations and their dependence on large-scale philanthropic organizations and external groups/community supporters.

In Figure 1, Roy Y. Chan's conceptual framework in the context of RDT portrays how professional fundraisers (e.g., board of trustees, the president, development officers) are highly dependent with their external environments in order to survive and grow as academic organizations. Specifically, leaders of higher education must establish cooperative arrangements with philanthropic organizations (e.g., foundations, corporations), external groups, and/or community supporters to acquire the

Figure 1. Conceptual model for research in higher education philanthropy: inter-organizational relations between higher education organizations and private funders in the context of Resource Dependency Theory (RDT)

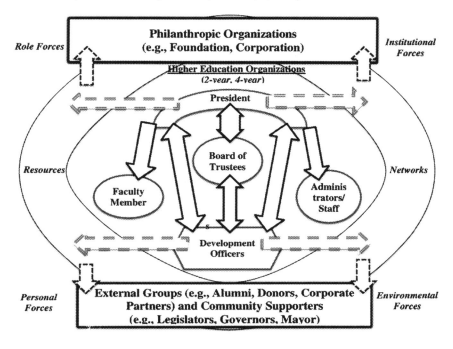

necessary resources for innovation and growth within its organization and field levels. As colleges and universities are becoming resource-insufficient as a result of environmental uncertainty and ambiguous goals, fundraising professionals are tempted give up power and control within their external environments in hopes of securing valuable resources (e.g., financial, physical, natural, information) and networks (i.e., linkage) they need for institutional survivability (i.e., myth-making). Though Chan's conceptual model does not explain the effects of environments on colleges and universities, the conceptual model does highlight four critical forces that impact professional fundraisers in higher education: 1) personal forces, 2) role forces, 3) institutional forces, and 4) environmental forces (Cook & Lasher, 1996)

Firstly, fundraising professionals (e.g., board of trustees, alumni and public relations, development officers) are highly influenced by the president or chancellor of a college or university. Notably, fundraising professionals must work with the president to interpret the educational environment of his or her institution. Because every president or chancellor brings in wide wealth of knowledge and expertise to each college or university, fundraising professionals must align their fundraising practice and strategy with the president traits, habits, preferences, attitudes, values, and beliefs if they are to remain successful in attracting large philanthropic gifts to the university (Cook & Lasher, 1996). That is, the president's vision and leadership style will largely influence the decision-making process of professional fundraisers, of which, in turn affects their ability to attract resources and networks from large-scale philanthropic organizations and external groups/community supporters.

Secondly, fundraising professionals are influenced by the president's expected role to raise great sums of money for the college or university (i.e., role forces). Notably, the president must take the lead role in defining and articulating the institution's mission and priorities. Because the president is the most 'powerful' position in the college or university, the president's relationship with development staff and board of trustees is pivotal to the success of obtaining major gifts from large-scale philanthropic organizations and external groups. That is, the ability of a president to secure major gifts, for example, can be influenced by the interests of trustees, the community, and the faculty. To prevent this ordeal, the president must provide administrative leadership and support to advancement professionals. Any decision the president makes within the academic structures of higher education may affect fundraisers ability to attract resources and networks to the institution. Consequently, the president must be a team player by balancing competing needs and special interests within the institution.

Thirdly, the institutional forces that shape modern colleges and universities in the 21st century influence fundraising professionals. This includes established traditions, history, culture, norms, sanctions, taboos, rituals, rewards, and other aspects of organizational life (Cook & Lasher, 1996). Because every higher education operates differently with regards to institutional type (private, public, for-profit) and population (2-year, 4-year, online), fundraising professionals must understand the histories, traditions, and governance structures of their institution prior to making any solicitation for major gifts (or transformational gifts) to the university. That is, the quality of the governing board, student body, faculty, and alumni along with size and prestige has a direct influence on fundraising performance by the president, board of trustees, and development professionals. As higher education organizations becomes more complex and dynamic within its organization and field level, professional fundraisers must make decisions that align with the institutional goals and mission of the university without compromising the history and culture of the institution.

Fourthly, and lastly, the environmental forces that shape modern colleges and universities in the 21st century influence fundraising professionals. This includes inflation rate, underemployment, state of the economy, as well as public attitude toward higher education (Cook & Lasher, 1996). Because the environment affects the organizational structure and behavior of institutional advancement, fundraising professionals must utilize their practical skills and experience to support and enhance the fundraising activity of trustees and the president through collaboration. Generally, collaboration and cooperation with different constituents and units can provide teambuilding opportunities and sustain regular communication between fundraising professionals and external groups. Notably, the role of collaboration may assist fundraising professionals to embed communication structures within their external environments that are critical in securing major gifts from elite philanthropists. That is, for an institution realize its fundraising potential, colleges and universities must establish inter-organizational cooperation within their external environments to deal with economic rationality (i.e., donor's behavior, donor-oriented attitudes) of large-scale philanthropic organizations (March & Simon, 1958). Furthermore, fundraising professionals must develop a "three-party relationship" between institutional players – the board of trustees, the president, development professionals – to ensure that the institution comply with fundraising requirements to the university, reflecting institutional theory (Kinnison & Ferin, 1989).

Nevertheless, while some areas of responsibility are and should remain exclusive to the board, the president, or the development staff, all four types of forces exert differing levels of influence on fundraising professionals and thus affect board of trustees and development professionals decision-making process in varying degrees (Cook & Lasher, 1996). Though Figure I do not examine the effects of environments on the organizational structures of institutional advancement, the conceptual framework paints the importance of how "partnership roles" can help support and sustain the mission and priorities of the institution. If fundraising professionals seeks to survive in the globally competitive marketplace, then they must support one another's effort through a collaborative partnership and involve others personally in the fundraising process to the university. Moreover, professional fundraisers must understand the interaction and power/dependence relationship between the university and philanthropic organizations or external groups in shaping government expectations and public responses to higher education philanthropy.

Institutional Theory and Academic Organizations

The institutional theory of organizations as a theoretical framework is practical to explain the barriers to diversity, responsiveness, and improvement in higher education. Notably, the concept of institutional theory (e.g., political, legal, social), often described as new institutionalism, is critical to understand how institutional environments affect the organizational structures and resource flows to higher education, and how they conform to similar cultural norms and values of higher education organizations in response to environmental uncertainty, unclear technologies, and/or ambiguous goals (March & Cohen, 1974; Sills, 1957; Tolbert, 1985).

Furthermore, institutional theory is useful for teacher-scholars and practitioners to explain why organizations such as institutional advancement change in structures and practices (e.g., fundraising activities, social events), and to explain the wider social and cultural environment as the ground in which organizations are rooted (Meyer & Rowan, 1977; Scott, 1995).

Paul J. DiMaggio and Walter W. Powell (1983) are perhaps the two main theorists who developed the concept of institutional theory, who argue that institutional theory is useful to understand the relationship between academic organizations and environments, and how educational organizations adopt symbol-like elements rather than acting rationally as a result to competitive external markets and social expectations (Hoy & Miskel, 2008). Generally, academic organizations change in structure, practice, and behavior as a result of homogenization (i.e., isomorphism) (Sporn, 1999). Homogenization in the context of higher education occurs when institutions resemble each other (i.e., alike) in respect to buildings, classroom design, instruction and curriculum, and other similar forms. Typically, organization of higher education engage in homogenization activity because they face intense competition (e.g., goals, priorities) and efficiency (e.g., performance, outcomes) among capitalist firms (or competitive market) to conform to social rules and cultural pressures held by individuals and other organizations that are acceptable and legitimate. For example, fundraising professionals at Penn State University may recruit new board of trustees to their institution in hopes of legitimizing the university due to intense competition for major gifts at both the organizational and field levels. DiMaggio and Powell (1983) define organizational field as "those organizations which, in the aggregate, constitute a recognized area of institutional life: key suppliers, resources and product consumers, regulatory agencies, and other organizations that produce similar services or products" (p. 148). Because fundraising professionals often compete for several goals or priorities (i.e., power imbalance) with other institutions, the concept of institutional theory is useful to explain why board of trustees, the president, and advancement professional engage in similar activities, practices, and behaviors between constituents to achieve organizational success and survival in higher education (Miller-Millesen, 2003).

INSTITUTIONAL ENVIRONMENTS AND HIGHER EDUCATION PHILANTHROPY

Defining Institutional Isomorphism

Historically, Weber (1978) argued that the marketplace forces academic organizations to be isomorphic in nature because they must model themselves after other educational organizations they see as being successful or prestigious (e.g., research universities). To clarify, DiMaggio and Powell (1991) defined isomorphism as "a constraining process that forces one unit in a population to resemble other units that face the same set of environmental conditions" (p. 66). Specifically, Hannan and Freeman (1977) argued that isomorphism is the result of individuals and groups responding to different behaviors and structures of organizations that is identified as elite or prestigious. Generally, once the field is established within an institution, there is an inexorable push towards similarity (i.e., alike) rather than innovation as a result of activities or events enacted within the administrative and academic units. For example, David Riesman (1956), the first eminent scholar to examine the concept of institutional isomorphism, noticed that many institutions replicated university course catalogues from other institutions to meet both social and societal expectations of university course offerings. Similarly, Drezner and Huehls (2014) observed that board members borrowed fundraising programs (e.g., billion-dollar campaigns, annual fund programs) and stewardship programs (e.g., legacy society, president's club) from other universities in order to strive and attract wealthy philanthropists for institutional prestige within the academic hierarchy (i.e., symbolic capital) (O'Meara, 2007). Such trend has led fundraising professionals to pursue higher level of complexity (e.g., new offices, new units), formalization (e.g., new policies, new rules), and centralization (e.g., authority, power) within higher education to meet the growing isomorphic pulls from local and global organization fields that are perceived to be elite (Suchman, 1995).

Types of Isomorphism in Higher Education

DiMaggio and Powell (1983) identified three mechanisms through which institutional isomorphic conformity occurs: 1) coercive, 2) mimetic, and 3) normative. Firstly, *coercive* isomorphism stems from political influence and the problem of legitimacy (e.g., image-building). Notably, academic organizations have high degree of legitimacy, in which the actions of the institution are appropriate within some socially constructed system of norms, values, and beliefs (Suchman, 1995). American colleges and universities are subject to institutionalization because government agencies or other political organizations (e.g., coercive sources) use sanctions or mandates to get academic organizations to adapt to specific structural arrangements (Tolbert & Hall, 2008). Typically, institutionalization occurs when fundraising professionals perform similar behaviors (e.g., self-assessment practices), structure (e.g., advisory committees) and/or processes (e.g., *Robert's Rules of Order*) (Miller-Millesen, 2003). For example, a university president may enforce a new regulation and policy on donor intent or incentive based compensation that prompt advancement professionals to conform to the new mandate that aligns closely with other institutional advancement. Similarly, organizations of higher education, such as Office of Admissions or Office of Student Affairs may hire affirmative action officers to prevent allegations of discrimination from other individuals or institutions. Comparatively, medical hospitals across the U.S. may adopt new Ebola prevention protocols according to the Centers for Disease Control and Prevention (CDC) guidelines to prevent an Ebola crisis in the U.S. In other words, *coercive* isomorphism results from both formal and informal pressures exerted on organizations by other organizations or individuals, and by cultural expectations in the society with which organizations function (DiMaggio & Powell, 2012). These pressures, in turn, become institutionalized where academic organizations create structures and hierarchies to gain normative acceptance as an institution. Thus, organizations of higher education such as institutional advancement or development office would become increasingly homogeneous in structure, climate, and behavior with other institutions in hopes of attracting larger philanthropic gifts (i.e., coercive authority) from more hierarchical organized donor organizations (e.g., Andrew Carnegie Corporation, Bill & Melinda Gates Foundation, Lumina Foundation, Rockefeller Foundation).

Secondly, educational organizations serve as a model for others to *mimetic* or imitate. Notably, symbolic uncertainty is a powerful force that encourages *mimetic* isomorphism. Often known as modeling, organizations mimic after similar organizations because of the high degree of uncertainty surrounding education technologies such as "best practices" or learning outcomes (Meyer & Rowan, 1978). Because organizations of higher education often create goals that are highly disputed (Birnbaum, 1988), academic organization such as university advancement may model themselves with other similar institution in order to conform to the social pressure of other elite institutions (Meyer & Scott, 1983). For example, the University of Pennsylvania may model, observe, and imitate the standardization of Columbia University online giving days (i.e., one day fundraising challenge) prior to launching their own online giving day at their institution. Similarly, several large-scale organized philanthropic organizations such as Pew Charitable Trust and Kellogg Foundation may fund several higher education research institutes (i.e., Institute for Higher Education Policy (IHEP), Center for Policy Studies in Higher Education, New America Foundation) in order to broaden access and completion for higher education in American society. Comparatively, Boston College's Office of Institutional Advancement may model, observe, and imitate the standardization of University of Notre Dame billion-dollar capital campaign prior to launching their billion-dollar capital campaign on-campus. Such *mimetic* behavior would help Boston College fundraising professionals identify the success and/or problematic issues that occurred during University of Notre Dame billion-dollar capital campaign with little risk or expense. Furthermore, Boston College reliance on an established, legitimated organization like Notre Dame would enhance their institutional legitimacy and survival characteristics while at the same time, minimize conflict over organizational goals between constituencies (e.g., donor relations, gift coordinators). In other words, organizations of higher education are highly dependent on the organizational structure of other institutions in order to achieve institutional legitimacy (e.g., university-based training programs, professional networks of organizations) and survival. In addition, fundraising professionals are more likely to seek new structures within their organization and field levels that are perceived to be legitimate in hopes of reducing uncertainty in times of constraint and support to higher education.

The last mechanism of institutional isomorphic change is *normative* pressures. *Normative* isomorphism is common when academic organizations such as institutional advancement staff advocate for certain organizational rules (e.g., gift arrangement procedures, principles of stewardship) and structures (i.e., professionalization) in order to become more institutionalized (e.g., status, power) (Terlaak, 2007). Generally, the concept of organizational rules is defined as "the routines and procedures around which human behaviors and rewards in an organization are defined" (Youn & Price, 2009, p. 208). In other words, rituals and rules (i.e., cultural, cognitive, normative, regulative) explain cumulative experience as well as actions of formal organizations in shaping the development of structural inertia (i.e., resistance) and institutional change (Allison, 1971; Cohen & Sproul, 1996; March et al., 2000). Once an organization occupies a "niche" (i.e., behavior), it will move toward the state of structural inertia by formulating new rules and routines for long-term survivability and effectiveness as a result of a competitive market, external pressures, or efficiency (Scott, 2001). While rules may maintain a sense of stability within an organization, structural inertia can inhibit organizational adaptability in times of great ecological change (Hannan & Freeman, 1984). This is highly evident in the context of higher education philanthropy, where fundraising professionals create new rules, rituals and procedures (e.g., donor-recognition policy, principles for corporate donations) to maintain a sense of stability and survivability. Furthermore, in-house advancement offices often incorporate widely held myths about fundraising activities by adhering to institutional scripts (e.g., hiring certified fundraisers) and ideals as a result of the professionalization (i.e., professional-organizational relations) of fundraising (Meyer & Rowan, 1978; Scott, 2001; Tempel, Seiler, & Adrich, 2010).

Today, higher education fundraising is now regarded as a profession in which professional fundraisers specializes in annual giving, foundation relations, corporate giving, planned giving, major gifts, or campaign fundraising (Proper & Caboni, 2014). The rise of professionalization for fundraising within the college setting has forced several higher education constituents to define their area of specialization of which, in turn, prompt fundraising professionals to define the conditions of their workplace environment, and to establish legitimation for their occupational autonomy (Larson, 1977; Collins, 1979). Tolbert and Hall (2008) define professionalization as "the formalization and conditions under which resistance to formalization occur in organizations" (p. 36). For example, the vice-president for institutional advancement at Boston College may hire a professional consulting firm, such as Grenzebach Glier & Associates, Marts & Lundy, or Ayers & Associates, Inc. (i.e., filtering of personnel) to enhance or change administrator roles due to possible comprise or conflict between constituencies (e.g., coordinators, managers, regulators). Similarly, development offices at Boston College may require their peers to attend professional seminars and workshops organized by the Council for Advancement and Support of Education (CASE) as a result of intense competition among elite colleges and universities in the United States. Because competition has caused colleges and universities to become more alike instead of distinctive, leaders of higher education must recruit several managers (e.g., director of gift planning, director of development) and specialized staff members (e.g., major gifts coordinator, assistant director of athletic development) to assist current newcomers and career changers with new fundraising responsibilities being placed for the welfare of both donors and institutions (Caboni, 2012). In other words, the professionalization of fundraising may serve to reinforce and act as an isomorphic force of socialization (i.e., standard methods of practice, normative rules about appropriate behavior), of which, in turn, prompt fundraising professionals to a commonly recognized hierarchy of status (i.e., formal and informal means) that is driven by status competition and institutional prestige (i.e., organizational identity). Ultimately, such *normative* pressure would foster homogenization in structure, process, and behavior of formal organizations as colleges and universities not only compete to provide the same benefits, services, and rewards for private donors and elite philanthropists but also because they would be defined as legitimate only if they can offer everything similar to what other institutions of higher education offers in modern society. To help visualize institutional theory in the context of higher education philanthropy, Figure 2 present a conceptual framework developed by the author in conceptualizing institutional isomorphism in higher education.

In Figure 2, Roy Y. Chan's conceptual model illustrates that fundraising professionals within the contexts of resource allocation, donor engagement, and fundraising are making decisions that foster or exhibit isomorphism on campus. Notably, fundraising professionals are striving for power and control within their external environments as a result of intense competition for elite philanthropists (i.e., power/dependence relationship). O'Meara (2007) defines striving "as the pursuit of prestige within the academic hierarchy" (p. 122). That is, the decision to strive for prestige prompts fundraising professionals to be conformist with institutional rules, rituals, and routines, and the prospective of major donors rights (i.e., *Donor Bill of Rights*) (Caboni, 2010).

Figure 2. Conceptual model for research in higher education philanthropy: academic environments in the context of institutional theory

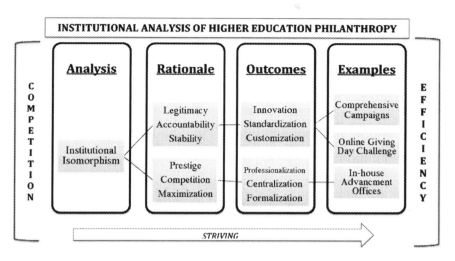

To enumerate, Figure 2 illustrates the role of institutional isomorphism in facilitating legitimacy, prestige, and stability have led to the intense competition for major donors in both the organization and field levels. Notably, competition and imitation have led to burgeoning staff, whereby professional fundraisers compete for efficiency and effectiveness in terms of the total dollars raised in higher education by customizing and standardizing their reward programs and structures that caters to the needs and interests of private donors. For example, Boston College may create comprehensive capital campaigns similar to the University of Notre Dame to generate the funds needed for capital improvements and endowment growth such as, new educational technologies in the classroom, libraries, and beyond the physical campus. Such process often requires a development professional that is multi-skilled (or "curious chameleons"), whereby in-house advancement professionals develop activities such as comprehensive capital campaigns and online giving day challenge that are personalized to the individual and/or organization interests. As many colleges and universities now have established offices of institutional advancement across the United States, leaders of university advancement must develop programs and activities that are creative and innovative to the core mission and identity of the institution. Furthermore, fundraising professionals must go beyond merely adopting the techniques of "best practice" if they are to increase institutional performance and efficiency that reflects the core needs of institution. While most activities and programs now require broad-based participation in both the local and national level, the campaign is likely to remain as the core element of higher education philanthropy because it provides people an unequaled opportunity to respond to specific goals and deadlines in an organized fashion.

Nonetheless, applying a theoretical lens of isomorphism may assist teacher-scholars and advanced practitioners to understand fundraisers decision-making process and their actual behavior to comprehensive capital campaigns in higher education. Furthermore, integrating a theoretical construct of isomorphism may assist leaders to better understand donor's intent to support colleges and universities through normative and social elements (e.g., conformity, isomorphism, loose-coupling) as well as the symbolic aspects of marketization than solely on self-interest. As institutional advancement offices develop more sophisticated and elaborate comprehensive campaigns, with top research universities often competing within their peer group for campaign dollars, fundraising professionals must *appear* legitimate and prestigious (i.e., logic of confidence) within the inter-organizational network in hopes of mobilizing additional funding from large-scale philanthropic organizations and external groups (Proper & Caboni, 2014). Nevertheless, the role of the board of trustees, the president, and development professionals in securing major resources and philanthropic gifts within the organization and field level is the result of coercive (state bodies), imitative (other organizations), and normative (professionals) conformity to institutional rule, institutional isomorphism, and normatively based decision making in higher education (Oplatka & Hemsley-Brown, 2010).

CONCLUSION

In essence, the potential for organizational theory such as, resource dependence theory (RDT) and new institutionalism, in contributing to research on higher education philanthropy is enormous. This chapter introduces and proposes teacher-scholars and advanced practitioners to utilize organizational analysis to understand the role of philanthropy in shaping major structural and formal changes to the field of higher education administration, such as gift management, endowment management, and institutional mission. Applying a theoretical construct would help colleges and universities make sense of the complex relationship between academic organizations and a set of actors in their technical environment (e.g., donor's demands, donor's rights), as well as the effects of their civic and social environment on legitimizing the work with external partners. As colleges and universities become highly homogeneous or isomorphic in nature as a result of institutionalization (e.g., inter-organizational arrangements, behavior dynamics of actors), teachers-scholars and advanced practitioners should apply resource dependence theory (RDT) and institutional theory along with other organizational theories – agency theory, contingency theory, network theory, control theory - to help answer the many unanswered research agenda in higher education philanthropy such as, donor intent and the effect of time on the relationship of donors; the effect of giving on institutional mission in shaping the ways campuses become involved with their communities; the engagement of non-traditional donors at historically black colleges and universities (HBCUs); and/or the relationship between tuition price and state subsidies to philanthropy (Bernstein, 2013). Needless to say, there is some excellent work being done in historical research, particularly as regards to the role of leadership in fundraising for colleges and universities. However, as editor-in-chief Scott L. Thomas of *The Journal of Higher Education* once noted, "During my four years as editor, I have yet to receive a well-developed manuscript on the role of philanthropy in academe." Consequently, new formal research that utilizes interpretive frameworks in philanthropy research will yield better studies on linking leadership to fundraising performance and functioning in higher education. Charles Keidan (2014) once stated, "Philanthropy's imprint on the fabric of university life is just emerging. As its profile rises, we should expect some celebration of its contribution to higher education – but we are also entitled to demand more rigorous and robust scholarship about its role in society." Subsequently, a thorough understanding of organizational theories is relevant for teacher-scholars and development professionals in conceptualizing how philanthropic organizations operate and how funding patterns influence academic organizations in the era of the knowledge economy and globalization. The future of philanthropy research will lie upon grounded theory method and case study research data from teacher-scholars and advanced practitioners if we seek to understand how funding has shaped the evolution of research universities in the evolving field of philanthropy and fundraising in American higher education (Drezner, 2013).

ACKNOWLEDGMENT

The author would like to kindly acknowledge Dr. Ted I. K. Youn, Dr. Joseph P. Zolner, Dr. Noah D. Drezner, Dr. Frances Huehls, Dr. Brad Weiner, and Madelyn Bell for providing substantial feedback and comments in this paper.

REFERENCES

Allison, G. T. (1971). *Essence of decision: Explaining the Cuban missile crisis.* Boston, MA: Little Brown.

Altbach, P. G. (2002). Knowledge and education as international commodities: The collapse of the common good. *Industry and Higher Education, 28*, 2–5.

ASHE. (2012). Philanthropy, volunteerism & fundraising in higher education (ASHE Reader Series). New York City, NY: Pearson Custom Publishing.

Bastedo, M. N. (2012). *The organization of higher education: Managing colleges for a new era.* Baltimore, MD: John Hopkins University Press.

Bender, T. (1997). Politics, intellect, and the US university, 1945-1995. *Daedalus, 126*, 1–38.

Bernstein, A. R. (2013). *Funding the future: Philanthropy's influence on American higher education.* New York City, NY: R&L Education.

Birnbaum, R. (1988). *How colleges work: The cybernetics of academic organization and leadership.* San Francisco, CA: Jossey-Bass.

Bloland, H. G. (2002). No longer emerging, fundraising is a profession. *The CASE International Journal of Education Advancement, 3*(1), 7–21.

Bremmer, R. (1988). *American philanthropy.* Chicago, IL: The University of Chicago Press.

Brittingham, B. E., & Pezzullo, T. R. (1990). *The campus green: Fund raising in higher education.* Washington, D.C.: ERIC Clearinghouse on Higher Education.

Brubacher, J. S., & Rudy, W. (1997). *Higher education in transition: A history of American colleges and universities* (4th ed.). New Brunswick, NJ: Transaction Publishers.

Caboni, T. C. (2012). Toward professionalization: Fundraising norms and their implications for practice. In *Found in ASHE, Philanthropy, volunteerism & fundraising in higher education* (pp. 725–746). New York City, NY: Pearson Learning Solutions.

Caboni, T. C., & Proper, E. (2007). Dissertations related to fundraising and their implications for higher education research. Louisville, KY: Association for the Study of Higher Education (ASHE) *Annual Conference.*

Caboni, T. C.Timothy C. Caboni. (2010). The normative structure of college and university fundraising. *The Journal of Higher Education, 81*(3), 339–365. doi:10.1353/jhe.0.0094

Caboni, T. C.Timothy C. Caboni. (2010). The normative structure of college and university fundraising behaviors. *The Journal of Higher Education, 81*(3), 339–365. doi:10.1353/jhe.0.0094

Carbone, R. F. (1986). *An agenda for research on fund raising*. College Park, MD: Clearinghouse for Research on Fund Raising.

Cohen, M., March, J. G., & Olsen, J. P. (1972). A garbage can model of organizational choice. *Administrative Science Quarterly, 17*(1), 1–25. doi:10.2307/2392088

Cohen, M. D., & Sproull, L. S. (Eds.). (1996). *Organizational learning*. Thousand Oaks, CA: Sage.

Collins, R. (1979). *The credential society: An historical sociology of education and stratification*. New York City, NY: Academic Press.

ConSCU. (2014). *BOR awarded $500,000 Kresge Foundation Grant*. Retrieved from: http://www.ct.edu/newsroom/bor_awarded_500000_kresge_foundation_grant

Cook, W. B. (1997). Fundraising and the college presidency in an era of uncertainty: From 1975 to the present. *The Journal of Higher Education, 68*(1), 53–86. doi:10.2307/2959936

Cook, W. B., & Lasher, W. F. (1996). Toward a theory of fund raising in higher education. *The Review of Higher Education, 20*(1), 33–51. doi:10.1353/rhe.1996.0002

Corbin, J., & Strauss, A. (2008). *Basics of qualitative research: Techniques and procedures for developing grounded theory* (3rd ed.). Thousand Oaks, CA: SAGE Publications.

Curti, M. E. (1958). The history of American philanthropy as a field of research. *The American Historical Review, 62*(2), 352–363. doi:10.2307/1845188

Cutlip, S. M. (1990). *Fundraising in the United States (Its role in America's philanthropy)*. New York, NY: Transaction Publishers.

Dee, J. R. (2014). *Organization, administration, and leadership: Addressing the relevance gap in higher education research*. Washington, DC: American Education Research Association (AERA) Division J Blog. Retrieved from: http://aeradivisionj.blogspot.com/2014/07/organization-administration-and.html

DiMaggio, P. J., & Powell, W. W. (1983). The iron cage revisited. Institutional isomorphism and collective rationality in organizational fields. *American Sociological Review, 48*(2), 147–160. doi:10.2307/2095101

DiMaggio, P. J., & Powell, W. W. (1991). *The new institutionalism in organizational analysis*. Chicago, IL: University of Chicago Press.

DiMaggio, P. J., & Powell, W. W. (2012). *The iron cage revisited. Institutional isomorphism and collective rationality in organizational fields (revised). In Philanthropy, volunteerism & fundraising in higher education (ASHE Reader)* (pp. 100–140). New York, NY: Pearson Learning Solutions.

Drezner, N. D. (2011). *Philanthropy and fundraising in American higher education.* Hoboken, NJ: Wiley.

Drezner, N. D. (2013). *Expanding the donor base in higher education: Engaging non-traditional donors.* New York, NY: Routledge.

Drezner, N. D., & Huehls, F. (2014). *Philanthropy and fundraising in higher education: Theory, practice, and new paradigms.* New York, NY: Taylor & Francis Group.

Edwards, K. (2004). The university in Europe and the US. In R. King (Ed.), *The University in the Global Age* (pp. 27–44). Houndmills, UK: Palgrave Macmillan.

Geiger, R. L. (1993). *To advance knowledge: The growth of American research universities, 1900-1940.* Oxford, UK: Oxford University Press.

Giroux, H. A. (2014). *Neoliberalism's war on higher education.* New York: NY Haymarket Books.

Gose, B. (2013). Strategic philanthropy comes to higher education. *The Chronicle of Higher Education, 19*(July). Retrieved from http://chronicle.com/article/Strategic-Philanthropy-Comes/140299

Gouldner, A. W. (1954). *Patterns of industrial bureaucracy.* New York, NY: Free Press.

Gumport, P. J. (2000). Academic restructuring: Organizational change and institutional imperatives. *Higher Education, 39*(1), 67–91. doi:10.1023/A:1003859026301

Hall, P. D. (1992). Teaching and research on philanthropy, voluntarism, and non-profit organizations: A case study of academic innovation. *Teachers College Record, 93*(3), 403–436.

Hannan, M. T., & Freeman, J. (1977). The population ecology of organizations. *American Journal of Sociology, 83*(5), 929–984. doi:10.1086/226424

Hannan, M. T., & Freeman, J. (1984). Structural inertia and organizational change. *American Sociological Review, 49*(2), 149–164. doi:10.2307/2095567

Hendrickson, R. M., Lane, J. E., Harris, J. T., & Dorman, R. H. (2012). *Academic leadership and governance of higher education: A guide for trustees, leaders and aspiring leaders of two- and four-year institutions.* New York, NY: Stylus Publishing.

Hoy, K. H., & Miskel, C. G. (2008). *Educational administration: Theory, research and practice*. New York, NY: Allyn and Bacon.

Jacobson, H. K. (1990). Research on institutional advancement: A review of progress and a guide to literature. *The Review of Higher Education, 13*(4), 433–488.

Johnson Grossnickle and Associates. (2013). *Million dollar ready assessing the institutional factors that lead to transformational gifts*. Indianapolis, IN: Indiana University-Purdue University Indianapolis (IUPUI) Lilly Family School of Philanthropy. Retrieved from http://www.philanthropy.iupui.edu/files/research/million_dollar_ready_executive_summary_booklet_low_res.pdf

Katz, M. (1975). *Class, bureaucracy, and schools: The illusion of educational change in America*. New York, NY: Praeger.

Keidan, C. (2014, October 23). Why philanthropy merits scholarly study. *Times Higher Education*. Retrieved October 20, 2014 from: http://www.timeshighereducation.co.uk/features/why-philanthropy-merits-scholarly-study/2016437.fullarticle

Keidan, C., Jung, T., & Pharoah, C. (2014). *Philanthropy education in the UK and continental Europe: Current provision, perceptions and opportunities*. London, UK: Centre for Charitable Giving and Philanthropy.

Kelly, K. S. (1991). *Fundraising and public relations: A critical analysis*. Hillsdale, NJ: Lawrence Erlbaum Associates.

Kelly, K. S. (2002). The state of fundraising theory and research. In *New strategies for educational fundraising* (pp. 39–55). New York, NY: Rowman & Littlefield Publishers.

Kerr, C. (2001). *The uses of the university*. Cambridge, MA: Harvard University Press.

Kezar, A. (2011). Understanding and facilitating Organizational change in the 21st century: Recent research and conceptualizations. *ASHE-ERIC Higher Education Report, 28*.

Kinnison, W. A., & Ferin, M. J. (1989). The three-party relationship. In J. W. Pocock (Ed.), *Fundraising Leadership: A Guide for Colleges and University Boards* (pp. 57–61). Washington, DC: Association of Governing Boards of Universities and Colleges.

Lagemann, E. C. (2002). Toward a fourth philanthropic response: American philanthropy and its public. In *The perfect gift: The philanthropic imagination in poetry and prose* (p. 103). Bloomington, IN: Indiana University Press.

Larson, M. S. (1977). *The rise of professionalism*. Berkeley, CA: University of California Press.

Let's Get Ready. (2014). *Let's get ready to launch college success program*. Retrieved from: http://letsgetready.org/index.asp?page=17&press=139

Levinthal, D. (2014). Inside the Koch brothers' campus crusade. Washington, DC: The Center for Public Integrity.

Lynch, K. (2006). Neo-liberalism and marketization: The implications for higher education. *European Educational Research Journal*, *5*(1), 1–17. doi:10.2304/eerj.2006.5.1.1

Mangan, K. (2013). How Gates shapes state higher-education policy. *The Chronicle of Higher Education*, *19*(July). Retrieved from http://chronicle.com/article/How-Gates-Shapes-State/140303

March, J. G., & Cohen, M. (1974). *Leadership and ambiguity: The American college president*. New York, NY: McGraw-Hill.

March, J. G., Schulz, M., & Zhou, X. (2000). *The dynamics of rules: Change in written organizational codes*. Palo Alto, CA: Stanford University Press.

March, J. G., & Simon, H. A. (1958). *Organizations*. New York, NY: Wiley.

Meyer, H., & Rowan, B. (1978). The structure of educational organizations. In M. Meyer (Ed.), Environments and organizations, (pp. 78-109). San Francisco, CA: Jossey Bass.

Meyer, J. W., & Scott, W. R. (1977). Institutionalized organizations: Formal structure as myth and ceremony. *American Journal of Sociology*, *83*(2), 340–363. doi:10.1086/226550

Meyer, J. W., & Scott, W. R. (1983). *Organizational environments: Ritual and rationality*. Beverly Hills, CA: Sage Publications.

Miller-Millesen, J. L. (2003). Understanding the behavior of nonprofit boards of directors: A theory-based approach. *Nonprofit and Voluntary Sector Quarterly*, *32*(4), 521–547. doi:10.1177/0899764003257463

O'Meara, K. (2007). Striving for what? Exploring the pursuit of prestige. Higher Education: Handbook of Theory and Research, 22, 121–179.

Oplatka, I., & Hemsley-Brown, J. (2010). The globalization and marketization of higher education: Some insights from the standpoint of institutional theory. In F. Maringe & N. Foskett (Eds.), *Globalization and Internationalization in Higher Education* (pp. 65–80). New York, NY: Continuum International Publishing Group.

Payton, R. L. (1988). *Philanthropy: Voluntary action for the public good*. New York, NY: American Council on Education/Macmillan Series on Higher Edu.

Perry, M., Field, K., & Supiano, B. (2013). The Gates effect. *The Chronicle of Higher Education*, *19*(July). Retrieved from http://chronicle.com/article/The-Gates-Effect/140323

Pfeffer, J. (1972). Size and composition of corporate board of directors. *Administrative Science Quarterly*, *21*, 218–228. doi:10.2307/2393956

Pfeffer, J. (1987). A resource dependence perspective on interorganizational relations. In M. S. Mizruchi & M. Schwartz (Eds.), *Intercorporate relations: The structural analysis of Business* (pp. 22–55). Cambridge, UK: Cambridge University Press.

Pfeffer, J., & Salancik, G. R. (1978). *The external control of organizations: A resource dependence perspective*. New York, NY: Harper & Row.

Proper, E., & Caboni, T. C. (2014). *Institutional advancement: What we know*. New York, NY: Palgrave Macmillan. doi:10.1057/9781137374288

Quinterno, J., & Orozco, V. (2012). *The great cost shift: How higher education cuts undermine the future middle class*. New York, NY: Demos.

Riesman, D. (1956). *Constraint and variety in American education*. Lincoln, NE: University of Nebraska Press.

Rowland, A. W. (1983). Research in institutional advancement: A selected, annotated compendium of doctoral dissertations. Washington, DC: Council for the Advancement and Support of Education (CASE).

Rowland, A. W. (1986). *Handbook of institutional advancement: A modern guide to executive management, institutional relations, fundraising, alumni administration, government relations, publications, periodicals, and enrollment management*. San Francisco, CA: Jossey Bass.

Schervish, P. G., & Havens, J. J. (1998). Embarking on a republic of benevolence: New survey findings on charitable giving. *Nonprofit and Voluntary Sector Quarterly*, *27*(2), 237–242. doi:10.1177/0899764098272007

Scott, W. R. (1987). *Organizations: Rational, natural and open systems*. Hoboken, NJ: Prentice-Hall, Inc.

Scott, W. R. (1995). Introduction: Institutional theory and organization. In W. R. Scott & S. Christnesne (Eds.), *The Institutional Construction of Organizations*. Thousand Oaks, CA: Sage.

Scott, W. R. (2001). *Institutions and organizations*. Thousand Oaks, CA: Sage.

Sporn, B. (1999). *Adaptive university structures: An analysis of adaptation to socioeconomic environments of U.S. and European higher education*. London, UK: Jessica Kingsley.

Suchman, M. C. (1995). Managing legitimacy: Strategic and institutional approaches. *Academy of Management Review, 20*, 571–610.

Tempel, E. R., Seiler, T. L., & Adrich, E. E. (2010). *Achieving excellence in fundraising*. San Francisco, CA: Jossey-Bass.

Terlaak, A. (2007). Order without law? The role of certified management standards in shaping socially desired firm behaviors. *Academy of Management Review, 32*(3), 968–985. doi:10.5465/AMR.2007.25275685

Thelin, J. R., & Trollinger, R. W. (2014). *Philanthropy and American higher education*. New York, NY: Palgrave Macmillan. doi:10.1057/9781137318589

Thompson, J. D. (1967). *Organizations in action*. New York, NY: McGraw-Hill.

Tolbert, P. S. (1985). Institutional environments and resource dependence: Sources of administrative structure in institutions of higher education. *Administrative Science Quarterly, 30*(1), 1–13. doi:10.2307/2392808

Tolbert, P. S., & Hall, R. H. (2008). *Organizations: Structures, processes and outcomes*. New York, NY: Pearson.

Villalonga, B., & McGahan, A. M. (2005). The choice among acquisitions, alliances, and divestitures. *Strategic Management Journal, 26*(13), 1183–1208. doi:10.1002/smj.493

Weick, K. E. (1976). Educational organizations as loosely coupled systems. *Administrative Science Quarterly, 21*(1), 1–19. doi:10.2307/2391875

Weitz, E., & Shenhav, Y. (2000). A longitudinal analysis of technical and organizational uncertainty in management theory. *Organization Studies, 21*(1), 243–265. doi:10.1177/0170840600211005

Worth, M. J. (1993). Educational fundraising: Principles and practice. Washington, DC: American Council on Education (ACE).

Worth, M. J. (2002). *New strategies for educational fundraising.* New York, NY: Rowman & Littlefield Publishers.

Yin, R. K. (2008). *Case study research: Design and methods* (4th ed.). London, UK: Sage Publications.

Youn, T. I. K., & Murphy, P. B. (1997). *Organizational studies in higher education.* New York, NY: Garland Publishing, Inc.

Youn, T. I. K., & Price, T. M.Ted I. K. Youn; Tanya M. Price. (2009). Learning from the experience of others: The evolution of faculty tenure and promotion rules in comprehensive institutions. *The Journal of Higher Education, 80*(2), 204–237. doi:10.1353/jhe.0.0041

Zunz, O. (2014). *Philanthropy in America: A history.* Princeton, NJ: Princeton University Press. doi:10.1515/9781400850242

Chapter 2
Philanthropy and the Character of the Public Research University:
The Intersections of Private Giving, Institutional Autonomy, and Shared Governance

Larry Catá Backer
Pennsylvania State University, USA

Nabih Haddad
Michigan State University, USA

ABSTRACT

Educational scholars have examined the relationship of philanthropy and its contributions to the public university. Yet, there has been little discussion of the influence of philanthropy on the governance space of the public research university, and specifically as conditional philanthropy may affect academic integrity and shared governance. In this chapter, we consider these larger issues in the context of a study of a recent case. Drawing on public records, interviews, and university documents, the chapter examines conditional donation of The Charles G. Koch Foundation (CKF) to the Florida State University (FSU). We suggest that the Koch Foundation gift appears to illustrate a new model of governance based philanthropy. It has done so by tying donations to control or influence of the internal governing mechanics of an academic unit of a public university. This model has generated controversy.

DOI: 10.4018/978-1-4666-9664-8.ch002

Though there was substantial faculty and student backlash, the model appears to be evidence of a new philanthropic relationship between the public university and substantial donors, one in which donors may change the nature of traditional shared governance relationships within the university. We maintain that instances of such "new" strategic philanthropy require greater focus on and sensitivity to shared governance and faculty input as a way to ensure accountability, especially to preserve the integrity of the academic enterprise and its public mission where donors seek to leverage philanthropy into choices relating to faculty hires, courses and programs traditionally at the center of faculty prerogatives in shared governance.

INTRODUCTION

The close relationship between philanthropy and higher education has played a substantial role within the American higher education system. Bonglia (2002, p. 9) notes that "Early in the 18th Century, private support of institutions of higher education by philanthropists became a trend." And indeed, this relationship is just as salient today as it has been in the colonial area. Drezner (2011), for example, noted that "American higher education as we know it today would not exist if it were not for the voluntary contributions of many individuals" (p. 26). Hall (1992) drew similar conclusions, suggesting that "[n]o single force is more responsible for the emergence of the modern university in America than giving by individuals and foundations" (p. 403). The recent economic downturn coupled with the steady decline of state support for public universities, for instance, has forced public institutions to position themselves to better harvest philanthropic donations (Speck, 2010; Cheslock & Gianneschi, 2008). As McAlexander and Koenig (2012) have noted, "The growing concern about the ability to glean necessary financial resources from the traditional sources of tuition, taxes (for public universities), and fees, has driven leaders of institutions of higher education to place a much sharper focus on developing the philanthropic capacity of alumni, friends, and other partners to provide the economic support necessary to deliver higher education in the modern millennium" (p. 122). Additionally, this steady decrease in state appropriations for higher education represents what many scholars have suggested as a "new paradigm" of higher education funding (Speck, 2010; McKeown, 1996). Increasingly, more and more public universities have started to describe themselves as state-assisted, rather than state-supported, institutions (Hossler, 2004). Naturally, this has created an environment where public institutions are now actively searching out alternative revenue sources because this has become "the only source of real discretionary money and in many cases is assuming a critical role in balancing institutional budgets" (Leslie & Ramey, 1988, p.115-116).

One substantial source of such alternative revenue sources are foundations. Unlike public bodies, foundations are highly centralized and closed systems. Public accountability is very limited and one of the few forms of accountability are done mainly through tax laws, which requires foundations to allocate funding for charitable purposes. They are also accountable to their own organizational by-laws and their trustees, but not to the general public. Many times, major foundations are guided by wide ranging social agendas which is collectively understood as strategic philanthropy (Dowey, 2001; Barrows, 1990). With over $700 billion in assets and over $50 billion in total giving per year (Foundation Center, 2014), foundations collectively have an immense amount of power to fund public policy initiatives at a national and global scale (see, e.g., Roelofs, 2003 and Dowey, 2001). According to Dowey (2001), governmental devolution coupled with increasing austerity measures have made these organizations even more powerful.

Though there has been much discussion on the influence of philanthropy on k-12 education (see, e.g., McKersie, 1999; Cohen, 2007), there has been a limited discussion within the higher education literature (Hall & Thomas, 2012). Although foundations have always taken an active role in American higher education (see, e.g., Barrows, 1990; Drezner, 2011; Dowie, 2001; Thelin, 2011), it has been much more concerted in recent years through a market-based approach where initiatives are funded by foundations using "engaged" or "advocacy" philanthropy (Katz, 2012). More importantly, a new form of philanthropy has emerged in recent years. Through forms of *strategic philanthropy*, the most powerful foundations "have taken up a set of methods -- strategic grant-making, public policy advocacy, the funding of intermediaries, and collaboration with government -- that illustrate their direct and unapologetic desire to influence policy and practice in numerous higher education arenas." (Hall & Thomas, 2012). The object is to leverage contributions to the university into a power to more directly determine university policy and practices that was once the sole domain of university administrators and faculty. Especially as these new strategic philanthropic strategies have sought to affect decisions about faculty hires, course offerings, pedagogy and academic programs, these strategies directly affect the traditional relationship between faculty, board and administration in the governance of universities. Despite this trend, scholarly discourse regarding the influence of philanthropy on public universities has been limited, at best. Naturally, the influence of philanthropy occupies a contentious space among key stakeholders of the public research university — professors, students, and the community—because the most pressing issues rests on the influence of philanthropy on institutional autonomy, shared governance, and the freedom of inquiry, ideals ingrained into the ontological fabric of the academy. The ideal of the university represents an autonomous generator of knowledge, free from external constraints, allowing the flow of knowledge to disseminate freely for the advancement of the public good (Thelin,

2011; Albach, 2001). While this ideal has only been partially reached, now more than ever, the influence of private funding on knowledge production has been an increasing concern for those within the higher education enterprise.

To that end, this chapter examines the relationship between philanthropy undertaken through foundations or by individuals, and the increasingly contested governance space of the public research university, and against the backdrop of academic integrity and shared governance. We do so by situating our analysis specifically on an agreement between The Charles G. Koch Foundation's (CKF) and Florida State University (FSU). In 2007, CKF approached Florida State with an initial pledge of $1.5 million that would be extended to over $6 million in the course of 6 years. In return, FSU's economics department would allow CKF representatives to sit on screening committees for new faculty hires, providing funding for doctoral students in economics as well as the creation of a new undergrad programs that would be based on curriculum based on the educational ideology of CKF. This deal eventually produced strong faculty and community backlash, especially with respect to the way the deal relegated substantial control of a public institution to an external actor. As the chair of FSU's economics, Bruce Benson, stated in an internal email, "Koch cannot tell a university who to hire.... [but] they are going to try to make sure, through contractual terms and monitoring, that people hired are [to] be consistent with 'donar Intent.'" And indeed, where donors traditionally had little to say how their grants would be used, this trend represented by the CKF is a major point of contention. In this chapter, we first provide background regarding the case of involving FSU and CKF's agreement. We first examine the FSU/CKF donation as the case basis for our analysis. We then consider its ramifications for university governance and philanthropy. We situate that discussion first within the analytical context of the university faculty senate, and its role within the public university. We then focus on the realities of shared governance and its functional challenges in light of academic integrity and university donors through that framework. On that basis we then flesh out the difficulties of shared governance within the a-symmetric power arrangements that are the hallmark of public universities, and then suggest where a faculty senate can fit into this governance enterprise when dealing with external influences of major donors.

CKF AND FLORIDA STATE UNIVERSITY

In these difficult economic times, it is more important than ever that public universities find ways to partner with the private sector to develop the sorts of programs that our society will need in coming decades. – Past President of Florida State University, T.K. Wetherell

Universities are no strangers to leveraging private donations for programmatic development. As the former FSU president T.K. Wetherell describes in the quote above, it may not be just financial need that drives universities to partner with donors. The "sorts of programs our society will need in the coming decades" language masks ideology. And that ideology is operationalized through the choices about which ideologically committed donors a university would be willing to engage with. CKF had a history of funding libertarian and anti-regulation causes throughout the nation (CKF's Academic Giving Principles notes: "We fund those activities that a university proposes that match our philanthropic priorities and have the greatest likelihood of success."). Charles Koch is described as having "continuously supported academic and public policy research (including a number of Nobel Prize winners) for 50 years, with a special focus on developing voluntary, market-based solutions to social problems. This interest led Mr. Koch to found or help build a number of organizations, including the Institute for Humane Studies, Cato Institute, Mercatus Center at George Mason University, Bill of Rights Institute, and Market-Based Management Institute." (CKF, About Charles G. Koch).

CKF and Florida State Agreement present a very interesting case which examines the issues surrounding faculty governance and administrative and philanthropic influences on the public research university. This section will examine the agreement, and what lead then President Eric Barron, to formally ask the faculty senate to set up a committee to examine the issues surrounding the Koch Foundation and academic integrity. The CKF donation was part of a gift (with conditions) made by it and the financial company BB&T Corp (Ray, 2008). CKF had a history of funding libertarian and anti-regulation causes throughout the nation.

When the grant was announced, then President Wetherell, the Dean of both, the College of Business, and the College of Social Sciences, along with BB&T Tallahassee President Paul Sullivan and Nan Hillis, president of BB&T's Orlando-based East Florida Region were all present (Ray, 2008). As then described, a portion of the gift went to both the Department of Finance, and the Department of Economics, to develop a joint BB&T Program of Free Enterprise as a way to expand free market education to undergrad students at Florida State University. When it came to CKF's portion of the grant, the agreement accumulated to a $6.59 million budget, with $1.5 million coming from the CKF. The grant money would go toward the Economics Department. Under The Memorandum of Understanding (MOU), CKF would have a direct say in the hiring of faculty members through a Koch appointed advisory-board. There would also be the creation of two undergraduate programs: *The Program for the Study of Political Economic and Free Enterprise (SPEFE)* and *The Program for Excellence in Economic Education (EEE)*, both located within *The Gus A. Stavros Center for the Advancement of Free Enterprise and Economic Education*, which defines itself as part of the Department of Economics. In this instance, the donor prescribed curricular content, primal through the development of undergraduate courses with Ayn Rand as required reading. This course would be offered to 108 students per term, and eventually increase to 500 students, also providing an online option. The MOU also provided graduate student support, such as fellowships, and undergraduate extracurricular activities, that would include an economics club, a speaker series, and support for the Director of the Koch Undergraduate Program, and small scholarships of $200 for students to participate. This all aimed to "develop and promote a free-enterprise curriculum; [that] will enable the development of a Web site that focuses on the program's free-enterprise principles and highlights a new Speaker Series with the inclusion of podcasts from previous speeches; and will fund the establishment of a new economics course, 'Morals and Ethics in Economic Systems" (Ray, 2008). There would also be the creation of a new certificate program: The Certificate in Markets and Institutions.

Thus under the MOU, CKF, the FSU Foundation, and the FSU economics department, there would be an appointment of five professors and staff, the creation of a Program for the Study of Political Economic and Free Enterprise and a Program for Excellence in Economic Education, and the creation of educational undergrad programs (Miller & Bellamy, 2012). Of course, the Koch Foundation would establishe an oversight mechanism in how this gift would be monitored, a practice that was almost unheard of in American universities. The most controversial piece of this agreement was the CKF sponsored advisory committee. An advisory board would be chosen by CKF which would determine what faculty candidates would be qualified for funding. By reviewing all publicly provided material by applicants for the new teaching positions this was a way to ensure that the scholarship of the professors met the ideological objectives of the foundation, and the potential professors who did not match the objectives of CKF would "not eligible to hold a Professorship Position or any other position in an Affiliated program and Position, without CKF's prior written consent" (Memorandum of Understanding, p.3). This stipulated that a Koch-appointed advisory committee would select professors and conduct annual evaluations (Levinthal, 2014; Hundley, 2011). The advisory board system worked like this: the faculty members would create a faculty appointed committee that will do the initially vetting of candidates. The CKF sponsored advisory committee would then review the list and make its recommendations on which members would be qualified for Koch funding. In the final stages, the faculty committee would select the finalists, where no funding for any program would be released without the review of Koch's advisory board.

It was contemplated that Bruce Benson, a well-respected libertarian economic theorist and Florida State University economics department chairmen would remain another three years as the department chairmen. CKF expressed its willingness to give Florida State an extra $105,000 to keep Benson in as the chairperson even though he told his wife that he would step down in 2009 after a one, three-year term. Ideologically, Professor Benson is a self-described "libertarian anarchist" who asserts that every government function he's studied "can be, has been, or is being produced better by the private sector." (Levinthal, D. (2014, September 12). Internal emails from Benson, eventually obtained and published by the Center for Public Integrity, evidenced some the internal decision making and discussions among the economic faculty. The emails sent on November 26, 2007 to the economics faculty detailing the Koch Foundation's proposal described the ideological aims: "The Koch Foundation agenda is to expose students to free-market ideas, and to provide opportunities for students who want to study with faculty who share Koch's appreciation for markets and distrust for government. This proposal is, therefore, not to just give us money to hire anyone we want and fund any graduate student hat we choose. There are constraints, as noted below" (Koch Foundation Proposal, 2007, p.1). In the proposal, Benson also pointed out some of the obvious influences of the Koch foundation's agenda within the academic process of the economics department. As he explains in the proposal, "As we all know, there are not free lunches. Everything comes with costs. In this case, the money for faculty lines and graduate students is coming from a group of funding organizations with strong libertarian views. These organizations have an explicit agenda. They want to expose students to what they believe are vital concepts about the benefits of the market and the dangers of government failure, and they want to support and mentor students who share their views. Therefore, they are trying to convince us to hire faculty who will provide that exposure and mentoring. If we are not willing to hire such faculty, they are not willing to fund us" (Koch Foundation Proposal, 2007, p.3).

Initially, when an agreement was reached, there was little to no publicity regarding the deal, on campus or elsewhere (Hundley, 2011). Yet, by 2011, there was an increasing concern among the university's stakeholders, mainly from the faculty and students, about the influence that the agreement gave to the donors especially with respect to academic matters. Dr. Ray Bellamy, a physician and a faculty member at FSU's College of Medicine, and Dr. Kent S. Miller, a professor of emeritus of psychology publicized their views in the May 2011 edition of the *Tallahassee Democrat*. Before that, however, they both went to the administration to air their concerns. As Bellamy & Miller (2012) write in the AAUP "Before publishing a coauthored op-ed in the *Tallahassee Democrat* in May 2011, we took our concerns to both the current FSU president, Eric Barron, and the Dean of the College of Social Sciences and Public Policy, David Rasmussen. Barron, who hadn't been president at the time the agreement was signed, said that he had reviewed the documents and didn't see a problem. Rasmussen told us that the university had not hired anyone who would not have been hired otherwise, that the grant had facilitated the recruitment of two excellent assistant professors and high-quality graduate students, and that it had created new postdoctoral opportunities. He told us, as he subsequently told the *St. Petersburg Times*, that not taking the money would have been 'irresponsible.'" (Miller & Bellamy, 2012). Both Miller and Bellamy eventually published their op-ed in the Tallahassee Democrat, arguing that "Public universities particularly need to raise money from donors. So much so, it has become a major function of university presidents, reinforced by tying pay to success in bringing in the money. The Kochs know this and have spent many millions of dollars working their way into higher education, impacting the hiring of faculty, supporting "correct" students, influencing the curriculum and generally advancing their agenda" (Bellamy & Miller, May, 2011) . The story was also eventually picked up by the Tampa Bay Times, which published an article in which it was reported:

Traditionally, university donors have little official input into choosing the person who fills a chair they've funded. The power of university faculty and officials to choose professors without outside interference is considered a hallmark of academic freedom. Under the agreement with the Charles G. Koch Charitable Foundation, however, faculty only retain the illusion of control. The contract specifies that an advisory committee appointed by Koch decides which candidates should be considered. The foundation can also withdraw its funding if it's not happy with the faculty's choice or if the hires don't meet "objectives" set by Koch during annual evaluations. (Hundley, 2011)

In 2009, the Koch Foundation rejected about 60% of the faculty's suggestions for the positions in the program called the Study of Political Economy and Free Enterprise and the Excellence in Economics Education. And though it is not unusual for foundations and donors to endow professorships, but what is unusual in this case, for instance, is the donors helping within the hiring process (Allen, 2014). As Rudy Fichtenbaum, an economics professor at Wright State University and AAUP's president stated: "You know, it amounts to the Koch brothers' foundation basically trying to buy a position on the faculty. And that certainly is a threat to academic freedom" (Allen, 2014).

The controversy continued through the summer. President Eric Barron, who had inherited the agreement, sent an email on May 18, 2011 to the Faculty Senate asking them to quickly examine the issues surrounding the Koch Foundation agreement and its implications on FSU's academic integrity. This was important since FSU was in the process of initiating a $1 billion fundraising campaign (Miller & Bellamy, 2012). In response to Barron's request, the Faculty Senate Steering committee appointed a five-person ad hoc review committee that included former faculty senate presidents and one former president of the university. The Faculty Senate steering committee appointed a five-member committee, who contacted as many relevant stakeholders as possible. The committee also reviewed as many documents as possible, such as the Memorandum of Understanding (MOU), the Donor Partner agreement, archived emails from the Department Chair, Dean, Provost's office, faculty members discussions, adoptions, and implementation of the agreement, new course approval paperwork for ECO 3131 – Market Ethics and the syllabus (spring 2011 section), and FSU foundation first agreement templates FSU governance documents FSU-UFF collective bargaining agreement (Faculty Senate Ad Hoc Committee Review Report, July, 2011).

After the faculty senate concluded their review, they found that the appointment of faculty did indeed meet university standards (Faculty Senate Ad Hoc Committee Review Report, July, 2011). They found that economics department had primarily control over the selection process, which was consistent with the FSU Faculty Handbook. However, the committee founded that the donor Memorandum of Understanding contained "several phrases that could open the possibility of undue outside influence in the hiring process" (p.4). In their report, the faculty senate proposed a series of recommendations, such as the ending of donor-funded hirings; prohibiting future donor agreements with external evaluations of faculty hirings; suspending Eco 313- market ethics; and resubmitting its proposal and recommending new mechanisms to review policies concerning future gifts and academic and university integrity (Faculty Senate Ad Hoc Committee Review Report, July, 2011).

As a result, the issue seemed settled. The changes made to the agreement changed the power the Koch foundation has over hiring. In the old agreement, there was a three-member advisory board to hired faculty position. The new deal, however, only included one Koch representative and does not hire faculty members. After a new hire is made, the board will consider if the Koch Foundation money will be used for their salary (Allen, 2014). President Barron was pleased with the outcome: "We acted with a high level of academic integrity and followed the normal course of events, in that the faculty picked the faculty they wanted to work with," said Barron (quoted in Chandler, 2011). Similarly, the director of higher education programs at the Koch Foundation, Ryan Stowers, publicly stated: "We are pleased that this review of the facts by the faculty committee confirms what FSU administrators have said – that the agreement with the foundation protected academic integrity and added significant value to FSU." (Chandler, 2011) And throughout the life of this funding arrangement, the economics department at FSU would allow Koch representatives to sit on screening committees for new faculty hires; and a year after the CKF provided FSU with the $1.5 million in 2008, with the foundation rejected roughly 60% of faculty candidates proposed by the faculty at FSU (Romero, 2014). While FSU administrators noted that Koch had little to no say in the hiring practices, the Faculty Senate argued otherwise, and the administration eventually altered the agreement to respond to faculty concerns. Though the Faculty Senate did undertake the reviews producing agreement revision, which retained for the faculty more control over the curriculum, nevertheless, the new agreement still maintained CKF's power over hiring practices, essentially providing them with "indirect veto power on some faculty hiring" (Romero, 2014).

PHILANTHROPY AND ITS IMPACT ON SHARED GOVERNANCE AND INSTITUTIONAL AUTONOMY

One of the most interesting issues facing public universities, as institutional actors, is the future of shared governance, especially in the effectiveness of shared governance as a means of institutionalizing the participation of faculty in university governance. Universities have sometimes succumbed to the temptation of invoking formal institutional structures to mask efforts (deliberate or unconscious) to undercut the role of faculty in university governance. In the Koch/Florida State case, President Eric Barron contacted the Faculty Senate, copying all FSU faculty, deans, and vice-president, as a way "to examine the issues surrounding the Koch Foundation agreement and its implementation to ensure that the integrity of Florida State University was protected" (FSU Faculty Senate Report, 2011).[1] This section, then, considers shared governance and university administration in a "conventional" public university. We will examine the institutional structures of the faculty senate in relation to the university system, and then see how the ideal of the faculty senate fits within the principles of shared governance.

Faculty Senate

The contextual focus in this section will be on its most fragile element, the faculty senate. "Servility rather than governance may be the most likely product of this system and cultures of retribution, of fear of marginalization for failure to adopt the appropriate position may arise organically, even if unintended. The incentives of such systems may be too powerful to resist." (Backer, May 4, 2012). This organ of governance is sometimes trotted out for photo opportunity moments as proof of democratic engagement within non-profit organizations with a teaching and research mission (Dill & Helm, 1988). "In order to reduce the likelihood of administrative capture and management, the faculty voice (spoken in the singular in decision making, but operated in the plural among all individuals who together constitute "the" faculty) requires consolidation." (Backer, May 9, 2012). On some occasions it plays a formal role as a source of advice and consultation on matters of direct concern to faculty, the substance of which might or might not be embraced in whole or in part to by those with authority to act. More rarely, some of its members could be invited to play a critical role, though one usually behind the scenes and limited to the expression of faculty sentiment with a chance of influencing decisions or influencing thinking about potential action by those with power. On the rarest occasions, some members of the Senate may find themselves permitted a very small space in which to hear and speak to the most pressing matters of administration in the wake of crisis.

Faculty members are increasingly understood as units of production to the administration —factors in an human production line that is meant to apply processes to students that stamp out graduates of uniform quality who are fit for specific purposes, and also to produce knowledge of some utility to the currently favored crop of knowledge consumers—commercial enterprises and the state. In this factory setting, faculty governance participation appears to be a distraction valued mostly as gesture, reduced to the service component of mandatory faculty responsibility (Silverman, 2004). " The currency of power is usually expressed as control over (1) factors in the production of university wealth and prestige, (2) the results of that production (usually measured in money). The exercise of that power is usually effectuated through mechanisms, the objectives of which are to (1) socialize subordinate factors of production within power regimes (e.g. to get labor to do what is commanded or to accept what is done), and (2) to mask the realities of control through elaborate systems of transparency that feigns engagement but offers only the provision of information." (Backer, May 1, 2015). This remains a marginal element of everything from annual reviews to the review of the sufficiency of tenure files, reflecting and simultaneously deepening the production line mentality that is usually clothed in more elegant language. Its exercise can result in retaliation, sometimes of the most sophisticated and subtlest kind, sometimes quite crude, especially far from the eyes or cares of even governance-sympathetic central administrators. Faculty governance is sometimes thought to serve best when its ambitions are quite humble—for example when governance is understood as service to low level administrators, or when it serves to more efficiently respond to issues of administrative organization and rule implementation for the management of students, staff and faculty themselves (Silverman, 2004; Minor, 2004).

High-level and policy governance is beyond the usual realm of the acceptable; as a consequence, faculty sometimes cultivate a deferential attitude that can appear to slide toward a servility of a kind that reminds more of the Commons in Tudor England than of modern notions of participation and engagement (Hutcheson, 2000). Servility is sometimes expressed as alienation and passivity (Backer, 2013). This tension between service and servility, and the influence of faculty governance cultures that favor one or the other, complicates the development of cultures of governance (Silverman, 2004; Minor, 2004). But this tension also reflects a reality in which the cultural parameters of corporate governance and state administration practices—grounded in power hierarchy, division of function, chain of command,

and obedience—have come to dominate thinking about the way a university, like a governmental administrative agency or a large multi-unit corporation, ought to be governed (Birnbaum, 2000; Backer, 2013; Silverman, 2004; Minor, 2004). Within these structures, the idea of faculty governance is a rare and sometimes unappreciated thing indeed. It suggests a culture of governance that posits more horizontal relationships among stakeholders in the enterprise, and a more sensitive degree of commitment to consultation, inclusion, engagement, and accountability, that is absent increasingly from emerging foundations of institutional cultures, especially outside the university (Minor, 2003; Backer, 2013).

There lies more formally as a set of tensions inherent in the position of a university faculty senate within a governance structure that places it between the *hierarchical structures* of university administration, the *political structures* of state and federal governments, the *fiduciary structures* of the Board of Trustees, and contests among them all, the *academic structures* of knowledge production and sharing from which administrators, politicians, regulators, board members and consumers (employers and alumni) derive benefits and from which the profitability of the enterprise is (un)conventionally but increasingly measured (Hutcheson, 2000; Minor, 2004). We will start with a very brief review of the foundations. The conceptual structures of shared governance are fairly well known but it is always useful to nod in the direction of sources.

The Framework of Shared Governance: Normative Structure and Operating Principles

The general principles that reflect the common culture of shared governance in the context of universities are well known (Minor, 2004). These emerged first in the early 20th Century. As Robert Birnbaum (2000) succinctly explained:

President Henry P. Tappan of the University of Michigan, for example, proposed in 1858 that the faculty should enjoy sovereignty over teaching methods and the curriculum since scholars "are the only workmen who can build up universities" . . . This principle, while broadly recognized, was honored more in the breach than in the observance by many institutions for the next fifty years. But the increasing professionalism of the faculty during the early decades of the 20th century, accelerated by the academic revolution following World War Two, led at many institutions not only to faculty control over the curriculum but to a strong faculty voice in other education-related matters as well.

The AAUP, of course, has been instrumental in developing and maintaining a good part of this culture (Hutcheson, 2000). Referring to the 1915 Declaration of

Principles on Academic Freedom and Academic Tenure (AAUP, 2015), the 1940 Statement of Principles on Academic Freedom and Tenure (AAUP, 194), the 1966 Statement on Government of Colleges and Universities, and the 1994 Statement on the Relationship of Faculty Governance to Academic Freedom (AAUP, 2006), we examine the role of faculty within the legal contours of the AAUP. For instance, from the 1915 Statement emerged the modern understanding of the special role of faculty within a modern research university, one that resists easy conversion to the routinized hierarchical relationship of employee and superior. The 1915 Statement characterized the relationship between faculty and the university as one in which the faculty "are the appointees, but not in any proper sense the employees, of the university trustees. For, once appointed, the scholar has professional functions to perform in which the appointing authorities have neither competency nor moral right to intervene. . . . (1915 Statement, p. 294). As a consequence, the relationship between faculty, administration and trustee are necessarily not strictly hierarchical, but instead invoke a sharing of responsibility for the work of the university:

A university is a great and indispensable organ of the higher life of a civilized community, in the work of which the trustees hold an essential and highly honorable place, but in which the faculties hold an independent place, with quite equal responsibilities—and in relation to purely scientific and educational questions, the primary responsibility. (1915 Statement, p. 294)

That responsibility extended to the production of knowledge based on independent inquiry, to the training of students, and to the development of expertise for the advancement of the general welfare of the state (1915 Statement, page 295-6; Hutcheson, 2000). The 1915 Statement, then, is grounded in another great principle of the academic establishment—academic freedom, an explanation of which was the primary objective of that statement (Finkin & Post, 2009; Hutcheson, 2000; Minor, 2004). While the normative conception and operationalization of academic freedom was ultimately elaborated in the 1940 Statement, the fundamental conception of the nature of the relationship between faculty and university—the idea of the academic as appointee but not employee, of the autonomy of the scholar's undertaking within the university—remains as strong today as it was in 1915, as a matter of internal practice to which a university may but need not subscribe as a matter of binding internal organization.

That idea of the faculty member as appointee and autonomous actor within the government of the university had another significant consequence. Inherent in that principle was another, that of shared governance—for if the academic was not to be understood as being in a conventional employment relationship with the university, and if the scholar was expected to contribute to the training of students and the public good, then those interests would require participation in the operation of the institution in which they conducted their work (Hutcheson, 2000). The idea of the fundamental importance of governance participation as central to the integrity of academic freedom was at the heart of the 1966 Statement on Government of Colleges and Universities (Hutcheson, 2000). Its basic premise was what it called "joint effort": the necessity for joint action among governing board, administration faculty and students to increase capacity to solve educational problems (AAUP, 1966). It followed from this premise that governance principles are necessary to avoid the confusion or conflict that would result from institutional usurpations by one of the coordinate governance bodies (AAUP, 1966). For our purposes here, we focus on the role of the 1966 Statement in clarifying two distinct aspects of the faculty role in governance. The first is the normative standard—the fundamental premises of the faculty role. The second is the operational standard—the fundamental premises of the organization required to permit the exercise of the faculty role in governance.

The fundamental normative standard is grounded in stakeholder engagement, understood as both an institutional commitment to transparency and an equally strong commitment to engagement in decision-making (AAUP, 1966; Hutcheson, 2000; Minor, 2004). Transparency is understood in its dual role—the provision of meaningful information at a meaningful time and in a meaningful form—and transparency as a mechanism for effective participation in governance. The 1966 Standard, for example, speaks to "Effective planning demands that the broadest possible exchange of information and opinion should be the rule for communication among the components of a college or university" (AAUP, 1966, p. 2a). For faculty, the principal substantive governance role centers on "such fundamental areas as curriculum, subject matter and methods of instruction, research, faculty status, and those aspects of student life which relate to the educational process" (AAUP, 1966, p.5).

The operational standard consists of two requirements: first, an institutionalized participation in decision making, either in an initiator or consultative role, and second, a principle of deference where the decision falls closest to the heart of the core governance role of the stakeholder (Hutcheson, 2000). In the case of faculty, primary responsibility for decision-making, and the greatest deference by governing boards and administration, center on the core normative governance role of faculty relating to curriculum, instruction, research, faculty status and educationally related student life (Ibid). As Minor (2004) has noted, "Functional senates primarily operate to represent and protect the interest of faculty in university decision making.... These senates can also involve deans or other administrators as members of the senate. Various committees have specific responsibilities and carry out the work of the senate. The senate's decisions or recommendations usually result from formal procedures and voting. Governing documents such as by-laws, a faculty handbook, a constitution, or statutes determine the extent of its authority" (p. 348). In these areas, the faculty's role in decision-making should be at its strongest and both governing board and administration should defer to the greatest extent. With respect to other aspects of university governance, where the responsibilities of governing board and administration are paramount—strategic planning, legal compliance and risk management, budgeting, selection of administrative personnel, physical resources management and the like—faculty engagement remains significant but deference to faculty views might be sometimes significantly reduced (Minor, 2004). The degree of deference, or put another way, the degree of responsibility for governance, is a function of the subject for decision and the context in which decision-making occurs—or as the 1966 Statement suggests, "differences in the weight of each voice, from one point to the next, should be determined by reference to the responsibility of each component for the particular matter at hand" (AAUP, 1966, p. 2a).

The 1966 Statement also speaks to the organization of the faculty voice in governance—after all there is little value in vesting authority without institutionalizing its exercise in some sort of efficient and representative manner. That institutionalization calls for the creation of a government internal to faculty so that the views of the body of the faculty could be articulated, presented and advanced effectively. In the words of the 1966 Statement: "Agencies for faculty participation in the government of the college or university should be established at each level where faculty responsibility is present. An agency should exist for the presentation of the views of the whole faculty" (AAUP, 1966, p.5). These agencies, then, can be constituted as faculty senates at the university level and as local faculty organizations within departments, colleges and units in a multi-campus, multidivisional research university—like Penn State. These institutions, like the faculty they represent, are meant to be constructed as autonomous entities, governed by their own terms and without interference by the coordinate governing groups—principally administration, governing board, or the organs of state government when acting as an internal stakeholder—though created in consultation with and jointly approved by all stakeholders (Ibid).

With the 1994 Statement, the AAUP added the last layer to governance within the university. In the context of institutionalizing shared governance and deepening its normative framework, the 1994 Statement sought to expand on the meaning of deference in shared governance. It was meant to remind all stakeholders, in part at least, that deference was not an invitation to ignore a coordinate partner in governance. It also reminded that the object of the shared governance model of the 1966 Statement was not to cabin, and by cabining, reduce the role of the faculty to a very narrow slice of university life—such as the construction and offering of courses. Instead, tying together the 1915, 1940 and 1966 Statements, it made a case for the broad construction of the faculty role in governance and the importance of faculty engagement in most aspects of university governance, even as that role varied from consultation to a principal role in the fashioning of rules and policy. It also included a warning, taken in part from the 1966 AAUP Statement on Professional Ethics, a warning that has been increasingly overlooked to the detriment of shared governance in this century—"'Professors accept their share of faculty responsibilities for the governance of their institution.' If they do not, authority will drift away from them, since someone must exercise it, and if the members of the faculty do not, others will" (AAUP, 1966, p.).

This integrated structure of governance focused faculty governance authority on those key areas in which faculty contributed to the enterprise—the protection of the integrity of the disciplines within which knowledge was divided through control over hiring, and the protection of the integrity of the dissemination of knowledge through the control of courses and shared control over academic programs. The donor deal at FSU represented a substantial potential incursion into that framework. And it provided for the development of a model in which administration would serve as a pass through ministerial role (deferring to donor power) while faculty would lose most authority to participate in those key areas where their expertise was greatest—hiring and course content. It is to a consideration of those issues that we turn to next.

THE REALITY OF SHARED GOVERNANCE: INSTITUTIONAL RESPONSES AND THE ROLE OF THE FACULTY SENATE

According to Miller & Bellamy (2012), "On the face of it, the memorandum of understanding seemed to have the potential to do serious damage to academic freedom and faculty governance." As then President Eric Barron to the Faculty Senate said in a May 18, 2011 email: "Given the importance of the issue of academic integrity, I would like to formally ask that the Faculty Senate set up a committee to examine the issues surround the Koch Foundation Agreement and its implementation to ensure that the integrity of Florida State University was protected. I believe it is essential for members of this committee to meet with the members of the faculty in Economics. I would appreciate receiving your findings in as timely manner as possible, as well as any recommendations you might have to ensure that we maintain the highest possible standards in ensuring academic integrity of our programs " (FSU Faculty Senate Report, 2011, p.1). And indeed, the committee engaged with the faculty of the Department of Economics, the former Economics faculty members present when the agreement was negotiated, the Chair of the Department, the Dean of the College of Social Sciences and Public Policy, the Dean of the College of Business, the Interim Provost, the Vice-President for Advancement, and the University Council.

Governance at the university is not grounded in the principles of the organization of economic enterprises or even of charitable and religious institutions—grounded in hierarchy, obedience, and power based differentiation of function and control

(Finkin & Robert, 2006). Instead, the university is conceived as a collaborative enterprise to a greater extent, one in which its coordinate branches—the governing board, the administration, the faculty and students, work together, exercising their authority in harmony and for the greater glory of the institution for whose interests they all work. As one study noted:

Research on institutional governance—intensive in the 1970s and resurgent in the 1990s—advanced a core set of values, including mutual respect between administrators and faculty, commonly defined issues, and equality in decision-making, responsibility, and accountability. Effective shared governance, most scholars noted, requires two-way communication and an ability for each "side" to relinquish decision-making to the other when necessary. But shared governance, goes the current standard thinking, may also placate faculty needs for involvement and consultation in decision-making, even when not resulting in specific actions. (Miller, 2002)

But reality sometimes paints a less gloriously bright picture (Lieberwitz, 2007). Of course, this picture was painted at FSU, where, at least as first, there was the tolerance of a culture of impunity and administrative overreaching. When in 2007 CKF considered providing funding for the economics department at Florida State, it came with strings, which was not vetting by the faculty, only the chair of the economics department and a few members appointed by him. This not only provided the Koch Foundation want oversight over faculty hiring, but also influence of the undergraduate curriculum. The administration and the Deans at Florida State even welcomed the grant. There was, however, little faculty oversight on how this grant would impact the academic integrity of the institution. And it was not until the agreements revision in 2013 that a CKF advisory board would be consulted on faculty hiring's. It was not until 2011 that President Eric Barron contacted the FSU faculty senate to examine the agreement. This was indeed a step in the right direction, providing faculty a voice in university affairs, especially regarding academic integrity. July, 2011, the Faculty Senate Ad Hoc Committee Review Report was released, suggesting that while there were many good results from this controversial process (hiring two quality hires, stronger new teachers in large entry level classes, an active undergraduate club, and more funds for graduate support), there were shortcomings in donor hiring practices, issues around transparency in undergrad curriculums, clarification of the agreement, and mechanism to ensure the role of faculty were represented in hiring and curriculum development. In sum, the faculty senate recommended some changes to the contract, but found that the faculty hiring compiled with university policies. The school and foundation revised their agreement in 2013 "for clarity" and to emphasize the "fact that faculty hires would be consistent with departmental bylaws and university guidelines."

In their report, the faculty senate proposed a series of recommendations, such as suggesting an end to donor funded appointments; restructuring the committee that oversaw faculty appointments; prohibiting future donor agreements which have donor evaluations of faculty; suspend course offerings advanced by the grant until a new agreement is created that separates conflicts of interests; reviewing FSU Foundation's policies concerning such gifts vis-a-vi faculty appointments, evaluation, and university curriculum (Miller & Bellamy, 2012). And though these recommendations were useful, and accumulated in a revised agreement that clarified areas relating to transparency and shared governance, the university failed to institutionalize methods to ensure all the recommendations were fulfilled.

They also failed to protect faculty by putting the onus on the faculty senate to essentially do the President's and the administrations work for them. For instance, here the FSU Senate played the role of the "heavy" player who had to respond to the local and national criticism. This was in many ways an awkward position because they had no real power and could be undermined by both the president, the administration and of course, the Board of trustees.

The President was pleased with the outcome and similarly, the director of higher education programs at CKF, Ryan Stowers, was also pleased. Though the Faculty Senate did helped make the reviews for the agreement revision, which provided faculty control over the curriculum, nevertheless, the new agreement still maintained the Koch Foundation's power over hiring practices, essentially providing them with "indirect veto power on some faculty hiring" (Romero, 2014). As a result, the administration and the Koch foundation essentially won, and while the faculty senate report did make recommendations that were generally efficient in curtailing the impacts of the agreement, many of them were not enforced. Among the most serious issues that occurred were the cultivation and tolerance of cultures of impunity, supported by administrative governance models that do little to provide avenues for remediation.

The administrative responses to CKF's demand might illustrate the potential dangers of administrative overreaching, and its threat to shared governance, especially in the context of the sometimes difficult search for funds. This included deliberate avoidance of consultation, or accidental failures to consult on matters of shared governance, resulting in the successful intrusions of administrators into the heart of the administrative organs of faculty governance. Since consultation is at the heart of shared governance, the management of that process, and the control of the use of consultation, both without accountability for abuse by administrators of that management and control, can significantly skew the contributions of faculty to discussion. If administrators can determine the time, place and manner of consultation by faculty, consultation itself becomes little more than theatre, and in this case theatre for the amusement of the governing board. It is true that sometimes administration officials know what is best—but many times consultation provides additional perspectives that might challenge even the most absolutely certain knowledge. Even the easy case, the low lying fruit, of administrative decision-making might profit from the sort of consultation that could lead to better or better accepted decision-making that preserves the integrity of the process of shared governance. Moreover, failures of consultation can have a significantly demoralizing effect, eventually corroding shared governance so that it remains a formal husk covering a rotted and shriveled body.

Yet equally damaging to the body of shared governance is what appear to be overt and covert efforts to *usurp and corrupt the internal processes of faculty governance*. Overt usurpation usually involves administrative efforts to expand control in matters where faculty authority is traditionally at its greatest. There is a noticeable tendency among university officials at the middle levels of administration—deans, chancellors, and their subordinates—to move to usurp the faculty role in governance. This can be effectuated formally—we have heard of cases in which such officials have insisted on the need for them to become leaders of the faculty governance organization, or where officials have insisted that they should have full authority over the development of courses and curricula. In the case of Florida State, the usurpation was incidental and a consequence of the determination to secure funding from CKF. But that might make the usurpation more dangerous—the administration appears blameless; helpless before the demands of a powerful financing body, with whose bidding it finds itself complicit. The effort is sometimes made to appear less damaging to traditional shared governance by embedding formal compliance with shared governance forms while undermining its forms. FSU administrators did not actively seek this usurpation of faculty governance space in their negotiations with CKF. They were, however, willing to waive these prerogatives in return for the donation. It is not clear that this waiver was the administration's to make.

Covert overreaching is more insidious. It can appear through a strategy of primus inter pares projection of administrative voices into policy and governance debates within faculty organizations. Thus, for instance, tenured administrators sometimes seek to speak as faculty during faculty deliberations, the conflict is unavoidable but dismissed because as a formal matter many administrators are tenured faculty. But administrators cannot serve two masters, they will serve the master who can terminate their administrative position first—purporting to speak as colleagues effectively privileges the administrative perspective (their own) in faculty debates about an issue. Debate is chilled where administrators become too eager to share their views within the debates of non-administration colleagues. Where participation might dictate self-control, an over-eagerness to project voice and manage outcomes becomes clear and clearly troubling. Both formal and informal intrusion by administrative officials in the internal governance of faculty organizations corrupts the integrity of any shared governance system as surely as any assertion, for example, by the U.S. President of power to appoint members of Congress ex officio to participate in their activities. FSU administrators avoided this trap. They permitted a space for faculty governance to participate without undue influence from within. And that greatly contributed to the ability of the FSU faculty to engage in the negotiation of the terms of the donation.

But faculty organizations sometimes share blame in equal measure for retaliatory practices. It is not unknown among faculties, and every faculty member is aware of instances of faculty bullying and mob behavior (Twale & Luca, 2008). These include instances of covertly enforced isolation, a disinclination to respect the views of colleagues, usually marginalized as offbeat, the social marginalization of the "cranky" or "unusual" colleague, and the cultivation of academic judgments based on notions of political advantage within a faculty. There are instances where an isolated faculty member becomes invisible—forgotten, not spoken to, and even lower level administrators feel no shame in walking by them without even the courtesy of an acknowledgement or "hello". Where these efforts are undertaken to curry favor with administration officials the corrupting effects are horribly pernicious. Interestingly, these instances of bad behavior are usually understood in hierarchical terms, something for a superior to control (even when she is the problem) and not a matter for faculty governance. Important as well might be the criticism that Nancy Rappaport gently made—because there are few consequences for irresponsible actions by faculty organizations, there is a tension in shared governance that is hard to avoid (Rapoport, 2010).

The FSU context suggests, however, the complexity of this potential for complicity. It is true enough that the CKF funds were helpful to the department, and that it would be easy for faculty to accept the terms under which they might be made available. However, the opposite is not necessarily the only possible measure of appropriate faculty reaction in the face of the sort of conditionality that CKF sought. The FSU case suggests that a more nuanced approach may preserve both the ability of institutions to seek donation, of donors to seek some influence in the use of their funds and on faculty to preserve their primary responsibility for hiring and for curriculum. Whether FSU got it right in this case or not, they appeared to have sought to move in the "right" direction. But it also suggests the contours within which such future discussion might be better managed in ways that maintain a strong fidelity to shared governance and the integrity of the public university as a shared enterprise.

FACULTY GOVERNANCE: RECOMMENDATION

When the FSU President asked the faculty senate to examine the issues of academic integrity around the Koch Foundation agreement and its implementation, he also asked for quick responses. Though the faculty senate was eventually called in to make recommendations, it was three years after the initially agreement was created, and after significant backlash. The Faculty Senate Ad Hoc Committee Review Report was released in July, 2011, with a set of recommendations. Many of these recommendations were aligned with principles of shared governance, as well as university norms and the FSU faculty handbook. And though many faculty members were happy with the recommendations, it must be noted that there was little to no enforcement mechanism to ensure they were followed through. This is, and has always been, one of the primary criticisms of the faculty senate, which, depending on this institution and their organizational history, have varying powers. The Faculty Senate Ad Hoc Committee made many recommendations, and substantive changes were indeed made, especially regarding faculty hiring, nevertheless, the core elements of the agreement remained in place, and the agreement between the administration, the economics department, and the Koch Foundation was legitimized. In this section, we will detail recommendations for faculty senate units in the future when dealing with external agencies and faculty governance. This begs the question: Is there a real and substantive role for a faculty Senate that is not obviated by local governance or the good intentions of the administration, or has this been a thin attempt to mitigate negative press to include some faculty say in the agreement.

The first are programs to enhance engagement. The University Faculty Senate must shed its increasingly single-minded concentration on issues of the facilitation of administrative mandates. For that purpose the Senate must begin to more consciously participate in dialogue at all levels of university decision-making. Additional avenues of consultation and engagement need to be pursued. Engagement is not useful when limited to being the first to hear about decisions that have already been taken. Perhaps enhanced joint committees reflect a structural innovation that, at the price of a certain loss of autonomy, also increases the role of the faculty in the development of critical policy (Birnbaum 1999). For Florida State's Faculty Senate, they were summoned by the President, and essentially did his bidding, unfairly. The administration had the resulting impact of putting the onus on the faculty senate to do the President's work for him, where the FSU Senate played the role of the "heavy" which was awkward because they had no real power and could be undermined by both the president and the Board. The Faculty Senate Ad Hoc Committee Review (2011) had recommendations that spoke to programs of enhanced engagement. For instance, recommendation (1) suggested that Florida State should have primary control in accordance the governing principles in Article 17 of the FSU Factual Handbook in hiring and curricular decisions. The three person Advisory Board should have at least two members of the faculty members from FSU's economics department (which was done), and should be specified in the MOU (which was not).

The second are programs to militate against retaliation. Retaliation affects all faculty in a governance role, but most especially it is the principle focus of the problems of engagement by fixed term faculty. But it also goes to the extent to which the university is willing to provide real protection, enforceable against its officers, for faculty exercising their shared governance duties—for example by the adoption of a code of governance rights. It has a cultural element as well—there ought to be as great a focus on cultures of retaliation as there is about the culture of drinking at public universities (Backer, 2010). Changing cultures of impunity, especially in the form of retaliation and overreaching is a critically important task. That requires some additional sensitivity on the part of the administration and less tolerance for the overreaching exuberance even by administrators that are otherwise meeting other goals and objectives dear to central administrator's priorities. Programs implementing 360-degree review of administrative personnel would be useful (Lublin, 2011). But more importantly it requires both a recognition that the ideals (and realities) of shared governance are not hard wired into law. Law does little to protect faculty engagement in shared governance. What little protection there is obtained at high cost—litigation after retaliation and subjection to after the fact second guessing by courts required to contort First Amendment distinctions onto an employment relationship that is distinct but not unique. Universities committed to shared governance, then, are required to prove it; and the proof is in the contractual provisions they are willing to subject themselves to protect activities that advance shared governance by contract and tenured faculty. While some courts have refused to recognize the binding effect of handbooks, (Stanton v. Tulane University, 777 So.2d 1242 (La.App. 2001); Raines v. Haverford College, 849 F.Supp. 1009 (E.D.Pa. 1994), and many courts have held that written employee handbooks, bylaws and similar documents could be enforced as contract (Woolley v. Hoffmann-La Roche, Inc., 491 A.2d 1257, mod. 499 A.2d 515 (N.J., 1985); Collins v. Colorado Mountain College, 56 P.3d 1132 (Ct.App.Colo. 2002)). The protection of shared governance starts with protection from retaliation; and protection from retaliation for acts of shared governance necessarily starts with the university's contractual commitment specified in its handbook and human sources policies, and made binding on all parties. That is the lesson that the state of U.S. law teaches. The problem with The Faculty Senate Ad Hoc Committee Review report was there was not discussion on mitigation against retaliation and while there is not discussion there are suggestions. Recommendation 10, for instance, notes that the new Provost should review its practices with all deans regarding the roles of faculty in shared governance in the development of curriculum. The mechanics behind this review process, however, is not properly fleshed out, but does provide a starting point for future negotiations with donors and institutions.

The third are programs enhancing transparency. There is no effective governance without thorough and effective transparency. But transparency, both understood as data and assessment, can sometimes be employed as a weapon to sharpen the disadvantages among parties to decision making. Where there are a-symmetrical power relationships—where administration controls the levers of access to information, it does little good to provide a certain enhanced level of information and data to administrative personnel and another, and less enhanced level of access to faculty engaged in governance. In that context, the excuse of privacy or sensitivity is hardy worthy—such data was not private enough to prohibit its use in making a determination, by some; if you use it you should be prepared to share it.

Transparency has been a constant theme within the debates and discourse around Florida State and the Koch Foundation. The issue, from an institutional view to a departmental one, is that there lacked meaningful transparency. And while The Faculty Senate Ad Hoc Committee Review Report did not discuss creating programs to enhance transparency, they did recommend approaches to enhance greater cooperation between departments and donors, which would result in greater transparency between the two parties. Recommendation (7), for instance, recommended that the college and the department should work with the Koch Foundation and work out the governing mechanics on how to work with donor's interest while insuring the integrity of the curriculum. If this was the starting point of the conversation, much of the controversy would have been mitigated. Recommendation (8) took this a step further, and suggested that the foundation itself should review its policies concerning gifts that focused on the conditions over the hiring of faculty, their evaluations of hired faculty, and the development of curriculum. They further stressed that they should update their documents to ensure autonomy and institutional integrity in future negotiations. Part of this was to also temporally suspend its approval of ECO 313 – "Market Ethics", and to then resubmit the proposal with an indication on how this course relates to the donor's intent and agreement, which was not present in the initial proposal for the course.

Perhaps one of the most powerful recommendations was recommendation (9), which recommended that the Provost's office to create some mechanism to review multiple donor agreements that involve more than one college. This would be most important to institutionalize this practice within the university as a way to mitigate the possibility of such an agreement to occur again in the future. Recommendation (10) also recommended that the new Provost should review with all deans regarding the roles of faculty in shared governance and the primary responsibility of faculty for the development of the curriculum. The majority of the discussion around the FSU/Koch Agreement has been around faculty hiring's, yet there has been a limited discussion on the influence of curriculum. This is perhaps one of the most significant blows to academic integrity and institutional autonomy, being a cornerstone of the modern university system of creating and promoting knowledge without external influence. But transparency means more than merely sharing selected information with groups of people. Transparency means opening proceedings to all stakeholders and engaging stakeholders through consultation; it means accountability to those in whose service one acts. It also means that Senate meetings might cease being well-managed staged affairs that make good theatre, and which follows corporate models, but which also discourages participation. Greater opportunities for comment on proposed action by Senate, board and administration would serve transparency well. But so would an HR 40 style requirement that front line administrators list their annual goals and account for their attainment.

The fourth involves flexing atrophied muscles. The Senate is at its strongest in its governance role when it carefully considers an issue. For that purpose the Senate can make greater use of its forensic powers. Some examples of ways in which the forensic power can be more usefully deployed include seeking to assess administrators informally through the application of its own metrics; producing programs discussing cultures of administrative overreach at the University, and discussing institutional approaches of equity for academic integrity and protection against overreaching by administrators in future agreements with powerful donors. It is not unusual for foundations to provide funding for professorships or endow chairs; this has been a common practice throughout the history of American higher education. What is unusual in this case, is not the gift itself but the donor's influence in the hiring process (Allen, 2014). Throughout The Faculty Senate Ad Hoc Committee Review Report (2011), there is little discussion on the future role of the faculty senate in future negotiations. This is perhaps one of the baggiest obstacles in future negotiations. A mechanism of including a faculty senate committee to review sizable grants would have been a recommendation worth noting. In a very similar case involving Yale University, a billionaire alumni provided $20 million to expand its Western civilization curriculum. The donor requited that he approve the faculty members for the proposed course and after substantial faculty backlash, Yale returned the $20 million dollar gift. Though this present a rare case of returning money to a donor, it threated a cornerstone of the university system, that is, faculty control of hiring and curriculum.

The fifth involves restructuring the Senate to respond to the functional realities of the modern university. But even as the functional role of the Senate has been changing with respect to its legislative, advisory and consultative and forensic authority, new functions are emerging that are more in line with the evolution of the relationship between academics and finance, between the administration and the faculty, and between the faculty and the board of trustees. The most important of these is the role of the Senate as an autonomous critical *monitor*, to be aware of and to assess the state of a system in which faculty now participate functionally in a more passive and *post facto* way in the development of policy and governance at the university but in which the faculty retains a strong role. That role is now functionally clear--to review, assess predict and judge the work of the administration, and to use that monitoring and assessment power to aid administration at all levels in the efficiency and coherence of their work. More importantly, the monitoring role serves the board of trustees as well. Monitoring and reporting provides the board with an independent source of information and assessment that is critical to the role of the broad to hold administrators accountable.

The Senate then can serve as an autonomous center for accountability with respect to those matters traditionally reserved to shared governance. But this role also requires support against retaliation as a matter of contract between the university and its faculty. This includes one that engages in routine and systematic data collection relating to performance, providing feedback and episodic and objective assessment. The monitoring function is designed to enhance accountability in those organizations where decision-making becomes harder to effectively share.

CONCLUSION

The influence of philanthropy occupies a contentious space among key stakeholders of the public research university — professors, students, and the community—because the most pressing issues rests on the influence of philanthropy on institutional autonomy, shared governance, and the freedom of inquiry, ideals ingrained into the ontological fabric of the academy. The ideal of the university represents an autonomous generator of knowledge, free from external constraints, allowing the flow of knowledge to disseminate freely for the advancement of the public good (Albach, 2001). While this ideal has only been partially reached, now more than ever, the influence of private funding on knowledge production has been an increasing concern for those within the higher education enterprise.

In this chapter, we examined the relationship between philanthropy and the increasingly contested governance space of the public research university, and against the backdrop of academic integrity and shared governance. CKF made a grant of $1.5 million to FSU's economics department which would allow CKF representatives to sit on screening committees for new faculty hires, provide funding for doctoral students in economics, and the creation of a new undergrad programs that would be based on curriculum based on the ideology of the Koch Foundation. This deal was eventually met with faculty and community backlash, since it relegated substantial control of a public institution to an external actor. We first provided a background regarding the case of involving Florida State University and the Koch Foundation's agreement, and from this perspective, we considered the realities of shared governance and its functional challenges in light of academic integrity and university donors. We then flesh out the difficulties of shared governance within the a-symmetric power arrangements that are the hallmark of public universities, and then consider where a faculty senate can fit into this governance enterprise when dealing with external influences of major donors. Though the faculty senate did eventually have a place to ensure that all stakeholders had some influence in the agreement, by the end, the agreement was not fully enforced and lacked real teeth. Of course, our recommendations could ensure that such cases do not occur in the future, but alas, institutions are slow moving creatures, and at times, require much resistance and pressure to make changes. Of course, faculty do not own or run the university but neither are they owned or run by it. Sadly, over the last century, radical ideologies, disguised as new notions have sought to abandon this basic relationship between the university and its faculty in favor of some flavor of paternalism. It remains to faculty with likeminded supporters within university administration and our governing boards, among students and state officials, that we can reject these radical incursions into the governance life of the university and preserve its role as an authoritative site for the production and sharing of knowledge (Steck, 2003).

REFERENCES

Allen, G. (2014, May 23). Koch Foundation Criticized Again For Influencing Florida State. *NPR*. Retrieved from http://www.npr.org/2014/05/23/315080575/koch-foundation-criticized-again-for-influencing-florida-state

American Association of University Professors. (1966). *Statement on government of colleges and universities*. Retrieved September 2002 from http://www.aaup.org/statements/Redbook/Govern.htm

American Association of University Professors. (2006). Statement of Principles on Academic Freedom and Tenure. In *AAUP Policy* (10th ed.; pp, 3-11). Available at http://www.aaup.org/AAUP/pubsres/policydocs/contents/1940statement.htm

American Association of University Professors (AAUP). (1915, December). Declaration of Principles on Academic Freedom and Academic Tenure. *AAUP Bulletin; Quarterly Publication of the American Association of University Professors*, *1*(Part 1).

Backer, L. (2013, January 29). *Monitoring University Governance*. Retrieved May 26, 2015, from http://lcbpsusenate.blogspot.com/2013/01/statement-of-senate-chair-made-at.html

Backer, L. C. (2010, September 17). *Law at the End of the Day: The University and the Panopticon: Naturalizing "New" Governance Forms for Behavior Control Beyond Law*. Retrieved from http://lcbackerblog.blogspot.com/2010/09/university-and-panopticon-naturalizing.html

Backer, L. C. (2012a, May 4). *Monitoring University Governance*. Retrieved June 9, 2015. Available http://lcbpsusenate.blogspot.com/2012/05/on-institutional-role-of-faculty-senate.html

Backer, L. C. (2012b, May 9). *Monitoring University Governance*. Retrieved June 9, 2015. Available http://lcbpsusenate.blogspot.com/2012/05/on-institutional-roel-of-faculty-senate.html

Backer, L. C. (2015, May 1). *Monitoring University Governance*. Retrieved June 8, 2015. Available http://lcbpsusenate.blogspot.com/2015/05/power-and-control-through-prism-of.html

Barrow, C. W. (1990). *Universities and the capitalist state: Corporate liberalism and the reconstruction of American.* Academic Press.

Bellamy, R., & Miller, K. (2014, May 14). My View: FSU learns from Koch association. *Tallahassee Democrat*. Retrieved March 3, 2015, from http://www.tallahassee.com/story/opinion/columnists/2014/05/14/view-fsu-learns-koch-association/9097603/

Birnbaum, R. (1991). *Faculty in governance: The role of senates and joint committees in academic decision making.* San Francisco: Jossey-Bass.

Birnbaum, R. (2000). *Management fads in higher education: Where they come from, what they do, why they fail.* San Francisco: Jossey-Bass.

Bongila, J.-P. K. (2002). *Funding Strategies for Institutional Advancement of Private Universities in the United States: Applications for Afro-Congolese Universities.* Retrieved from dissertation.com

Callahan, D. (1999). *1 billion for ideas: Conservative think tanks in the 1990s.* Washington, DC: National Committee for Responsive Philanthropy.

Cash, S. B. (2005). Private voluntary support to public universities in the late nineteenth century. *International Journal of Educational Advancement, 5*(4), 343–358. doi:10.1057/palgrave.ijea.2140225

Chandler, J. (2011, July 18). FSU Faculty Approves Koch Deal, With Caveats. *WCTV.tv*. Retrieved March 3, 2015, from http://www.wctv.tv/news/floridanews/headlines/UPDATE_FSU_Faculty_Senate_Releases_Review_of_Koch_Deal.html

Cheit, E. F., & Lobman, T. E. (1979). *Foundations and higher education: Grant making from golden years through steady state.* Berkeley, CA: Carnegie Council on Policy Studies in Higher Education.

Cheslock, J. J., & Gianneschi, M. (2008). Replacing State Appropriations with Alternative Revenue Sources: The Case of Voluntary Support. *The Journal of Higher Education, 79*(2), 208–229. doi:10.1353/jhe.2008.0012

Clotfelter, C. T. (2007). Patron or bully? the role of foundations in higher education. In R. Bacchetti & T. Ehrlich (Eds.), *Reconnecting education and foundations* (pp. 213–248). San Francisco, CA: Jossey-Bass.

Covington, S. (1997). *Moving a public policy agenda: The strategic philanthropy of conservative foundations.* Washington, DC: National Committee for Responsive Philanthropy.

Dill, D., & Helm, K. (1988). Faculty participation in strategic policy making. In Higher Education: Handbook of Theory and Research (vol. 4, pp. 319-355). New York: Agathon Press.

Drezner, N. (2006). Recessions and Tax-Cuts: Economic Cycles' Impact on Individual Giving, Philanthropy, and Higher Education. *International Journal of Educational Advancement, 6*(4), 289–305. doi:10.1057/palgrave.ijea.2150036

Drezner, N. (2011). *Philanthropy and fundraising in American higher education.* San Francisco, CA: Jossey-Bass.

Drezner, N. D. (2011). The Influence of Philanthropy on American Higher Education. *ASHE Higher Education Report, 37*(2), 17–26.

Finkin, M., & Post, R. (2009). *For the common good: Principles of American academic freedom.* New Haven, CT: Yale University Press.

Flaherty, C. (2014, June 25). Not Interested in Koch Money. *Inside Higher Ed.* Retrieved March 3, 2015, from https://www.insidehighered.com/news/2014/06/25/professor-says-brooklyn-college-missed-chance-get-millions-koch-foundation

Foundation Center. (2014). *Foundation Yearbook.* New York, NY: The Center.

Gold, M. (2014, January 5). *Inside the Koch-backed political network, an operation designed to shield donors.* Retrieved June 10, 2015, from http://www.washingtonpost.com/politics/koch-backed-political-network-built-to-shield-donors-raised-400-million-in-2012-elections/2014/01/05/9e7cfd9a-719b-11e3-9389-09ef9944065e_story.html

Gumport, P. (2000). Academic Restructuring: Organizational Change and Institutional Imperative. *Higher Education,* (39), 67-91.

Hall, C., & Thomas, S. (2012, April). *Advocacy philanthropy and the public policy agenda: The role of modern foundations in American higher education.* Paper presented at the American Education Research Association, Vancouver, BC.

Horsley, S. (2006). *Wal-Mart's hypocrisy: A free enterprise 'success' story that's not so free.* United for a Fair Economy. Retrieved September 20, 2006, from http://www.faireconomy.org

Hossler, D. (2004). Refinancing Public Universities: Student enrollments, incentive-based budgeting, and incremental revenue. In E. P. S. John & M. D. Parsons (Eds.), *Public Funding of Higher Education: Changing Contexts and New Rationales* (pp. 145–163). Baltimore, MD: Johns Hopkins Press.

Hundley, K. (2011, May 9). Billionaire's role in hiring decisions at Florida State University raises questions. *Tampa Bay Times.* Retrieved March 3, 2015, from http://www.tampabay.com/news/business/billionaires-role-in-hiring-decisions-at-florida-state-university-raises/1168680

Hutcheson, P. A. (2000). *A professional professoriate: Unionization, bureaucratization, and the AAUP.* Nashville, TN: Vanderbilt University Press.

Katz, S. N. (2012, March 25). Beware Big Donors. *The Chronicle of Higher Education.* Retrieved from http://chronicle.com/article/Big-Philanthropys-Role-in/131275/

Leslie, L. L., & Ramey, G. (1988). Donor Behavior and Voluntary Support for Higher Education Institutions. *The Journal of Higher Education, 59*(2), 117–132. doi:10.2307/1981689

Levinthal, D. (2014, September 12). *Koch foundation proposal to college: Teach our curriculum, get millions.* Retrieved March 3, 2015, from http://www.publicintegrity.org/2014/09/12/15495/koch-foundation-proposal-college-teach-our-curriculum-get-millions

Lublin, J. S. (2011, December 3). Transparency Pays Off In 360-Degree Performance Reviews. *WSJ.* Retrieved from http://online.wsj.com/article/SB1000142405297020350130457708659207513 6080.html

McAlexander, J. H., & Koenig, H. F. (2012). Building communities of philanthropy in higher education: Contextual influences. *International Journal of Nonprofit and Voluntary Sector Marketing, 17*(2), 122–131. doi:10.1002/nvsm.1415

McKeown, M. P. (1996). State Funding Formulas: Promise Fulfilled? In D. S. Honeyman, J. L. Wattenbarger, & K. C. Westbrook (Eds.), *A Struggle to Survive: Funding Higher Education in the Next Century* (pp. 49–85). Thousand Oaks, CA: Corwin Press.

Michael T. Miller, Faculty Governance Units and Their Leaders: A National Profile, The NEA 2002 Almanac of Higher Education 51, 52. (2002). Available http://www. nea.org/assets/img/PubAlmanac/ALM_02_07.pdf

Miller, K., & Bellamy, R. (2012). Fine Print, Restrictive Grants, and Academic Freedom. *Academe*, *98*(3).

Minor, J. T. (2003). Assessing the senate: Critical issues considered. *The American Behavioral Scientist*, *46*(7), 960–977. doi:10.1177/0002764202250122

Minor, J. T. (2004). Understanding faculty senates: Moving from mystery to models. *Review of Higher Education*, *27*(3), 343–363. doi:10.1353/rhe.2004.0004

Mittal, A. ((2006). Turning the tide: Challenging the Right on campus. Oakland, CA: The Institute for Democratic Education/Speak Out and The Oakland Institute.

Mulhere, K. (2014, November 4). Students want Koch, corporate influence off campus. *InsideHigherEd*. Retrieved from https://www.insidehighered.com/news/2014/11/04/ students-want-koch-corporate-influence-campus

Osei-Kofi, N. (2010). Coercion, possibility, or context? questioning the role of private foundations in american higher education. *Discourse (Abingdon)*, *31*(1), 17–28. doi:10.1080/01596300903465393

Rasmussen, D. (2011, May 6). Opinion Columnist. *Florida Today*. Retrieved from http://www.floridatoday.com/article/CD/20110508/OPINION05/105080315/David-Rasmussen-Philanthropy-academic-freedom-can-co-exist?odyssey=mod_section-stories

Rasmussen, D. W. (2011, May 8). David Rasmussen: Philanthropy, academic freedom can co-exist. *Tallahassee Democrat*.

Ray, B. (2008, January 1). Florida State receives major gifts for studies in free enterprise, ethics. *Florida State University News*. Retrieved March 3, 2015, from https://fsu.edu/news/2008/11/10/bbt.gift/

Risa, L. (2007). Faculty in the Corporate University: Professional Identity, Law and Collective Action, 16 Cornell J. L. & Pub. *Pol'y*, *263*, 306–310.

Roelofs, J. (2003). *Foundations and public policy: The mask of pluralism*. Albany, NY: State University of New York Press.

Romano, J. (2014, April 19). Column: Some fear Charles Koch's influence damages FSU's integrity. *Tampa Bay Times*. Retrieved from http://www.tampabay.com/news/education/college/some-fear-charles-kochs-influence-damages-fsus-integrity/2175919

Schulman, D. (2014). *Sons of Wichita: How the Koch brothers became America's most powerful and private dynasty*. Academic Press.

Silverman, F. (2004). *Collegiality and service for tenure and beyond acquiring a reputation as a team player*. Westport, CT: Praeger.

Speck, B. W. (2010). The Growing Role of Private Giving in Financing the Modern University. *New Directions for Higher Education*, 8–16.

1994 Statement quoting in part, American Association of University Professors, 1966 Statement on Professional Ethics, at ¶ 3. (n.d.). Available at http://www.aaup.org/AAUP/pubsres/policydocs/contents/statementonprofessionalethics.htm?PF=1

Steck, H. (2003). Corporatization of the University: Seeking Conceptual Clarity. *The Annals of the American Academy of Political and Social Science*, 585(1), 66–83. doi:10.1177/0002716202238567

Strauss, V. (2014, March 28). *The Koch brothers' influence on college campus is spreading*. Retrieved June 10, 2015, from http://www.washingtonpost.com/blogs/answer-sheet/wp/2014/03/28/the-koch-brothers-influence-on-college-campus-is-spreading/

Sulek, M. (2010). On the Classical Meaning of Philanthôpía. *Nonprofit and Voluntary Sector Quarterly*, 39(3), 385–408. doi:10.1177/0899764009333050

Thelin, J. (2011). *A History of American Higher Education*. Baltimore, MD: The Johns Hopkins Press.

Twale, D. J., & Luca, B. M. (2008). *Faculty incivility: The rise of the academic bully culture and what to do about it*. San Francisco, CA: Jossey-Bass.

ENDNOTES

[1]   Available here: http://www.aaup.org/NR/rdonlyres/E741FFA6-CAFD-4089-A782-14B12490AD0F/0/SenateReport.pdf

Chapter 3
Tweeting for Donors:
How Institutions of Higher Education Use Social Media to Raise Funds

Leigh Nanney Hersey
University of Memphis, USA

ABSTRACT

Universities and colleges are embracing social media as a tool to spread the message about their institutions. Common uses include recruiting new students, connecting with current students, and staying connected with alumni. Nonprofit organizations in the United States also consider social media an important part of their fundraising toolbox, but use it more for recruiting volunteers, advocacy, and fundraising. Colleges and universities are also seeing the need to use social media for development purposes, whether they are private or state-supported institutions. This chapter explores how universities are using Twitter to promote year-end giving. Findings from this research suggest that while some universities seem to effectively use social media, others are inconsistent and even dormant in their messaging.

INTRODUCTION

Institutions of higher education in the United States are turning more to social media as a way to communicate with both internal and external audiences. Nearly all colleges and universities have adopted social media as part of their communications plans (Barnes & Lescault, 2013). Universities are using these interactive tools to

DOI: 10.4018/978-1-4666-9664-8.ch003

recruit students (Barnes & Lescault, 2013), to engage students in the classroom (Davis, et. al, 2012; also see edited volumes by Benson & Morgan, 2014; Pătruţ & Pătruţ, 2013; Pătruţ, Pătruţ, & Cmeciu, 2013), to engage alumni (Slover-Linett & Stoner, 2012), and to improve their overall image (Slover-Linett & Stoner, 2012). Universities are also using social media to fundraise, but do not know how to take full advantage of it (Stoner, as quoted in Lavrusik 2009).

While approximately 40 percent of four-year universities are private, nonprofit institutions (U.S. Department of Education, 2012), almost all colleges and universities depend on philanthropic support. In 2014, colleges and universities in the United States raised more than $37 billion in private gifts (Council for Aid to Education, 2015). In this way, even publically-supported universities operate like nonprofit organizations, actively fundraising to secure donations. Some colleges and universities have established separate nonprofit foundations to support their educational missions through private giving. As budgets continue to be limited, universities are depending more on private donations to operate (ASHE 2011). Both private and publically-supported institutions are looking for additional ways to attract these donors.

Alumni make up the core of individual giving to universities. More than 26 percent of private giving to universities comes from alumni, compared to 18 percent from non-alumni (Council for Aid to Education, 2015). Social media appeals to younger generations, making it an important tool for building a foundation of giving for young alumni (Longfield, 2014), a population that many universities feel is the most difficult group to contact and engage (Slover-Linett & Stoner, 2012). However, keeping young alumni engaged is important to long-term fundraising strategies as it encourages life-long giving, benefiting the university for years to come (Association for the Study of Higher Education, 2011). Traditional methods of communication are no longer sufficient for reaching the supporters (Wymer & Grau, 2011). New pathways for giving, such as those provided by social media, can also be important during times of financial concerns (Wymer & Grau, 2011).

Nonprofit organizations have also embraced social media, though in many different ways. The largest 200 nonprofit organizations in the United States had adopted social media as a communications tool by 2010 (Barnes, n.d.). Nonprofit organizations commonly use social media to increase awareness of the organization's mission (Barnes, n.d.) and build relationships (Briones, et al., 2011). Nonprofit organizations also find that social media can help them enhance their accountability and transparency, as well as fundraising efforts (Waters, Burnett, Lamm & Lucas, 2009). Some nonprofit organizations use social media to educate the public about the organization's cause and establish credibility (Levinson, Adkins, & Forbes, 2010). Nonprofit organizations are also engaging social media for advocacy activities (Guo & Saxton, 2014). The research suggests that universities tend to use social media for a more internal audience – prospective, current, and former students. In a nonprofit context, this group could be considered clients, or recipients of the service (education) provided by the university. In contrast, nonprofit organizations tend to direct their social media messages toward a more external audience, using the tool to garner support, whether it be volunteers, advocates, or donors. While a number of studies have explored how nonprofit organizations use social media, few of them include institutions of higher education in the research, partly because of the complex system that makes up higher education. However, when it comes to fundraising, nonprofit organizations and universities have many similarities.

This chapter bridges the gap in research focusing on how colleges and universities use social media to fundraise. In addition to making the connection between the education and nonprofit sectors, a special focus is placed on the use of Twitter by colleges and universities for fundraising. The research question for this study is straight-forward: How do institutions of higher education use Twitter to encourage year-end giving? The chapter analyzes fifty Twitter feeds of colleges and universities to access not only whether they use Twitter to promote year-end giving, but also how they are using it based on the types of messages they use. Going beyond Saxton & Wang (2013) suggest more research should be conducted on the message characteristics of Tweets "organizations are sending to strategically engage stakeholders, build relationships, and request donations and volunteer support" (p.865). The research reveals that the use of Twitter by universities varies widely and lack consistently. Most of the tweets posted by the fundraising departments of the universities do not directly address fundraising needs nor do they provide an avenue for giving.

The chapter continues as follows. The next part provides an overview of how nonprofit organizations and universities are using social media to fundraise. An overview of the fundraising process provides background for how the tweets were classified. The following section describes the methodology and data collection for the research. After a presentation of the results, further discussion suggests future research in this area.

BACKGROUND

This section presents the key factors to understanding the use of social media for fundraising by universities. As little research has been focused directly how universities use social media to fundraise, examples from nonprofit organizations help bridge this gap. A breakdown of the fundraising process lays the framework for the role social media can play in securing donations.

Nonprofit Organizations, Universities, and Social Media

Nonprofit organizations have long depended on the ability to reach mass target audiences with their fundraising appeals. For decades, direct-mail was the primary solicitation tool, requiring a large investment of money and time. Then e-mail became the leading fundraising tool, providing a quick and inexpensive way to reach supporters. Now, e-mail is losing some of its appeal. Although the number of people that subscribe to nonprofit e-mail updates continues to grow, the number of people who open these emails continue to drop (M+R, 2014). In its annual review of nonprofit social media use, M+R (2014) sampled 53 U.S.-based national nonprofit partners. M+R (2014) found that just 0.07 percent of fundraising emails sent from the sample organizations were opened in 2013. They also found that the nonprofit organizations in their study saw an increase in social media numbers, with Facebook fans increasing by 37 percent and Twitter followers by 46 percent from the previous year. The focus now is shifting to social media as an evolving tool for fundraising, particularly for reaching younger audiences. As

For universities, social media is often part of a multichannel campaign tool, where social media messaging is paired with more traditional communication methods to reach stakeholders (Slover-Linett & Stoner, 2012). Today's college students were "born into a world in which technology was a well-established and rapidly intensifying part of everyday life" (Martínez Alemán & Wartman, 2009, p. 1). Furthermore, social media allows alumni to remain connected to the virtual campus after graduating ((Martínez Alemán & Wartman, 2009). For these future alumni, providing an opportunity to connect digitally early in their academic careers can lead to longer term interaction and maintained loyalty. As students have been exposed to other organizations who use social media to promote fundraising, it is important that universities include themselves in the conversation.

Once a social media presence has been created, it is important for the organization to maintain activity. Potential supporters could be turned off by a social media account with little activity (Waters, Burnett, Lamm & Lucas, 2009). Lovejoy, Waters, & Saxton (2012) suggest that an active Twitter posts on average three tweets per week. As they note, it is important to finding a balance in the number tweets posted, enough to keep followers engaged without cluttering the Twitter feed.

Twitter is a social media tool that has gained prominence in recent years. The highest rates of Twitter use are with adults 18 – 29 (37 percent) and 30 – 49 (25 percent) (Duggan, Ellison, Lampe, Lenhart, & Madden, 2015). Use of Twitter is increasing with adults who live in households with a $50,000 income and are college graduates, two characteristics appealing to development officers in higher education (Duggan, et al., 2015). As a micro-blogging application, it allows for instant messages, sent in real-time that are wide disseminated and easily shared. Although seemingly easy with its 140 character limit, it can be surprisingly complex as non-profit organizations try to provide meaningful information and remain responsive to their stakeholders (Lovejoy, Waters, & Saxton, 2012). Twitter is becoming a more important tool for communications, with the number of higher education institutions using it increasing from 67 percent in 2010 to 80 percent in 2012 (Slover-Linett & Stoner, 2012). Smitko (2012) found that Twitter can be helpful in building social capital and trust, important components of fundraising. "A failure to develop and maintain the public's trust may lead to long-term difficulties for non-profit organizations to raise sufficient funds to support their work" (Burt, 2012, p.317).

One of the key features is the ability to engage in two-way conversation in a short response time. However, research by Linvill, McGee, & Hicks (2012) found that less than one-third (29.5 percent) of university tweets in their study were engaged and maintained conversations with their audiences. Most of these two-way conversations occurred when the university retweeted someone else's tweet.

Despite the increase of adoption of social media to promote an organization's mission, results of these efforts are mixed at best. In their case study of an animal rescue organization, Schaefer & Hersey (2015) found the integration of social media positively impacted the marketing efforts, brand awareness, stakeholder support, and the promotion of events and fundraising. But in a survey of mid-sized nonprofit organizations, Ogden & Starita (2009) found than more than 70 percent of the respondents had raised less than $100 from social media. More than half of universities (57 percent) surveyed found social media to be most successful in increasing engagement with their target audiences (Slover-Linett & Stoner, 2012). But the satisfaction is much lower in the fundraising realm as university development staff members do not find social media effective in meeting their goals (Slover-Linett & Stoner, 2012). Some consider social media better suited for donor acquisition than dollar acquisition (Longfield, 2013).

The Fundraising Process

To understand the role social media can play in fundraising, it is important to understand the steps in fundraising process. While many people think of fundraising as only asking for money, there are many steps in a successful fundraising campaign: Research, Planning, Cultivation, Solicitation, Stewardship, and Evaluation (Lindahl 2010). Evaluation is often seen as the end of the fundraising process, but fundraising is not always linear and the steps may overlap along the way (Lindahl, 2010). Research plays an important role in the fundraising process. This step includes researching prospective donors by gathering information on their giving history and possible connections to the organization (Lindahl 2010). This step helps nonprofit organization determine to whom it should reach out for support. The next step is creating a strong plan that will guide the fundraising efforts. This step should include setting fundraising goals and creating plans to reach those goals (Lindahl 2010). Although these steps are very important to a successful fundraising campaign, they are often done behind the scenes and difficult to identify through social media.

Cultivation, solicitation, and stewardship are much more visible actions of the fundraising process. Cultivation engages prospective donors with the organization, creating and maintaining an interest in the plans and goals of the organization (Association of Fundraising Professionals, 2003). This step is used more often when targeting donors with the anticipation of asking for a larger gifts, as the cultivation of a prospective donor can often be involved and lengthy. Common cultivation activities include having lunch meetings, inviting them to events, or giving tours of the site (Lindahl, 2013), limiting the number of people an organization can cultivate at one time. Broader scale cultivation activities may include sending newsletters or holding open houses. However, the advances of social media make cultivating a larger group of people, including those that are more likely to make smaller gifts, more cost effective (Wymer & Grau, 2011).

Solicitation is the stage of fundraising that comes to most people's mind, however, it is only a small part of the process. Yet, it is the act of asking someone for a donation that turns someone for a sideline supporter to donor (Lindahl, 2010). Solicitation can come in many forms, from a letter, to a phone call, to an in-person ask. While the most effective form of solicitation is the personal ask (Maxwell, 2003), there is an increase in peer-to-peer fundraising and impulse giving, particularly for smaller gifts.

Peer-to-peer fundraising methods use the social networks of an organization's supporters to encourage donations (Castillo, Petrie, & Wardell, 2014). A familiar example of peer-to-peer fundraising is the Leukemia & Lymphoma Society's (LLS) Team in Training program which encourages participants to raise money from their friends for LLS while training for an endurance event like a half-marathon. Since the program's inception in 1988, team members have raised more than $1.4 billion for blood cancer research (Leukemia & Lymphoma Society, n.d.). The ice bucket challenge, which raised more than $115 million for the ALS Association in 2014 (ALS Association, 2014), is an example of a peer-to-peer fundraising campaign that used social media to challenge friends and spread the message quickly. Donors participate in impulse giving when they make quick decisions to give, dedicating minimal time to researching the organization (Smith 2012). Donations made after a natural disaster are often the result of impulse giving as donors are compelled to give after seeing the images of destruction. Engaging social media in fundraising leads to efforts that are "largely a decentralized endeavor, where the scope and success of the campaign depends as much on the abilities, preferences, and connections of the organization's fans as it does on the organization" (Saxton & Wang, 2012,

p. 860). By asking supporters to participate in social media strategies, not only are organizations asking them to donate, they are also asking them to share their capital with the organization (Castillo, Petrie, & Wardell, 2014). Saxton & Guo (2014) refer to this as social media capital where "social capital is reflected in the size of the organization's social media network, its degree of influence over that network, and the extent to which its publics are engaged in that network" (p. 287). The success of both peer-to-peer fundraising and impulse giving depends on the social network effect, where "the organizations' fans reaching expanding circles of online friends in their own social networks, which ultimately increases charitable contributions" (Saxton & Wang, 2014, p. 862 – 863).

While many think the fundraising process ends after the solicitation, there are two more steps, stewardship and evaluation. Institutions of higher education that are successful at fundraising also have a strong stewardship program that keeps donors engaged, even the younger ones (MacLaughlin, 2014). The Association of Fundraising Professionals (2003) defines stewardship as "a process whereby an organization seeks to be worthy of continued philanthropic support, including the acknowledgement of gifts, donor recognition, the honoring of donor intent, prudent investment of gifts, and the effective and efficient use of funds to further the mission of the organization." As the relationship-building aspect of fundraising has recently become more prevalent, relationship-building is also seen as an important aspect of stewardship (Lindahl, 2010). Some stewardship activities are very individualized, like writing a thank you note or providing endowment reports. However, social media can contribute to more public forms of stewardship, including transparency, donor recognition, showing how funds are being used, and continued relationship building.

Evaluation determines if the previous steps in the fundraising process were effective. It includes not only meeting financial goals, but also the evaluation of the process to make sure all efforts were maximized. A review of the process can lead to an understanding of the successes and failures and improve efforts in the future (Lindahl, 2010). It is important to establish the objectives while developing the social media plan (Wymer & Grau, 2011). Handley & Chapman (2011) suggest organizations set clear goals that can be objectively measured. Although institutions may share achievements of goals with donors, the full evaluation process is often conducted internally; therefore it is hard to measure it by reviewing tweets.

Nonprofit organizations depend heavily on charitable giving that happens at the end of the year. Most charitable giving is made at the end of the year, with one-third of donations made in the final three months of the year and more giving in December (17.5 percent) than any other single month (MacLaughlin, 2014). In addition to making a push for final gifts before the tax deadline, two national philanthropic promotions take place in the final two months of the year – National Philanthropy Day ® and #GivingTuesday. First celebrated in 1986, National Philanthropy Day®

is "set aside to recognize and pay tribute to the great contributions that philanthropy – and those people active in the philanthropic community – have made to our lives, our communities and our world" (Association of Fundraising Professionals, 2009, paragraph 1). This stewardship event is help annually on November 15 and many nonprofit organizations recognize and thank their donors during this week.

A more recent phenomenon is #GivingTuesday, "a global day dedicated to giving back" (GivingTuesday.com, 2014, paragraph 1). Following on the heels of Black Friday, Small Business Saturday, and Cyber Monday, #GivingTuesday is held the Tuesday after Thanksgiving. The campaign depends heavily on social media promotion, using the hashtag (#) symbol to highlight the conversation and drive donors to online giving sites. Initial results show that more than $45 million was raised on December 2, 2014, in just the third year of the #GivingTuesday movement (Lilly Family School of Philanthropy, 2014).

RESEARCH QUESTION

Based on literature, an overarching research question developed: How are institutions of higher education using Twitter to raise funds for their university? Twitter was chosen over other social media platforms because of its growth in popularity among young adults and teens, representing the age categories of recent alumni and the next wave of college students. As noted earlier, reaching younger donors is increasingly important to colleges and universities. To examine the research question, a number of smaller benchmarks were measured. Outlined in Table 1, the benchmarks include measurements for both social media use and for fundraising strategy. The benchmarks can help identify if the university Twitter account incorporates some of the best practices that have emerged in the literature. They can also provide a measurement tool for other universities to track their own use of Twitter.

Table 1. Research benchmarks

Benchmark	Measurement	Corresponding Literature
Twitter account active	Was there a post during the three-month study period?	Waters, Burnett, Lamm, & Lucas, 2009
Frequent posts	Was there an average of three tweets per week?	Lovejoy, Waters, & Saxton, 2012
Fundraising Process	Did posts incorporate various steps of the fundraising process? (Donor Recognition, Stewardship, Events)	Lindahl, 2010
Campaigns & Initiatives	Did the university participate in targeted campaigns and intiatives? (National Philanthropy Day/Week, Giving Tuesday, Year-End Giving, University-Specific Campaign)	Association of Fundraising Professionals, 2009 GivingTuesday.com, 2014

METHODOLOGY

Fifty twitter accounts affiliated with fundraising at universities in the United States were selected to address the question of how institutions of higher education use Twitter to encourage year-end giving. This research focused only on the accounts that included references to fundraising in their profile descriptions. While most nonprofit organizations have only one or two social media accounts, universities often have numerous accounts, representing the different departments, student clubs, and sporting activities on campus. For example, Harvard University, ranked as the top social media college by StudentAdvisor.com (n.d.), lists 174 social media accounts affiliated with the university (Harvard University, 2015). The accounts were identified by using Twitter keyword searches on terms like annual giving, university fundraising, university foundation, and university development. The dataset includes public and private universities, as well as separate nonprofit support foundations that exist to help fund the university. Analysis of the content of tweets posted between November 3, 2014, and January 2, 2015, demonstrates how colleges and universities use Twitter to encourage donations and interact with current and prospective donors. While many studies on the use of Twitter use a one-month study period (e.g., Lovejoy, Waters, & Saxton, 2012; Guo & Saxton, 2014) this study used two months to capture common fundraising initiatives that fall during this time span. Each tweet, including retweets, was classified to identify the different ways that universities used the fundraising Twitter account. While other categories emerged during the coding process, the categories of National Philanthropy Day ®, #GivingTuesday, and year-end giving were established from the beginning to capture the universities' participation in these initiatives.

RESULTS

The fifty accounts analyzed represented 43 universities located in 27 states plus the District of Columbia. Seven universities had two accounts in the study. For four of these universities, one of the accounts was dormant, not posting any tweets during the time period. One university maintained an alumni account and a student philanthropy account; one maintained a comprehensive campaign account and an annual fund account; the final university hosted a foundation account and an athletics account. Eleven (22 percent) of the accounts represented private universities, with the remaining accounts representing publically-supported universities. The accounts focused on a variety of types of fundraising efforts by the university. Most of the accounts were either general fundraising accounts (17) or annual giving accounts (16). Nine (9) twitter accounts supported athletic fundraising. Other accounts focused on specific fundraising campaigns (3), alumni and fundraising offices (2), and leadership giving, student philanthropy and individual academic departments within the university (1 account each). The earliest Twitter account was created in July 2008, with the most recent starting in December 2014. Most accounts were started in 2009 (10) or 2010 (8). Thirteen accounts did not have a date listed on their profile stating when they joined Twitter. Nine accounts did not respond to a tweet requesting more information. Two of these accounts were dormant during the study period. One of the accounts retweeted the request, but did not answer the question. Three accounts without a start date responded to the tweet and provided information on when they joined.

The accounts had a wide-range of followers, from 12 – 7,634. The mean number of followers was 973; the median was 358. Interestingly, the number of followers did not always reflect the inactivity of the account. Four dormant accounts had more than the mean of 358 followers. In contrast, one of the more active accounts only had 129 followers. The number of tweets per account also varied widely, ranging from 0 to 228 tweets during the time period, for a total of 2,043 tweets analyzed. Sixteen of the accounts were dormant during the study period and posted no tweets. The 34 active accounts averaged 60 tweets during the two-month study, with a median of 20. Less than half (22) of the accounts posted at least 27 tweets during the study period, the minimum amount needed to be considered active by Lovejoy, Waters, & Saxton (2012).

The posted tweets shared a variety of information with their followers, as can be seen in Figure 1 and discussed in detail below. Although some tweets could be

Figure 1. Frequency of fundraising tactics present in University Tweets, Year-End 2014

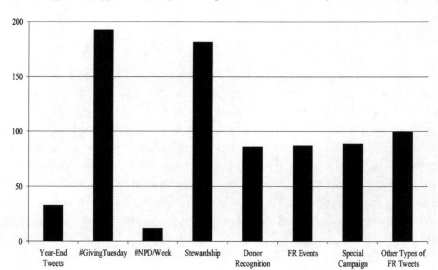

categorized in multiple categories, each one was only tallied once. The most common instances of tweets that fit multiple categories occurred with the special focus areas of this chapter, such as #GivingTuesday. In these instances, the tweet was classified in the special focus area. For example, a tweet might show a picture of a donor (donor recognition) and include #GivingTuesday in the tweet. This tweet would be classified as a #GivingTuesday tweet.

On one hand, all tweets could be considered as either engaging prospective donors or strengthening relationships with existing donors, important activities for cultivation and stewardship. However, a more in-depth analysis of the specific messages tweeted out provides a deeper understanding of how universities use Twitter. Nine primary categories emerged from the coding: National Philanthropy Day/Week, Giving Tuesday, Year-end Giving, Stewardship, Donor Recognition, Fundraising Events, Special Fundraising Campaigns, Other Types of Fundraising Tweets, and Other Tweets (not directly related to fundraising). Overall 38 percent of the 2,043 tweets were directly related to fundraising. The remaining 62 percent of tweets were categorized as Other. Table 2 provides more detailed information on the distribution of the tweets.

The results were also compared between public and private universities, and a presented in Table 3. Of the original fifty accounts reviewed, 11 were private universities and the remaining 39 were public. Four (36 percent) private university

Table 2. Distribution of Fundraising Tactics present in University Tweets, Year-End 2014*

Fundraising Tactic	Uni. Accounts Participating	Mean	Min.	Max.	SD	Frequency	%
Year-End Giving	11	1	1	9	56.72	33	2
#GivingTuesday	20	6	1	55	1.98	193	9
#NPD/Week	4	0.4	1	8	11.22	12	1
Stewardship	29	5	1	42	1.41	182	9
Donor Recognition	20	3	1	11	7.65	86	4
Fundraising Events	21	3	1	24	3.22	87	4
Special Campaign	10	3	1	47	4.71	89	4
Other Types of FR Tweets	19	3	1	21	8.48	100	5
Total Fundraising Tweets	34	23	1	108	24.57	782	38
Total All Tweets	34	60	1	228	1690.18	2043	100

* The data represents the 34 active accounts and does not include the dormant accounts in the calculations.

Table 3. Comparison of Private and Public University Fundraising Tweets, Year-End 2014*

	Private Universities	Public Universities
Number of Accounts	11	39
Dormant	36%	31%
Average Followers	384	1139
Average Tweets	70	33
Average FR Tweets	34 (49% of average tweets)	20 (60% of average tweets)
Year-End Giving	29%	33%
#GivingTuesday	57%	59%
#NPD/Week	14%	11%
Stewardship	57%	93%
Donor Recognition	57%	63%
Fundraising Events	57%	63%
Special Campaign	43%	22%
Other Types of FR Tweets	43%	59%
Total Fundraising Tweets	29%	33%

accounts were dormant compared to twelve (31 percent) of the public university accounts. While data was similar between private and public universities in many areas, there were some notable differences. First of all, public universities had nearly three times the average number of followers (1139 to 384). This difference in followers could be in part due to the likelihood that the public universities have more alumni. However, private universities averaged more tweets (70 compared to 33). In contract, public universities averaged a higher percentage of fundraising tweets that the private universities (60 percent compared to 49 percent). Public universities were much more likely to post tweets related to stewardship than private universities (93 percent compared to 57 percent). Private universities were nearly twice as likely to participate in special Twitter-based fundraising campaigns, with 43 percent of the private universities reviewed holding such a campaign, compared to only 22 percent of public universities. This comparison suggests that private and public universities may have different goals for their Twitter-based fundraising campaigns.

The next step is to compare how this data measures up against the research question benchmarks established earlier in the chapter. Table 4 outlines the results of these benchmarks. While most universities met the benchmarks of being active (68 percent) and posting at least one step in the fundraising process (66 percent, with

Table 4. Benchmark results, n=50

Benchmark	Measurement	Percentage met Benchmark
Twitter Account Active	Was there a post during the three-month study period?	68%
Frequent Posts	Was there an average of three tweets per week?	48%
Fundraising Process	Did posts incorporate various steps of the fundraising process? (Donor Recognition, Stewardship, Events)	Donor Recognition – 40% Stewardship – 58% Events – 42% At least one type – 66% All three types – 20%
Campaigns & Initiatives	Did the university participate in targeted campaigns and initiatives? (National Philanthropy Day/Week, Giving Tuesday, Year-End Giving, University-Specific Campaign)	Nat'l Philanthropy Day – 8% Giving Tuesday – 40% Year-End Giving – 22% University Campaign – 20% At least one type – 44% All four types – 2%
Met all benchmarks	Achieved at least one benchmark in each category	36%

stewardship messages being the most common at 58 percent), none of the other benchmarks achieved 50 percent success. Collectively, only 36 percent of the accounts in the study achieved success based on these benchmarks.

National Philanthropy Day/Week

National Philanthropy Day/Week tweets recognized National Philanthropy Day on November 15 and were regularly tagged #NationalPhilanthropyDay. In this study, #NationalPhilanthropyDay only garnered twelve tweets from four accounts. This count includes one school that celebrated National Philanthropy Week. Universities not only celebrated National Philanthropy Day ® on campus, but recognized stakeholders that were being recognized for their effort, as demonstrated in the tweet below (posting Twitter account in italics):

@WrightGiving Congrats to #AFPDayton #NationalPhilanthropyDay honorees Larry and Marilyn Klaben, HORAN and #WSURaiderthon! http://ow.ly/EuyA9

#GivingTuesday

More tweets (193) were categorized as #GivingTuesday tweets than any other type. Universities used this hashtag to encourage people to make a donation on the Tuesday after Thanksgiving, as well as retweet donors that had posted their donation to Twitter. Some universities also added their own hashtag to the #GivingTuesday conversation to localize the national initiative. This practice can be seen in the example below with the inclusion of the #SRUUnselfie:

@SRUannualgiving With your help we were able to raise $348.14 so far for #GivingTuesday! Post #SRUunselfie and why you give to SRU! (with graphic)

Year-End Giving

Year-end giving tweets reminded people that the end of the calendar year was approaching, encouraging them to make a donation soon. Eleven schools encouraged year-end giving, posting 33 tweets focusing on gifts made by December 31, 2014. The appeal of making a gift by year-end for tax purposes was often a theme of the tweet, as can be seen in the example as follow:

@UMGiving Yikes! It's almost 2015! Still time to make a gift to UM that'll be counted for your 2014 taxes... http://www.miami.edu/CanesGiving

Stewardship

For this analysis, stewardship tweets addressed accountability of funds raised and showed examples of the impact of donations. Most schools (29 of the 34 active accounts) shared a tweet related to stewardship. Nine percent of all the tweets were stewardship tweets. The general thanking of a broad group donors for their support was also a feature of stewardship donors, as can be seen in the following example:

@RedRaiderClub Hear from our amazing student-athletes about how #YourSupport helped make their dreams come true! Thank you, donors! http://youtu. be/6XsyECy5cRA (with video)

The relationship-building aspect of stewardship was not included as most of the tweets fit this category. Donor recognition, also a form of stewardship, was separated into its own category.

Donor Recognition

Donor recognition tweets publically acknowledged donors and thanked them for their donations. While donor recognition is a form of stewardship, for the purposes of this study they were categorized separately. Donor recognition tweets thanked and recognized a single donor or small group of donors for their support, as can be seen in this example:

@UWFoundation Generous #WisAlumni, the Morgridges, donate landmark $100 million gift to invest in @UWMadison faculty. http://bit.ly/1EFK2wt

Twenty universities used donor recognition as a fundraising tactic, posting 86 tweets which recognized individual or small groups of donors.

Fundraising Event

Fundraising event tweets highlighted specific events aimed at raising money for the university and its affiliated entities or events that were for donors only. Twenty-one universities spread the news about a fundraising event through Twitter, representing 4 percent of all tweets. The following example is of a fundraising event hosted by the university's alumni association with proceeds supporting "the work of the Young Alumni and its commitment to building a stronger University and a stronger city" (RacesOnline, n.d. paragraph 2).

@MemAnnualGiving Don't forget about the True Blue 5K tomorrow! The Young Alumni Committee invites all runners, walkers, alumni, students and friends to... The alumni association did not announce the fundraising results, but the race drew 380 participants (University of Memphis Alumni Association, 2014).

Special Fundraising Campaign

Special fundraising campaign tweets focused on giving opportunities unique to that school. The senior class gift campaign was popular as four universities encouraged graduating seniors to make a gift. The following example of a senior class gift tweet was posted by the Twitter account dedicated to student philanthropy:

@WeBackApp #seniorclassgift donors are invited to the Toast with the Chancellor! Don't miss out! Donate today! #cheersandthanks

Ten universities used social media to promote their own fundraising campaigns, resulting in 4 percent of all tweets. Texas Christian University's #TCUGivesDay represents a growing trend of 24-hour fundraising campaigns driven by social media. Held on November 6, 2014, the university challenged its followers to make 500 gifts in a 24-hour period, tagging their posts #TCUGivesDay. After reaching its goal, a new challenge was issued for 700 gifts. A total of 594 gifts were made (Texas Christian University, 2014), nearly twice the number of followers of the account (302). More than half (47) of TCU's 90 tweets included #TCUGivesDay.

Other Fundraising

Other fundraising tweets addressed fundraising opportunities not addressed in the previous categories, such as the promotion of honorarium gifts or challenge gifts.

@MemAnnualGiving Make a gift to the U of M in honor of someone special, and they will receive a notecard letting them know! http://www.memphis.edu/give

Other Tweets

All remaining tweets were considered to be Other. These tweets included anything from updates on sporting events, general news about campus activities, or messages from other departments on campus. The example below congratulates those students that will be graduating:

@asufoundation Congratulations to all the Sun Devils graduating next week! https:// asunews.asu.edu/20141205-asu-commencement-fall-2014 …

These initial results show just the beginning of how universities are using social media to raise funds. Although these results cannot be applied to the entire higher education system, they do suggest an area for continued research. Understanding how universities currently use social media is the first step to identifying best practices that can make social media a more effective tool for fundraising. The research can also help create evaluation strategies so colleges and universities can determine which actions are working for each university.

DISCUSSION

This attempt to categorize university fundraising tweets provides an interesting snapshot of current practice. University administrators can use this information to help determine if Twitter has a place in their own fundraising strategy. Universities must dedicate time, effort, and funds to have a Twitter account that produces results. To understand if the investment is worth it, a university must first determine its own goals. Twitter can be effective for recruiting younger donors and raising smaller dollar amounts. If this results are an area where the university wants to expand, then it might be the right decision to include Twitter as a fundraising tool. However, if a university's goal is to grow major gifts or endowments, attention should be focused on other types of fundraising tools. While some universities have created Twitter accounts for comprehensive fundraising campaigns, Twitter best aligns with the goals of annual fund campaigns. Twitter has the capability of starting relationships with new donors with smaller gifts. Additionally, as social media use on campus is becoming more prominent, the continuing communications with recent graduates via social media will seem like a natural transition. If a university can get a student to follow the Twitter account before graduating, it can also help maintain contact during this transitional time period. Recent alumni often move a number of times following graduating, accommodating for new jobs, married life, or graduate education. However, few alumni keep their alma mater informed of these address changes. Twitter can serve as a bridge, enabling the university and alumni to maintain contact.

Like all fundraising initiatives, potential adopters of Twitter on campuses must determine if the tool fits the goals and objectives of the university. Administrators considering adding Twitter to their fundraising toolbox should treat it as they do other annual fund campaigns. In advance of establishing the account, leaders should determine who will manage the account and be responsible for the posts. Consideration should often be given to the expected frequency of the posts and the content material. At the same time, flexibility must be given to take advantage of the instantaneous messaging that Twitter provides. Once the decision has been made to include Twitter in the fundraising strategy, then a commitment must be paid to keep the account active. A dormant account suggests poor planning and may turn away potential donors. After initiating the account, an active campaign should be conducted to gain followers. Alumni and development websites should have links to the Twitter account. Written communication, both printed and electronic, should also promote the account. Twitter-based campaigns should be included in the general fundraising calendar. Goals for the campaign should be outlined and measured. These results should be reviewed and strategy adapted when necessary. By following some of the Twitter accounts as the examples provided here, university administrators can get ideas on how to best use Twitter on their own campuses.

FUTURE RESEARCH

The study also leads to some possible further research to expand the knowledge of university social media use. The results support Stoner's (as quoted in Lavrusik, 2009) comments that universities are not maximizing the potential that exists in social media. Nearly one-third (32 percent) of the accounts examined did not post one tweet during the two-month time period. Twelve (24 percent) additional accounts averaged less than three tweets per week. Regular and consistent use of social media leads to improved results when engaging people. The irregular use of social media and the prevalence of abandoned accounts suggest that many universities opened their Twitter accounts without fully incorporating them into their communication plans and creating a strategy for use.

As noted earlier, Waters, Burnett, Lamm & Lucas (2009) suggest that regular activity on social media can also be important for gaining followers. At first glance this research does not support this finding as four dormant accounts have more followers that the sample mean of 358. However, it could suggest that dormant accounts gained followers early in their lifecycle, but as the tweets fell off, the followers forgot about them and did not go back to unfollow the account. From a fundraising standpoint this inactivity can be detrimental. In essence the organization is ignoring a group of people who have already stepped up and announced their interest in the organization.

The results also suggest that universities do not use their fundraising Twitter accounts to participate in common fundraising initiatives that fall in November and December. This finding reinforces that belief that universities are not using social media to its full extent. During the 24-hour period of #GivingTuesday more than 698,000 tweets joined the conversation (Lilly Family School of Philanthropy, 2014). Such active engagement by more than 15,000 organizations make it likely that donors will see a request to give every time they look at their Twitter account on that day. Universities need to join the conversation and take advantage of the heightened awareness of giving.

The study does have its limitations. First of all, only the Twitter accounts of the fundraising departments of the universities were consider for review. However, fundraising is not only conducted by the fundraising staff members. Other Twitter accounts hosted by other university departments may be actively engaged in fund-raising, but not included in this study. Second, only fifty accounts were examined, not enough to make a broad generalization of how all universities use Twitter to fundraise. In fact, these fifty accounts showed a too wide a variety of trends to suggest that Twitter use is anything but inconsistent.

Despite these limitations, the results have set a baseline for research and suggest opportunities for future research. One area that was not investigated in depth is how interactive the universities were with their followers. The results were presented as if Twitter was an outwardly focused communications tool. What makes Twitter so valuable is the ability to engage in two-way communications. To further explore this aspect, future research can look at how universities engage with their followers.

Do they retweet messages? Do they reply to questions asked of them via Twitter? How many people to they follow? The research would expand on the work done by Linvill, McGee, & Hicks (2012) by focusing on fundraising tweets and including donors as a target audience.

Research on special campaigns that are driven by social media could help determine how effective these campaigns are long-term and what practices lead to success. The increase in daylong campaigns like the #TCUGivesDay suggest that there is preliminary success, but what do they accomplish? Do they recruit new donors? Do these new donors remain donors? How did the university prepare for the campaign? What evaluation tools are used to measure the success? Further analysis in these areas can help other universities strengthen their social media presence and organize improved social media driven fundraising activities.

A final thread of research revolves around the internal aspects of social media campaigns. The research presented here focused on the external product of social media, specifically the tweets. As noted earlier, the research and planning steps are an important part of the fundraising process and should be better understood to assess However, a successful social media presence does not come without planning. How do universities decide to incorporate social media into their overall communications and development plan? What resources are in place to ensure that communication is consistent and relevant? What policies are in place to help guide the social media conversation? On the flip side, why have some universities abandoned their social media accounts? Presenting best practices on social media use that are specific to universities will help maximize resources for the best performance.

Social media is an evolving communications tool. Research in the area needs to keep up with the practices to help gain a better understanding of the tool and how it relates to previous literature. To maintain a donor pool, nonprofit organizations and universities alike must continue to be responsive to new prospective donors and their preferred mode of communications. This study has added to the literature on the use of social media for fundraising by providing a baseline on where social media use currently stands in universities and possible avenues for future research.

REFERENCES

ALS Association. (2014). *The ALS ice bucket challenge*. Retrieved from http://www.alsa.org/fight-als/ice-bucket-challenge.html

Association for the Study of Higher Education. (2011). ASHE Higher Education Report. *Special Issue: Philanthropy and Fundraising in American Higher Education*, *37*. doi:10.1002/aehe.3702

Association of Fundraising Professionals. (2003). *The Fundraising Dictionary Online*. Retrieved from http://www.afpnet.org/ResourceCenter/ArticleDetail.cfm?ItemNumber=3380

Association of Fundraising Professionals. (2009). *About National Philanthropy Day*. Retrieved from http://www.afpnet.org/content.cfm?ItemNumber=4033

Barnes, N. G., & Lescault, A. M. (2013). *College presidents out-blog and out-tweet corporate CEO's as higher ed delves deeper into social media to recruit students*. Center for Marketing Research. University of Massachusetts Dartmouth. Retrieved from http://www.umassd.edu/cmr/socialmediaresearch/

Benson, V., & Morgan, S. (2014). *Cutting-Edge Technologies and Social Media Use in Higher Education* (pp. 1–436). Hershey, PA: IGI Global; doi:10.4018/978-1-4666-5174-6

Burt, C. D. (2012). The importance of trust to the funding of humanitarian work. Humanitarian work psychology. In S. C. Carr, M. MacLachlan, & A. Furnham (Eds.), *Humanitarian Work Psychology* (pp. 317–331). Basingstoke, UK: Palgrave Macmillan.

Castillo, M., Petrie, R., & Wardell, C. (2014). Fundraising through online social networks: A field experiment on peer-to-peer solicitation. *Journal of Public Economics*, *114*, 29–35. doi:10.1016/j.jpubeco.2014.01.002

Council for Aid to Education. (2015, January 28). *Colleges and Universities Raise $37.45 Billion in 2014*. New York, NY: Author.

Davis, C. H. F. III, Deil-Amen, R., Rios-Aguilar, C., & Canche, M. S. G. (2012). *Social Media in Higher Education: A Literature Review and Research Directions*. The Center for the Study of Higher Education at the University of Arizona and Claremont Graduate University.

Duggan, M., Ellison, N. B., Lampe, C., Lehnart, A., & Madden, M. (2015). *Social Media Update 2014*. Washington, DC: Pew Research Center Internet, Science & Tech. Retrieved from http://www.pewinternet.org/2015/01/09/social-media-update-2014/

Guo, C., & Saxton, G. D. (2014). Tweeting social change: How social media are changing nonprofit advocacy. *Nonprofit and Voluntary Sector Quarterly*, *43*(1), 57–79. doi:10.1177/0899764012471585

Handley, A., & Chapman, C. C. (2011). *Content Rules: How to Create Killer Blogs, Webinars, (and More) that Engage Customers and Ignite Your Business*. Hoboken, NJ: John Wiley & Sons, Inc.

Harvard University. (2015). *Social media*. Retrieved from http://www.harvard.edu/social-media

Lavrusik, V. (2009, July 23). 10 Ways Universities are Engaging Alumni using Social Media. *Mashable*. Retrieved from http://mashable.com/2009/07/23/alumni-social-media/

Leukemia & Lymphoma Society. (n.d.). *Team in Training*. Retrieved from http://www.teamintraining.org/ March 14, 2015.

Lilly Family School of Philanthropy. (2014, Dec. 3). *Significant growth in online giving seen on #GivingTuesday 2014, initial data from major donation processing platforms show*. Retrieved from http://www.philanthropy.iupui.edu/news/article/significant-growth-in-online-giving-seen-on-givingtuesday-2014-initial-data-from-major-donation-processing-platforms-show

Lindahl, W. E. (2010). *Principles of Fundraising: Theory and Practice*. Sudbury, MA: Jones and Bartlett.

Linvill, D. L., McGee, S. E., & Hicks, L. K. (2012). Colleges' and universities'' use of Twitter: A content analysis. *Public Relations Review*, *38*(4), 636–638. doi:10.1016/j.pubrev.2012.05.010

Longfield, C. (2014). *The Blackbaud Index for Higher Education: Higher Education Fundraising Performance in 2013*. Blackbaud.

Lovejoy, K., Waters, R. D., & Saxton, G. D. (2012). Engaging stakeholders through Twitter: How nonprofit organizations are getting more out of 140 characters or less. *Public Relations Review*, *38*(2), 313–318. doi:10.1016/j.pubrev.2012.01.005

MacLaughlen, S. (2014). *Charitable Giving Report: How Nonprofit Fundraising Performed in 2013*. Blackbaud.

Martínez Alemán, A. M., & Wartman, K. L. (2009). *Online Social Networking on Campus: Understanding What Matters in Student Culture*. New York, NY: Routledge.

Maxwell, M. M. (2003). Individuals as donors. In E. R. Tempel (Ed.), *Hank Rosso's Achieving Excellence in Fund Raising* (pp. 161–176). San Francisco, CA: John Wiley & Sons.

M+R. (2014). *2014 M+R Benchmarks*. Available from http://www.mrbenchmarks.com

Ogden, T. N., & Starita, L. (2009). *Social Networking and Mid-size Non-profits: What's the Use?* Philanthropy Action.

Pătruţ, B., Pătruţ, M., & Cmeciu, C. (2013). *Social Media and the New Academic Environment: Pedagogical Challenges* (pp. 1–511). Hershey, PA: IGI Global; doi:10.4018/978-1-4666-2851-9

Pătruţ, M., & Pătruţ, B. (2013). *Social Media in Higher Education: Teaching in Web 2.0* (pp. 1–474). Hershey, PA: IGI Global; doi:10.4018/978-1-4666-2970-7

RacesOnline.com. (n.d.). *True Blue 5K*. Retrieved from http://trueblue5k.racesonline.com/ on March 14, 2015.

Reuben, R. (2008). *The use of social media in higher education for marketing and communications: A guide for professionals in higher education*. Academic Press.

Saxton, G., & Wang, L. (2013). The social network effect: The determinants of giving through social media. *Nonprofit and Voluntary Sector Quarterly*, *43*(5), 850–868. doi:10.1177/0899764013485159

Saxton, G. D., & Guo, C. (2014). Online stakeholder targeting and the acquisition of social media capital. *International Journal of Nonprofit and Voluntary Sector Marketing*, *19*(4), 286–300. doi:10.1002/nvsm.1504

Schaefer, G., & Hersey, L. N. (2015forthcoming). Enhancing Organizational Capacity and Strategic Planning Through the Use of Social Media. In H. Asencio & R. Sun (Eds.), *Cases on Strategic Social Media Utilization*. Hershey, PA: IGI Global.

Slover-Linett, C., & Stoner, M. (2012). *Socialmedia and Advancement: Insights from Three Years of Data*. The Council for Advancement and Support of Education.

Smith, A. (2012). *Real time charitable giving*. Washington, DC: Pew Internet & American Life Project.

StudentAdvisor.com. (n.d.). *Top 100 social media colleges*. Retrieved from http://www.studentadvisor.com/top-100-social-media-colleges

Texas Christian University. (2014). *#TCUGivesDay*. Retrieved from http://tcugivesday.tcu.edu/

University of Memphis Alumni Association. (2014). *Young Alumni*. Retrieved from http://memphis.edu/alumni/youngalumni/index.php# on

U.S. Department of Education. (2012). *National Center for Education Statistics, Education Directory, Colleges and Universities, 1949-50 through 1965-66; Higher Education General Information Survey (HEGIS), "Institutional Characteristics of Colleges and Universities" surveys, 1966-67 through 1985-86; Integrated Postsecondary Education Data System (IPEDS), "Institutional Characteristics Survey"(IPEDS-IC:86-99); and IPEDS Fall 2000 through Fall 2011, Institutional Characteristics component.* Retrieved from http://nces.ed.gov/programs/digest/d12/tables/dt12_306.asp

Waters, R. D., Burnett, E., Lamm, A., & Lucas, J. (2009). Engaging stakeholders through social networking: How nonprofit organizations are using Facebook. *Public Relations Review*, *35*(2), 102–106. doi:10.1016/j.pubrev.2009.01.006

Wymer, W., & Grau, S. L. (2011). *Connected Causes: Online Marketing Strategies for Nonprofit Organization*. Chicago: Lyceum Books, Inc.

KEY TERMS AND DEFINITIONS

Annual Giving: The organized effort to raise funds on an annual basis. These gifts tend to be smaller in nature and serve as the entry point of giving for many donors. Can also be referred to as the annual fund.

Campaign: A coordinated effort of multiple messages that support a single goal.

Engage: The interaction between people via social media.

Follower: Someone who signs up to follow another Twitter account, opting to receive information that the account holder sends out.

Hashtags: Noted by the use of the symbol # at the beginning these words or phrases are used to denote themes of social media posts and contribute to a larger conversation.

Retweet: The act of sharing someone else's tweet with one's own followers.

Stakeholder: Someone that has an interest in the nonprofit organization or university, such as a board members, alumni, or students.

Twitter Feed: The stream of tweets to which you have subscribed.

Chapter 4
Senior Leaders as Effective Fundraisers:
A Toolbox for Dealing with Complexities in the New Ecology

Morgan R. Clevenger
Wilkes University, USA

ABSTRACT

Funding in higher education continues to be volatile and complex, so senior leaders must focus on fundraising among a host of other key roles (Bornstein, 2003, 2011; Cheng, 2011; Clevenger, 2014; Cohen, 2010; Drezner & Huels, 2014; Essex & Ansbach, 1993; Gould, 2003; Hodson, 2010; Kaufman, 2004; Rhodes, 2001; Tromble, 1998). The goal is creating win-win relationships with a donor and the institution (Bornstein, 2003, 2011; Bruch & Walter, 2005; Carroll & Buchholtz, 2015; Clevenger; Eddy, 2010; Levy, 1999; Prince & File, 2001; Siegel, 2012). There is "a new ecology—a context deeply different from that in which many of today's institutions, assumptions, and habits were formed" (Fulton & Blau, 2005, p. 4). Senior leaders must have a toolbox filled with expertise to be effective fundraisers.

INTRODUCTION

Higher education continues to face resource challenges; therefore, creating win-win, long-term relationships of all kinds are of high importance (Clevenger, 2014; Cohen, 2010; Essex & Ansbach, 1993; Gould, 2003; Kaufman, 2004; Meyer & Rowan, 1977; Rhodes, 2001). Resource dependence (Pfeffer & Salncik, 2003) pushes

DOI: 10.4018/978-1-4666-9664-8.ch004

higher education leaders to devise keen relationships to gain access to appropriate resources. While it is the primary function of the development office to raise funds, senior leaders—such as presidents, board members, provosts, deans, advancement officers, community and government relations officers, corporate and foundation relations officers, and key volunteers—must spend time building relationships with individuals (e.g., alumni and alumnae, major donors, philanthropists, elected officials, and community friends) and other organizations' leaders (e.g., corporations, foundations, governments, and other community initiatives) who can contribute to the needs and programs of the institution (Bauer, 1993; Bunce & Leggett, 1994; Clevenger; Cook, 1997; Flanagan, 2002; Hunt, 2012; Norton, 2009; Prince & File, 2001; Sanzone, 2000; Saul, 2011; Siegel, 2007, 2008, 2012; Slinker, 1988; Weidner, 2008; Weinstein, 2009). Drezner and Huels (2014) summarize the challenge:

Within a philanthropic context, academic leaders must convince both internal (professional fundraisers, faculty, staff, and students) and external (alumni and other donors) stakeholders of their long-term vision of the institution. Fundraising success is only achieved if all of these constituents partner in the efforts. (p. 68)

Further, Kaufman (2004) indicated, "Fundraising is one of the most visible and demanding roles expected from campus leaders today" (p. 50). The process of fundraising and philanthropy is "relationship intensive" (Day, 1998, p. 37).

To be effective, higher education leaders "need to *develop key strategies for fundraising techniques, provide multiple opportunities* with several areas of the institution, *create clear value propositions, invest in stewardship of relationships, prioritize key people*, and *always act ethically*" (Clevenger, 2014, p. 468). Therefore, senior leaders must have a toolbox filled with expertise to be effective fundraisers including: maturity, a visionary thinking, an inspirational attitude, optimism, personal commitment and connectivity, excellent communications, ethical integrity, professionalism, sensitivity, "a systematic perspective to create strong relationships" (Kinnicutt & Pinney, 2010, p. 27), powerful influence, determination, flexibility, and patience. Additionally, these senior leaders "model appropriate behavior to their entire organizations" (Clevenger, 2014, p. 146). All members of an organization give emphasis to key goals and policies set by leaders.

BACKGROUND

Higher education is funded by a basic combination of tuition, investment income, and support from both individuals and other organizations (both private and public) such as alumni and alumnae, corporations, foundations, and strategic partnerships

(Clevenger, 2014; Drezner, 2011; Drezner & Huels, 2014; Essex & Ansbach, 1993; Hunt, 2012; Walton & Gasman, 2008). Private sector resources are key to help fund higher educations' purposes and goals (Arulampalam & Stoneman, 1995; Carroll & Buchholtz, 2015; Ciconte & Jacob, 2009; Clevenger, 2014; DeAngelo & Cohen, 2000; Drezner, 2011; Gould, 2003; Hearn, 2003; Hodson, 2010; Hunt, 2012). Goal implementation occurs as appropriate resources become available. Today, the competition for these resources continues to increase.

Colleges and universities also seek a myriad of "nontraditional revenue-generating initiatives" (Hearn, 2003, p.7) including "instructional initiatives such as online programming and special-interest programs, research, pricing strategies for various constituents, investment tools, franchising, licensing, third-party activities, auxiliary enterprises, special financing arrangements and discounts, and facility rental and other user fees" (Clevenger, 2014, p. 98). These initiatives illustrate the manifestation of Meyer and Rowan's (1977) institutional theory, which addresses socially constructed practices and norms relating to cultural and environmental influences, as well as Pfeffer and Salancik's (2003) resource dependence theory, which stresses that organizations must exchange resources with other organizations for survival. Funding is required to operate academic institutions, so senior leaders must understand these complex dynamics and their impact on how they approach philanthropy, fundraising, and resource development (Clevenger, 2014; Drezner & Huels, 2014).

Why Higher Education Leaders Must Perform: Resource Dependence

Meyer and Rowan (1977) explained that institutional theory increases three types of pressures for organizations—including academic institutions—as (a) coercive pressures from legal mandates and/or influence from the other organizations upon whom they are dependent, (b) mimetic pressures to copy other successful models (e.g., other college and universities' practices) during times of high uncertainty (e.g., like the two economic recessions already experienced in the 21st Century), and (c) normative pressures that tend to create homogeneity, which are promulgated by similar attitudes and approaches of various professional groups and/or associations brought into an organization through hiring practices. Aldrich's (1979) resource dependence theory (further refined by Pfeffer and Salancik, 2003) explains thoroughly how higher education must scan outside itself for necessary resources—including state and federal governments, various organizations, and individuals' support, which vividly manifests Meyer and Rowan's (1977) explanation of institutional theory pressures. These organizational demands impact senior leaders' prioritization to scan the environment for needed resources and to create collaborations and partnerships with a wide range of constituents. Aiken and Hage (1968) claimed that

...as the need for resources intensifies, organizations are more likely to develop greater interdependencies with other organizations...in order to gain resources... [However, in the process]...organizations attempt to maximize their gains and minimize their losses...they want to lose as little power and autonomy as possible in their exchange for other resources. (pp. 915-916)

This balance is experienced by both organizational and individual relationships in resource development and philanthropy, respectively.

Senior leaders are the main administrators to set priorities, to manage expectations, and to actively engage constituents in fostering the institution's mission, vision, and wide range of goals. Higher education leaders are expected to "present a clear and strong case" (Pollard, 1958, p. 182). This case statement aids in effective fundraising. Fundraising provides opportunity and resources to survive and thrive, expand, establish long-term programs and scholarships, build the constituency base, create viability, grow, be competitive, and perpetuate (Clevenger, 2014; Flanagan, 2009; Weinstein, 2009). To meet those goals, institutional resources are invested in the process. The resources include time, money to operate the fundraising function, and opportunity costs (Weidner, 2008). One concern on opportunity costs is the liability placed on an organization to be able to implement a new program or initiative (Bornstein, 2011). Each academic institution must be assured of their own ROI and leverage as to not create an undue burden on their own organization at the cost of gaining resources whether from individuals or other organizations.

A new era with a new ecology must be accommodated. Major forces of privatization, broad accessibility and connection, acceleration of opportunities, multiplication and diversification of opportunities, reflection of society's directions, accountability, and planning strategic and cooperative advantages will provide senior leaders opportunities for effective fundraising.

The New Ecology

There is "a new ecology—a context deeply different from that in which many of today's institutions, assumptions, and habits were formed" (Fulton & Blau, 2005, p. 4). Various dynamics have created a new era of resource development in the world in a new century pushing senior leaders to higher standards and greater performance. "Seven major forces—privatization, connection, acceleration, multiplication, diversification, observation, and reflection—and the ways they are combining...create a new ecology of social benefit" (Fulton & Blau, 2005, p. 4). These forces expedite both demand for senior leaders' performance as well as create additional opportunities.

- **Privatization:** In the United States and some other countries, there has been a "shift of power away from governments or other public institutions toward businesses [and other private entities]" (Fulton & Blau, 2005, p. 11). This privatization has shifted financial strength to many individuals, corporations, foundations, and other organizations. "Some corporations have grown to a size and reach that exceeds that of many national governments…Walmart was the sixth largest revenue-producing entity in the world, behind only the governments of the U.S., Germany, the U.K., Italy, and Japan" (Fulton & Blau, p. 11). This prioritization creates an opportunity for senior leaders to explore additional resources and partnerships.

- **Connection:** The new century has greatly increased the "advances in communication and transportation that promote global connection and commerce" (Fulton & Blau, 2005, p. 12). This availability and expediency creates broad opportunity and awareness for institutions—including higher education. However this depth of connection is increasing public scrutiny on accountability, transparency, and ethical behavior of all individuals, corporations, and other organizations. Higher education and nonprofits have also come under scrutiny and received pressure to measure outcomes and prove their impact on society. Most everyone—individuals, corporations, foundations, and other funders—have greater information and comparative data to aid choices on which organizations to support and partner. Such connection has increased competition among colleges and universities and nonprofits. "The information to pass judgment is widely available: on the Web, in the mainstream media, and in the growing number of trade press publications dedicated to nonprofits and philanthropy" (Fulton & Blau, 2005, p. 16).

- **Acceleration:** The expediency of information has increased exponentially each year since the advent of the Internet. Fulton and Blau (2005) said,

By increasing the density, speed, and scope of connection, our society has accelerated the rate at which information is communicated, the rate at which it can be incorporated into other processes, and the number of people who can use that information to create new ideas, make new discoveries, and synthesize new inventions. Not only is the creation and diffusion of knowledge accelerating, but so is everything that depends on it: science, technology, commerce, fads, culture, and efforts to create social benefit. Even the pace of acceleration is, itself, accelerating. (p. 13)

And Clevenger (2014) observed,

Who better than universities, colleges, and research organizations to continue to be the primary source for information, innovation, and solutions to key needs, op-

portunities, and problems as well as to prepare the next generation of workers and leaders? Corporations become the vehicle to harness that information to expedite its delivery into the world. Thus the partnership between corporations and higher education continues to grow and be vital in the new century—with added pressure for acceleration of ideas and answers for the country and world's most pressing issues. (p. 87)

While acceleration creates more pressure for higher education and its organizational leaders, it also provides new and wider venues to solicit assistance and resources.

- **Multiplication and Diversification:** "Everything associated with the domain of social benefit has grown significantly in the last 25 years, making it both a more active and more crowded environment" (Fulton & Blau, 2005, p. 14). Yet "the environment in which any individual actor chooses issues, formulates strategies, and makes contributions is increasingly crowded with competitors, potential collaborators, and even people or organizations working at cross-purposes" (Fulton & Blau, 2005, p. 14). Such multiplication creates additional pressure for performance to become the differentiator among all organizations. This factor can be leveraged by higher education to focus on core values and programs.
- **Reflection:** "In the last 25 years, people in the social sector have benefited from the enormous advances in their ability to reflect on their own work and the work of others" (Fulton & Blau, 2005, p. 17). This reflection increases the knowledge base, the knowledge of best practices to create ideas, and the implementation of solutions in nearly all fields. These resources allow senior academic administrators to create ongoing dialogue with all constituents and stakeholders, to build long-term relationships harnessed for producing measurable and effective impact, and to transform institutional emphases and societal outcomes (Clevenger, 2014).
- **Accountability:** "Accountability addresses what an organization does with its resources and reports on such" (Clevenger, 2014, p. 88). Most governments require organizations to report on certain information, but the transparency of more detailed information has become available in the information age. Accountability is "the responsibility…to provide evidence to stakeholders and sponsors" (Rossi, Lipsey, & Freeman, 2004, p. 200). "Where evaluation was historically done only retrospectively, many funders are now conducting formative evaluations, which review programs in progress to help grantees and funders identify problems and make mid-course corrections" (Fulton & Blau, 2005, p. 30). In order to perform, organizations have created infrastructures for planning, organizing, implementing, and record keeping

to summarize their inputs, outputs, outcomes, and impact (Clevenger, 2014; Katz & Kahn, 2005; Rossi et al., 2004). Corporations, foundations, and higher education institutions have had to develop "a much closer and more active relationship…[and] achievement of measurable goals" (Fulton & Blau, 2005, p. 24). Accountability "is creating new codes of ethics, new standards for basic compliance, new governance recommendations, and renewed interest by the IRS and Congress" (Fulton & Blau, 2005, p. 45).

- **Strategic and Cooperative Advantages:** Finally, organizations have been forced to develop strategic advantages, cooperative advantages, ability to respond to complexity, and navigate scrutiny (Fulton & Blau, 2005). The dialogues have shifted from a hands-off approach to philanthropy to organizationally centered attention of program development by colleges and universities and partnered execution to create "a lasting and collaborative relationship between a donor or collection of donors and an organization or group of organizations devoted to a shared set of goals and objectives" (Fulton & Blau, 2005, p. 23).

However, both fundraisers at all levels and constituents—such as individuals, corporations, and foundation counterparts—have indicated that it is an increased "time to build relationships" (Mayer, 2010, p. 3). Higher education has had to continue to be creative in the new millennium on how it navigates acquiring and stewarding resources (Clevenger, 2014; Eddy, 2010). Eddy (2010) summarized, "With calls for accountability, innovation, and expanding access coupled with significant economic recession and increased public skepticism about institutions' ability to deliver effective and efficient educational experiences for increasingly diverse learners, the future looks no less demanding" (p. xiii).

NAVIGATING THE COMPLEXITIES OF SENIOR LEADERSHIP FOR EFFECTIVE FUNDRAISING

Leaders define priorities. A major priority for higher education is fundraising, and senior leaders must champion the importance of these relationships (Bornstein, 2003, 2011; Cheng, 2011; Hearn, 2003; Hodson, 2010). Senior leaders, trustees, and key stakeholders work together to foster a philanthropic and positive fundraising environment (Clevenger, 2014; Essex & Ansbach, 1993; Sturgis, 2006). Fundraising must be removed "from the periphery to the center of the academy…integrated and seamless with other administrative functions, not discrete and disconnected" (Bornstein, 2003, p. 126). Leaders create organizational culture and reinforcement of behavior based on what they "pay attention to, measure, and control" (Schein,

1985, p. 224); their reactions "to critical incidents and organizational crises" (Schein, 1985, pp. 224-225); how they role model, teach, and coach others; how they allocate "rewards and status" (Schein, 1985, p. 225); and their "criteria for recruitment, selection, promotion, retirement, and excommunication" (Schein, 1985, p. 225) of employees. Senior leaders must learn about key issues and demonstrate personal involvement, engage others internally and externally, be strategic, set objectives and expect results, and recognize and reward good work (MacAllister, 1991). Emphasis on fundraising by senior leaders reinforces organizational commitment and the importance of resource development organization-wide.

The Role of Senior Leaders

Senior leaders lead; "it's what the institution and its many constituents expect of them" (Hodson, 2010, p. 39). Ideally, the best leaders have a combination of high concern for people and a high concern for task, which is described as integrative management on Blake and Mouton's (1985) managerial grid model. During the past 40 years, higher education boards have emphasized the need for senior leaders to actively engage in fundraising and resource development (Bornstein, 2003, 2011; Cook, 1997; Drezner & Huels, 2014; Essex & Ansbach, 1993; Hunt, 2012; Miller, 1991; Sturgis, 2006; Tromble, 1998). Hodson (2010) said, "it's a part of the job that is not well defined or understood" (p. 39). Fundraising and philanthropy cannot be merely delegated to development staff. Essex and Ansbach (1993) admonished:

Development directors can and should be expected to generate major donor funding for their college or school. They should be part of setting the goals and budgets for their operations. They should be effective in identifying donor and volunteer prospects, training volunteers, planning and managing events and mailings, maintaining donor records, developing suggestions for recognitions and maintaining communications with donors over time. They should help identify and clarify those aspects of campus programs that will be most appealing to donors and packaging those appeals with input from all concerned. Development directors should be able to show progress in not only the amounts raised, but also the levels to which they are helping to move donors in their giving. But there are several important things development directors cannot do that must be done by the college president or trustee. (p. 3)

Thus, development team members carry out the administrative functions (Bornstein, 2011; Essex & Ansbach; Hodson, 2010). Senior leaders have the capacity to set a personal example and "to shape policy" (Carroll & Buchholtz, 2015, p. 237). These actions are mimicked by other fundraisers and employees in general. Such positive actions help to increase the overall bottom line. Senior leaders guide the fundraising and philanthropy process, identify constituencies, set goals, provide budgets and needed staffing, create a positive image, cultivate major donors, actively solicit major requests, and provide a high level of personal recognition as warranted (Bornstein, 2003, 2011; Clevenger, 2014; Cook, 1997; Essex & Ansbach; Hodson, 2010; Hodson, 2010; Kaufman, 2004).

While some leaders love dealing with constituents and soliciting funds, others merely tolerate the process, and yet others are uncomfortable with the activity—donors read all of these attitudes (Bornstein, 2003; Bunce & Leggett, 1994; Cook; 1991; Hodson, 2010; Hunt, 2012). A major concern of higher education leaders is distraction from their main job function of providing vision and strategy (Clevenger, 2014; Hodson, 2010; Hunt, 2012; Weinstein, 2009). The role of these leaders is to provide personal commitment and passion as well as the availability to readily discuss the college or university's current and future plans. The key is balancing roles and perspectives (Kinnicutt & Pinney, 2010).

Ways Senior Leaders Lead

"Researchers usually define leadership according to their particular conceptual background or field of interest, including traits, behavior, influence, interaction patterns, roles, and power" (Day, 1998, p. 246). Avolio, Walumbwa, and Weber, (2009), Bornstein (2003), Day (1998), and Drezner and Huels (2014) have reviewed literature from classic business and leadership authors. Those researchers summarized and discussed important considerations of higher education leaders' management styles (e.g. transactional, transformative, transformational, servant, shared, authentic, distributed, leader-member exchange, etc.) and their implications on fostering strategic and philanthropic cultures. Likely, the three most important leadership styles for effective fundraising by senior leaders are *authentic*, *shared*, and *transformational*.

Authentic leadership focuses on the authentic self (Avolio et al., 2009; Drezner & Huels, 2014). This characterization is "one that reflects a leadership style that is in harmony with the leader's personality and character and is grounded in a genuine desire to serve others" (Drezner & Huels, p. 64). George (2004) indicates the five dimensions of this authentic focus are passion, values, heart, emphasis on relationships, and self-discipline. These are the qualities that make good leaders effective fundraisers. Accountability and transparency require authentic leadership (Clevenger 2014; Drezner & Huels, 2014).

Shared leadership (also known as distributive or collective leadership) is a willingness to have joint ownership of authority to manage (Hodson, 2010; Yukl, 2012). Success of co-sharing responsibilities include centralized and shared goals, on-going collegial support, and *voice*, the consideration that each member has equal

90

involvement and input into making decisions (Avolio et al., 2009; Carson, Tesluk, & Marrone, 2007; Drezner & Huels, 2014; Hodson; Yukl). Shared leadership is likely the key for senior leaders to effectively fundraise by creating shared purpose and holistic outreach on behalf of the academic institution (Avolio et al., 2009; Clevenger, 2014; Cook, 1997; Drezner & Huels, 2014; Glier, 2004; Weidner, 2008).

The 21st Century mandates change, growth, accessibility, and improvement, making *transformational* leadership the focus. Transformational leadership is taking people, causes, and organizations to a higher level (Burns, 1978). Such levels meet "more universal needs and purposes" (Bolman & Deal, 2008, p. 368). "Leaders with charisma are more likely to lead through persuasion rather than position" (Day, 1998, p. 250). These charismatic transformational leaders "motivate employees to achieve organizational goals and to put aside self-interest for the good of the organization" (Drezner & Huels, 2014, p. 60).

SOLUTIONS AND RECOMMENDATIONS

Senior leaders' attitudes, behaviors, personal commitment, and involvement in constituent engagement set the tone and send the message both internally and externally about the importance, emphasis, and prioritization of resource development (Benioff & Adler, 2007; Clevenger, 2014; Drezner & Huels, 2014; Essex & Ansbach, 1993; Freeman, 1991; Garvin, 1975; MacAllister, 1991; Sirsly, 2009). Quantifying impact is of high importance for academic leaders to be able to compete successfully in today's complex resource environment (Brock, 2007; Clevenger, 2014; Fulton & Blau, 2005; Saul, 2011). Colleges and universities typically measure "success by student achievement, faculty research and scholarship, alumni accomplishments, and contributions to society" (Clevenger, p. 415). However, fundraising must also be measured and stewarded (Clevenger; Drezner & Huels, 2014; Eckert & Pollack, 2000; Essex & Ansbach, 1993; Hodson, 2010). Eckert and Pollack (2000) indicated that partners and donors are looking for results. Individuals want to know impact: exactly how many students benefitted from their gifts. Tracking and reporting on this type of information helps in the stewardship process.

Ineffective leaders are bureaucratic, petty, weak, charlatans, or unethical (Bolman & Deal, 2008). Bornstein (2011) said, "There is nothing more important than the good reputation of an institution and its leaders. Once lost, public trust is difficult to regain" (p. 77).

Senior leaders must have a toolbox filled with the expertise to be effective fundraisers (Clevenger, 2014). The attitudes, policies, and behavior of senior leaders sets the tone for the rest of the organization's emphasis on fundraising and philanthropy (Clevenger, 2014).

The Senior Leaders' Toolbox

"People give money [and other resources] to people" (Bauer, 1993). Friend-raising is therefore a key to effective fundraising (Weinstein, 2009). With this caveat in mind, senior leaders need to understand other people, to know that they consummately represent their academic institution, and to realize people represent interests, companies, foundations, and other organizations. Building individual relationships is what leads to shared interests, mutual understanding and commitment, and ultimately access to resources (Clevenger, 2014). Kaufman (2004) identified authentic institutional belief, investment of external relationships, strategic goal setting, vision, passion, and credibility as key leadership emphasis areas to support fundraising. Some of Kinnicutt and Pinney's (2010) and Pinney and Kinnicutt's (2010) personal attributes from their leadership competency models are applicable for higher education senior leaders: maturity, optimism, vision, understanding systems, collaboration, initiative, passion, balance, strategy, and influence. Senior leaders must have a toolbox filled with expertise to be effective fundraisers: maturity, a visionary thinking, an inspirational attitude, optimism, personal commitment and connectivity, excellent communications, ethical integrity, professionalism, sensitivity, a systematic perspective, transparency, powerful influence, determination, flexibility, and patience. This wide range of qualities and attributes, competencies, knowledge, skills, abilities, personality, intelligence, and experience dimensions should provide for effective fundraising.

- **Maturity:** Individuals arrive in senior leadership with a wide range of experience, knowledge, and vision. These tools allow a sense of maturity to permeate their thinking and actions. Senior leaders use "patience and pragmatism to maintain confidence in the face of change and adversity, knowing the organization or cause will benefit from efforts" (Pinney & Kinnicutt, p. 11). This maturity is what provides consideration of all the other toolbox attributes.
- **Visionary Thinking:** Leaders must understand the big picture and all the individual parts to connect the dots to promote creative and innovate thought in support of organizational direction (Bornstein, 2011; Kaufman, 2004; Kinnicutt & Pinney, 2010). "Vision, mission, and money are intertwined. Fulfilling a vision and mission is not possible without resources, and raising money is challenging without an exciting vision and mission" (Bornstein, 2011, p. 13). Leaders combine "vision with the persistence and drive to mobilize people around a higher purpose" (Pinney & Kinnicutt, 2010, p. 22). This vision must then be communicated organization-wide. Morgan (2006) explained this organization-wide concept (called *corporate DNA*) this way:

The visions, values, and sense of purpose that bind an organization together can be used as a way of helping every individual understand and absorb the mission and challenge of the whole enterprise. Just as DNA in nature carries a holographic code that contains the information required to unfold the complete development of the human body, it is possible to encode key elements of a complete organization in the cultural and other codes that unite its members. (p. 99)

- **Inspirational Attitude:** Passion and the ability to convey vision to others is inspirational attitude (Essex & Ansbach, 1993; Kaufman, 2004). Optimistic passion engages others and builds community (Clevenger, 2014; Pinney & Kinnicutt, 2010). An inspirational attitude permeates senior leaders' actions to promote the academic institution's many causes. A positive attitude aids in creating optimism, sharing personal satisfaction, and exciting others about important opportunities and initiatives.
- **Optimism:** Optimism pushes organizations to better standards and higher performance (Clevenger, 2014; Kinnicutt & Pinney, 2010; Pinney & Kinnicutt, 2010). Organizations' optimism or pessimism often extends from the tone, aura, actions, and attitudes of its leaders. Optimism is therefore a key element to success in effective fundraising and philanthropy. After goals are set, senior leaders and other fundraisers work together in a positive way to achieve objectives, celebrate milestones, and steward the individuals and organizations who contributed resources to the work.
- **Personal Commitment and Connectivity:** Leaders are committed to their vision and purpose (Clevenger, 2014; Kinnicutt & Pinney, 2010; Pinney & Kinnicutt, 2010). Senior leaders are expected to support fundraising goals in spirit and in action. Personal financial commitment creates an unspoken conscientiousness for senior leaders' involvement in the fundraising and philanthropy process. Flanagan (2002) explains it best:

If the cause does not seem important to you, then how can you convey to others the importance and urgency of doing something about it? You must really believe in the cause you are addressing and in the work that your organisation is doing. Your enthusiasm and commitment will encourage others to become equally committed through their giving. (p. 23)

Additionally, leaders have a wide range of peers and liaisons in their network. These connections multiply senior leaders' impact by bringing additional effort and funds into important causes based on their own personal commitment and action (Clevenger, 2014).

- **Excellent Communications:** Senior leaders communicate "well with stake-holders, adapting to their issues, concerns, and level of understanding" and deliver "well-timed and effective presentations" (Pinney & Kinnicutt, 2010, p. 22). Communication is the key to exploring curiosity; learning about constituents; listening and responding to ideas, issues, concerns, and opportunities; and promoting the vision, mission, and goals of the institution and its programs, causes, platforms, and research (Clevenger, 2014).
- **Ethical Integrity:** Carroll and Buchholtz (2015) and Reichart (1999) advocate that organizations are expected to avoid questionable practices, to respond to the spirit and letter of the law, and to protect employees and the environment. Instead of making right decisions, Bolman and Deal (2008), Bornstein (2003, 2011), and Levy (2012) promoted that the responsibility of organizational leaders is to be role models and catalysts for values in all activities, thus setting both the tone and modeling an appropriate example to everyone. However, "ethics must be rooted in soul" (Bolman & Deal, p. 409). This ethical integrity promotes the authentic leadership and provides for concrete actions with good conscience.

Ethics is not a science. Ethics falls into three main categories: descriptive ethics, metaethics, and normative ethics (Weinstein, 2009). *Descriptive ethics* are records and reports—often required by boards, governments, and sometimes, agreements with donors. *Metaethics* are more complex; they deal with abstracts that must be considered and appropriately applied. Such complexity can involve variances in acceptable practice stemming from an organization or a leader's particular views and practices of culture, religion, or science. Finally, *normative ethics* are judgments addressing moral dilemmas or basically distinguishing right from wrong.

Several professional associations promote self-regulation to ensure ethical behavior of fundraisers and of higher education leaders including: the Association of Fundraising Professionals (AFP) Code of Ethical Principles and Standards of Professional Practice, the Association of Private College and University Alumni Directors (PCUAD), the Council for Advancement and Support of Education (CASE) Statement of Ethics, the Donor Bill of Rights (jointly developed by the American Association of Fund Raising Counsel, the Association of Healthcare Philanthropy, AFP, and CASE), the National Association of Independent Schools (NAIS), and National Committee on Planned Giving (NCPG) Model Standards of Practice for the Charitable Gift Planner.

Bornstein (2003) discussed threats to leaders' ethics and legitimacy, including lack of organizational fit, incompetence, misconduct, devaluing social capital, inattentiveness to priorities, and grandiosity. Clevenger's (2014) dissertation research exploring organizational behavior and ethics between higher education and companies revealed three current concerns with academic leaders including "an entitlement attitude from university administration," a "concern of culture change when top management changes," and "personality-driven" agendas in organizational relationships (p. 348). These issues are a direct result of today's pressure on senior leaders to fundraise and increase resources.

- **Professionalism:** Professionalism includes a mix of persona, behavior, and reputation. Extending common courtesy to others, having sincere respect and interest for situations and people, attending to personal grooming and habits, providing thoughtful actions, and allowing for open communication builds professionalism. These actions contribute to legitimacy as a professional. The main professional aspect for senior leaders is building this legitimacy or validity (Bornstein, 2003; Carroll & Buchholtz, 2015.) Ultimately, professionalism inspires confidence with those who interact with a senior leader (Hodson, 2010).
- **Sensitivity:** Leaders use "empathy and interpersonal understanding to build mutually beneficial relationships and connect and engage diverse groups of people" (Kinnicutt & Pinney, 2010, p. 29). Sensitivity is the comfort to read people and situations and appropriately respond or take action. The attribute and skill of sensitivity provides thoughtful considerations, keen articulation, and empathy to promote authentic solutions and actions. This empathy nurtures relationship, which contributes to effective fundraising and philanthropy (Clevenger, 2014; Weinstein, 2009).
- **Systematic Perspective:** Senior leaders must invest extensive time and energy in "a systematic perspective to create strong relationships" (Kinnicutt & Pinney, 2010, p. 27). Leaders use "an understanding of how elements of a system relate and interact to frame risks and opportunities" (Kinnicutt & Pinney, p. 29). Being strategic in fundraising and philanthropy leverages resources to create win-win for both parties (Clevenger, 2014). Organizations' internal systems influence how they interact with other organizations and their environments (Bolman & Deal, 2008; Day, 1998; Morgan, 2006; Shafritz, Ott, & Jang, 2005). Four internal systems include (1) structure, which varies depending on the size of the academic institution and includes policies; (2) human resources roles and hiring of leadership, management, and employees; (3) politics; and (4) organizational culture—specifically as mission, vision, and values (Bolman & Deal; Clevenger; Herman, 2008; Morgan, 2006; Saiia, 2001). Finally, a key component of effective fundraising is measuring and reporting (Brock, 2007; Cleland et al., 2012; Fulton & Blau, 2005; Saul, 2011; Weinstein, 2009).

- **Transparency:** Because of "increased media attention to ethical violations by a few organizations" (Day, 1998, p. 214), senior leaders must safeguard practices through transparency. Transparency includes open processes to divulge goals, intents, fair disclosure, proper ethical behavior by stakeholders at all levels, compliance, and reporting of institutional behavior (Clevenger, 2014; Weinstein, 2009). Many governments require several compliances and regulations as part of societal demands. For example, in the United States, the Internal Revenue Service (IRS), the Securities and Exchange Commission (SEC), and state and federal revenue offices provide regulations and disclosure requirements for both non-profit and for-profit organizations to provide extensive transparency and reporting on significant financial transactions. Additionally, the age of technology and communication provides easy-access venues for communicating organizational goals (i.e., intended behaviors) and periodic or annual reporting (i.e., actual behaviors) (Clevenger, 2014).

- **Powerful Influence:** Leaders employ a combination of authority, influence, and power to execute their roles (Clevenger, 2014; Day, 1998). Authority stems naturally from a person's role, title, and office. "Power refers to the ability and capacity to produce an effect—to get something done that otherwise may not be done" (Bolman & Deal, 2008, p. 70). Leaders begin with their personal and positional power to leverage influence (Bolman & Deal; Kinnicutt & Pinney, 2010). Through collaboration, alliances, and networks they build a reputation for success that promotes legitimacy (Bolman & Deal; Bornstein, 2011; Kinnicutt & Pinney; Pinney & Kinnicutt, 2010). Leaders' influence makes things happen (Day, 1998). Their span of influence develops others, pushes people and programs to innovate, builds trust, motivates, inspires, shapes ideas, sets direction, aligns people, seeks opportunities for change, and assesses risks (Day).

- **Determination:** Leaders are in their roles because of their ability to lead (Hodson, 2010). Their span of control is wide. Senior leaders must therefore understand each situation, person, or organization's depth and have a keen sense of navigating the situation. This process is determination. Determination provides leaders with an unwavering commitment to the situation, person, or organization being addressed.

- **Flexibility:** Circumstances of individuals and organizations change. Goals and milestones change. The economy changes. Internal staff members change positions and roles. Key liaisons with corporations and foundations change. Senior leaders must have the flexibility to adjust their thought processes, actions, and policies dynamically to change with circumstances.

- **Patience:** Building relationships takes time, persistence, and patience (Bornstein, 2003; 2011; Burnson, 2009; Ciconte & Jacob, 2009; Clevenger, 2014; Flanagan, 2002; Garecht, 2015). Patience also comes from persistence with key follow-up, appropriate and timely interactions, and on-going mutual commitment (Day, 1998). Fundraising often is delayed, and frustration can result. However, it is patience that commits senior leaders to invest for a longevous viewpoint in the fundraising and philanthropy process. Typically, the larger the resource at stake, the longer negotiating a win-win agreement may take.

Effective Fundraising and Resource Development

The most successful, effective senior leaders as fundraisers are those who are committed in spirit and to the amount of time required for the process (Hodson, 2010; Hunt, 2012). Senior leaders such as presidents spend between 50-80% of their time on resource development (Cook, 1997). To be effective, higher education leaders "need to *develop key strategies for fundraising techniques, provide multiple opportunities* with several areas of the institution, *create clear value propositions, invest in stewardship of relationships, prioritize key people*, and *always act ethically*" (Clevenger, 2014, p. 468).

- **Develop Key Strategies for Fundraising Techniques:** Leaders may find themselves called upon to assist in any part of the fundraising relationship process: identification, cultivation, engagement, solicitation, or stewardship (Bornstein, 2011; Bunce & Leggett, 1994; Clevenger, 2014; Cook, 1997; Hodson, 2010; Hunt, 2012; Kaufman, 2004; Weidner, 2008). Fundraising must be removed "from the periphery to the center of the academy…integrated and seamless with other administrative functions, not discrete and disconnected" (Bornstein, 2003, p. 126).
- **Provide Multiple Opportunities with Several Areas of the Institution:** Having a wide range of programs, capital improvement projects, new ventures, scholarships, and other initiatives increases the likelihood of matching interest with a donor (Clevenger, 2014). Outcomes for higher education are measured in any or all of three categories: (1) change in status, (2) change in condition, and/or (3) systemic change (Saul, 2011). Embedding those outcomes into funding opportunities increases the likelihood for funding (Clevenger; Saul). Understanding constituents' values and needs; speaking their language; creating solutions for problems, opportunities, and needs;

and assuring efficiency and effectiveness aid in creating success (Clevenger; Brock, 2007; Rhodes, 2001; Saul). Institutions wanting resources need to be relevant and "Understand important trends and directions driving the industry. Understand their key measures of success. Try to anticipate the problems, challenges, and opportunities they face" (Brock, p. 2).

- **Create Clear Value Propositions:** Academic institutions must think more like businesses to provide value propositions that excite and assist funding partners, whether individual, corporations, foundations, governments, or other organizations (Clevenger, 2014; Flanagan, 2002; Norton, 2009; Saul, 2011). These value propositions create clarity, direction, and intentions.

- **Invest in the Stewardship of Relationships:** *Stewardship* is a process that includes follow-up, acknowledgement, recognition, and accountability with donors (Bunce & Leggett, 1994; Hunt, 2012; Sheldon, 2000). These processes must occur "in ways that are meaningful to the donors" (Weidner, 2008, p. 397). Eckert and Pollack (2000) said, "Donors are looking for results. Individuals want to know exactly how many students benefitted from their gifts. This desire for greater accountability is a result of decreased public confidence in educational institutions" (Clevenger, 2014, p. 47). "Stewardship activities supporting existing relationships" are "important" (Cleland et al., 2012, p. 6). Sanzone (2000) said, "the institution must prove its ability to consistently use and manage gifts and other corporate revenue responsibly" (p. 324).

- **Prioritize Key People:** Involving the right people within higher education in the fundraising or philanthropy process is vital to establishing key relationships (Clevenger, 2014). Boards, fundraising staffs, and senior leadership must define roles and responsibilities and work together to foster a healthy fundraising environment, which creates positive results from individuals and organizations being fully committed and engaged (Clevenger; Essex & Ansbach, 1993; Hodson, 2010; Tromble, 1998). Clevenger (2014), Sanzone (2000), and Weidner (2008) observed that successful relationships are built through engaging individuals such as senior leaders, management, researchers, faculty, and alumni and alumnae of educational institutions with constituents as appropriate.

- **Always Act Ethically:** Ethics is the ability to distinguish between right and wrong decisions and choosing to do right (Clevenger, 2014; Day, 1998). Ethics are embodied through peoples' actions and rooted in values, beliefs, morals, laws, and acceptable best practices, norms, and standards collectively shared by stakeholders. Credibility is established and maintained through high ethical standards, transparency, accountability, and stewardship of resources (Bornstein, 2003; Clevenger; Hunt, 2012; Kaufman, 2004). Ethics are the basis for human interaction, dignity, and social interaction regardless of origins from Buddhism, Christianity, Chinese religions, Hinduism, Judaism, Muslim, Zoroastrianism, or other faiths (Day).

Organizational Modeling

Senior leaders build strong trusting relationships both internally and externally (Clevenger, 2014; Pinney & Kinnicutt, 2010). These leaders "model appropriate behavior to their entire organizations" (Clevenger, 2014, p. 146). Bolman and Deal (2008) observed that successful leaders engrain virtue and ethics into their organization's character. This behavior contributes to the culture of the organization and other leaders' and employees' behaviors (Bornstein, 2003; Clevenger, 2014; Morgan, 2006).

"Organizational culture refers to the ground on which the organization and its employees stand. The commitments made, the beliefs held, the values shared, the unspoken understandings all contribute to the shape, form, and content of an organization's culture" (Day, 1998, p. 37). Robbins and Stylianou (2003) said that "culture can be defined as a shared set of values that influence societal perceptions, attitudes, preferences, and responses" (p. 206). Key areas of concern in developing organizational culture include philosophy, values, mission, strategy, structure, resource commitment, and style (Clevenger, 2014; Hall, 1991). These elements are governed by policies and practices created, implemented, monitored, and measured by senior leaders.

To understand organizational culture, it is important to understand the essence of an academic institution, which includes the purpose(s) typically communicated in vision and mission statements, values that are enacted in organizational behaviors through individual action, and relevant artifacts that create and celebrate how the organization functions (Bolman & Deal, 2008; Clevenger, 2014; Morgan, 2006; Spradley, 1980). The essence of culture is intangible and deep; culture operates unconsciously in "an environment's view of itself and its environment" (Schein, 1985, p. 6). Morgan (2006) explained, "The visions, values, and sense of purpose that bind an organization together can be used as a way of helping every individual understand and absorb the mission and challenge of the whole enterprise" (p. 99).

Senior leaders set the tone of an organization and create a culture of resource development in fundraising, philanthropy, and ethics (Brief & Motowidlo, 1986; Clevenger, 2014; Evans, 2000; Herman, 2008; Sirsly, 2009). Schein (1985) said leaders create culture and reinforcement of cultural behavior based on what they "pay attention to, measure, and control" (p. 224); how they react "to critical incidents and organizational crises" (pp. 224-225); how they role model, teach, and coach others; how they allocate "rewards and status" (p. 225); and their "criteria for recruitment, selection, promotion, retirement, and excommunication" (p. 225) of employees.

"Organizational culture shapes and defines staff response to the several stimuli at work on and in the organization" (Day, 1998, p. 37). So senior leaders' priorities, policies, and behavior end up being manifested in an organization's culture and ultimately mimicked in employees' behaviors.

FUTURE RESEARCH DIRECTIONS

Prior research on presidents and fundraising leaders from 1975 to 2000 could be replicated for comparative analysis of expectations, behaviors, and adoption of best practices. These same studies could be replicated in several countries to compare and contrast practices based on culture, governmental frames, or economics. Research on 21st Century senior academic leaders' response to the new ecology would highlight how colleges and universities address the seven major forces for organizations' resource development. A meta-analysis of studies in development and advancement may shed light on additional variables adding to senior leaders' success. Expansion of Clevenger's (2014) research to more colleges and universities would add additional breadth and depth of inter-organizational behavior including senior leaders' behaviors and ethical actions. Specifically, additional consideration of the Carnegie© Classification of academic institutions may shed light to compare and contrast doctoral research university, comprehensive masters institutions, traditional 4-year schools, faith-based schools, Historically Black Colleges and Universities (HBCUs), and other classifications. Finally, more qualitative exploration of academy boards, current and retired fundraisers, and current and retired senior leaders would provide additional understanding of the attributes they believe should be in today's senior leaders' toolbox and management of such high expectations as effectiveness in fundraising.

CONCLUSION

New expectations in the 21st Century have mandated change, growth, accessibility, and improvement in societies and their organizations. Higher education continues to face resource challenges, which continues to create expectations and pressures for effective fundraising from senior leaders. To achieve effectiveness in fundraising, it must be an institutional priority. The effort is team-oriented and enhanced with shared responsibility. Fundraising is a daunting task with high time commitment, emphasis on relationships, and attention to details. Success centers on authentic leadership and transformational intentions. Senior leaders ought to embrace their roles and show personal involvement, engage others internally and externally, be innovative, be strategic, set objectives, and expect strong fundraising and philanthropy results. Displaying a conscientiousness of professionalism, friend-raising relationship skills, and proper ethics aid in advancing fundraising, philanthropy, and resource development efforts. Senior leaders require a toolbox filled with qualities and attributes, competencies, knowledge, skills, abilities, personality, intelligence, and experiences to provide a fertile environment for effective fundraising and philanthropy. Effective fundraising leaders are mature, optimistic, ethical visionaries who simultaneously function as architects, strategists, catalysts, advocates, influencers, negotiators, servants, and poets (Bolman & Deal, 2008; Bornstein, 2003, 2011; Clevenger, 2014; Essex & Ansbach, 1993; Kinnicutt & Pinney, 2010). Leaders need to recognize and reward good work (Clevenger, 2014; MacAllister, 1991). As Weidner (2008) said, "Good luck with this important work, and have some fun in the process!" (p. 398).

REFERENCES

Aiken, M., & Hage, J. (1968). Organizational interdependence and intra-organizational structure. *American Sociological Review*, *33*(6), 912–930. doi:10.2307/2092683

Aldrich, H. E. (1979). *Organizations and environments*. Englewood Cliffs, NJ: Prentice-Hall.

Arulampalam, W., & Stoneman, P. (1995). An investigation into the givings by large corporate donors to UK charities, 1979-86. *Applied Economics*, *27*(10), 935–945. doi:10.1080/00036849500000073

Avolio, B. J., Walumbwa, F. O., & Weber, T. J. (2009). Leadership: Current theories, research, and future directions. *Annual Review of Psychology*, *60*(1), 421–429. doi:10.1146/annurev.psych.60.110707.163621 PMID:18651820

Bauer, D. (1993). *The fund-raising primer*. New York, NY: Scholastic Inc.

Blake, R., & Moulton, J. S. (1985). *Managerial grid III*. Houston, TX: Gulf.

Bolman, L. G., & Deal, T. D. (2008). *Reframing organizations: Artistry, choice, and leadership* (4th ed.). San Francisco, CA: Wiley.

Bornstein, R. (2003). *Legitimacy in the academic presidency: From entrance to exit*. Washington, DC: Roman & Littlefield Publishers.

Bornstein, R. (2011). *Fundraising advice for college and university presidents: An insider's guide*. Washington, DC: AGB Press.

Brock, D. (2007, July 5). Focus on a customer's need to buy, not on your need to sell. *EyesOnSales*. Retrieved from http://www.eyesonsales.com/content/article/focus_on_a_customers_need_to_buy_not_your_need_to_sell/

Bruch, H., & Walter, F. (2005). The keys to rethinking corporate philanthropy. *MIT Sloan Management Review, 47*(1), 48–55.

Bunce, R. L., & Leggett, S. F. (1994). *Dollars for excellence: Raising private money for private schools and public schools*. London: Precept Pr.

Burns, J. M. (1978). *Leadership*. New York: Harper Collins.

Carroll, A. B., & Buchholtz, A. K. (2015). *Business & society: Ethics and stakeholder management* (7th ed.). Mason, OH: Thomson South-Western.

Carson, J. B., Tesluk, P. E., & Marrone, J. A. (2007). Shared leadership in teams: An investigation of antecedent conditions and performance. *Academy of Management Journal, 50*(5), 1217–1234. doi:10.2307/20159921

Cheng, K.-M. (2011). Fund-raising as institutional advancement. In P. G. Altbach (Ed.), *Leadership for world-class universities: Challenges for developing countries* (pp. 159–175). New York, NY: Routledge.

Ciconte, B. L., & Jacob, J. G. (2009). *Fundraising basics: A complete guide* (3rd ed.). Sudbury, MA: Jones and Bartlett.

Cleland, T. A., Colledge, B., Ellerbrock, M., Lynch, K., McGowan, D., Patera, S., . . . See, J. (2012). *Metrics for a successful twenty-first century academic corporate relations program*. White Paper, Network of Academic Corporate Relations Officers Benchmarking Committee, August 2, 2012. Retrieved from http://www.nacroonline.org/assets/metrics%20whitepaper%202012%20final.pdf

Clevenger, M. R. (2014). *An organizational analysis of the inter-organizational relationships between a public American higher education university and six United States corporate supporters: An instrumental, ethnographic case study using Cone's corporate citizenship spectrum* (Unpublished doctoral dissertation). University of Missouri-Columbia, Columbia, MO.

Cohen, A. M. (2010). *The shaping of American higher education: Emergency and growth of the contemporary system* (2nd ed.). San Francisco, CA: Jossey-Bass Publishers.

Cook, W. B. (1997). Fund raising and the college presidency in an era of uncertainty: From 1975 to present. *The Journal of Higher Education, 68*(1), 53–86. doi:10.2307/2959936

Day, D. L. (1998). *The effective advancement professional: Management principles and practices.* Gaithersburg, MD: Aspen Publishing.

DeAngelo, L., & Cohen, A. (2000). *Privatization: The challenge ahead for public higher education.* Washington, DC: U.S. Department of Education.

Drezner, N. D. (2011). *Philanthropy and fundraising in American higher education. ASHE Higher Education Report, 37(2).* San Francisco, CA: Wiley.

Drezner, N. D., & Huels, F. (2014). *Fundraising and institutional advancement: Theory, practice, and new paradigms.* New York, NY: Routledge.

Eckert, G., & Pollack, R. (2000, September). Sowing the seeds of philanthropy. *CASE Currents*, 26(7), 46–49.

Eddy, P. L. (2010). *Partnerships and collaborations in higher education. ASHE Higher Education Report, 36(2).* San Francisco, CA: Wiley.

Essex, G. L., & Ansbach, C. (1993, June). Fund raising in a changing economy: Notes for presidents and trustees. *Foundation Development Abstracts, 3*(2), 2-4.

Evans, G. A. (2000). Ethical issues in fund raising. In P. Buchanan (Ed.), *Handbook of institutional advancement* (3rd ed.; pp. 363–366). Washington, DC: CASE.

Flanagan, J. (2002). *Successful fundraising: A complete handbook for volunteers and professionals.* New York, NY: McGraw-Hill.

Freeman, H. L. (1991). Corporate strategic philanthropy: A million here, a million there, it can add up to real corporate choices. In *Vital Speeches of the Day* (pp. 246-250). Salt Lake City, UT: Academic Press.

Fulton, K., & Blau, A. (2005). *Looking out for the future: An orientation for twenty-first century philanthropists.* Cambridge, MA: The Monitor Group.

Garecht, J. (2015). Major donor fundraising 101. *The Fundraising Authority.* Retrieved from http://www.thefundraisingauthority.com/individual-fundraising/major-donor-fundraising-101/

Garvin, C. C. Jr. (1975). *Corporate philanthropy: The third aspect of social responsibility.* New York, NY: Council for Financial Aid to Education.

George, B. (2004). *Authentic leadership: Rediscovering the secrets to creating lasting value.* San Francisco, CA: Jossey Bass.

Glier, J. (2004, May 13). *Higher education leadership and fundraising*. Remarks to the Council for Industry and Higher Education. CIHE Council meeting, London, England.

Gould, E. (2003). *The university in a corporate culture*. New Haven, CT: Yale University Press.

Hall, M. S. (1991). Linking corporate culture and corporate philanthropy. In J. P. Shannon (Ed.), *The corporate contributions handbook: Devoting private means to public needs* (pp. 105–118). San Francisco, CA: Jossey Bass.

Hearn, J. C. (2003). *Diversifying campus revenue streams: Opportunities and risks*. Washington, DC: American Council on Education.

Hodson, J. B. (2010). Leading the way: The role of presidents and academic deans in fundraising. In J. B. Hodson & B. W. Speck's (Eds.), Perspectives on fund raising: New directions for higher education, number 149 (pp. 39-49). San Francisco, CA: Jossey-Bass.

Hunt, P. C. (2012). *Development for academic leaders: A practical guide for fundraising success*. San Francisco, CA: Jossey-Bass.

Katz, D., & Kahn, R. L. (2005). Organizations and the system concept. In J. Shafritz, J. Ott, & Y. Jang (Eds.), *Classics of organization theory* (6th ed.; pp. 480–490). Boston, MA: Thomson Wadsworth.

Kaufman, B. (2004). Juggling act: Today's college or university president must be a champion fundraiser and a strong internal leader. *University Business, 7*(7), 50–52.

Kinnicutt, S., & Pinney, C. (2010). Getting to the roots of success: The leadership competencies that grow corporate citizenship pros. *The Corporate Citizen, 4*, 26–30.

Levy, B. R. (2012). *Defining your leadership role in promoting ethical practice*. Presentation at the Association of Fundraising Professionals' 49th AFP International Conference on Fundraising, Vancouver, BC. Retrieved from http://conference. afpnet.org/

MacAllister, J. A. (1991). Why give? Notes to a new CEO. In J. P. Shannon (Ed.), *The corporate contributions handbook: Devoting private means to public needs* (pp. 121–125). San Francisco, CA: Jossey Bass.

Meyer, J. W., & Rowan, B. (1977). Institutionalized organizations: Formal structure as myth and ceremony. *American Journal of Sociology, 83*(2), 340–363. doi:10.1086/226550

Miller, M. T. (1991). *The college president's role in fund raising*. (Unpublished thesis). University of Nebraska-Lincoln, Lincoln, NE.

Norton, M. (2009). *The worldwide fundraiser's handbook: A resource for mobilisation guide for NHOS and community organisations*. London: Directory of Social Change.

Pfeffer, J., & Salancik, G. R. (2003). *The external control of organizations: A resource dependence perspective*. Stanford, CA: Stanford University Press.

Pinney, C., & Kinnicutt, S. (2010). *Leadership competencies for community involvement: Getting to the roots of success*. Boston, MA: The Boston College Center for Corporate Citizenship.

Pollard, J. A. (1958). *Fund-raising for higher education*. New York, NY: Harper & Brothers, Publishers.

Prince, R. A., & File, K. M. (2001). *The seven faces of philanthropy: A new approach to cultivating donors*. San Francisco, CA: Jossey-Bass.

Reichart, J. (1999). *Corporate ethics and environmental values: Issues, perceptions, and the logic of stakeholder action*. (Unpublished dissertation). University of Virginia, Richmond, VA.

Rhodes, F. H. T. (2001). *The creation of the future: The role of the American university*. Ithaca, NY: Cornell University.

Robbins, S., & Stylianou, A. C. (2003). Global corporate web sites: An empirical investigation of content and design. *Information & Management, 40*(3), 205–212. doi:10.1016/S0378-7206(02)00002-2

Rossi, P. H., Lipsey, M. W., & Freeman, H. E. (2004). *Evaluation: A systematic approach* (7th ed.). Thousand Oaks, CA: Sage.

Saiia, D. H. (2001). Philanthropy and corporate citizenship: Strategic philanthropy is good corporate citizenship. *Journal of Corporate Citizenship, 2*(2), 57–74. doi:10.9774/GLEAF.4700.2001.su.00009

Sanzone, C. S. (2000). Securing corporate support: The business of corporate relations. In P. Buchanan (Ed.), *Handbook of Institutional Advancement* (3rd ed.; pp. 321–324). Washington, DC: CASE.

Saul, J. (2011). *The end of fundraising: Raise more money selling your impact*. San Francisco, CA: Jossey-Bass.

Schein, E. H. (1985). *Organizational culture and leadership*. San Francisco, CA: Jossey-Bass.

Shafritz, J. M., Ott, J. S., & Jang, Y. S. (2005). *Classics of organization theory* (6th ed.). Boston, MA: Thomson Wadsworth.

Siegel, D. (2007). Constructive engagement with the corporation. *Academe, 93*(6), 52–55.

Siegel, D. (2008). Framing involvement: Rationale construction in an inter-organizational collaboration. *Journal of Further and Higher Education, 32*(3), 221–240. doi:10.1080/03098770802220413

Siegel, D. (2012). Beyond the academic-corporate divide. *Academe, 98*(1), 29–31.

Sirsly, C.-A. T. (2009). 75 years of lessons learned: Chief executive officer values and corporate social responsibility. *Journal of Management, 15*(1), 78–94.

Slinker, J. M. (1988). *The role of college or university presidents in institutional advancement.* (Unpublished doctoral dissertation). Northern Arizona University, Flagstaff, AZ.

Sturgis, R. (2006). Presidential leadership in institutional advancement: From the perspective of the president and the vice president of institutional advancement. *International Journal of Higher Educational Advancement, 6*(3), 221–231. doi:10.1057/palgrave.ijea.2150019

Tromble, W. W. (1998). *Excellence in advancement: Applications for higher education and nonprofit organizations.* Gaithersburg, MD: Aspen Publishing.

Walton, A., & Gasman, M. (Eds.). (2008). *Philanthropy, volunteerism, and fundraising.* Upper Saddle River, NJ: Pearson.

Weidner, D. J. (2008). Fundraising tips for deans with intermediate development programs. *University of Toledo Law Review. University of Toledo. College of Law, 39*(2), 393–398.

Weinstein, S. (2009). *The complete guide to fundraising management.* San Francisco, CA: Wiley. doi:10.1002/9781118387061

Yukl, G. A. (2012). *Leadership in organizations.* New York, NY: Prentice Hall.

KEY TERMS AND DEFINITIONS

Ethics: The core behaviors made in good conscience complying with moral, legal, and reasonable person actions.

Fundraising: The process of building long-term relationships with funding partners (e.g., individuals, corporations, foundations, and other organizations) through a series of interactions to create win-win outcomes for both parties involved.

Philanthropy: The love of human kind. Individuals and organizations are philanthropic when they selflessly invest in causes to benefit society in some way.

Senior Leaders: Include key individuals aiding the orchestration and execution of fundraising such as presidents, board members, provosts, deans, advancement officers, community and government relations officers, corporate and foundation relations officers, and key volunteers.

Vision: The aim of leaders: scanning the environment, choosing direction, and creating passion and excitement for others to join an institution in its endeavors.

Section 2
Community, Culture, and Economic Development in Higher Education Fundraising and Philanthropy

Chapter 5
Higher Education and Philanthropy Potential in the GCC States:
Analysis of Challenges and Opportunities for FDI and Venture Philanthropy in the MENA Region

Henry C. Alphin Jr.
Drexel University, USA

Jennie Lavine
Higher Colleges of Technology, UAE

ABSTRACT

In this chapter we aim to discuss the opportunities for FDI and venture philanthropy in higher education for the Middle East and North Africa. The MENA region has gathered interest due to the large population and increasing governmental influence on improving higher education in general in the region, and creating partnerships with organizations to better match higher educational options and employment. The GCC plays a large role in the impetus of foreign institutes wanting to invest in the economically developing MENA region. There are many challenges to overcome, some of which are great enough to discourage FDI; but overlooking the initial challenges, there are a wealth of opportunities awaiting exploration.

DOI: 10.4018/978-1-4666-9664-8.ch005

INTRODUCTION

This chapter will attempt to create an overall analysis of opportunities and challenges for foreign direct investment (FDI) and venture philanthropy for institutions of higher education (IHEs) in the Middle East and North Africa (MENA) region.

Higher education systems and their policies are affected by globalization, which is "the widening, deepening and speeding up of worldwide interconnectedness" (Held, McGrew, Goldblatt, & Perraton, 1999, p. 2). Higher education has become more of a focus in emerging nations, "in which worldwide networking and exchange are reshaping social, economic and cultural life" (Marginson & van der Wende, 2006, p. 4).

Higher Education philanthropy has been gathering traction in the wealthy Gulf States in recent times (Hertog, 2013). The need for funding has increased with the rapid growth rate the region has undergone and is continuing to undergo. Supporting and investing in higher education has become increasingly important in a globalized world, and to secure a competitive nature of the MENA region and future leaders (Hertog, 2013).

Before organized philanthropy in the twentieth century, philanthropy was conducted on a much smaller scale, largely financed by a few very wealthy individuals in response to personal appeals (Cutlip, 1990). Education philanthropy in the United Arab Emirates (UAE), and some other MENA countries, was predominantly orchestrated by governmental bodies ensuring that all citizens, up until university age, were educated under their funding.

Different countries have differing attitudes on philanthropy, especially regarding philanthropy in education. More recently, the growth of the focus on higher education in the Arab world has attracted the attention of many private companies (Wilkens, 2011). Major private Arab institutions donated more than $1.9 billion USD in the years 2010-2012 to finance global education (The World Bank, 2015) – the largest being the Islamic Development Bank and the Saudi Fund for Development, which have generously given $740 million USD and $690 million USD (Zawya, 2015), respectively. The phenomenon of philanthropy in higher education is one that has the potential to be developed further and, moreover, encouraged in the Arab world (Kapur & Crowley, 2008).

The rise of philanthropy in Arab higher education can be attributed to a number of factors. Heavy reliance on oil revenues is not a sustainable way to fund higher education, so alternatives must be sought and implemented (Luomi, 2009). Globalization has had a profound effect on the economies of the world (Gilpin, 2001). Previously, the UAE and other Gulf states relied significantly on low skilled labor from Asia due to its abundance and lower expected wage compared with other nationalities (Elhiraika, 2007). This was the way forward for rapid growth and to prosper. The changes in the economic climate and an increasingly hyper competitive market, both domestically and internationally, have introduced a new environment. Knowledge, including education and skills, has emerged as an imperative factor that companies must sustain for competition and growth. This requires a workforce capable of understanding, producing and utilizing knowledge-intensive goods and services and adopting and adapting modern methods of technological innovation, in order to remain competitive (International Labour Organization, 2011).

Currently, the financial support to MENA higher education from non-governmental entities is unknown and can be logically interpreted as modest (Cohen & Khan, 2013). The majority of Emiratis prefer to work in governmental institutes due to higher salaries and more accommodating working hours. The introduction of Emiratization by the UAE government as an affirmative action employment policy aimed at Emiratis to be able to achieve employment in the private sector has, so far, not reached quotas (Alnaqbi, 2011). The reasons are plentiful, with many opinions being directed at cosmetic approaches (Trenwith, 2013), and Professor William Scott-Jackson of Oxford Strategic Consulting, stating in a conference in Abu Dhabi, that employers must train future employees before they apply for jobs (Salama, 2013).

The establishment of majority American investors, and fewer from British or Australian universities, particularly focusing on the Gulf States of Qatar, Saudi Arabia and the UAE, are all pointing towards an influx of international financial investment and a push towards educational improvement (Thacker & Cuadra, 2014). Whether the latter is indeed the strategy is a cause for questioning. It has been speculated that the respective governments are using the investments as a method of diversifying the economy from the dwindling oil reserves to one featuring education and sustainability at the forefront, without really focusing on the standard of education itself.

The current environment provides an opening for FDI in higher education. However, many potential investors or philanthropists – particularly from the West, do not understand enough about the local cultures and economies to make accurate assessments of the investment potential. An analysis of opportunities and challenges for higher education investment in the MENA region will provide investors with a better ability to understand the risks with the investment and also provide IHEs and MENA countries with a better ability to improve their potential for investment. The transformation of higher education from elite to a mass system and the inability of the government to take responsibility for the ever increasing burden and cost of higher education are several initial reasons for adopting the philanthropic route to higher education and treating students as consumers, all open to further exploration.

Research Questions:

1. What are the challenges in obtaining FDI and venture philanthropy for higher education in the MENA region?

2.   What are the current opportunities and incentives for foreign-based higher education investors in the MENA region?
3.   What can the MENA region do, individually and as a whole, to minimize challenges and maximize opportunities for FDI and venture philanthropy for higher education in the MENA region?

BACKGROUND

Introduction

The MENA region includes the following countries: Algeria, Bahrain, Djibouti, Egypt, Iran, Iraq, Israel, Jordan, Kuwait, Lebanon, Libya, Malta, Morocco, Oman, Qatar, Saudi Arabia, Syria, Tunisia, United Arab Emirates (UAE), West Bank and Gaza, and Yemen.

The specific topic of higher education philanthropy through FDI or venture philanthropy methods in the MENA region has not been studied extensively. Higher education philanthropy, overall, is a small field that is only beginning to explore a theory-based approach from disciplinary perspectives (Drezner & Huehls, 2014).

FDI in MENA

The Middle East is the major region of the world that receives the lowest FDI in-flow (Varghese, 2009). Al-Asaly (2003) argues that factors inhibiting FDI flow into the MENA region include: fragmented social systems; an undeveloped economic system; imbalances of constitution and financial law; the rate of growth of public expenditure; lack of well-developed objective criteria; and exogenous agreements that are required, such as IMF intervention. Bouoiyour (2003) cites other difficulties in obtaining FDI in the MENA region, including a backdrop of growing competition from EU countries, lack of education and illiteracy, and a need to move to higher value added, skill intensive, and high wage industries.

Eid and Paua (2002) found that FDI flows into MENA countries have been weak and unevenly distributed. FDI flows out from the Arab World are influenced by the foreign exchange rate, interest rates, and inflation (Onyeiwu, 2000).

Brahim & Rachdi (2014) developed nine measures of quality institutional frame-works to better understand the potential for FDI to flow into the MENA region. These nine measures include law and order, corruption, socioeconomic conditions, external conflicts, internal conflicts, military in politics, bureaucracy quality, religion in politics, and ethnic tension. Their paper further develops the connection of

FDI with country and political stability. Onyeiwu (2003) uses measures that also include the rate of return on investment, openness of the economy, political rights, infrastructures, natural resource availability, corruption and bureaucratic red tape, human capital, and macroeconomic fundamentals. For this study, the factors we will focus on include a mixture of each: political stability and individual rights, conflict and tension, religion or military in politics, human capital, level of economic freedom, infrastructure and natural resources, and corruption.

Investors use available information to make investment decisions. At times, and within certain environments, information may be unavailable, skewed, or simply unreliable. Access to the country or region is important, whether in the form of travelling to the site, obtaining first-hand information from inside reporters or scholars, or analyzing data provided by government, quasi-government entities, NGOs, or academic researchers. Negative affiliations of any sort can be detrimental, as Haddad & Hakim (2003) note the increase in sovereign spreads for the MENA region after the September 11, 2002 attacks.

One of the dominant factors in FDI is the stability of the receiving government. In the MENA region, factors that affect the stability of country and local governments and their budgetary systems are myriad. In Oman, the two most important motives for FDI are political and economic stability (Mellahi, Guermat, Frynas, & Al Bortamani, 2003). In the MENA region, particularly the Gulf Cooperation Countries (GCC) – which include Bahrain, Oman, Kuwait, Qatar, Saudi Arabia, and the UAE, have been unable to better integrate their economies largely due to socio-political reasons, rather than primarily economic concerns (Darrat & Al-Shamsi, 2003).

Oil revenues are primary government income (65 percent in Yemen), while the country's oil reserve is limited (Al-Asaly, 2003). Some Persian Gulf countries are considered developing countries because of their reliance on natural resources, particularly the windfall of oil revenues, even while the UAE has one of the world's highest per capita incomes (Burden-Leahy, 2009). The UAE aspires to be a global investment hub, and both the public and private sector understand that diversification of the economy is crucial to achieving that goal (Mina, 2014).

The Environmental Sustainability Index (ESI) is a ranking system, best equipped to worst equipped, based on the country's state of environmental systems, stresses on those systems, human vulnerability to environmental change, social and institutional capacities to cope with such change, and the ability to respond to the demands of global stewardship (Alpay, 2003). In the 2005 ESI, the highest ranking MENA countries were Tunisia at 55 and Israel at 62, the UAE was ranked at 110, and those countries ranking near the bottom (above 125), included Libya at 126, Lebanon at 129, Iran at 132, Saudi Arabia at 136, Yemen at 137, Kuwait at 138, and Iraq at 143 (Yale University & Columbia University, 2005). The UAE, along with Kuwait and

Saudi Arabia, are noted as having limited participation in international cooperative efforts, yet these countries perform better than other MENA countries in reducing economic stress indicators (Alpay, 2003).

The UAE has been making steps in this area by developing institutes and initiatives to address this issue. Alpay (2003) developed a model, based on the ESI, that includes economic development and openness to trade. Alpay (2003) shows that per capita income has a significant and positive impact on ESI, and that positive impact is higher for developing countries, particularly for MENA countries. This means that economic growth can occur in the MENA region without a negative impact on the environment.

Kuemmerle (1999) found that multinational firms based in different countries or regions follow similar stimuli when seeking research and development sites abroad, including local and national commitment of public and private entities to R&D in the target country. Nour (2014) found a positive relation in Egypt between the share of public spending on R&D and spending on education, leading to a greater transfer of knowledge.

Higher Education Philanthropy in MENA

The MENA region, particularly Egypt, is home to the world's oldest continuous higher learning center, Al-Azhar University (Teferra, 2008). While the MENA region has a rich higher education history, some of that richness is tarnished by colonialization (Teferra, 2008), as well as an overall lack of qualified instructors coupled with outdated academic resources (Rupp, 2009). The World Bank (1999) argues that returns to education by level differ more in the MENA region than anywhere else. In addition, universities in developing countries are at risk for political instability, threatening perceptions of internationalization (Alphin Jr., 2014), lack of resources, and the potential for being peripheral institutions in the scope of international higher education (Altbach, 1998). Developing countries in the MENA region, particularly those that are ethnically diverse and under centralized government control, are at risk of reduced higher education expansion (Schofer & Meyer, 2005), and thus a decreased potential for an improved economy through higher education enrollment. Turmoil in the MENA region has led to conflict between the Middle East and the United States (Rupp, 2009), and it is unlucky that that investment can occur without socio-political stability taking shape (Teferra, 2008).

Higher education philanthropy in the MENA region is difficult to assess quantitatively and qualitatively primarily due to it not being a part of the culture, lack of government transparency and reporting, and lack of a true IHE push for investment. Developing a culture of philanthropy in higher education is an investment of its own, as institutional advancement requires commitment to the short and long term goals of the development team and approach; adequate staffing and professional development; a data infrastructure conducive to prospect management; a culture of outreach and developing alumni and potential donors; and the support of higher education leaders, community leaders, and the government to pattern a holistic approach to higher education sustainability coupled with economic and regional development.

Drezner (2011) provides a report on philanthropy and fundraising in American higher education, but many of the topics, including annual giving and campaigns, can be utilized as a structure for beginning to understand philanthropy and fundraising in MENA higher education. The link between the two seems to be effective leadership that can bring together donors and causes, including boards of trustees (Drezner & Huehls, 2014) and women in leadership positions (Sperling, Marcati, & Rennie, 2014). As an example, Shimoni (2008) connects mega donors in Israel to patriotic philanthropy focused on the public good on a national level. Higher education fundraising leadership could utilize this type of approach with donors from each of the MENA countries who feel a kinship with their respective people.

In Tunisia, students contribute less than one percent to fund their education, which results in a regressive tax benefitting high income groups (Johnstone, 1998). Johnstone (1998) argues that cost restructuring in higher education is resulting in systems having a difficult time closing inefficient and outdated campuses. As higher education tends to be a reflection of world cultures (Schofer & Meyer, 2005), the MENA region has much to prepare for in terms of accessibility and equality of opportunity. Part of the answer may lie in ICT growth, whereas such growth may have a positive effect on economic growth (Shirazi, Gholami, & Higon, 2009), which could correspond with increased higher education attainment and knowledge production. Murphy and Salehi-Isfahani (2003) developed a model of human capital accumulation based on knowledge versus creativity, with individuals in rigid labor markets – supported by education systems and employer-defined rewards – focusing on knowledge accumulation and credentialing rather than developing their creativity skill set.

Academic freedom is an ongoing issue in MENA higher education, most recently making headlines when New York University professor Andrew Ross was barred from entering the UAE to conduct research (Mangan, 2015). Also noticed by the international higher education community is Iran's foray into branch campuses across the Arab states (Sawahel, 2015a).

Privatization of higher education has become an important discussion in the MENA region. Public higher education institutions often offer low salaries and inadequate academic resources. In addition, with the increased prevalence of rapid transportation combined with the internationalization of higher education, many students do not need to rely on their home countries to fulfill their higher education needs.

Leslie and Ramey (1988) argue that prominence and public visibility are vital in the decision making process of higher education donor groups. MENA IHEs, with a healthy mix of well-established and nascent institutions, have yet to reach the prominence and visibility of Western institutions. Some countries have very few higher education philanthropists, with higher education philanthropy in Oman being almost nonexistent (Al-Lamki, 2002). Non-philanthropic private contributions to higher education can be detrimental to growth because of the reduction of autonomy (Tilak, 2005). However, liberty-oriented philanthropists have the potential to increase autonomy by allowing the institution to rely less on government support and more on charitable giving that reinforces voluntary exchange (Ealy, 2012).

Quality in higher education is a vague term, but for the purposes of this chapter, Tarawneh's (2011) description of the following factors is sufficient: managing the changing perception of society toward higher education, satisfying the needs of students' and employers' expectations of graduates, structure and context of academic programs, study conditions and implementation of the academic process, and the balance between research and teaching. It is important to restate the importance of perception and prominence within the description of quality in higher education, as noted earlier, Leslie and Ramey (1988) point out that prominence of the institution or system is vital to obtaining donors. Garvin (1980) developed a model of universities as economic institutions led by individuals with self interest in mind, in which faculty members and administrators focus on prestige as a market-enhancing element. For the MENA region, prestige is a priority, but Raines and Leathers (2003) caution that within an economic model, IHEs focusing on prestige need to be able to balance a quantity and quality tradeoff of expanded enrollments and increased salaries versus poorly prepared students and budgetary restraints, respectively.

Quality assurance in higher education is a peer review process, generally with self-evaluation initiatives and site visits by peer teams. Independent accreditation boards, particularly in the MENA region, are crucial to the success of monitoring quality in both public and private higher education (The World Bank, 1999). Private higher education, alone, presents specific challenges regarding autonomy, including equity issues (Tilak, 2005) and student stratification (Varghese, 2009). Inequities in higher education tend to result in inequities in employment (Varghese, 2009).

Higher education accreditation in the MENA region is lacking a central, authoritative, and cohesive authority with contacts deeply invested in the region. The most developed effort at accreditation within the region is membership in the International Network for Quality Assurance Agencies in Higher Education (INQAAHE), which is a voluntary international association with purposes to gather and disseminate assessment information, undertake or commission research on higher education quality, promote the theory and practice of higher education quality improvement, and provide advice and expertise, among others (INQAAHE, 2013).

While INQAAHE processes and procedures provide a step closer toward well-developed accreditation efforts, Knight (2008) argues that there has been a lack of cohesive policies and results, and Blackmur (2008) argues that the network merely encourages compliance on a national level. One of the issues facing INQAAHE is its ability to change and update according to new challenges, which has been an ongoing problem in higher education worldwide. Blackmur (2008) criticizes the INQAAHE Guidelines of Good Practice (GGP) from 2007 for disregarding cultural differences, making compliance difficult. As of March 2015, the GGP were last updated in 2007. However, the INQAAHE is making an attempt to better understand cultural differences in higher education assessment, as the 2015 conference has keynotes subthemes on diversity in higher education and internationalization (INQAAHE, 2015).

The INQAAHE has regional networks that attempt to better address higher education quality issues at a deeper and intimate level. The Association of Quality Assurance Agencies of the Islamic World (QA-Islamic) was established at a conference in Syria in 2009, and exists to strengthen the quality of institutions in the Islamic region, including raising the level of underperforming institutions and developing and maintaining human resources in the form of world-class scientists and technologists, and to promote cooperation amongst quality assurance agencies in the Islamic world (Tarawneh, 2011).

The Arab Network for Quality Assurance in Higher Education (ANQAHE) exists to support and enhance Arab quality assurance organizations, develop human resources and quality assurance cooperation in the Arab region, and sustain regional and international cooperation in quality assurance (ANQAHE, 2015). ANQAHE was conceived in 2004 and the constitution drafted in 2006, all in Cairo. ANQAHE membership includes half of the MENA countries, including Bahrain, Egypt, Jordan, Kuwait, Lebanon, Libya, Morocco, Oman, Palestine, Saudi Arabia, Sudan, UAE, and Yemen. The ANQAHE works in collaboration with INQAAHE and the Association of Arab Universities (AArU) to disseminate information, apply good practice, and establish mutual recognition (Tarawneh, 2011). Ultimately, higher education accreditation in the MENA region has much to improve upon so that quality can be a universal concept with which higher education leadership can utilize to solicit funds from philanthropists.

Venture Philanthropy

Venture philanthropy is a relatively new style of philanthropy centering around four primary characteristics: a close relationship between the investor and individual or organization, a long term commitment between the parties, the investor's commitment to strengthen the organization, and developing an ability to measure the outcomes of the investment (Boverini, 2006). Venture philanthropy is an ongoing relationship between the donor and the donee, whereas the donor uses his or her expertise to assist in improving the organization's mission. Venture philanthropy is also known as high impact philanthropy and the new philanthropy, as a large proportion of venture philanthropists are younger investors who offer a hands on approach to philanthropy. The Lumina Foundation and similar groups tend to focus on grant making with engagement, part of a hands on strategic philanthropy approach (Gose, 2013). Venture philanthropy builds off of Duncan's (2004) model of impact philanthropy as the donor making a difference in the final outcome of the mission, rather than simply providing funding for an organization that is pursuing the mission's end result.

While venture philanthropists of differing persuasions have been actively involved with their investments since Andrew Carnegie and John D. Rockefeller in the late nineteenth century (Boverini, 2006), venture philanthropy wasn't adequately defined as a discipline until Grossman, Letts, and Ryan (1997) came along. Grossman et al. (1997) use the venture capital model to develop a comprehensive investment approach for nonprofit organizations. Their approach focuses on six practices of venture capitalism, including: risk management, performance measures, closeness of the relationship, amount of funding, length of the relationship, and the exit.

Risk management is an important component concerning the potential for FDI in the MENA region. Venture philanthropists may be willing to take on a riskier higher education investment if the potential for reward is high. As higher education philanthropy in Oman is almost nonexistent, a venture philanthropist seeking social status or fulfilling a personal commitment to Oman may be willing to invest to improve the country's higher education system if the potential for reward or success is high. However, a foundation may either not be willing to take the risk or may donate to the higher education system without having an adequate performance measurement system in place.

Measuring the performance of MENA higher education institutions is not a clear cut process. In the MENA region, international higher education funders – including The World Bank and IMF – have obtained significant influence (Alphin Jr., 2014). Accreditation provides a method to review the quality of the system, but institutional leadership is responsible for the direction of IHEs. While the accreditation process generally offers a set of guidelines or best practices, it is incumbent upon leaders within the IHEs to build rapport with potential donors and alumni. In this sense, executive leadership ties into venture philanthropy because venture philanthropists want to be sure that leadership at the top is open to their recommendations.

Institutional leadership is largely responsible for securing financial support. Lasher and Cook (1996) argue that IHE presidents can utilize a presidential hand of cards for raising funds, including: stature of the office or position, quality and

118

prestige of the institution, importance of higher education to society, interpersonal and human relations skills, appealing to donor motives, strength of the relation between the donor and institution and representatives, and stature and prestige of the solicitation team. Harbaugh (1998) expands upon Becker's (1974) and Andreoni's (1988) arguments that donations buy the donor a warm glow – internal satisfaction, as well as the prestige that coincides with Garvin's (1980) analysis, arguing that reporting plans that reward donors seeking internal satisfaction and prestige could present an opportunity for more donors who seek to be included in the respected club. Duncan (1999) developed a public goods production model noting that individuals can contribute both time and money.

Ultimately, venture and strategic philanthropy are nascent approaches in higher education. In the MENA region, there is much potential for this type of approach to take hold. As the world becomes more open through ICT and rapid transportation, students are increasingly willing to travel for education and other career-specific opportunities. Patriotism and a warm glow can lead these future leaders to become lifelong learners while simultaneously leading them to connect with their home IHEs and become actively involved in philanthropy through a hands on approach.

ANALYSIS OF HIGHER EDUCATION AND PHILANTHROPY IN THE MENA REGION

Matching Culture and Natural Resources with Workforce Development

The challenges in education in the Middle East are generally well known to the rest of the world. Besides poverty, there are rising political and religious tensions. Education is also an area that remains unstable and fluctuates from region to region. Literacy rates vary as shown below. There is a huge gender gap with respect to education in many countries – the highest in Yemen, with a literacy rate of 65.3 percent and speculated to be 35 percent for females. Other regions in the MENA area differ. Female literacy among 15-24 year olds is close to 100 percent in the Gulf Countries, including Oman, as well as in Saudi Arabia, Jordan, Syria and Tunisia, and between 70-75% in Egypt, Morocco and Yemen (Egypt, Morocco and Yemen) (World Bank, World Development Indicators). One of the highest literacy rates is in the occupied Palestine, where UNICEF reports literacy as 99.3 for males and 99.4 for females (UNICEF 2013).

The lack of females being educated is a common phenomenon in some countries in the MENA region due to cultural traditions. Schultz (1997) affirmed that the low investment in girls' education is not economically effective in any country.

Access to secondary and tertiary education is a challenge in several MENA countries due to a variety of reasons, and the majority lay with political biases amongst the elites. In Lebanon, the late Prime Minister Rafic Hariri had his own foundation whereby he ensured education was a priority for Lebanese nationals. The foundation in the United States also pledged millions of dollars in donations to Georgetown University in 2009 (Georgetown University Press, July 2009). On the other hand, Palestinian refugees in Lebanon have limited access to public secondary education, and higher education is strictly reserved for the elites or those with connections (Hanafu & Tiltnes, 2008). Most of the population are not able to afford the high cost of private secondary education, and higher education is even less possible. UNRWA operates three secondary schools in Beirut, Saida and Tyre. Accessing education can be described as inequitable. The main determinants in the Middle East are by region, by gender and socio-cultural issues (Moghadam, 2003). The tremendously unstable regions plagued by war, religious tensions and poverty have created a major gap in educational access and, moreover, attitudes toward education. More rural inhabitants do not see the need to enter into higher education as their role is that of cultivating the land, and for the women, it is child rearing. The more urban students have a greater access, but this can be hindered by sudden political changes or decisions. With each new leader, prime minister, or similar, the rules surrounding who can and cannot gain education alters.

Traditionally, women in the Middle East have been predominantly groomed for being a wife and mother, and education after primary school was seen as something wasted. The rising cost of education meant the men of the family were more likely to be educated in order to provide for the family. The late Sheikh Zayed strongly encouraged educating the female population of the UAE, which research has shown a 45 percent decline in uneducated women in not only the UAE, but Jordan, Bahrain and Algeria (Steer, Ghanem, & Jalbout, 2014).

Birth rates are higher in the MENA areas, population size is growing and more and more women are entering higher education (Clawson, 2009). The focus on quality has made students, both male and female, across the Middle East become much more selective in educational choices. Those from the more affluent backgrounds are able to fund private education in the country or abroad – countries of choice being UK or USA. Students from less strong socio-economic backgrounds opted in the past for a government education, which is paid in full until a bachelor degree is achieved, in most of the MENA region (UNESCO, 2010). The UAE government's response to improving education and encouraging more and more private organizations to invest has created a large market of nationals who would now not only prefer to be educated in their own country, but are increasingly interested in a variety of non-traditional subjects for employability, hence creating a heightened interest in attracting investors. Johnstone (1998) argues that there is greater demand for quality and efficiency equating to an increased relevance and learning.

The more oil-rich Gulf States have taken appropriate and innovative methods in an attempt to ensure a sustainable future for nationals focusing on health, education, and sustainable resources in an attempt to focus on a move from their dependency on oil. As part of its strategic development plan, at the Abu Dhabi Economic Vision 2030, the government stated ambitious focus to transform the economy of the emirate of Abu Dhabi into a knowledge-based economy by focusing on sectors requiring high skills such as energy, aviation and biotechnology.

The growing population and the need for an increasingly competitive, technologically sophisticated nature (Johnstone, 1998) has altered the shape of education in the region. Education philanthropy in the UAE, especially, was predominantly orchestrated by governmental bodies that ensured all its citizens until completing tertiary education to a bachelor level were eligible for their full educational funding.

Different countries have differing attitudes in philanthropy, especially towards education. Orr (1999) has proposed that through Western education, citizens are losing vernacular knowledge, referring to knowledge of one's own identity. With many foreign institutes either opening or funding education in the region, the internationalization of higher education has become one of the key targets of educational policy and planning in many Arab Countries. This is the case particularly in the GCC countries that are anxious to appear modern, forward thinking, and promote education as a symbol of modernity and accepting Western standards of education. Godwin (2006) recommends an "acceleration of the articulation and accreditation programme" (p. 1) and not so much on educational establishments already present in the country. In such a vast land populated with enormous youth and ambition, growth in donations and education establishments could never have been more important.

The growth of the focus on higher education in the Arab world has attracted the attention of many private organizations and institutes. Altbach (2007) states that some developing nations have an advantage economically, and hence are more successful at establishing private institutions. A growing population and a cultural commitment to philanthropy means that the Middle East is now one of the most fertile lands for fundraising, delegates at the Council for the Advancement and Support of Education Europe stated at a conference in Glasgow in 2010 (Fearn, 2010). A recent announcement in the UAE is the opening of a Dubai-based campus developed by the University of Balamand (UoB), a non-profit higher education institute with headquarters in Lebanon (Khaleej Times, 2014). The market for higher education in the UAE is a dynamic market and a fast growing area of the UAE economy (Reuters, 2014).

With the emergence of knowledge-based and technology driven economies in the Gulf States, there is a surge in the demand for a highly skilled and technologically competent workforce. International higher education enrollment is expected to double to more than 262 million by 2025 (Maslen, 2012). Zayed University's provost, Dr. Daniel Johnson, states that the university predicted that enrollment of Emirati students would increase from the current 4,820 to more than double the amount to around 9,000 in 2014 (Zayed University, 2013). This expectation is according to the demographics of the population and in the number of Emiratis reaching university age (Mahani & Milki, 2011). The demand for places in higher education is rapidly increasing, yet the support from governments in the Gulf states in terms of funding per student as a unit, is declining (Wilen-Daugenti, 2009). The push towards higher education funding has never been as attractive and, indeed, lucrative.

Employers are increasingly concerned with maximizing financial gains by ensuring they are recruiting and retaining only the best talent to further their business and maintain a competitive advantage, pushing them to invest their money in the education of much needed and wanted individuals. Qatar has developed several strong ties with higher education institutes outside of the Gulf in a push for educational excellence, and to create individuals that are employable (Gill, 2008). For example, Cornell and Georgetown Universities each have a branch campus in Doha.

The rise of philanthropy in education can be attributed to a number of factors. Heavy reliance on oil revenues is not a sustainable way to fund higher education in the future, so alternatives must be sought and implemented. According to (Shuaa Capital, 2008), Abu Dhabi contributed 55 percent of the UAE GDP through oil revenues. The number of UAE nationals wanting to enter the federal university system has increased, yet places are limited, resulting in a push for donations from private organizations (The National, 2013). A rising population, a greater emphasis on quality in education, and the fact the UAE has been taking steps to model their education on the collaborations with western institutes – like Kuwait and Saudi Arabia before them, have allowed access and opened markets. Previously, all subjects were taught predominantly in Arabic, and now English is the medium in order to prepare leavers of secondary education for the world of global business. There is a massive untapped potential for growth, which has caused many international institutes to gain an interest in the region. A presentation made by The Parthenon Group in 2014, declares the UAE as having the largest market opportunity for international IHEs in the K-12 and higher education segments (Wam, 2014).

Currently, in the UAE, there are 18 IHEs. They are divided into 3 categories, federal, public non-federal, and private. Federal institutes are funded by the UAE government and are located all across the UAE. The two largest are the Higher Colleges of Technology and UAE University, followed by Zayed University. The public non-federal can either be funded directly by the government or indirectly. The Petroleum Institute is funded directly by ADNOC, however, this is privately owned government oil company.

The push for more privately funded higher education in the UAE coincides to a noticeable lacuna between the "qualifications provided by the education & training system and labor market requirements" (Raven, 2011, p. 30) . There is a considerable difference in education between privately funded institutes and government institutes, which is why there is a need for more fundraising and philanthropy to bridge the gap and allow graduates to confidently enter the workplace with the required skills. Traditional approaches to learning were employed, which did not especially encourage independent learning or application of what had been learned. The market is attractive in the UAE as it provides new lines of investment, coupled with the major changes that are being implemented to modernize education and align it with international standards, which sets the path for better accreditation efforts.

The large number of expatriates in the country created a need for an influx of foreign schools and IHEs with the standards expected in their home countries. Knowledge Village, based in Dubai, is home to the UAE's majority foreign higher education institutes. It was established in 2003 by TECOM investments and enables organizations from outside the UAE to operate without the requirement of a local sponsor. This led to institutes from the UK, USA, New Zealand and India opening up small campuses to fulfill the needs of the market.

In 2009, MASDAR Institute, a not-for-profit, independent, graduate level and research-driven higher education institute opened in Abu Dhabi, with Massachusetts Institute of Technology (MIT) support and cooperation. It supports the government focus on educational reforms for jobs of the future by offering a range of sustainability-focused courses. According to a report from the American Management Association (AMA), the primary goal of sustainability is to ensure that "whole systems remain healthy so that people as individuals, societies, and organizations improve their overall chances of wellbeing" (AMA, 2011). Diversifying of the economy from oil to one based on health and education requires investment into areas not previously offered, such as sustainable development, energy and maritime studies. In addition to an international affiliation, qualified students were accepted into the postgraduate program from around the world and are offered full tuition, accommodation, monthly stipend, personal computers, all text books, and travel reimbursements (Mahani & Milki, 2011).

In order for these foreign institutions to be academically and economically successful, they must recognize the cultural and legal differences in the host country. The MENA region is not as uniform as first suggested, as each country has its own dialect, food and history, which has shaped the people, their attitudes, behavior and culture. Failure to comply with these cultural differences could result in civil or criminal liability, culture clash, and an outraged host government. In order to prevent such problems, institutions must recognize and understand the host country's laws, regulations and cultural differences (Mahani & Milki, 2011). The more modern UAE has lesser restrictions on education, as opposed to Saudi Arabia, and education is increasingly featuring in government initiatives. Traditionally, certain jobs or careers were bifurcated based on gender. Women scientists or engineers from the Gulf states are rarely employed. Despite 57 percent of graduates from university in Saudi Arabia being female, only 17 percent of women gain employment (Booz Allen Hamilton, 2013), despite Saudi Arabia being the largest education market in the GCC (Alpen Capital, 2014b). A conservative attitude towards women in the workplace could purport an explanation, but also lack of opportunities, in certain sectors.

In a global competitiveness report (Alpen Capital, 2014b), the UAE was graded 34 in quality of scientific research institutions and 13 overall for availability of scientists and engineers. On the other hand, the Saudi Arabian government is now observing how this higher education segment is necessary to produce home grown talent and have set strategic goals such as international collaborations and investment, and a number of visiting professors, to increase the wide spectrum of ideas. Although this is currently in place, the number of students in tertiary education in Saudi Arabia is just over 50 percent enrollment (Choudaha & Chang, 2012).

The higher education market in Saudi Arabia is attracting a large number of private investors, with a further interest in that of vocational training. Encouraging this investment has allowed the Saudi government to set targets in this industry to reach in excess of a 30 percent share by 2018, currently at 12 percent (Choudaha & Chang, 2012). Private investors are expected and encouraged to bring in professional education institutions to operate schools and universities, in addition to their international experience and best practices. Increasing competition in the higher education sector will also present an opportunity to enhance the quality of education offered in the country by raising curriculum standards and enhancing student experience. Majors such as business management and IT will fuel innovation and research in the industry, presenting new teaching methods and nurturing new ideas.

The current market in some areas of the GCC and MENA region can be described colloquially as a free for all, as there is now an increasingly different type of student evolving who wants to relate education and the industry, and a strong push from the respective governments. Government employment only has a limited amount of positions and it is clear from research that Emirati graduates do not have the transferable skills to enable them to successfully integrate into private organizations (McLean, 2010). A new, updated government request in all higher education establishments is the inclusion of courses on innovation and entrepreneurship. This is to ensure its nationals have the tools required in the future should the availability of positions rapidly decline due to economic cycles. Full employment in countries like the UAE can actually increase GDP by 12 percent (Paschyn, 2013). We expect the same result for other countries in the region.

Diversifying from Oil and Attracting FDI

The MENA region is attempting to diversify its respective economies and reduce the need for oil and natural resources as the main source of revenues. Abu Dhabi is attempting an ambitious project worth approximately 25 million AED, the Khalifa Industrial Zone Abu Dhabi (KIZAD). The free zone has been designed to allow international investors the chance to own an industrial property without the need of an Emirati national. The zone, which is based on the Abu Dhabi and Dubai border, is 160 square miles, providing office facilities, storage, and land specifically for industrial use (Abu Dhabi Ports, 2015).

The aim is to attract FDI partnerships with the lure of tax exemptions, facilities and modern infrastructure coupled with reduced rates for necessities such as water and electricity. KIZAD is marketing itself in selected regions across the globe to attract private companies to open and manage businesses in the area. The UK, USA and Germany are among the Western countries targeted, and China, South Korea, and India are among the Eastern countries encouraged to invest. Asia is a key component in attracting philanthropy. China, India, and South Korea are the world's leading sources of international students. One out of six internationally mobile students is from China (ICEF, 2014), and together these three top countries account for more than a quarter of all students studying outside their home countries (ICEF, 2014). Asian students account for 53 percent of all students studying internationally (ICEF, 2014). Encouraging investment from Asian counties will enable the MENA region to develop their higher education systems further and equip students with knowledge required and the work skills necessary for employment and career success.

The Khalifa Fund and the Abu Dhabi Council of Economic Development (ADCED) are offering full training and support in funding to local SMEs and the private sector for purposes of growth, alongside investing in higher education establishments to produce nationals of an acceptable and employable standard. The corollary here is the businesses will invest directly in the education of the employees to their specification, who are then able to gain employment.

All throughout the Arab world, standards and accessibility to higher education is different. Egypt has a range of very well established universities such as Al Azhar and the American University of Cairo. In general, there is an overall lack of quality in higher education in Egypt (Abi-Mershed, 2010). This can be attributed back to Nasser's reforms, which were largely continued by his predecessors. Nasser wished to create a more equitable society by increasing the access to higher education for the masses (Council on Foreign Relations, 2014). However, the reforms of greater access, although well-intentioned, led to poor quality of public university education today. Most Egyptian students attend state run universities, and currently there are 12 state-run universities, as well 10 private universities (The American University in Cairo, 2012b).

Private universities have tapped into foreign resources including universities overseas, technical experts, and donor funding. Private universities are thriving in Egypt and are generally perceived as a success story (The American University in Cairo, 2012b). Egypt began the mission of seeking out private institutes that focus on attracting talent in specific areas of education, such as business-related degrees.

One of the oldest not for profit educational establishments is the American University of Cairo. It was established in 1919 and is now ranked the number one university in Egypt (The American University in Cairo, 2012b). The John D. Gerhart Centre for Philanthropy and Civic Engagement at the American University in Cairo in 2012 launched a conference titled Takaful. The conference is based on Arab philanthropy and civic engagement, and is a platform for academics and practitioners to engage in an intellectual exchange on the latest trends in citizenship, youth leadership and agency, volunteerism, philanthropy in transition, transnational philanthropy and Muslim philanthropy. 'This conference introduces new research on civic participation and links scholars with professionals working in this vital arena," notes Barbara Ibrahim, director of The John D. Gerhart Center for Philanthropy and Civic Engagement (The American University in Cairo, 2012a). Since the Arab Spring in 2010 that swept through Tunisia, Libya and Egypt, amongst other Arab states, ensuring a smooth transition for the Arab youth in the region requires collaboration and support from society as a whole.

In some areas of the MENA region, there is the lack of fully evolved education and the requirement of several missing parts that have failed to link graduating students with employment in industries. Alpen Capital (2014a) reports that only 29 percent of employers believe that graduates in the GCC region meet current job market requirements. In approach to tackle this problem, Saudi Arabia established many technical colleges to increase the transferability of quality education directly into the workplace.

A consistent concern in attracting FDI to the MENA area is the frequent political turmoil the region experiences, and the number of wars that are still ongoing, including those in Iraq, Syria, Lebanon, and Yemen. Many countries in the MENA regions are too encompassed with a daily fight to survive to focus on education. Despite this, research by UNICEF has shown that the occupied Palestinian territory has a 95 percent literacy rate despite the restrictions and unstable environment the people live under (UNICEF, 2013). A high population density and the loss of access to traditional work life has motivated education amongst the youth in an attempt to further their studies at foreign institutes in a foreign country as a means of escaping poverty and a daily fight to exist. Many of the universities in Palestine are government- and UN-funded with a little amount of fundraising (UNICEF, 2013).

The number of globally mobile students will nearly triple to eight million by 2025 (Mahani & Milki, 2011). The advancements in technology and access to the world have stimulated the university students of today to seek a global education overseas to gain a greater perspective on life, education, and the world. The phenomenon will also continue to be a widespread trend among future generations. The emergence of the Gulf states as global players in the business field, diversification of the ruling families into not only other countries, but industries – Qatari owned Harrods in London, Abu Dhabi owned Manchester City Football Club – has been enough for an emergence for a potential surge of not for profit foreign organizations investing in higher education institutes in the region.

In 2012, there was an 11 percent increase in enrollment in private higher education institutes, specifically in Dubai – which hosts the majority (KHDA, 2013). Dubai has an ambitious vision to be a higher education hub in the very near future. An added bonus for private organizations wanting to invest in this area of MENA is the ease of application for visas for other non GCC Arabs and the close proximity geographically, not including other cultural landscapes such as religion, food, art, music, and more.

Information extracted from a UNESCO research demonstrates that enrollment in higher education is the highest in MENA with a rate, as of 2013, at 50.9 percent (OECD, 2012). It further demonstrated that the growth rates in the region surpassed the world average of 30.1 percent (OECD, 2012).

Currently, there is an employment shortage in a number of sectors in the majority of the GCC region. Engineering and medical graduates are not as represented in the GCC regions, with the majority of medical doctors in the region hailing from other Middle Eastern states such as Syria, Egypt, Lebanon and Jordan and other Western states. The aim is to attract students from the region to study in this sector in order to fulfill future requirements. It is estimated 42 percent of the GCC's local population are under the age of 15 and will shortly be embarking on a career (Alpen Capital, 2014b).

An increasing population and increasing unemployment amongst the GCC nationals has shaped the hand of the governments who are now actively fundraising and donating funds for students in the medical field. Existing investment in education in the medical sector is ongoing with private institutes such as Cornell's undergraduate medical program in Qatar and The Royal College of Surgeons of Ireland have opened postgraduate facilities in Bahrain (RCSI, n.d.). These institutes are not producing enough medical doctors in order to maintain the surge in population expected. There is a gap in this market for education in the UAE. Currently, there are no affiliations with any private higher education institute, leaving a huge lacuna. This gap is not only evident in the UAE, but Oman also has a huge gap between job availability and skilled local manpower (Alpen Capital, 2014a). Some international players in the training industry have already entered the Omani market and are making an impact, but still require some investment, which all GCC states are now viewing as important in accomplishing their objectives. The Kuwaiti, Bahraini and Qatari education markets are currently growing at a relatively modest pace attributed to a combination of gaps in the education market in many areas, and with strong positive encouragement from the respective governments, private institutions are being attracted into the region.

Special Needs

The Gulf has opened to special needs education only since the last decade. Those with special needs or disabilities were largely hidden from society and therefore restricted from any form of education. Schools do not have children with varying disabilities, such as Down Syndrome, and in the case of a child with special needs wanting further education, they are often placed in different rehabilitation centers reserved specifically for the more affluent in society.

The Ministries of Education of the GCC member nations have begun to embrace a broader policy view of inclusive education, which seeks to provide learning opportunities to special needs students. Each nation has adopted a different approach towards offering support and learning for students who fall into this category. Currently, it is practically non-existent and unclear how the process will go forward, when employers are still unsure of the provisions required for those employees and future employees with disabilities. However, considering this segment in the region, the private sector can play a key role in enhancing the quality and availability of special needs learning and training.

The government in the UAE, with an aim to reform the education system across the country and deepen the reach and quality of education, established the Dubai Education Council (DEC) and the Abu Dhabi Education Council (ADEC) in 2005. The DEC's strategy was to enhance the quality of education in Dubai by attracting more prestigious private schools and focusing on availing international accreditation (The Cultural Division of the Embassy of the United Arab Emirates, 2011).

Similarly, ADEC began to focus on improving educational standards and facilities, curriculums and ICT usage, by engaging investors from the private sector. The government was reasonably successful and many top class higher education providers opened campuses in both Dubai and Abu Dhabi, which are the two main cities in the UAE.

The current higher education segment is still requiring investment, and UAE is also witnessing an increase in the number of private investors in the higher education segment, which has to cater to a growing number of youth, in the UAE, GCC and greater MENA region in general.

SOLUTIONS AND RECOMMENDATIONS

In this study, the factors affecting FDI include: political stability and individual rights, conflict and tension, religion or military in politics, human capital, level of economic freedom, infrastructure and natural resources, and corruption. Current opportunities and incentives for foreign-based higher education investors include: a large student base, increasing level of democratization, an increase in the amount of women entering higher education, increasing level of economic freedoms, and an attempt by MENA governments to work with IHEs to improve academic freedom concerns.

This leads us to the final research question: what can the MENA region do, individually and as a whole, to minimize challenges and maximize opportunities for FDI and venture philanthropy for higher education in the MENA region?

Government, Legal, and Policy

MENA governments will have to begin or continue to develop policies and legal initiatives that promote transparency and equity. As an example, the budgetary process could be separated and handed over to different agencies (Al-Asaly, 2003). This type of arrangement will provide a balance of powers that would be a step toward better transparency and decreasing corruption. Under strong and inclusive leadership, IHEs and government entities can come together to promote a competitive environment in which everyone has an opportunity to thrive.

Specifically concerning higher education and economic development, government recommendations include: assuming startup costs, then transferring ownership to the private sector; subsidies for private sector higher education participation (Al-Lamki, 2002); promoting entrepreneurial activities within IHEs – industry collaboration (Sawahel, 2015b); and developing a culture of philanthropy and endowment to better endow IHEs (Al-Lamki, 2002).

Government-promoted philanthropy is an important component in this process. Even if the government cannot provide funding for higher education, it still has a role in planning and regulation (Varghese, 2009). If government agents take the time to listen to the concerns of donors and consider legislation that decreases donor fears and concerns, then there is an element of harmony that shows other potential donors that the government is open to collaboration. However, governments must follow through and maintain stability, particularly concerning policies that promote FDI. Unfair practices including nepotism and blatant cronyism will hinder the process, as will disallowing competition from dwindling down the best ideas through Schumpeter's creative destruction.

If foreign investors are provided with an equal or fair opportunity to develop private IHEs, then the needs of students and the nation will play a large role in the success of the efforts. For all its concerns, private higher education offers choice to students – if they can afford the options (Tilak, 2005). Governments can moderate the public/private dichotomy by ddressing equity and access in determining how to pass along costs to students and families during privatization initiatives (Al-Lamki, 2002). Private institutions and the search for profit may make governments and citizens wary, but a highly developed system of accreditation will assist in making sure that students are provided with credible and quality options and quality programs, respectively.

Higher Education and Human Capital

MENA region higher education does not need to emulate Western higher education, but leaders can learn from the successes and failures of the West. One of the efforts that will calm the nerves of potential investors is a well-developed peer-review accreditation system.

Some higher education systems would be better served by consolidating to reduce costs and improve accountability (Al-Lamki, 2002), while others need to grow in order to thrive. MENA governments can assist in the consolidation process, but faculty input should be a priority. The education world is watching MENA higher education development closely, and any concerns over academic freedom should be openly discussed and resolved transparently. Otherwise, fewer international academics will be open to relocating to the MENA region and helping to build existing and new systems.

It would be optimal for each MENA country to develop a comprehensive strategic plan for its higher education system, and then share that plan. Investors would be able to look for opportunities, and then seek government assistance and direction in acting on those opportunities. Again, transparency would be the impetus for such an initiative, and then investors would begin to feel more confident that their goals could align with that of the national system (Al-Lamki, 2002). Together with employers, IHEs and their respective systems can serve as collaboration hubs, forging stronger networks between higher education, research institutions, and overall investment in R&D (Emirates Competitiveness Council, 2011), leading the way in boosting investor confidence.

Higher education systems have the potential to create positive economic spill-overs, improving conditions such as characteristics of investors, local firms, human capital, and the policy framework (Bouoiyour, 2003). As an example, expansion and diversification of current higher education systems can meet the needs of the student population (Al-Lamki, 2002) in order to develop a deeper reserve of human capital that can promote success in knowledge-intensive markets. Each country will need to analyze its system to see whether consolidation of expansion is the right path for their vision.

Together with government, IHEs should work to promote an inclusive environment within, similar to the vision and mission of King Abdullah University of Science and Technology (KAUST) to diversify the Saudi economy and also "root and grow a culture of excellence embracing openness with purpose, passion with focus, debate with respect, and diversity with respect" (KAUST, 2015). It is understandable that turning such a vision into reality is difficult, and should not be only permissible within guarded walls, but such an initiative is a starting point and opens a dialog to further inquiry.

Economic and Individual Freedom

The MENA region is in a strong position to show the rest of the world that an increase in economic and individual freedom can result in strategic higher education economic development and growth. Further development of existing resources and gaining new ones will promote stability and show investors that the MENA region offers a solid footing for FDI. Existing resources include human capital and a dynamic workforce, and new resources include youth working their way through the education system and developing their career skills, yet it also includes opportunities for unemployed and underemployed workers, each of whom will benefit from a better developed higher education system. Developing existing resources includes diversifying the economy beyond that of natural resources, and yet also serving as a proponent of sustainability. Following Alpay (2003), there is potential for an increase in GDP per capita to increase the ESI, which could increase the potential for FDI investment in higher education.

Along with a robust and attractive investment environment, government officials can implement knowledge economy focused education policies (Emirates Competitiveness Council, 2011). An increase in ICT growth in the MENA region could lead to economic growth and increased higher education attainment (Shirazi et al., 2009). Development of existing higher education systems supplemented with technology and deeper connections to foreign IHEs willing to build collaborations or branch campuses offers potential for the large amount of students in the region seeking higher learning. The UAE has been a leader in this area, and much of the MENA region may be open to these changes as they see the benefits.

Providing students with quality options and offering academics the freedom to develop and promote their expertise without consequence is the individual freedom path to growth. Some donors may be offended by criticisms by academics, but the long term growth of the higher education systems and the quality of education will allow new donors to step up. Donors can be quite specific in their requests, such as contributing to endowed professorships or deanships, resources, or capital for new construction. Development officers in the MENA region need to be able work well with both home and international donors. Venture philanthropists will want to apply a hands-on approach, and senior leadership should be willing and able to accept input from donors. Venture philanthropy also provides an element of individual freedom, as donors are not only offering input, but shaping the future of the higher education system for current and future students – shared governance will only make MENA region IHEs stronger. Accordingly, investors will be increasingly willing to become part of economic development efforts that are transparent and planned strategically.

FUTURE RESEARCH DIRECTIONS

Research into the quality of MENA higher education, considering the accreditation process, is ongoing, and would be a further direction of study. The marrying of the educational system with employer needs is another area to ascertain to see if it is meeting expectations and succeeding, or requires further development. The diversification of the economy from oil revenues opens doors for higher education growth, and thus reveals the importance of higher education and quality.

Other information could be researched from the opening of a second and larger New York University Campus in Saadiyat Island Abu Dhabi. The university has recruited staff worldwide and is housed in the cultural area, which will also open the Guggenheim and Lourve in 2016 and 2017 respectively. This is, potentially, a lucrative area of investment. INSEAD have acquired a plot in the neighboring area and will begin construction for a second campus in Abu Dhabi. The opening of the two universities will aim to attract not only Emirati nationals, but talent from the greater MENA and Asia regions alike. Research could be directed towards the impact of two major Western universities opening bigger campuses in a MENA region where economic freedom is increasing, and the talent and philanthropy it is attracting.

Research into the effect the recent political issues and wars have had on attracting philanthropy in the MENA region would be beneficial. The Arab Spring in December 2010 caused a complete turmoil after several countries in the MENA region were catapulted into political unrest and several presidents and prime ministers were removed from power. The aftermath of this relating to education and FDI could be a further area of investigation. It is easy to see how higher education, economic development, FDI, and political science are all intertwined and thus interdisciplinary studies of this region are of the utmost importance.

CONCLUSION

To summarize, there is potential for educational development via FDI in the majority of the MENA region, the focus being on the Gulf States. There is a large population of Arab youth who are keen to develop not only human capital within themselves, but the workforce and societies within their countries. There are challenges in understanding the many bifurcating cultures and traditions in the MENA region, and for some philanthropists, the risk may be too much to consider for investing. But there are many investors willing to take that risk and they can be reassured that they will have a fair chance to succeed.

The increased importance of a few countries in the MENA region in the world economy and politics has generated a mutual interest in what the West is willing to provide and promote, and what the MENA region can offer investors. The importance of the Gulf States, specifically, which are increasingly becoming more and more noticeable, will lead FDI into the MENA region. Active government initiatives to improve institutions and offer an educational system that could compete with Europe and Asia will only serve to attract investors to the region. Other research has stipulated the importance to provide quality institutes in order to attract FDI (Daude & Stein, 2007), which in turn will improve economic growth, creating the vision the government has of the UAE more specifically – to diversify from oil.

Issues remain with the impact that democracy and corruption have on FDI investment, and generally high corruption countries do not attract investors (Brahim & Rachdi, 2014). The nature of the region and the plagues of war and turmoil are negatives that tend for investors to search for alternative locations. The emergence of Qatar and the UAE as global front runners in business—and now a move towards education, prepares the region to attract FDI. With Qatar hosting the world cup in 2022 and Dubai hosting the Expo in 2020, this will allow tourists and businesses alike the opportunity to visit the two countries, and business investors to pledge millions of dollars for the construction of much needed infrastructure. The growth in population and the governments' attempting to compete in educational reforms can only be observed to be positive. The attempt at reducing corruption, relaxing stringent laws and reducing complex bureaucratic procedures can improve the attractiveness to FDI investors.

The MENA region is in an enviable position, preparing to take great strides in business and education. Internally, an increase in alumni of quality programs and institutions provides a substantial donor base of patriotic investors, likely venture philanthropists. Across the globe, wise investors will continue to view the MENA region as a less risky investment, as each MENA country begins to increase FDI and put it to good use, particularly in higher education. Higher education philanthropy requires an investment of adequate resources and a commitment to the time it takes to develop donors and create a culture of philanthropy, involving higher education leadership, regional and local leadership, and government support. A well-educated workforce with strategic philanthropy in mind would position the MENA region to establish itself as a solid foundation in need of FDI to grow its prestige and continue the growth and economic development trajectory.

REFERENCES

Abi-Mershed, O. (2010). *Trajectories of education in the Arab world: Legacies and challenges*. New York, NY: Routledge.

Abu Dhabi Ports. (2015). *Kizad*. Retrieved from http://www.adports.ae/en/article/industrial-zone/kizad-1.html

Al-Asaly, S. (2003). *Political reform and economic institutional building: A case study of budgetary institutional reform in Yemen*. Presented at the ERF 10th Annual Conference, Marrakech, Morocco.

Al-Lamki, S. M. (2002). Higher education in the Sultanate of Oman: The challenge of access, equity and privatization. *Journal of Higher Education Policy and Management, 24*(1), 75–86. doi:10.1080/13600800220130770

Alnaqbi, W. (2011). *The relationship between human resource practices and employee retention in public organisations: An exploratory study conducted in the United Arab Emirates*. Perth: Edith Cowan University.

Alpay, S. (2003). *Economic development, openness to trade and environmental sustainability in the MENA countries*. Presented at the ERF 10th Annual Conference, Marrakech, Morocco.

Alpen Capital. (2014a). *GCC education industry*. Retrieved from http://www.alpen-capital.com/downloads/GCC_Education_Industry_Report_July_2014.pdf

Alpen Capital. (2014b). *GCC Education sector undergoing an exciting phase of growth, says Alpen Capital's latest report*. Retrieved from http://www.alpencapital. com/news/2014-July-2.html

Alphin, H. C. Jr. (2014). Global accreditation for a knowledge-oriented community: Foundational change breeds global access to educational and economic opportunity. In *Handbook of Research on Transnational Higher Education* (Vol. 1, pp. 303–328). Hershey, PA: IGI Global. doi:10.4018/978-1-4666-4458-8.ch016

Altbach, P. G. (1998). *Comparative higher education: Knowledge, the university, and development*. Westport, CT: Ablex Publishing.

Altbach, P. G. (2007). Peripheries and centres: Research universities in developing countries. *Higher Education Management and Policy, 19*(2), 111–134. doi:10.1787/ hemp-v19-art13-en

AMA. (2011). *Management Centre Europe to open Middle East office in Abu Dhabi*. Retrieved from http://www.amanet.org/news/5201.aspx

Andreoni, J. (1988). Privately provided public goods in a large economy: The limits of altruism. *Journal of Public Economics, 35*(1), 57–73. doi:10.1016/0047-2727(88)90061-8

ANQAHE. (2015). *History*. Retrieved from http://www.anqahe.org/index.php/ about/history

Becker, G. (1974). A theory of social interactions. *Journal of Political Economy, 82*(6), 1063–1094. doi:10.1086/260265

Blackmur, D. (2008). A critical analysis of the INQAAHE Guidelines of Good Practice for higher education quality assurance agencies. *Higher Education, 56*(6), 723–734. doi:10.1007/s10734-008-9120-x

Booz Allen Hamilton. (2013). *Booz Allen Hamilton to support business and economic growth in the Kingdom of Saudi Arabia*. Retrieved from http://www.boozallen.com/ media-center/press-releases/2013/02/booz-allen-to-support-economic-growth-in-saudi-arabia

Bouoiyour, J. (2003). *The determining factors of foreign direct investment in Morocco*. Presented at the ERF 10th Annual Conference, Marrakech, Morocco.

Boverini, L. (2006). When venture philanthropy rocks the ivory tower. *International Journal of Educational Advancement, 6*(2), 84–106. doi:10.1057/palgrave. ijea.2150011

Brahim, M., & Rachdi, H. (2014). Foreign direct investment, institutions and economic growth: Evidence from the MENA region. *Journal of Reviews on Global Economics*, *3*, 328–339. doi:10.6000/1929-7092.2014.03.24

Burden-Leahy, S. M. (2009). Globalisation and education in the postcolonial world: The conundrum of the higher education system of the United Arab Emirates. *Comparative Education*, *45*(4), 525–544. doi:10.1080/03050060903391578

Choudaha, R., & Chang, L. (2012). *Trends in international student mobility*. World Education Services. Retrieved from http://www.uis.unesco.org/Library/Documents/research-trends-international-student-mobility-education-2012-en.pdf

Clawson, P. (2009). *Demography in the Middle East: Population growth slowing, women's situation unresolved*. The Washington Institute. Retrieved from http://www.washingtoninstitute.org/policy-analysis/view/demography-in-the-middle-east-population-growth-slowing-womens-situation-un

Cohen, M. L., & Khan, E. (2013). Scientific engagement defining gaps and creating opportunities for cooperative research and global security in the broader Middle East and North Africa (BMENA) region. In K. M. Berger (Ed.), *Future Opportunities for Bioengagement in the MENA Region*. Washington, DC: AAAS.

Council on Foreign Relations. (2014). *Egypt info service: The Egyptian Women and Economy*. Retrieved from http://www.cfr.org/world/egypt-info-service-egyptian-women-economy/p24141

Cutlip, S. M. (1990). *Fund raising in the United States: Its role in America's philanthropy*. New Brunswick, NJ: Transaction Publishers.

Darrat, A. F., & Al-Shamsi, F. S. (2003). *On the path to integration in the Gulf region: Are the Gulf economies sufficiently compatible?*. Presented at the ERF 10th Annual Conference, Marrakech, Morocco.

Daude, C., & Stein, E. (2007). The quality of institutions and foreign direct investment. *Economics and Politics*, *19*(3), 317–344. doi:10.1111/j.1468-0343.2007.00318.x

Drezner, N. D. (2011). Special issue: Philantropy and fundraising in American higher education. *ASHE Higher Education Report*, *37*(2), 1–155.

Drezner, N. D., & Huehls, F. (2014). *Core concepts in higher education: Fundraising and institutional advancement: Theory, practice, and new paradigms*. Florence, KY: Routledge.

Duncan, B. (1999). Modeling charitable contributions of time and money. *Journal of Public Economics*, *72*(2), 213–242. doi:10.1016/S0047-2727(98)00097-8

Duncan, B. (2004). A theory of impact philanthropy. *Journal of Public Economics*, *88*(9-10), 2159–2180. doi:10.1016/S0047-2727(03)00037-9

Ealy, L. T. (2012). Investing in the ideas of liberty: Reflections on the philanthropic enterprise in higher education. *Independent Review*, *17*(2), 177–191.

Eid, F., & Paua, F. (2002). *Foreign direct investment in the Arab World: The changing investment landscape* (Working Paper Series). Beirut: School of Business, The American University.

Elhiraika, A. M. (2007). Explaining growth in an oil dependent economy: The case of the United Arab Emirates. In J. B. Nugent & M. H. Pesaran (Eds.), *Explaining Growth in the Middle East*. Oxford, UK: Elsevier.

Emirates Competitiveness Council. (2011). *Policy in action: The UAE in the global knowledge economy: Fast-forwarding the nation*. Retrieved from http://www.ecc.ae/docs/default-source/ecclibrary/ecc_policy_in_action_issue_01_knowledge_economy_jan_2011_english.pdf?sfvrsn=0

Fearn, H. (2010). *Fundraisers recommended to tap Eastern promises of financial aid*. Times Higher Education. Retrieved from http://www.timeshighereducation.co.uk/news/fundraisers-recommended-to-tap-eastern-promises-of-financial-aid/413396.article

Garvin, D. A. (1980). *The economics of university behavior*. New York: Academic Press.

Gill, J. (2008). *Oiling the learning machine*. Times Higher Education. Retrieved from http://www.timeshighereducation.co.uk/403223.article

Gilpin, R. (2001). *Global political economy: Understanding the international economic order*. Princeton, NJ: Princeton University Press.

Godwin, S. M. (2006). Globalization, education and Emiratisation: A study of the United Arab Emirates. *The Electronic Journal of Information Systems in Developing Countries*, *27*(1), 1–14.

Gose, B. (2013). *Strategic philanthropy comes to higher education*. The Chronicle of Higher Education. Retrieved from http://chronicle.com/article/Strategic-Philanthropy-Comes/140299/

Grossman, A., Letts, C. W., & Ryan, W. (1997). Virtuous capital: What foundations can learn from venture capitalists. *Harvard Business Review*, *75*(2), 36–50. PMID:10165448

Haddad, M. M., & Hakim, S. R. (2003). *Did September 11 alter the sovereign risk in MENA? An empirical investigation*. Presented at the ERF 10th Annual Conference, Marrakech, Morocco.

Hanafu, S., & Tiltnes, A. A. (2008). The employability of Palestinian professionals in Lebanon: Constraints and transgression. *Knowledge, Work and Society, 5*(1), 1–15.

Harbaugh, W. T. (1998). What do donations buy? A model of philanthropy based on prestige and warm glow. *Journal of Public Economics, 67*(2), 269–284. doi:10.1016/S0047-2727(97)00062-5

Held, D., McGrew, A., Goldblatt, D., & Perraton, J. (1999). *Global transformations: Politics, economics and culture*. Stanford, CA: Stanford University Press.

Hertog, S. (2013). *The private sector and reform in the Gulf Cooperation Council (No. 30)*. London: London School of Economics and Political Science.

ICEF. (2014). *Summing up international student mobility in 2014*. ICEF Monitor. Retrieved from http://monitor.icef.com/2014/02/summing-up-international-student-mobility-in-2014/

INQAAHE. (2013). *Constitution*. Retrieved from http://www.inqaahe.org/main/about-inqaahe/constitution/constitution-html

INQAAHE. (2015). *INQAAHE 2015*. Retrieved from http://www.acbsp.org/page/inqaahe2015

International Labour Organization. (2011). *A skilled workforce for strong, sustainable and balanced growth: A G20 training strategy*. Geneva: International Labout Office.

Johnstone, D. B. (1998). *The financing and management of higher education: A status report on worldwide reforms*. The World Bank.

Kapur, D., & Crowley, M. (2008). *Beyond the ABCs: Higher education and developing countries* (No. Working Paper Number 139). Washington, DC: Center for Global Development.

KAUST. (2015). *Our vision at KAUST*. Retrieved from http://www.kaust.edu.sa/vision.html

Khaleej Times. (2014). *Dubai Investments signs deal with University of Balamand*. Retrieved from http://www.khaleejtimes.com/biz/inside.asp?xfile=/data/uaebusiness/2014/November/uaebusiness_November329.xml&section=uaebusiness

KHDA. (2013). *The higher education landscape in Dubai 2012*. Dubai: Knowledge and Human Development Authority.

Knight, J. (2008). The internationalization of higher education: Complexities and realities. In D. Teferra & J. Knight (Eds.), *Higher Education in Africa: The International Dimension*. Chestnut Hill, MA: Boston College Center for International Higher Education.

Kuemmerle, W. (1999). The drivers of foreign direct investment into research and development: An empirical investigation. *Journal of International Business Studies*, *30*(1), 1–24. doi:10.1057/palgrave.jibs.8490058

Lasher, W. F., & Cook, W. B. (1996). Toward a theory of fund raising in higher education. *The Review of Higher Education*, *20*(1), 33–51. doi:10.1353/rhe.1996.0002

Leslie, L. L., & Ramey, G. (1988). Donor behavior and voluntary support for higher education institutions. *The Journal of Higher Education*, *59*(2), 115–132. doi:10.2307/1981689

Luomi, M. (2009). Abu-DFhabi's alternative-energy initiatives: Seizing climate-change opportunities. *Middle East Policy*, *16*(4), 102–117. doi:10.1111/j.1475-4967.2009.00418.x

Mahani, S., & Milki, A. (2011). Internationalization of higher education: A reflection on success and failures among foreign universities in the United Arab Emirates. *Journal of International Education Research*, *7*(3), 1–8.

Mangan, K. (2015). *UAE incident raises questions for colleges that open campuses in restrictive countries*. The Chronicle of Higher Education. Retrieved from http://chronicle.com/article/UAE-Incident-Raises/228565/

Marginson, S., & van der Wende, M. (2006). *Globalisation and higher education*. OECD. Retrieved from http://www.oecd.org/edu/research/37552729.pdf

Maslen, G. (2012). *Worldwide student numbers forecast to double by 2025*. University World News. Retrieved from http://www.universityworldnews.com/article.php?story=20120216105739999

McLean, M. (2010). Citizens for an unknown future: Developing generic skills and capabilities in the Gulf context. *Learning and Teaching in Higher Education: Gulf Perspectives*, *7*(2), 9–30.

Mellahi, K., Guermat, C., Frynas, G., & Al Bortamani, H. (2003). *Motives for foreign direct investment in Gulf coopoeration countries: The case of Oman*. Presented at the ERF 10th Annual Conference, Marrakech, Morocco.

Mina, W. (2014). United Arab Emirates FDI outlook. *World Economy*, *37*(12), 1716–1730. doi:10.1111/twec.12169

Moghadam, V. M. (2003). *Modernizing women: Gender and social change in the Middle East* (2nd ed.). Boulder, CO: Lynne Rienne Publishers, Inc.

Murphy, R. D., Jr., & Salehi-Isfahani, D. (2003). *Labor market flexibility and investment in human capital*. Presented at the ERF 10th Annual Conference, Marrakech, Morocco.

Nour, S. S. O. M. (2014). *Overview of knowledge transfer in MENA countries - The case of Egypt (No. #2014-017)*. Maastricht, The Netherlands: United Nations University.

OECD. (2012). *OECD Week 2012*. Retrieved from http://www.oecd.org/social/family/50423364.pdf

Onyeiwu, S. (2000). Foreign direct investment, capital outlflows, and economic development in the Arab World. *Journal of Development and Economic Policies*, 2(2), 27–57.

Onyeiwu, S. (2003). *Analysis of FDI flows to developing countries: Is the MENA region different?*. Presented at the ERF 10th Annual Conference, Marrakech, Morocco.

Orr, D. W. (1999). Education for globalization (modern Western education system). *The Ecologist*, 29(3), 166.

Paschyn, C. M. (2013). *Women in the Gulf: Better educated but less employed*. Al-Fanar Media. Retrieved from http://www.al-fanarmedia.org/2013/10/women-in-the-gulf-better-educated-but-less-employed/

Raines, J. P., & Leathers, C. G. (2003). *The economic institutions of higher education: Economic theories of university behavior*. Cheltenham, UK: E. Elgar.

Raven, J. (2011). Emiratizing the education sector in the UAE: Contextualization and challenges. *Education. Business and Society: Contemporary Middle Eastern Issues*, 4(2), 134–141. doi:10.1108/17537981111143864

RCSI. (n.d.). *RCSI Bahrain*. Retrieved from https://www.rcsi.ie/rcsi_bahrain

Reuters. (2014). *Dubai Investments plans investments in education, healthcare*. Gulf Business. Retrieved from http://gulfbusiness.com/2014/10/dubai-investments-plans-investments-education-healthcare/

Rupp, R. (2009). Higher education in the Middle East: Opportunities and challenges for U.S. universities and Middle East partners. *Global Media Journal, 8*(14).

Salama, S. (2013). *Emiratisation quotas won't work, warns academic*. Gulf News. Retrieved from http://gulfnews.com/business/sectors/employment/emiratisation-quotas-won-t-work-warns-academic-1.1262779

Sawahel, W. (2015a). *More cross-border campuses in the Arab states*. University World News. Retrieved from http://www.universityworldnews.com/article.php?story=20150320011437374

Sawahel, W. (2015b). *Universities urged to develop links with industry*. University World News. Retrieved from http://www.universityworldnews.com/article.php?story=20150326160428148

Schofer, E., & Meyer, J. W. (2005). The worldwide expansion of higher education in the twentieth century. *American Sociological Review*, 70(6), 898–920. doi:10.1177/000312240507000602

Schultz, T. P. (1997). Asssessing the productive benefits of nutrition and health: An integrated human capital approach. *Journal of Econometrics*, 77(1), 141–158. doi:10.1016/S0304-4076(96)01810-6

Shimoni, B. (2008). *The new philanthropy in Israel: Ethnography of major donors (No. Article 2)*. Jerusalem: The Hebrew University of Jerusalem.

Shirazi, F., Gholami, R., & Higon, D. A. (2009). The impact of information and communication technology (ICT), education and regulation on economic freedom in Islamic Middle Eastern countries. *Information & Management*, 46(8), 436–433. doi:10.1016/j.im.2009.08.003

Shuaa Capital. (2008). *Vision 2008: UAE equity markets*. Retrieved from http://www.arabruleoflaw.org/compendium/Files/UAE/104.pdf

Sperling, J. M., Marcati, C., & Rennie, M. (2014). *GCC women in leadership: From the first to the norm*. McKinsey & Company.

Steer, L., Ghanem, H., & Jalbout, M. (2014). *Arab youth: Missing educational foundations for a productive life?* Washington, DC: Center for Universal Education at Brookings.

Tarawneh, E. (2011). Assessing and understanding quality in the Arab region. In T. Townsend & J. MacBeath (Eds.), *International Handbook of Leadership for Learning* (Vol. 2, pp. 1107–1124). New York: Springer. doi:10.1007/978-94-007-1350-5_60

Teferra, D. (2008). The internationalization of dimensions of higher education in Africa: Status, challenges and prospects. In D. Teferra & J. Knight (Eds.), *Higher Education in Africa: The International Dimension*. Chestnut Hill, MA: Boston College Center for International Higher Education.

Thacker, S., & Cuadra, E. (2014). *The road traveled: Dubai's journey towards improving private education*. Washington, DC: The World Bank.

The American University in Cairo. (2012a). *AUC holds second annual conference on Arab giving and civic participation*. Retrieved from http://www.aucegypt.edu/news/Pages/NewsRelease.aspx?rid=294

The American University in Cairo. (2012b). *The chronicles 2012*. Cairo: The American University in Cairo. Retrieved from http://www.aucegypt.edu/research/ebhrc/publications/Documents/Chronicles2012/2012_chronicles_final-version.pdf

The Cultural Division of the Embassy of the United Arab Emirates. (2011). *Education in UAE: K-12 education*. Retrieved from http://uaecd.org/k-12-education

The National. (2013). *Room to improve private universities in the UAE*. Retrieved from http://www.thenational.ae/thenationalconversation/editorial/room-to-improve-private-universities-in-the-uae

The World Bank. (1999). *Education in the Middle East and North Africa: A strategy towards learning for development*. Human Development Network.

The World Bank. (2015). *Middle East and North Africa*. Retrieved from http://www.worldbank.org/en/region/mena

Tilak, J. B. G. (2005). *Private higher education: Philanthropy to profits*. Barcelona: Global University Network for Innovation and Palgrave Macmillan.

Trenwith, C. (2013). *Emiratisation failing to cut UAE jobless rate - Al Mulla*. ArabianBusiness.com. Retrieved from http://www.arabianbusiness.com/emiratisation-failing-cut-uae-jobless-rate-al-mulla-526191.html

UNESCO. (2010). *Towards an Arab higher education space: International challenges and societal responsibilities* (B. Lamine, Ed.). Cairo: UNESCO.

UNICEF. (2013). *At a glance: State of Palestine*. Retrieved from http://www.unicef.org/infobycountry/oPt_statistics.html

Varghese, N. V. (2009). *Globalization, economic crisis and national strategies for higher education development*. Paris: International Institute for Educational Planning.

Wam. (2014). *UAE more attractive for higher education institutions than China, Singapore.* Emirates 24|7. Retrieved from http://www.emirates247.com/uae-more-attractive-for-higher-education-institutions-than-china-singapore-2014-09-19-1.563512

Wilen-Daugenti, T. (2009). *Edu: Technology and learning environments in higher education.* New York, NY: Peter Lang Publishing, Inc.

Wilkens, K. (2011). *Higher education reform in the Arab world.* Washington, DC: Saban Center at Brookings.

Yale University & Columbia University. (2005). *2005 Environmental Sustainability Index: Benchmarking national environmental stewardship.* Yale Center for Environmental Law and Policy; Center for International Earth Science Information Network at Columbia University.

Zawya. (2015). *UAE.* Retrieved from https://www.zawya.com/middle-east/countries/uae/

Zayed University. (2013). *Zayed University self-study report.* Retrieved from http://www.zu.ac.ae/main/files/contents/assessment_resource/Accreditation/MSCHE_Self-Study_2013.pdf

KEY TERMS AND DEFINITIONS

Emiratisation: A government initiative in the United Arab Emirates to ensure all nationals were employed in all sectors, actively reducing the unemployment rate.

EXPO 2020: The event being held in Dubai in 2020 with the theme *Connecting Minds, Creating the Future*, will be a platform for hundreds of nations to showcase their thinking in architecture, science and technology.

MENA: Middle East and North Africa.

NGO: A nongovernmental nonprofit organization that is not part of a government and not part of a for-profit business.

UNRWA: United Nations Reliefs and Works Agency.

Chapter 6
Rebirth of a Program via Community, Industry, and Philanthropic Support

Cathleen Brandi Ruch
Lake Region State College, USA

ABSTRACT

In 2002, Lake Region State College closed their "Agricultural Farm Business Management" program, due to low enrollment and lack of interest. However considering that agriculture is one of the leading economic developers in North Dakota, Lake Region State College (LRSC) leaders and the community felt this might have been a premature closing, and decided to look at other agriculture workforce initiatives, considering ways to revitalize the agriculture workforce and its needs. This was an ambitious goal considering how rural LRSC is, with roughly 2000 in student matriculation in a given year. Before looking at reinventing, or "rebirthing" the ag program, challenges and steps needed to be addressed and employed. The following chapter will provide a case study on how LRSC leaders, its community, and the alignment of philanthropic support was able to revitalize or "rebirth" the agriculture program to the new cutting edge of Precision Agriculture.

DOI: 10.4018/978-1-4666-9664-8.ch006

INTRODUCTION

The fiscal relationship between higher education and its respective state has been eroding for a number of years. In fact, according to Mortenson (2004) there have been huge cuts with state appropriated funding for higher education in the last two and a half decades. In FY 2004, states appropriated $60.3 billion for operations, and this was down from FY2003 at $61.5 billion, and down from FY 2002 at $62.8 billion (p. 3). In fact, since 1978, state appropriated funding has declined by 40%. There are many factors that contribute to this nationwide decline for state funding, the biggest factor has been contributed to the economic recessions noted in the last 25 years, and two-year institutions are not immune to this decline in funding (Weerts & Ronca, 2006, p. 936).

The first and oldest community college was Joliet Junior College, founded in 1901 in Illinois. Community colleges then flourished nationally in the 1960's with 457 active campuses. Community colleges historically focused on liberal arts, however, during the depression took a more pragmatic turn, offering job-training programs in order to offset widespread unemployment (Community Colleges Past and Present, 2015). Two-year institutions are known to be 'open enrollment' and serve a range of students (Thelin, 2004). Local funds primarily funded and supported two-year institutions at 94 percent, however was soon to be insufficient, and other revenue streams were mainstreamed- state revenue, tuition and fees, federal funds, and gifts and grants. In the 70's came the awareness that public funding was not going to be sufficient for community colleges to meet their missions (Strauss, 2001).

Today, community colleges enroll nearly half the nation's undergraduate students (Worth & Smith, 1993) and funded primarily from state, local government, and student fees (p. 347). When it comes to fundraising, rarely see the "megagifts" at the two-year institution that four-year institutions have come to know and count on for philanthropic giving. However, reported by the "$70 Million Gift to Help California Students" (cited in Ramano, Gallagher, & Shugart, 2010) in 2008 a $70 million donation was presented to a community college system, to assist scholarships for California's 109 two-year colleges. However the gift was focused on scholarships, and as reported by Gose (cited in Ramano, Gallagher, & Shugart, 2010), "most community college donations are earmarked for scholarships" (p. 59). Additionally, in the 2014 CASE Survey of Community College Foundations (Paradise, 2015) reported that when it comes to a comprehensive or capital campaign, 80 percent of surveyed participants cited scholarships as the top destination (p. 27).

Two-year institutions are divided and recognized by three different types of de-mographics, categorized by the Carnegie Classifications of Institutions of Higher Education™. Carnegie defines community colleges by *service areas*; rural, suburban, and urban. This type of classification was set in place to demonstrate that nearly all public community colleges are place-based institutions, with geographic service delivery areas defined by state statute, regulation, or custom (Hardy & Katsinas, 2007, p.6). The Carnegie Foundation for the Advancement of Teaching (as cited from Hardy & Katsinas, 2007) defined that *serving*, whether the student is from an urban, suburban, or rural areas, depends on the physical location of that campus.

When it comes to fundraising, two-year institutions are not viewed the same, despite what service area they serve, and rural community colleges face the greatest budgetary strain. In fact, according to one study provided by Katsinas, Tollefson, & Reamey (2007), reported "rural community colleges lacked access to a good stream of local support" (p.4). For example when it comes to alumni and future support, students who attend two-year and matriculate to a four-year institution transfer their alumni loyalties, and later become donors to that four-year institution (Worth & Smith, 1993). Additionally, Worth and Smith (1993) further reported that since two-year institutions are program based and not research focused have constraints on where and what kinds of foundations and donors to solicit. In fact, a survey provided by The Marts & Lundy reported to *The Chronical for Philanthropy* (Daniels, 2015) that fifty-one percent of the large gifts to higher education went to university hospital centers and health programs, up from 41 percent in 2013. John Cash, Marts & Lundy's chairman said that "Instead of being driven by a sense of loyalty to their alma mater, Mr. Cash said, many of his clients prefer to give to institutions that are on the cusp of big breakthroughs."…"Donors are giving their big gifts to support research," he says. "They're much more opportunistic. They're not building buildings and creating monuments to themselves" (Daniels, 2015; https://philanthropy.com/article/Mega-Gifts-on-the-Rise-at/227955). Comparing prestigious and well-known four year agricultural institutions, such as Purdue where gifts are provided by the Bill and Melinda Gates Foundation (Austin, 2011), two-year institutions cannot compete, and therefor need to look at other avenues. Therefor to assist with philanthropy and fundraising, two-year institutions align themselves with the workforce, as is their mission, and solicit gifts supporting their unique programs and industry. To assist in this process, community college foundations have learned to align themselves to philanthropic opportunities via their foundation boards. In fact, Paradise (2015) reported in a CASE whitepaper that community college boards are composed of 98 percent of business and industry.

Reinventing a program in higher education, especially one that needs to be tied to a rural community presents a myriad of programs and challenges. However, such efforts have become necessary. A case study of a recent program reconstructed at a rural community college is presented. It will highlight the needed outreach nature of a close alignment of philanthropy, community, and higher education. By way of example will be a case study of the reinvented traditional agriculture program to the new cutting edge of Precision Agriculture.

Precision Agriculture (Precision Ag) is the combination of agriculture and technology. In the agriculture arena, the demand on farmers to continuously produce more food, fiber, and fuel for this world has made it imperative to become more efficient. In turn this need for efficiency has prompted the adoption of various forms of precision agriculture technologies. The use of precision agriculture technologies is the tool to allow farmers to manage small areas, and treat these areas uniquely in regards to their individual characteristics. Technology allows for the collection of immense amounts of data that assists in making necessary management decisions. The demand does support a workforce with these new skills.

The precision ag industry was very new and cutting edge. Initial research provided by key leaders at Lake Region State College (LRSC) indicated that there was not another institution regionally or nationally undertaking this type of workforce and developing a viable accredited program. However, the question was how to get industry to support this program, when there was no other model regionally, nationally or internationally? How much industry and community interest was there to support this type of program? Without proof that there was going to be a return on investment, and the fact that Lake Region State College (institution that housed the program) had initially closed their "Agricultural Farm Business Management" program, local industry was not interested in committing funding. Where was the revenue going to be generated from in order to implement and sustain this program? Other revenue would have to be considered and applied for, such as statewide grants that supported equipment and program funding.

The following chapter will discuss the following: 1) data collected in order to support a new and cutting edge workforce program, 2) local community funding committed in order to support the program, 3) overview of the Trade Adjustment Assistance Community College and Career Training federal grant, which required local support, that launched the program 4) other statewide grant funding that was used to support the program, such as the Workforce Enhancement Grant (North Dakota Department of Commerce), and 5) what the current efforts in place from the community in order to continue to provide support.

BACKGROUND: TRENDS IN REGARDS TO HIGHER EDUCATION AND THE WORKFORCE

Two-year institutions are recognized as a vital backbone in economic and workforce development (Bailey & Kienzal, 1999, p. 1), especially in rural locations. Push for two-year institutions to work with specific industries and offer content-specific courses or programs continues (Zinser, 2003, p. 1). Business leaders continue to voice their disapproval regarding higher education not producing the necessary workforce. With this kind of censure, two-year institutions eliminate programs that are not closely related to workforce. Fain (2014) reported that the two-year system, Louisiana Community and Technical College, made large programmatic cuts in recent years as state appropriated funding went from 70 percent to 30 percent. The system eliminated close to 700 programs, which were not closely tied to workforce needs. For example, the system cut its cosmetology program, since it no longer supported a workforce need (p. 2).

These funding cuts not only took place in Louisiana, but nationally. In the article, *Signs of hope for state funding* (2014, November 20), it was reported that during the last recession, 11 states had higher education funding cuts of more than 30 percent. Other states had decreases between 20 and 30 percent.

The trend of cutting higher ed programs not closely tied to workforce is not just a response to the last recession, but has been taking place many years. State appropriated funding has dwindled, and institutions of higher education, especially the two-year institutions, have had to align themselves closer to the workforce. Lake Region State College (LRSC) had to make the same type of cut in the early 2000's, and closed their "Agricultural Farm Business Management" program since it was not seeing student enrollment or retention. Like many institutions (two or four-year) looking to cut and save state appropriated funding, the closing of the program seemed like a logical strategy. However, in a state where agriculture is one of its prime economic developments, the community and agriculture industry of Devils Lake questioned the decision of discontinuing the program. Leaders and stakeholders revisited the closed program, and considered a bold move of reinventing the closed program, constructing and launching a new program, which would be tightly coupled with the community and local workforce industry.

REBIRTH OF A PROGRAM

In 2005, LRSC leaders and stakeholders revisited the agricultural program, to consider if there was a way to reinvent the ag program, providing a new prospective in the industry. After researching the agricultural needs statewide and nationally, it was concluded that agriculture was seeing considerable workforce needs within *Precision Agriculture*. In fact, precision agricultural careers continue to expand in occupational diversity and are numerically increasing as reported by the US Bureau of Labor Statistics in the Ag Leader Insights Magazine (2014, Spring), "employment opportunities will increase by more than 29 percent and create more than 100,000 new jobs by 2020" (p. 8).

Precision ag technology has been evolving since 1995 (Greene, 2011). Producers within the central regions of the U.S. recently reported in communication that

92 percent use one or more precision agriculture technologies, and have had such technology on their farm for an average of 5 years. Sixty percent plan to increase use of such technology within the next two years, and the majority of producers turn to their local agricultural implement dealer for information assistance when acquiring, installing, servicing such technology (P. Gunderson, personal communication, 2011).

Regionally and locally, precision agricultural was also considered a workforce need since approximately 32,000 farms/ranches are located in North Dakota however, of that number 3,000 are "limited resources", 5,000 are "retirement farms/ranches", and 8,100 are "residential lifestyle farms/ranches." These farms/ranches generated at least $250,000 or more in sales annually, and the children of these agricultural enterprises would be targeted as potential students for the program (U.S. Censes of Agriculture, 2007, Table 64). This in turn concluded that this new agricultural program could potentially impact a constituent of 29,000. This was a significant finding for a small regional institution, averaging an enrollment of 2,000 comprised of traditional and non-traditional students.

ISSUES, CONTROVERSIES, PROBLEMS: THE CLOSING OF ONE PROGRAM AND THE REBIRTH OF ANOTHER...CAN IT BE DONE AND RECEIVE LOCAL PHILANTHROPIC SUPPORT?

The Dakota Precision Ag Center (DPAC), Center of Excellence, was first created under the auspices of the ND Governor's Center of Excellence grant initiative in 2006. It was one of the first Centers to initiate research and job creation activity.

It was a long road before DPAC became to fruition. After the writing, and funded Center of Excellence (COE) grant, the program was underway. Answer Farms, an agricultural research facility, was recruited to assist DPAC in assessing current precision agriculture technology on local farms. The plan involved recruiting local farmers and producers from the cohort of adult farm management trainees directly involved in LRSC's Adult Farm Management program. With this selection, leaders of the DPAC program would be able to do research on farms, discovering which 'precision technology' was effective in order to base the reinvented agriculture degree program, Applied Associates of Science in Precision Agriculture. However resistance form the local agricultural community was encountered since LRSC had previously closed its agriculture training program- Agriculture Farm Business Management. Workforce and the local community was apprehensive in providing resources or assistance to an institution that closed a program that was providing much needed education and training in a field that was one of leading economic drivers of the state- agriculture.

Meetings and renewing relationships led by DPAC and LRSC leaders of local agricultural producers, establishing that once the newly reinvented ag program was in place, and successful, it would not be closed. However, only 3 (three) ag producers was willing for DPAC to use plots of their land for research, finding out what 'precision technology' was going to be the most needed and used as training and educational platforms for future precision ag students.

While three producers vested into the research and program was a good start, it was hardly the indication needed to ensure that the local community and workforce was vested into the DPAC program. An endeavor of this magnitude was going to need a vested community and workforce in order to build and sustain the program, which was going to need vast amount of equipment and other expenditures to get the program reinvented and launched. More research would have to be deployed, demonstrating need and sustainability before the ag workforce and local community would once again support an ag program at a small rural two-year institution.

Data Collected In Order to Support a New and Cutting Edge Workforce Program

According to the site, Bureau of Labor Statistics (North Dakota) North Dakota is the most rural of all the states, with farms covering more than 90 percent of the land with a strong economy and a low unemployment rate which stands at 2.8 percent, the lowest in the country (Bureau of Labor Statistics-North Dakota, 2015). During the country's most recent economic downturn where many states had few jobs, North Dakota was creating jobs and hiring. In fact, the state added 21,300 new jobs since 2005 earning a top position in the nation for growth (Murphy, 2010, p.116).

Considering North Dakota has such a high farm population, it could be concluded that the economic impact of a reinvented cutting edge agriculture program was within scope. However, intense research was deployed since the institution already had low enrollment numbers in past agriculture training programs which led to the closing of the program. This, in turn, produced a cautious local agriculture workforce and an institution needing a 'sound investment' before commitments would be forthcoming. Additionally, when it came to sustaining this type of program, other implications needed to be addressed; 1) any educational program in this arena will not be successful unless the target audience, agriculture producers, are directly involved in its design and 2) agricultural industries must possess economic clout, both locally and regionally in order to provide support.

In response, DPAC and LRSC leaders provided research in support for a new agriculture program in precision ag and the following key points were addressed; 1) what type of precision ag training was needed; 2) earnings for future employment; and 3) what were current industry economic profits in order to support future employees. In 2010, the following data was collected via surveys provided by the North Dakota Implement Dealers Association (NDIDA). They surveyed and compiled the following data:

- There are 126 retail farm equipment dealerships in North Dakota
- Annual total retail sales of new and used farm machinery and repair parts in North Dakota is over $495 million
- Over 3,120 people statewide are employed by retail farm equipment dealership.
- The average dealership employee earns over $43,000 per year
- The average annual payroll per dealership is over $1.1 million
- Dealership payroll statewide is over $132 million annually
- Dealer payroll comprises 12% of ND's total retail payroll
- Dealers statewide pay over $17.5 million in payroll takes and employee benefits annually (NDIDA, 2010)

Based on preliminary research, the need and support for a new agriculture workforce seemed promising, however, more in-depth research needed to be deployed. LRSC and DPAC leaders with specific questions created a survey in order to understand what the needs are from farmers, producers, and other ag workforce to build a successful program. Seventy-eight producers and dealerships responded to a survey conducted through the North Dakota Agriculture Association, which included the following inquiries:

1. Estimate the number of employees you will be hiring in the next 5 years who will specialize in precision farming technology.
2. How many new employees will you be hiring in the next 5 years that need basic precision ag knowledge but won't necessarily specialize in it?
3. Where would you expect future employees to receive training in technical areas of precision ag?
4. Where would you expect future employees to receive training in consultation of precision ag?
5. Where would you expect future employees to receive training in agronomics, businesses management, and soft skills?

Results from the survey included in Table 1 indicated that precision ag skills and knowledge would be a necessary and required skillset of 187 new employees across the next 5 years in North Dakota. Table 2 indicated that an additional 272 job openings in agribusinesses will require basic precision agriculture skillset. Table 1 and 2 combined indicated 459 jobs would be added where individuals could benefit from

Table 1. Estimate the number of employees you will be hiring in the next 5 years who will specialize in precision farming technology. (Data source: DCTOA (c). N.D. Agricultural Implement Dealer Survey. Devils Lake, ND. Lake Region State College – Dakota Center for Technology-Optimized Agriculture. November, 2011. 8 pages.)

Answer	Number of responses	Number of people that will be hired
None	16	0
1-3	44	88
4-6	12	60
6-8	1	7
8+	5	32
	Total	187

Table 2. How many new employees will you be hiring in the next 5 years that need basic precision ag knowledge but won't necessarily specialize in it. (Data source: DCTOA (c). N.D. Agricultural Implement Dealer Survey. Devils Lake, ND. Lake Region State College – Dakota Center for Technology-Optimized Agriculture. November, 2011. 8 pages.)

Answer	Number of Responses	Number of people that will be hired
None	6	0
1-3	42	84
3-6	15	75
6-8	7	49
8+	7	64
	Total	272

precision ag training. Additionally, results concluded that ag industries were looking towards and expecting state colleges to step up and provide the necessary training.

For survey question 3, "Where would you expect future employees to receive training in technical areas of Precision ag?" Table 3 indicated that 58 percent said college courses, however 92 percent responded with *industry sponsored* – which was not a surprising result considering the lack of a program locally or regionally that could support this type of program.

Table 3. Where would you expect future employees to receive training in technical areas of precision ag? (Data source: DCTOA (c). N.D. Agricultural Implement Dealer Survey. Devils Lake, ND. Lake Region State College – Dakota Center for Technology-Optimized Agriculture. November, 2011. 8 pages.)

Answer	Number of Responses	Response Percent
Industry Sponsored	69	92%
Self-Training	35	46.7%
Mentor/Coworker	45	60%
Formal Training (College Courses)	43	57.3%
Training is not applicable to my future employees	2	2.7%
(Skipped Question)	3	

Survey question 4, "Where would you expect future employees to receive training in consultation of precision ag?" Results from Table 4 indicated 73.3 percent in favor of *industry sponsored* however the second strongest response was *formal training (college courses)* with 64.5 percent.

Survey question 5, "Where would you expect future employees to receive training in agronomics, businesses management, and soft skills?" The results from Table 5 indicated employees would be getting their training from the *formal training (college courses)* at 86.8 percent, and *industry sponsored* was second, with 40.8 percent.

Table 4. Where would you expect future employees to receive training in consultation of precision ag? (Data source: DCTOA (c). N.D. Agricultural Implement Dealer Survey. Devils Lake, ND. Lake Region State College – Dakota Center for Technology-Optimized Agriculture. November, 2011. 8 pages.)

Answer	Number of Responses	Response Percent
Industry Sponsored	56	73.7%
Self-Training	28	36.8%
Mentor/Coworker	38	50%
Formal Training (College Courses)	49	64.5%
Training is not applicable to my future employees	4	5.3%
(Skipped Question)	2	

Table 5. Where would you expect future employees to receive training in agronomics, businesses management, and soft skills? (Data source: DCTOA (c). N.D. Agricultural Implement Dealer Survey. Devils Lake, ND. Lake Region State College – Dakota Center for Technology-Optimized Agriculture. November, 2011. 8 pages.)

Answer	Number of Responses	Response Percent
Industry Sponsored	31	40.8%
Self-Training	30	39.5%
Mentor/Coworker	35	46.1%
Formal Training (College Courses)	66	86.8%
Training is not applicable to my future employees	2	2.6%
(Skipped Question)	2	

Quantitative responses were also captured from equipment dealers, which said that, "The guys on staff right now in the state (N.D.) are not up to date on knowledge of precision agriculture." Some dealerships indicated that, "No employee is currently trained in precision agriculture technology" (P. Gunderson, personal communication, 2011).

Another industry leader indicated the following in an interview:

INTERVIEW WITH INDUSTRY LEADER

We need you (the Techs and Universities) to be bringing the next

…generation of precision worker to the workforce. There are not enough hours in the day to try to train people on the go, it usually takes a year to get them up to speed. To have them come in the door with the basic skills and knowledge, priceless. Additionally, the following statement was captured during an interview with a local N.D. agricultural cooperative, I don't know what I'm going to do; my guys aren't training, none of the other guys are out other (n=5) locations are training to use this stuff either. (Company name) doesn't provide the training, a local precision ag firm doesn't provide the training, but they want a special pricing agreement in exchange for providing the training, and we don't have any other source for training. You guys at Lake Region know how to do this stuff…why aren't you involved in training statewide for us? Every ag co-op in the state is in the same shape we are (P. Gunderson, personal communication, 2011).

DPAC and LRSC leaders disseminated qualitative and quantitative data and concluded that a precision ag program needed to be started and implemented at LRSC. However, 'wanting' and 'needing' this type of program was not going to get the program off the ground without local philanthropic support.

Local Community Funding Committed In Order To Support the Program

Devils Lake resides beside the largest natural body of water in North Dakota. The lake covers more than 160,000 acres, and has earned the reputation of being the "Perch Capital of the World." The city consists of 8,000 people, with 500 businesses (Devils Lake North Dakota, 2015, p. 20), which includes the necessary businesses to support the program. At least six ag businesses located in or around the city proper, including CASE-IH, John Deere, and Butler-Cat®. The state of ND houses the largest CASE-IH agricultural dealer network in the world, and the largest John Deere agricultural dealer network in the U.S. Hence, its agricultural implement dealer networks were not only poised to recruit and place large numbers of precision agriculture technicians, those networks also were capable of providing paid internships and other training opportunities in partnership with LRSC and DPAC.

With the need established within the workforce, the next step was to find and solicit local community support and funding. Considering the program was not up and implemented, and the institution could not prove the program would be viable with producing the workforce needed, funding from the community was going to be a challenge. As noted by Milliron & Browning (2003) that compared to four-year institutions, community colleges are relatively new to 'high stakes' fundraising (p. 90), and LRSC is no exception. LRSC was not known as an institution to solicit and receive large donations, or 'megagifts'; and with little validity that the program would work, soliciting donations needed to provide sustainability was going to be a challenge. Philanthropy for the program was going to have to come in the way of 'gifts in kind' via local industry; and few local industries were interested in supplying 'gift-in-kind' to assist in the development of the program. High Plains Equipment (HPE) of Devils Lake, N.D. had 27 employees and is the CaseIH Agricultural/AFS-Advanced Farming Systems™ / Borgaults ®/ Unverferth ® farm machinery dealer in the Devils Lake area. HPE had recently moved to a new location and constructed an ultra-modern facility. DPAC leaders developed a relationship convincing HPE that DPAC was poised to train the next generation of precision ag employees, however needed a viable building to implement the program. LRSC could not house the program on its campus since it did not have the necessary space needed. With the newly formed relationship in place, HPE provided complete access and use of their 4,480 square foot building 1 mile north of the LRSC campus for instructional and staff purposes and part of the 6,160 square foot shop space for student hands on training. Additional facility space would also provide for faculty and staff.

Farming is a risky business, considering a good yield (how much money a crop produces) could produce a huge return on investment or a below par yield could potentially bankrupt a farmer, its family, and future family for life. With such high risks involved, producers and farmers rely on accurate input from the land and the equipment they invest. Understanding and correctly interpreting the technologies used in precision ag, (this goes beyond the use and mechanical upkeep of a tractor or combine), was critical. DPAC leaders built and reinvented a program not only around the basic upkeep and maintenance of ag equipment, but the advanced technologies used in order to farm efficiently- and thus developing an Associate of Applied Science in Precision Ag. DPAC leaders looked outside of the scope of the 'basic equipment needs' of the program, and started talking and achieving buy-in from other industries where technologies would be utilized to achieve the precision in agriculture. Two local industries where cultivated to provide 'gift-in-kind' with access to software critical to the development and implementation of the precision ag program.

A local industry was approached to provide satellite remote sensing, which provides inferred mapping. Inferred mapping is a valuable tool when providing insight to a farmer's yield. When inferred pictures are captured, developed and stitched together to form a complete picture of a field, it can indicate the best and most profitable yield while assessing problems within the field itself, such as lack of nutrients and water. Again, in the high risk life of farming, every square inch of a field needs to be scrutinized and evaluated for yield production consistencies and inconsistencies.

Additional support was solicited from a company that built and sold Unmanned Aerial Vehicles (UAV). Gift-in-kind was provided in the purchase of UAVs in order to provide training for DPAC students in the flying and accessing inferred pictures (inside the Center). Like satellite remote sensing, UAVs can provide inferred photos that can assist producers and farmers with the necessary understanding of what their yield is or is not producing in the way of food. Without understanding and having training on these types of technologies, graduates of the program would be handicapped to assist farmers and producers when assessing fields and overall profit of their yield.

Additional support came from local industries from Butler-Cat®, John Deere®, FarmWorks Software®, and other high tech industries - each one providing gift-in-kind, from the use of high-tech precision ag equipment, to accessing needed software. All support provided an imperative need and support to implementing the program and providing necessary job training to future DPAC students.

Overview of the Trade Adjustment Assistance Community College and Career Training Federal Grant, Which Required Local Support

What ultimately launched the Dakota Precision Ag Center (DPAC) was seed funding from the Trade Adjustment Assistance Community College and Career Training (TAACCCT) grant. According to the Department of Labor- TAACCCT website, in 2010, President Barack Obama signed the Health Care and Education Reconciliation Act, which included $2 billion over four years to fund the TAACCCT grant program (DOL, 2010). The TAACCCT grant program, funded through the Department of Labor and partnered with the Department of Education, was implemented to "assist community colleges and other institutions of higher education with funds to expand and improve their ability to deliver education and career training programs. Training programs are geared for individuals to complete their education in two years or less, and focused on workers who are eligible for training under the TAA for Workers program" (DOL, 2010).

The TAACCCT grant was written and submitted by DPAC leaders in the spring of 2012, and awarded the following fall. The grant project was entitled Training Precision Agriculture Technicians (TPAT) and was geared to create career pathways through coursework and training through technology in precision agriculture. The project's major purpose was to deliver training and assistance to TAA-impacted workers, unemployed Veterans, unemployed and underemployed persons seeking to increase their skills for new and higher-paying jobs in the state of North Dakota. Lake Region State College would support and provide online learning and personalized instruction. Through competency based skill assessments, use of cognitive tutors, and developmental educational services, students would have the ability to accelerate progress for certifications and degrees.

The grant was developed to fiscally launch the precision ag program, which also solidified more community and local workforce support. In order to submit the grant, DPAC leaders had to ensure that the support from the institution and the community was in place. While data supported the need to reinvent the closed agriculture program, the federal government was not going to fund LRSC and DPAC $2.9million dollars in funding unless the local community and workforce were supporting the effort. With diligence, and the building of the foundation for the program over the last few years, the community and institution was ready to move forward behind the grant. A partnership was created with Job Service North Dakota (JSND), the State agency that administers the TAA for Workers program. DPAC had solicited and sustained a network of agriculture industry employers and businesses and created The Council of Consultants. In 2012-2013 The Council of Consultants consisted of 5 (five) individuals from implement dealerships, agronomy firms, and precision agricultural consulting firms, providing recommendations for curriculum development and technical, job skill-set banking, post-training assessment, on the job training opportunity, and resources such as precision technology test equipment and job opportunities. Today, with a membership of 15 (fifteen), the Council has expanded to a Board of Directors, composed of agricultural implement dealership management-level staff, precision agriculture software vendors, agronomists, crop consultants, producers, and agricultural cooperative representatives who provide overall training and research program advice and linkage to employees.

After a year of funding from the TAACCCT grant, the TPAT program at the Dakota Precision Agriculture Center (DPAC) had met and surpassed its expectations and was seeing success as a statewide, regional, and international program, providing services to students from Montana, Iowa, South Dakota, Michigan and Canada. In its first year of launching the program (2013), the program had enrolled 29 (twenty-nine) students and 27 (twenty-seven) completed their first year.

These key ingredients were needed in order to land the funding and launch the Precision Ag program. However, initial seed money can only reinvent and launch the program, more work needed to be deployed in order for the program to survive the next phase and reach sustainability.

Other Statewide Grant Funding That Was Used To Support the Program, Such As the Workforce Enhancement Grant (North Dakota Department of Commerce)

Seed money from the TAACCCT grant assisted in the launching of the precision ag program, however other local and statewide funding needed to be solicited considering program's needs were expensive, and $2.9 million in federal funding was not going to be able to cover all the initial costs.

DPAC leaders looked at the state for the next round of funding, which included the Workforce Enhancement Grant (WEG), administered through the North Dakota Department of Commerce. The Workforce Enhancement Grant Program provides funding for a demand driven response to workforce training needs for the five (Bismarck State College, Bottineau College, Lake Region State College, North Dakota State College of Science, and Williston State College) two-year institutions in North Dakota.

DPAC leaders knew that this program needed to be more than just a training program for those wishing to achieve an associates degree. The WEG was constructed not only to help supplement the program fiscally, but also provide another vital need; DPAC needed to provide outreach and training to those already in the precision ag business by providing workshops and training opportunities for local constituents. This, in turn, would start to bridge the gap towards producers and local ag workforce who were skeptical in providing necessary verbal or financial support for the program, and creating long term partnerships.

Again, through survey efforts provided by LRSC and DPAC leaders, identified necessary workforce skills that ag producers, farmers, and other ag businesses were lacking. In fact, identified that some agricultural equipment dealers, grain merchandising services, and independent agronomists/precision agriculture consultants needed necessary basic skills to manage farms in this high tech age of precision ag. Through Workforce Enhancement Grant funding, DPAC leaders constructed training needs in basic computer skills, basic precision agriculture, enhanced electronics skills, and customer relation skills. Grant funded efforts was able to provide DPAC leaders extended outreach and educational outreach to 55 (fifty-five) farmers in need of assistance and refresher classes in precision ag. This also continued to rebuild the torn relationships among the local workforce within farmers and producers.

What Are the Current Efforts in Place from the Community In Order To Continue To Provide Support?

The collaboration among institutions that is facilitated by consortia is a vital lever for transformational change—the type of change that will enable colleges and universities to not just survive but to prosper. (Forcier, 2011, p. 1)

CHANGE, COLLABORATION, AND CONSORTIA

Change, collaboration, and consortia – 3 C's - have become the watchwords of contemporary higher education. The one element that state and federal policy-makers, major foundations (Lumina, Kresge, Gates, and others), and government agencies all share is the firm belief that higher education must change in order to remain effective. One increasingly common strategy to promote such transformation is an intense focus on collaboration between and among institutions, including the creation of consortia arrangements. Indeed, in many cases, collaboration and/ or the formation of consortia are now requisite for the receipt of external funding. (Krotseng & Ruch, 2013, p.18)

Identifying and connecting with natural partners is the first step in developing long-lasting collaborations. (Krotseng & Ruch, 2013, p. 19)

DPAC was successful with the Workforce Enhancement Grant, providing educational outreach to farmers in need of assistance and refresher classes in precision ag. However, this was local, and DPAC wanted to move beyond the regional borders and provide this type of educational outreach statewide with a mobile training lab. This type of large-scale training was beyond the limits of the current program, and was time to employ the next phase to build support for the DPAC program. DPAC leaders knew that in order to provide change the next obvious step was collaboration building towards consortia. DPAC leaders looked towards their natural partner to collaborate with which was TrainND Northeast. TrainND is part of the North Dakota Workforce Training System, which provides and delivers training where the business needs it.

In collaboration with TrainND, DPAC leaders assisted in writing the Career Technical Education (CTE) grant in order to support workforce training in precision ag with a mobile training lab. With this collaboration, DPAC and TrainND would be able to offer non-credit workforce training developed specifically for the agricultural industry statewide. Small Business Computer Skills, GIS Systems, Basic Precision Agriculture, Enhanced Electronic Skills, Introduction to Welding, and Service to Customer Communication Skills will be available to producers, implement technicians, equipment operators, and other agriculture employees. Grant efforts would enable collaborative partners to purchase and equip a mobile high-tech training laboratory that will enable the delivery of precision agriculture technology training to the rural areas in the state of North Dakota.

SOLUTIONS AND RECOMMENDATIONS

The birth or rebirth of a program takes time, research, investment of a community, solicitation and commitment of the industry who will support it, extramural funding, and then collaboration of partnerships. The rebirth of the ag program took 8 years, troubleshooting and learning 'best practices.' The following take-away(s) could provide rural higher education institutions through philanthropy and other promising strategies ways to birth or rebirth a program tied to the community and workforce.

1. Research. Know the program you are trying to birth or rebirth. Talk with those in the industry. Ensure there is a need, and support for the program. You do not want to be a program that gets funded and implemented, only to have to close the program down in two-years, and to become another statistic like the ones stated at the start of the chapter. Some other items to consider:
    a. Is this a program your local constituents want? Talk with those who are involved and not involved in the industry and get their perspectives.
    b. Do not stay local when it comes to researching the proposed program. Go outside the area to ensure this is a program needed locally, regionally

and statewide. Once support has been provided locally, efforts will be needed outside the area for continued support and build sustainability.

    c.   Enlist the support of your local legislature. Securing funding and support in the state, whether through political actions or statewide grants, is another vital way to build sustainability.

2.   Start looking at external support. Federal grants are a good place, especially in the Department of Labor (DOL) or the US Department of Education. The current US federal administration is geared towards workforce development, and now is the time to capitalize on it. Current research and articles provided via the DOL indicates that this is a focus that will not be going away anytime in the near future.

    Also, look at statewide grants that support career and workforce developments, such as your CTE (Career Tech and Education) grants. Most states have these types of grants in place, or pools of money institutions can apply and compete for.

3.   Continue to work with local workforce as programmatic activities are solidified. Develop a steering committee comprised of those who are vested either financially (workforce), legislatively (state), and who can provide guidance and extramural support.

4.   And according to Krotseng & Ruch (2013), if you have not already considered or initiated collaborations with key partners or other like-minded institutions – start now. This is not a trend that will fade; it is becoming the norm to qualify for grants and extramural funding from federal, corporate, and private foundation sources. Begin today to identify potential partners and solidify productive alignments in preparation for the next major grant opportunity (Krotseng & Ruch, 2013, p. 19).

FUTURE DIRECTIONS AND RESEARCH TO BE CONSIDERED

Tight coupling between workforce and higher education is not a fad, and is becoming more of an emerging trend. As institutions continue to look for ways to develop or rebirth a program, whether in small rural locations or in an urban setting, this chapter speaks to all types of institutions and leaders, i.e. administration, faculty, legislatively, community and local workforce. Philanthropy and higher education is now an 'all hands on deck' practice, were everyone from the President down the chain of an institution is a fundraiser of some sort. No one is immune or not included in the process. All are involved with cultivating relationships. According to Ashford (2015, January, 5), "Rural colleges face plenty of challenges, such as a smaller pool of donors and fewer large corporations and wealthy donors nearby, but they actually have some advantages" reported Rich Gross, a consultant hired by the Danville Community College foundation. Such as being a "critical component in the community's workforce development, economic development, healthcare and quality of life," Gross reported (Ashford, 2015). LRSC DPAC leaders considered the 'community's workforce development' when rebirthing the program, Precision Ag. Furthermore, these are the areas a rural community college should focus on when it comes to cultivating relationships and building philanthropic donations- whether developing or rebirthing a program, building endowments, etc.

CONCLUSION

Rural institutions and community philanthropy support, while difficult to obtain, is the future of institutions of higher education to gain financial stability. However, key stakeholders and leaders should not dive into the process serendipitously. As this chapter demonstrated, steps and other issues need to be considered before moving forward. Again, data collection is vital; and most institutions rely heavily on data collection in order to make changes or decipher directions or missions. In the process of collecting data via quantum methods, do not forget qualitative; discussing and talking with local constituents, obtaining their ideas, thoughts and opinions is also important to knowing what is going to be sustainable in the way of programs. The development and sustainability of the Dakota Precision Ag Center was not developed, built and implemented overnight, or with little understanding of the workforce, community needs and philanthropic opportunities. Building workforce relationships, which provided the necessary foundation for the program, in order to achieve 'gifts-in-kind' in the way of expensive agriculture equipment, and internship and employment opportunities for graduating students.

However, when building or 'rebirthing' a program, rural or urban, leaders and key stakeholders need to look 'outside' there borders, and think of other ways to bring in funding for support; such as federal and statewide grants which align with efforts. Also, working with local legislative representatives, aligning with their efforts is another necessary process.

And last, for future sustainability, collaboration and consortium with natural partners with similar visions and missions is key- especially for rural institutions. The sharing and collaboration of resources demonstrates the commitment needed to ensure future sustainability.

ACKNOWLEDGMENT

Paul D. Gunderson is acknowledged for his contributions to this chapter.

REFERENCES

Ag Leader Insights. (2014, Spring). *Mapping New Classroom Opportunities; Rewarding careers in precision agriculture.* Author.

American Association of Community Colleges. (2000). *Community Colleges Past to Present (Based on material from National Profile of Community Colleges: Trends & Statistics, Phillippe & Patton, 2000).* Retrieved from http://www.aacc.nche.edu/AboutCC/history/Pages/pasttopresent.aspx

Ashford, E. (2015, January 5). *Fundraising is all about cultivating relationships.* Retrieved from http://www.ccdaily.com/Pages/Funding/Fundraising-is-all-about-cultivating-relationships.aspx

Austin, J. B. (2011, July 12). *Purdue fundraising shows growth.* Purdue University News Service. Retrieved from http://www.purdue.edu/newsroom/general/2011/11 0712CalvertYearend.html

Bailey, T., & Kienzal, G. (1999). *What Can We Learn About Postsecondary Vocational Education From Existing Data?.* Retrieved from http://ccrc.tc.columbia.edu/media/k2/attachments/vocational-education-existing-data.pdf

Bureau of Labor Statistics. (2015). *North Dakota.* Retrieved from http://www.bls.gov/regions/midwest/north_dakota.htm)

2007 . Census of Agriculture, United States Summary and State Data. (2007). *Summary of Farm by Typology: 2007.* Retrieved from http://www.agcensus.usda.gov/Publications/2007/Full_Report/usv1.pdf

Community College Daily- American Association of Community Colleges. (2014, November 20). *Signs of hope for state funding.* Retrieved http://www.ccdaily.com/Pages/Campus-Issues/Signs-of-hope-for-state-funding.aspx

Daniels, A. (2015, February 19). Mega-Gifts on the Rise at Colleges, Study Says. *The Chronical of Philanthropy.* Retrieved from https://philanthropy.com/article/Mega-Gifts-on-the-Rise-at/227955

Devils Lake North Dakota. (2015). *Visitor Guide,* 1-20.

Fain, P. (2014, August 7). Linking Business and Budgets. *Inside HigherEd.* Retrieved from https://www.insidehighered.com/news/2014/08/07/new-workforce-fund-louisiana-ties-money-jobs-and-private-donations

Forcier, F. M. (2011, September/October). Innovation Through Collaboration: New Pathways to Success. *Association of Governing Boards of Universities & Colleges, 5*(19). Retrieved from http://agb.org/trusteeship/2011/9/innovation-through-collaboration-new-pathways-success

Greene, R. (2011). *LightSquared Wireless Broadband – A Detriment to rural America?* Retrieved from http://precisionpays.com

Hardy, D. E., & Katsinas, S. G. (2007). Classifying Community Colleges: How Rural Community Colleges Fit. *New Directions for Community Colleges, 13*(137), 5–17. doi:10.1002/cc.265

Katsinas, S. G., Tollefson, T. A., & Reamey, B. A. (2008). *Funding Issues in U.S. Community Colleges: Findings from a 2007 Survey of the National State Directors of Community Colleges.* Retrieved from http://www.aacc.nche.edu/Publications/Reports/Documents/fundingissues.pdf

Krotseng, M. V. & Ruch, C. (2013). *Promoting and Sustaining Change Through Collaboration and Consortia.* American Association of State Colleges and Universities.

Milliron, M. D., De los Santos, G. E., & Browning, B. (2003). Feels like the third wave: The rise of fundraising in the community college. *New Directions for Community Colleges, 2003*(124), 81–93. doi:10.1002/cc.137

Mortenson, T. (2004, January). State Tax Fund Appropriations for Higher Education FY1961 to FY2004). *Postsecondary Education Opportunity* (no. 139). Oskalossa, IA: Mortenson Research Seminar on Public Policy Analysis of Opportunity for Post-Secondary Education. Retrieved from http://www.postsecondary.org/last12/139TAXFY04.pdf

Murphy, M. (2010). *An Energized Future.* Delta Sky Magazine.

North Dakota Implement Dealers Association. (2010) *Economic Impact of North Dakota's Retail Farm Equipment Dealers.* Paper presented at the North Dakota Implemented Dealers Association, Bismarck, ND.

Paradise, A. (2015). *Results from the 2014 CASE Survey of Community College Foundations* [White paper]. Retrieved May 19, 2015, Council for Advancement and Support of Education: http://www.case.org/Documents/WhitePapers/CCF_Survey2014.pdf

Romano, J. C., Gallagher, G., & Shugart, S. C. (2010). More than an Open Door: Deploying Philanthropy to Student Access and Success in American Community Colleges. *New Directions for Student Services*, *2010*(130), 55–70. doi:10.1002/ss.360

Signs of Hope for State Funding. (2014, November 20). *Community College Daily-American Association of Community College*. Retrieved from http://www.ccdaily. com/Pages/Campus-Issues/Signs-of-hope-for-state-funding.aspx

Strauss, L. (2001, December). *Trends in Community College Financing: Challenges of the Past, Present, and Future*. Retrieved from ERIC database. (ED467983)

Thelin, J. R. (2004). *A History of American Higher Education*. Baltimore, MD: The Johns Hopkins University Press.

United States Department of Labor. (2010). *Trade Adjustment Assistance Community College Career Training Program Summary*. Retrieved from http://www. doleta.gov/taaccct/

Weerts, D. J., & Ronca, J. M. (2006, November/December). Examining Differences in State Support for Higher Education: A Comparative Study of State Appropriations for Research I Universities. *The Journal of Higher Education*, *77*(6), 935–967. doi:10.1353/jhe.2006.0054

Worth, M. J., & Smith, N. J. (1993). Raising Funds for Community Colleges. In M. J. Worth (Ed.), *Educational Fund Raising: Principles and Practice* (pp. 347–356). Phoenix, AZ: American Council on Education and the Oryx Press.

Zinser, R. (2003, Winter). Evaluation of a Community College Technical Program by Local Industry. *Journal of Industrial Teacher Education*, *40*, 1–8. Retrieved from http://scholar.lib.vt.edu/ejournals/JITE/v40n2/zinser.html

KEY TERMS AND DEFINITIONS

Agricultural Producers or Producers: Another word for farmer.

Answer Farms: An agricultural research facility located near Fort Dodge, Iowa.

Career Tech Education Grant: North Dakota grant administered via the Career Technical Education department for the development and support of workforce enhancement.

Dakota Precision Ag Center: One of Lake Region State College's programs, which houses the Associates of Applied Science in Precision Ag.

Lake Region State College: Two-year higher education institution located in Devils Lake, North Dakota.

Precision Agriculture: This is the combination of agriculture and technology.

Trade Adjustment Assistance Community College Career Training Grant: Federal grant that was signed by President Barack Obama, and administered by the Department of Labor and Department of Education, in order to assist two-year and other higher education institutions in the development and expansion of education and career training programs.

Unmanned Aerial Vehicles (UAV): This is also known as a Drone, which is an unpiloted aerial vehicle.

Workforce Enhancement Grant: Grant administered via the North Dakota Department of Commerce in the development and support of workforce enhancement.

Chapter 7
Dynamics of Collaboration between U.S. Foundations and African Universities

Fabrice Jaumont
New York University, USA

ABSTRACT

The question of interest in this chapter is the recent project referred to as the Partnership for Higher Education in Africa, and the partner Foundations' goal to contribute to the transformation of a select number of universities in selected African countries. Can public universities in sub-Saharan Africa fully accept the solutions proposed by a private donorship from the West? In exploring the question this chapter draws upon the theoretical frameworks of neo-institutionalism and resource dependency to analyze the related issues. It also reviews, within a neo-institutional perspective, the long-standing debate on U.S. foundations' international activities, and discusses these foundations' perceived influence over Africa's higher education system. Applied to the relationship between U.S. foundations and African universities, this lens seeks to shed new light on the debate about donor funding and its influence on educational reforms.

DOI: 10.4018/978-1-4666-9664-8.ch007

SUMMARY

The case study that is developed in this chapter is a project referred to as the Partnership for Higher Education in Africa, a group of private American foundations that joined forces to transform a select number of African universities. This chapter draws upon the theoretical frameworks of neo-institutionalism and resource dependency to examine how and if universities in Africa, whether directly funded or not, fully accept the solutions proposed by private American foundations and actually expect to benefit from them. The findings point out the complex relationship and interaction between grantors and grantees, as well as resource scarcity that forced universities to adapt their research agendas in order to access the available funds. In addition, there is competition for resources amongst recipient institutions and pressure from national governments for institutions to be responsive to economic and development priorities. Furthermore, donor-initiated normative standardization generates a status-creating academic field, with successful institutions differentiating themselves from the rest. University-led autonomy-oriented policies and ownership claims are not always taken into consideration by the community of international donors and higher education developers. And resistance to change inherited from years of institutional upheavals is deeply engrained mechanisms that need to be taken into consideration.

INTRODUCTION

Questions concerning the impact of private donors on education and education reform resurface regularly in both the local and global arenas. In the United States, public school initiatives supported by established foundations such as The Bill & Melinda Gates Foundation, The Walton Family Foundation, or W.K. Kellog Foundation, among many others, and by individual donors such as Eli Broad, Michael Bloomberg or Mark Zuckerberg, to name but a few, often make headlines that criticize the donors' choices and question their legitimacy.[1] In general, critics question the effectiveness and fairness of the philanthropists' pet-project approach, a strategy that takes control away from local communities as foundations unilaterally set the course of education reform using their financial weight as a powerful incentive. Critics also argue that many donor-led education projects are utopian, not scientifically-based, and succumb to the schools' institutional environments, producing limited results and ignoring the link between education and poverty.

A similar set of questions and criticisms must be raised with regard to U.S. foundations' funding of education-based initiatives outside of the United States. The case study that is developed in this chapter the Partnership for Higher Education in Africa, a group of private American foundations that joined forces to transform a select number of African universities between 2000 and 2010. The consortium included seven of the most prominent foundations in the United States: Carnegie Corporation of New York, The Ford Foundation, The John D. and Catherine T. MacArthur Foundation, The Rockefeller Foundation, The William and Flora Hewlett Foundation, The Andrew W. Mellon Foundation, and The Kresge Foundation. Overall, the Partnership invested close to $500 million and supported institutions and research networks in nine countries.[2]

Although most of these foundations were already involved in education reform and had strong ties to the African continent, they decided to concert their efforts in order to tackle the major issues confronting the development of African universities, including: "technical obstacles to participation in increasingly global intellectual communities; redefining the nature of quality within international and local contexts; lowering costs through economies of scale; increasing access and gender equity; and positioning higher education as a responsible partner in building democratic societies"[3]. A report published by the Partnership at the end of its decade-long, collaborative effort claims that it had "directly or indirectly improved conditions for 4.1 million African students enrolled at 379 universities and colleges" (Grant Lewis et al., 2010).

While these figures may seem exaggerated, the Partnership "capitalized on the distinctive contribution that each foundation could make through shared learning, and enhanced the ability of grant-makers to support sustainable improvements in university performance".[4] As such, about 40 universities [5] received direct support from these donors, and as a result the entire field of higher education in Africa increased in desirability among international funders and higher education developers. However, the Partnership's claims and anticipated outcome raise several questions with regard to the relationship between grantors and grantees. Can all universities in Africa, whether directly funded or not, fully accept the solutions proposed by private American foundations and actually expect to benefit from them? In answering this question this chapter draws upon the theoretical frameworks of neo-institutionalism and resource dependency to avoid certain recurring ideological interpretations which are discussed in the following sections. Both neo-institutionalists and resource dependency theorists emphasize the effects of the social environment on organizations. Neo-institutionalists consider social rules and expectations, cultural norms, and values to be the primary source of pressure on organizations. Resource dependency theorists, on the other hand, focus on the material conditions of the institutions' environment and the constraints this imposes on their structures and practices, paying particular attention to issues of power, interests, and the institutions' strategic choices. Applied to the relationship between U.S. foundations and African universities, this institutional lens seeks to shed new light on the debate about donor funding and its influence on educational reforms. It also reviews, within a neo-institutional perspective, the long-standing debate on U.S. foundations' international activities, and discusses these foundations' perceived influence on higher education in Africa.

PHILANTHROPY IN THE U.S. CONTEXT

Early in the twentieth century philanthropists saw education as worthy of their support, particularly because they believed education gave individuals the opportunity to be successful. Since then, the development of higher education in the United States has been largely supported by private foundations. These foundations' investments contributed not only to the development of American universities, but also to these universities' influence - and, more generally, the influence of American values - throughout the world today. Prominent scholars have examined the relationship between philanthropy and universities in the United States (Hollis, 1938; Curti & Nash, 1965; Sears, 1990; Bacchetti & Ehrlich, 2007; Bernstein, 2013; Thelin & Trollinger, 2013). These notable studies present convincing examples of foundations that have increased their impact on society by building human capital and investing significantly in the universities' infrastructure, technology, research, faculty and student conditions, and professional development throughout the century.

In contrast to many European countries, the importance ascribed to civil society in the United States has encouraged Americans to be philanthropically entrepreneurial, thus explaining the ever-increasing number of private foundations being established each year. As a consequence, more and more U.S. foundations are working overseas to advance social change and to tackle global issues. U.S. private foundations represent the fastest growing and largest foundation community in the world. In 2012, the number of registered private foundations filing form 990PF was close to 97,000 [6], which represents a 70 percent growth since 2000.[7] The foundations' international grant-making has increased steadily since 2000, especially in the areas of international affairs, international development, and relief; human rights and civil liberties; education and health; public affairs and society benefit, environment and animal protection.[8] This community of funders is also the richest in the world, and it plays an increasingly active role internationally. Overall, U.S. foundation giving is estimated to be around $52 billion annually.[9]

Several studies question, through various theoretical lenses, the benefits and drawbacks of foundation work in the United States (Whitaker, 1974; Arnove, 1980; Dowie, 2002; Roelofs, 2007). At times, these studies conclude that older foundations such as Carnegie, Rockefeller, and Ford have a corrosive influence on U.S. society. Joan Roelofs (2007), for instance, argues that foundations are prime constructors of hegemony, by promoting consent and discouraging dissent against capitalist democracy, obscuring the frontiers of power and influence and supplanting democratic institutions with a "new feudalism." This view echoes earlier studies (Whitaker, 1974) which often considered foundations as relatively unfettered and unaccountable concentrations of wealth and power, perceived as entities that are able to buy intellectual capital, advance causes and outline what a society's attention should focus on. Darknell (1980) even argues that Carnegie's programs in higher education have been consistent with the interests of U.S. corporations. This view is echoed by Masseys-Bertoneche (2006), who argues that the foundations' networks of influence over higher education institutions are reinforcing the elites' grip on the sector.

Nonetheless –and without yielding to pro-foundation propaganda– many well-regarded scholars have demonstrated that private foundations have a strong track record of funding innovative research and path-breaking ideas in the United States and abroad (Gaudiani, 2003, Salamon, 2004, Fleishman, 2007). For instance, through its partnerships in communities across the United States, the Bill and Melinda Gates foundation is committed to raising the high school graduation rate and helping all students—regardless of race or family income—graduate as strong citizens ready for college, and work. The Gates' Education initiative also works to provide children with opportunities for quality early learning. Overall, more than 2,000 schools benefited from the foundation's support in the United States. Though privately controlled, foundations perform essential roles that serve society at large. They spearhead some of the world's largest and most innovative initiatives in science, health, education, and the arts, fulfilling important needs that could not be addressed adequately in the marketplace or the public sector. Still, many people have little understanding of what foundations do and how they continue to earn public endorsement (Prewitt, 2006).

U.S FOUNDATIONS AND AFRICA

Several studies (Arnove, 1980; Berman, 1983; Brison, 2005; Amutabi, 2013) question the aspirations and motivations of these large foundations that are active both at home and abroad. Arnove (1980), for example, depicts foundations as pervasive infiltrators of policy infrastructures in university systems, the public health sector, and the social sciences. He argues that foundations "help maintain an economic and political order, international in scope, which benefits the ruling-class interests of philanthropists." He criticizes foundations for promoting set agendas, serving the interests of industrial capitalism, and acting, in a sense, like "agencies of hegemony, imposing cultural imperialism on minorities and subordinate classes at home and abroad." In his study of Rockefeller, Ford and Carnegie, Parmar (2002) concludes that these foundations developed international knowledge networks and exercised intellectual influence over the research agenda "to build policy-relevant research and training institutions that would produce graduates with skills and ideas that fit Western notions of development."

However, none of these studies properly consider the inner workings of foundations, their program officers' commitment to their grantees, or the complexity of international grant-making, relying all too often on annual reports and secondary sources to justify their claims. As a result, the discussions have often underlined the hegemony of U.S. foundations. More recently, for instance, Amutabi (2013) casts NGOs, and the Rockefeller Foundation in particular, as "the 'economic and cultural bombs' in Africa, which are continuing Northern hegemonic tendencies, by codifying and continuously defining Africa's place in development without Africa having such as privilege to define the North". This view echoes Berman (1971) who states that Carnegie Corporation of New York's initial African programs in the 1920s could not have succeeded without the foundation's close cooperation with the British Colonial Office, thereby showing that the foundation's overseas work was fettered by ideological insinuation and restrictive national concerns.

However, the models that the Carnegie Corporation was considering for Africa did not embrace the precepts of the British education but actually followed those tested in the southern United States for native American and African-American children in the first half of the century thanks to the pioneering ventures of the Phelps-Stokes fund. Phelps-Stokes had embarked on educational philanthropy in Africa a few years prior to the Carnegie Corporation's first visit to schools and universities in Africa in 1927, and influenced the foundation greatly. Indeed, the Carnegie Corporation supported the transition of several vulnerable institutions "out of colonization and into modernization" (Murphy, 1976), tempering the elitism of the British educational model and moving universities towards a more practical, U.S.-inspired approach which called on university leaders to participate in national policy-making processes.

The question of hegemony, coercion and foundation activity has often been debated by scholars who pinpoint the foundations' fostering of pro-U.S. values and their reinforcement of American influence over developing nations. At times, foundations are found to be working both with and against U.S. foreign policy, seizing opportunities to operate internationally. For instance, the Rockefeller Foundation awarded grants for sending medical literature and small items of equipment to Soviet institutions in the 1920s, providing medicine to the people when their own government could not. During the Cold War, the Ford Foundation instituted a non-governmental cultural diplomacy program to offset Communism (Rosenbaum, 1989). Due to the increasing power that the U.S. had attained, the U.S. influence abroad developed in the first part of the twentieth century to reveal its full force after 1945, helping the spread of Western medicine around the world, including the first medical school in China (Bullock, 1980) or promoting international relations. Hewa & Stapleton (2005) argue that during this period, foundations took a more active role in instigating change. Indeed, Tournès (2002) shows that Ford's funding of intercultural publications, with publishing houses established in 52 countries, was the first major effort demonstrating the foundation's determination to play a role in international relations. Whitaker (1974) attacks the foundations for their multiple connections with the CIA over the years. More recently, Brison (2005) discusses the hegemonic influence of U.S. foundations over Canada's higher education institutions where scholars were not able to pursue their research as freely as they wanted once they had received support from U.S. foundations.

But are U.S. foundations always fostering a pro-Western agenda? Are their interventions perceived as hegemonic by their grant recipients? The hegemonic approach to the study of foundation work does not account for the complexity of the grantor-grantee relationship. Nigerian scholar Christiana Tamuno (1986) concludes that "there is nothing wrong in incorporating into the Nigerian university foreign models of education." Although she acknowledges that not all programs carried out by the Rockefeller, Carnegie and Ford foundations were successful in the institutional development of Ibadan University, she does not judge these foundations as being hegemonic. By questioning whether the involvement of U.S. independent foundations with African universities is a form of hegemonic influence, most studies tend to discard the particular dynamics that operate between both sets of institutions. Moreover, reorganizing an educational system according to norms of efficiency and cost effectiveness may have the effect of stymieing social mobility (Darknell, 1980). It is wrong, however, to make inferences about motives based on these possible effects.

Paul Di Maggio suggests that these studies' ideological lens "blinds the authors, at times, to the reality of organizational life in foundations: too often, foundations are conceived as purposeful and rational unitary actors." This tendency, he says, is reinforced by the disappointing absence of interviews with officers, grantees, and unsuccessful applicants, and by an overreliance on official documents. In a review of Arnove's *Philanthropy and Cultural Imperialism,* Di Maggio (1983) concludes that much of the discussion of foundation behavior in the less developed world suggests a "thoughtless application of Western models, rather than conscious efforts to impose hegemony." This again reinforces the need for a neo-institutional interpretation of U.S. foundations that clearly focuses on the environmental, institutional and actor-led factors which influence these institutions. Major foundations, for instance, do attempt to adapt to their grantees' environment. Incremental results from the grantees are essential for they struggle to deliver social change. But results are also essential for a grantor's credibility and reputation. Over the course of a century, the Carnegie Corporation's Africa programs evolved considerably, turning the foundation into one of the leading experts in the field.

Recent studies, for instance, discuss the activities of U.S. foundations abroad in relations to globalization processes. Kiger (2008) provides a historical account of U.S. foundations' international work and attempts to assess the impact of globalization on foundations and philanthropists. But his conclusions only briefly discuss the absence of global restriction on the foundations' freedom, which benefits their operations and reputation. Lester Salamon (in Hewa & Stapleton, 2005) highlights findings from the massive comparative civil society project he directs, documenting the size (number of employees and volunteers), scope (service vs. expressive functions), and funding sources by region for nonprofit and civil society organizations world-wide. He argues in a convincing way that the growth in such organizations is both a product of, and a reaction to, globalization. One should also take into consideration the internal phenomena at play within African universities, as well as their regional environment, because they compete with one another to catch the attention of donors.

MECHANISMS AT PLAY IN THE FOUNDATION-UNIVERSITY RELATIONSHIP

Higher education in Africa has been characterized by a small number of universities per country and low enrollment rates at the primary, secondary, and tertiary levels. The sector is plagued by challenges such as an aging faculty and a lack of incentives to attract younger staff, as well as the brain drain that continues to sap the intellectual capital of most African countries. Moreover, scholars such as Benneh, Awumbila & Effah (2004) argue that the inadequate financial and logistical support from national governments, along with weak private sector support and few private contributions to universities could be seen as insurmountable obstacles to any form of institutional development.

In opposition to the rather simplified view that international philanthropies are vehicles of Western hegemony, there are several institutional mechanisms at work that reveal a more complex relationship between U.S. foundations and African universities. Although the universities negotiate their similarities and differences through mimetic processes and normative pressures, the result is not only isomorphism—as DiMaggio and Powell (1991) demonstrate —but also institutional differentiation. Makerere University in Uganda offers a good example. In 1963, Makerere became the University of East Africa, offering courses leading to general degrees of the University of London. The special relationship with the University of London came to a close in 1970 and the University of East Africa instituted its own degree programs. On July 1, 1970, Makerere became an independent national university, offering undergraduate and postgraduate courses leading to its own degrees. Carnegie first initiated grants to Makerere University in 1937 and supported a variety of programs at the university. [10]

Between 2000 and 2010, Makerere University received $42 million from Carnegie, Rockefeller, Ford, MacArthur, and Mellon through the Partnership for Higher Education in Africa and other foundation-led initiatives. The university runs on an annual budget of approximately $100 million. Today, Makerere is a fee-based institution whose ambition is to become "a centre of academic excellence, providing world-class teaching, research and service relevant to sustainable development needs of society", as stated by its mission statement. In this particular case, hegemony-oriented theorists may argue that Makerere's relationship with U.S. foundations pushed the university towards an American model. However, Makerere's shift towards high tuition rates and its global ambitions might be a result of the university's interdependence with *Western* models more generally, in response to globalization and the demands of an internationally relevant education, or the process of integrating an internationalized dimension into the purpose and delivery of its education. It could also have stemmed from the pressures of internal players, competing universities or the State. Makerere's successful bids for grants from large foundations led the university to differentiate from peer institutions and become a standard for the African higher education sector as other universities sought to reproduce Makerere's success. Makerere has also used its successful fundraising to legitimize its autonomy from state control, and advance to new levels of development, while gaining influence over the whole field of higher education on the continent.

Furthermore, institutional differentiation has important consequences in creating levels of status among universities and in affecting organizational success. Pfeffer and Salancik (2003) argue that institutional status is determined by the status of the other organizations with which the organization interacts. Network relations and social ties are therefore an essential part of improving one's standing. There is little incentive for a high status organization to form alliances with lower status ones. The dynamic interaction and evolution of universities with their environments can help explain inter-organizational relations over time as the various social actors maneuver for advantages. Thus, external resource dependence affects both internal and trans-organizational dynamics.

Universities such as Makerere act strategically to manage their resource dependencies. Resource-dependent universities must interact with other institutions in their environment to acquire needed resources. Problems arise not merely because organizations are dependent on their environment, but because this environment is not dependable. The need for resources, including financial and physical resources as well as information, makes universities potentially dependent on the external environment as a supplier of these resources. The environment, including local actors, is a strong factor influencing inter-organizational variation. This view suggests that universities are embedded in networks of interdependencies and social relationships. As they try to alter their environments, they become subject to new and different constraints as their patterns of interdependence change. African universities attempt to manage the constraints and uncertainty that result from the need to acquire resources from the environment using various co-optive strategies. Because of external constraints on revenue and autonomy of decision-making organizations possess both the desire and the ability to negotiate their position within those constraints using a variety of tactics. Co-opting sources of constraint to obtain more autonomy and the ability to pursue organizational interests is therefore a process central to understanding African universities.

RESISTANCE TO INSTITUTIONAL CHANGE

Another aspect to take into account in the foundation-university relationship is the capability for both sets of institutions to resist institutional change. Historical institutionalists argue that resistance to change is embedded within institutions. According to this theory, an institution's norms and values are a function of the material context from which it emerged. In this light, institutions appear to have a logic of their own as their creation and growth result in consequences unintended and unpredicted by their actors. They reflect the societal situation prevailing at the time of their birth because, once created, they have autonomy from society and their institutional development follows a largely independent pattern.

Higher education has a much older history in Africa than is generally realized, beginning long before the establishment of Western-style universities in the 19th century. From the Alexandria Museum and Library in the third century B.C. to Christian monasteries in Ethiopia and Sankore Madrasah in Timbuktu, many of these centers of higher learning were influenced by religion. Africa claims distinction as the center of the world's oldest Islamic universities and some of the world's oldest surviving universities (Ez-Zitouna madrassa founded in Tunis in 731; al Qairawiyyin Mosque University in Fez in 859; Al-Azhar Mosque University in 969 in Cairo; Sankore Mosque University in Timbuktu in the 12th century. Y. G-M Lulat (2003) argues that the modern university that was brought to Africa by the colonial powers is as much Western in origin as it is Islamic.

Modern Western-style colleges and universities were started in the early 19th century by missionaries and largely concentrated in European settler colonies such as South Africa and Algeria, as well as in newly established territories of African

Diaspora resettlement such as Sierra Leone and Liberia. In colonial Africa, the development of higher education was limited until World War II because colonial authorities were generally wary of a modern and educated African elite and their nationalist demands, and colonial civil servants feared African competition. After independence, higher education was a key challenge for the newly independent states. The few existing universities were patterned on European models and were elitist. There was a need to make them more relevant to Africa's developmental needs and sociocultural contexts and more accessible to students of different social backgrounds.

The role of universities in Africa's socio-economic development has been a subject of debate throughout the post-independence era as scholars and many African governments search for ways to ensure that universities contribute to Africa's development. At times, universities were seen as central for national prestige, training a highly skilled labor force, and creating and reproducing a national elite (Yesufu, 1973). Universities became larger in size than their colonial predecessors, broader in mission, with expanded disciplinary and curricula offerings from the arts and social sciences to include professional fields of study (business, medicine, and engineering) and graduate programs. But decades of financial and structural decline led many of these institutions to a breaking point at the end of the 1990s.

Foundations such as those involved in the Partnership for Higher Education in Africa have put pressure on African universities to break with outmoded traditions —although several foundations do not accept this assertion and claim that their grantees had already broken free from old models before they were selected. In its selection process the PHEA looked for universities "on the move in countries on the move" (Parker, 2010) in order to implement its grant strategy. Still, these foundations encouraged universities to embark on major institutional and academic reform, including developing new financial formulas and means of income generation, reviewing course structures, encouraging collaborative research, and setting better governance practices. The Partnership's goal was to produce or reproduce African "knowledge centers" by directing the foundation's financial support to building the core institutional capacity of a select group of universities. This process has mainly benefited institutions which are either located in richer countries (South Africa's urban institutions and/or historically white institutions.) or which have been in contact with U.S. foundations for decades (Makerere University, University of Dar es Salaam, Ibadan University, University of Cape Town, to name but a few).

However, the recent literature on African higher education confirms that African scholars are calling for more ownership in the inception and implementation of programs (Mamdani & Diouf, 1994; Tiyambe & Olukoshi, 2004; Afolayan, 2007). As John Ssebuwufu, former director of research and programs at the Association of African Universities in Ghana writes: "The African institution must fully own the programs, and not be left feeling that the programs are an imposition with minimum input from their side." [11] The notion of program ownership is an underestimated and understudied aspect of the institutional interaction, which occurs between the recipient of a grant and the foundation. To a certain extent, this phenomenon reflects a resistance to an undesired transformation, i.e. a donor's vision of change implemented through its grant program. It also reflects the universities' inability to generate its own endogenous model, thus replicating what Eric Ashby (1964) described as the "mechanism for the inheritance of the Western style of civilization."

African scholars ask how universities are to be made African so that they can take on a proactive role in Africa's economic development (Ajayi, Goma & Johnson, 1996). But recent trends in grant-making seem to countenance the emergence of African universities as engines for Africa's development on Western terms. Since 2000, private donors have tried to shape the role that universities have to play in socio-economic development, and they have contributed to the debate by steering and directing the priorities set by the universities, transforming them according to priorities aligned to those of the foundations and the World Bank. An indicator of success in the PHEA case study, amongst others, is the ability to attract additional funding pledges from development agencies and the World Bank (Parker, 2010).

The development agenda for Africa is still highly influenced by donor countries and remains contested. The New Partnership for Africa's Development (NEPAD) is an example of Africa's attempt to chart its own development agenda and break out of the dependency mold. NEPAD represents a step in the right direction but these types of programs are hard to implement as the projects are typically funded by private donors or loans which come with their own pre-determined priorities and conditions. Cloete et al. (2011) conducted a groundbreaking study that tried to understand the relationship between higher education and economic development in Africa. One of the conclusions of this study is that donor funding does not support the academic core of the institution and actually destroys it whilst supporting individuals as grant holders or consultants. The study suggests that resistance to change is deeply rooted in the African university, and that understanding this resistance's origin and mechanism is critical for success in institutional development.

CONCLUSION

This discussion encompassed the specifics of a partnership between leading U.S. foundations – the Carnegie Corporation of New York, the Ford Foundation, the John D. and Catherine T. MacArthur Foundation, the Rockefeller Foundation, the William and Flora Hewlett Foundation, the Andrew W. Mellon Foundation, and the Kresge Foundation – and African universities. The considerable influence of these foundations, accumulated over decades of strategic grant-making in the field of African higher education, remains unrivaled and remarkable considering the relatively small size of their investments to academic institutions. These foundations have demonstrated a certain level of expertise in maximizing their investments, impact, influence, and legitimacy particularly in relation to institutions of higher learning in Africa. They explain the dynamics of collaboration in the Partnership for Higher Education in Africa and ways in which collaboration served the foundations involved. They are also informative in regards to the discourse of philanthropic foundations in African higher education and the extent to which impact-seeking philanthropic foundations need elaborate legitimation mechanisms in order to operate.

It is critical to ask if public universities in sub-Saharan Africa in a position to fully embrace the solutions and strategies supported by private donorship from the West. This chapter points out the complex relationship and interaction between grantors and grantees, as well as resource scarcity that forced universities to adapt their research agendas in order to access the available funds. In addition, there is competition for resources amongst recipient institutions and pressure from national governments for institutions to be responsive to economic and development priorities. Furthermore, donor-initiated normative standardization generates a status-creating academic field, with successful institutions differentiating themselves from the rest. University-led autonomy-oriented policies and ownership claims are not always taken into consideration by the community of international donors and higher education developers. Finally, resistance to change inherited from years of institutional upheavals is deeply engrained in mechanisms that need to be taken into consideration. Thus, all these factors indicate that it is impossible —even for a consortium of wealthy foundations— to assert with certainty that their funding produced positive impact on the universities' institutional development without an in-depth impact study to support the findings.

That said, in educational philanthropy, one needs only to look at the history of major foundations such as Carnegie Corporation of New York to recognize that positive changes are not easily achieved, and that it takes years for results to become apparent. Much to their credit the investments of the PHEA foundations led to the successful development of research initiatives across the African continent, as well as to the strengthening of pan-African organizations such as the Association of African Universities (AAU) and the Council for the Development of Social Science Research (CODESRIA). Other victories can be found in the Partnership's programs that were directed towards information technology and the provision of internet bandwidth at affordable prices to African universities. For example, with co-funding from the Partnership for Higher Education in Africa, universities in several sub-Saharan countries formed a consortium to purchase a six-fold increase in bandwidth and share Internet capacity at lower rates. Several regional organizations are now investing in the development of this sub-sector. In addition, these universities are offering African women unprecedented access to opportunity, expanding the pool of African experts who will contribute to the continent's efforts to reduce poverty and address other crucial challenges.

Foundations have also stimulated interest in areas such as capacity building and have worked with universities to reduce their dependency on donor funding. Since the launch of the Partnership for Higher Education in Africa in 2000, additional U.S. foundations have positioned themselves strategically as key stakeholders in the field of African higher education by focusing on capacity building, and treating universities as partners. They have invited African higher education networks and academic institutions to define the empowering them, although the success of these initiatives has yet to be measured. The role of universities in the economic development of Africa has been under close scrutiny since the post-independence era and is likely to remain so until scholars and African governments can identify a role for higher education in Africa's development.

Universities such as Makerere have become a primary locus for Western innovation and exert a strong degree of influence on the continent's future leaders in the public and private sectors. American foundations have also been in a position to propose new directions for policy and reforms to a number of institutions. This last observation suggests that foundations' influence over a small, elite group of African universities will either drive a divisive wedge within the field of higher education in Africa or push institutions to enter a competitive race for which they might not yet be ready. There are more questions to be raised concerning the role of foundations in developing countries, and their influence over resource-seeking universities. There is also a need for increased documentation of past experiences, such as the Parker (2010) report produced at the end of the partnership or the Lewis et al. (2010) report on the Partnership's accomplishments.

In his study of foundations Fleishman (2007) writes that most large foundations that are serious about their fields of grant-making show a preference for strategies that build on prior experiences in the same field, thus accumulating knowledge as they go forward. Bacchetti and Ehrlich (2007) argue that, in shaping strategies for grants to education, foundations should make their goal the building of "educational capital"—that is, the generation and accumulation of knowledge about how to best address the issues with which they are grappling. Moreover, the authors strongly urge that such strategies be developed *jointly* by foundations and groups of beneficiary educational institutions. They present a persuasive case that, in order to do so, foundations must first become "relentless learning organizations," by continuously studying their own impact and the processes that produce it. Moreover, Bacchetti and Ehrlich correctly point out that foundations cannot become "learning organizations" without becoming more public, visible, and transparent about their work, without subjecting themselves to critical review and discussion, and without building on their own and on others' learning in guiding future practice in the field.

In a climate that is critical of the ways in which development priorities are often set by various governmental and international agencies in the West, this study finds that major, trend-setting international foundations constantly rethink their philanthropically entrepreneurial solutions. For instance, the Partnership for Higher Education in Africa spearheaded new ways of power sharing in development work by including grantees in certain decision processes. This, in turn, maximized their legitimacy (Jaumont, 2014). However, questions remain concerning the degree of grantee participation in the foundations' agenda. It will take more effort from U.S. foundations to nurture institutional agency in the local organizations that they fund, and reinforce the role of African universities in the early stages of their decision-making processes and development strategies. Only then will we know if private donors can embrace Africa's development on Africa's terms, and if African universities can fully own their participation in the global economy.

REFERENCES

Ajayi Ade, J. F., & Goma Lameck, K. (1996). The African Experience with Higher Education. Accra: The Association of African Universities.

Amutabi, M. N. (2013). *The NGO Factor in Africa: The Case of Arrested Development in Kenya.* London: Taylor and Francis.

Arnove, R. F. (1980). *Philanthropy and Cultural Imperialism: The Foundations at Home and Abroad.* Boston, MA: G.K. Hall.

Berman Edward H. (1971). American Influence on African Education: The Role of the Phelps-Stokes Fund's Education Commissions. *Comparative Education Review, 15*(2), 132-145.

Berman Edward, H. (1983). *The Ideology of Philanthropy. The Influence of the Carnegie, Ford, and Rockefeller Foundations on American Foreign Policy.* Albany, NY: SUNY Press.

Bernstein, A. R. (2013). *Funding the Future: Philanthropy's Influence on American Higher Education.* Lanham, MD: Rowman & Littlefield.

Brison, J. D. (2005). *Rockefeller, Carnegie, and Canada: American Philanthropy and the Arts and Letters in Canada.* Montreal: McGill-Queen's University Press.

Bullock, M. B. (1980). *An American Transplant: The Rockefeller Foundation and Peking Union Medical College*. Berkeley, CA: University of California Press.

Carole, M.-B. (2006). *Philanthropie et Grandes Universités Privées Américaines: Pouvoir et Réseaux d'influence*. Bordeaux: Presses Universitaires de Bordeaux.

Claire, G. (2003). *The Greater Good: How Philanthropy Drives The American Economy and Can Save Capitalism*. New York, NY: Times Books.

Cloete, Bailey, Pillay, Bunting, & Maassen. (2011). *Universities and Economic Development in Africa.* Wynberg: CHET.

Di Maggio, P. (1983). Review: A Jaundiced View of Philanthropy. Philanthropy and Cultural Imperialism: The Foundations at Home and Abroad by Robert F. Arnove. *Comparative Education Review, 27*(3), 442–445. doi:10.1086/446388

Eric, A. (1964). *African Universities and Western Tradition*. Cambridge, MA: Harvard University Press.

Fleishman, J. (2007). *The Foundation: A Great American Secret; How Private Wealth Is Changing The World*. New York, NY: Public Affairs.

Frank, D. A. (1980). The Carnegie Philanthropy and Private Corporate Influence on Higher Education. In Philanthropy and Cultural Imperialism: The Foundations at Home and Abroad. Boston, MA: G.K. Hall.

George, B., Mariama, A., & Paul, E. (2004). *African Universities, the Private Sector and Civil Society, Forging Partnerships for Development*. Accra: African Regional Council of the International Association of University Presidents.

Hammack, D. C., & Anheier, H. K. (2013). *A Versatile American Institution: The Changing Ideals and Realities of Philanthropic Foundations*. Washington, DC: Brookings Institution Press.

Hollis Ernerst, V. (1938). *Philanthropic Foundations and Higher Education*. New York, NY: Columbia University Press.

Inderjeet. (2002). American Foundations and the Development of International Knowledge Networks. *Global Networks, 2*(1), 13–30.

Jaumont, F. (2014). *Strategic Philanthropy, Organizational Legitimacy, and the Development of Higher Education in Africa: The Partnership for Higher Education in Africa (2000-2010)*. (Ph.D. dissertation). New York University.

Jeffrey, P., & Gerald, S. (2003). *The External Control of Organizations. A Resource Dependence Perspective*. Stanford, CA: Stanford University Press.

Joseph, K. (2008). *Philanthropists & Foundation Globalization*. New Brunswick, NJ: Transaction Pub.

Lewis, G., et al. (2010). Accomplishments of the Partnership for Higher Education in Africa, 2000–2010. New York, NY: New York University.

Mahmood & Mamadou (Eds.). (1994). *Academic Freedom in Africa*. Dakar: CODESRIA.

Mark, D. (2002). *American Foundations: An Investigative History*. Cambridge, MA: MIT Press.

Merle, C., & Roderick, N. (1965). *Philanthropy in the Shaping of American Higher Education*. New Brunswick, NJ: Rutgers University Press.

Michael, A. O. (2007). *Higher Education in Postcolonial Africa: Paradigms of Development, Decline, and Dilemmas*. Trenton, NJ: Africa World Press.

Murphy, J. (1976). *Carnegie Corporation and Africa, 1953-1973*. New York, NY: Teachers College Press.

Parker, S. (2010). *Lessons from a Ten-Year Funder Collaborative. A Case Study of the Partnership for Higher Education in Africa*. Clear Thinking Communication.

Powell, W., & DiMaggio, P. (1991). *The New Institutionalism in Organizational Analysis*. Chicago, IL: Univ. of Chicago Press.

Prewitt, K., Mattei, D., Steven, H., & Stefan, T. (Eds.). (2006). *The Legitimacy of Philanthropic Foundations: United States and European Perspectives*. New York, NY: Russell Sage Foundation Publications.

Ray, B. (2007). Reconnecting Education & Foundations, Turning Good Intentions into Educational Capital. Stanford, CA: Carnegie Foundation for the Advancement of Teaching.

Roelofs, J. (2007). Foundations and Collaboration. *Critical Sociology, 33*(3), 479–504. doi:10.1163/156916307X188997

Rosenbaum, T. E. (1989). *Rockefeller Philanthropies in Revolutionary Russia*. Rockefeller Archive Center Newsletter.

Sears, J. B. (1990). *Philanthropy in the History of American Higher Education*. New Brunswick, NJ: Transaction Publishers.

Soma, H., & Darwin, S. (2005). *Globalization, Philanthropy & Civil Society*. New York, NY: Springer.

Tamuno, C. (1986). *The Roles of the Rockefeller Foundation, Ford Foundation and Carnegie Corporation in the Development of the University of Ibadan 1962-1978.* (Ph.D. dissertation). The University of Pittsburgh.

Thelin, J. R., & Trollinger, R. W. (2013). *Philanthropy and American Higher Education.* New York, NY: Palgrave Macmillan.

Tiyambe, Z. P., & Olukoshi, A. (2004). *African Universities in the Twenty-First Century* (Vol. 2). Dakar: Council for the Development of Social Science Research in Africa.

Tournès, L. (2002). La diplomatie culturelle de la fondation Ford, Vingtième Siècle. *Revue d'histoire, 4*(76), 65–77.

Whitaker, B. (1974). *The Philanthropoids. Foundations and Society.* New York, NY: Morrow.

Yesufu, T. M. (Ed.). (1970s). *Creating the African University: Emerging Issues of the.* Ibadan: Oxford University Press.

ENDNOTES

[1] See for instance Valerie Strauss' numerous articles in The Washington Post or Richard Rothstein in the New York Times, both of whom have frequently questioned the role of private donors in public education.

[2] South Africa, Ghana, Kenya, Nigeria, Mozambique, Uganda, Tanzania, Madagascar, and Egypt.

[3] Partnership for Higher Education in Africa. *Partnership Core Statement – Principles of the Partnership.* Retrieved August 9, 2015 from http://www.foundation-partnership.org/core.php

[4] Partnership for Higher Education in Africa. *Partnership Core Statement – Principles of the Partnership.* Retrieved August 9, 2015 from http://www.foundation-partnership.org/core.php

[5] Among the top recipients: Makerere University, Uganda ($23m); University of Cape Town, South Africa ($23m); University of KwaZulu-Natal, South Africa ($22m); University of the Western Cape, South Africa ($20m); University of Pretoria, South Africa ($18m); University of the Witwatersrand, South Africa ($17m); University of Dar es Salaam, Tanzania ($16,5); University of Ghana, Ghana ($10m); Rhodes University, South Africa ($9m); University of Natal, South Africa ($8m); University of Ibadan, Nigeria ($8m), etc.

[6]   Based on The National Center for Charitable Statistics's 2012 report Number of Registered Private Foundations Filing Form 990PF in the Past 2 Years by State. However, in its 2014 Key Facts on U.S. Foundations, the Foundation Center presents a larger number with 86,192 foundations that reported giving in 2012 and 17,000 foundations that did not report any giving in their last fiscal year, or an approximate total of 103,192 foundations.

[7]   In 2000, there were 56,582 foundations reported by the Foundation Center in Grantmaker Information, 2000 Foundation Center Statistics, p. 15.

[8]   2012 Grants by Issue Focus. Foundation Center. Key Facts on US Foundations. November 2014. p. 6.

[9]   Type of Foundations. Foundation Center. Key Facts on US Foundations. November 2014, p. 2. However massive this number may seem, foundation giving "only" represents 15% of all 2014 charitable giving in the United States, dwarfed by individual giving which represents 72% of the total, followed by bequests 8%, and corporation giving 5% (Giving USA 2015: The Annual Report on Philanthropy for the Year 2014)

[10]   The East African Institute for Social Research (1951-1957); Leadership Study (1952-1955); the Development of Teaching and Research (1954-1975); Extramural programs (1960-1964); the National Institute of Education (1963-1977); Social Psychology, Research, and Training in Collaboration with Syracuse University (1966-1977); the Association of Teacher Education in Africa (1969-1972); Program of Research, Curriculum Revision, and Staff Development for Primary Teacher Training in Uganda (1971-1972); Educational Programs (1979-1992); Redevelopment of the Institute (1979); Seminar on Economic and Social Development in Uganda (1985-1994).

[11]   Fisher Karin & Lindow Megan. "Africa Attracts Renewed Attention from American Universities" in *The Chronicle of Higher Education*, July 18, 2008

Chapter 8
Islamic Philanthropy as a "Discursive Tradition"

Sabithulla Khan
Virginia Tech, USA

ABSTRACT

By examining philanthropy towards Zaytuna College, the first Muslim liberal arts college in the U.S. and ISNA, and contextualizing it in the discourses of giving among American Muslims, this paper seeks to offer a theoretical framework for contextualizing Islamic philanthropy during 'crisis'. I argue that philanthropy in this context should be seen as a gradually evolving 'discursive tradition,' and not an unchanging one. Given the discourse of Islam in America being one framed in the rubric of 'crisis,' and the attempts by American Muslim organizations to gar-ner philanthropic support using this framework; it is important to understand how certain crisis situations impacted discourses of philanthropy towards this sector. This paper attempts a Foucaldian analysis of how American Muslims negotiate this discursive tension in the realm of giving. I build on the work of various scholars and offer a framework that treats philanthropy towards Islamic schools, cultural and educational institutions as a 'discursive tradition' to understand how the dynamics of philanthropy are changing in this sector. I propose that a discursive approach could also offer us new insights into how philanthropy is being transformed, under certain institutional constraints and relations of power.

INTRODUCTION

Speaking during a lecture organized by Zaytuna College, C.A., the first Muslim liberal arts college in the U.S. Dr. Hatem Bazian said: "Al-Waqf is to designate a particular property or land and to donate the proceeds that are driven from that to

DOI: 10.4018/978-1-4666-9664-8.ch008

donate for the general public.[1]" The development of architecture in Spain, the modes of funding higher education, independent of the state can be attributed to the Islamic concept of Waqf, Dr. Bazian points out. He was referring to the tradition of Islamic endowments towards education, that makes it possible for them to enjoy academic freedom and independence; so they could produce scholarship and original research, which may be at odds with the establishment.

Waqf is the term used to denote Islamic endowments that have been around from the time of the Prophet Muhammad. Dr. Bazian points out that this form of religious endowment built on the existing forms of pre-Islamic endowments to form some of the first universities in the world, including Al-Qarawwiyin, established in 859 A.D., much before Oxford University and others, in Europe. While *Zakat* and *Sadaqa* are the two religiously ordered forms of charitable giving, and are considered obligatory on Muslims, *Waqf* is any form of individual endowment, that wealthy individuals set up for perpetual benefit of society (Singer, 2008). In this paper, I will discuss primarily how religiously inspired philanthropy among American Muslims towards two institutions of culture and higher education, respectively - Islamic Society of North America (ISNA) and Zaytuna College – has been and continues to be re-interpreted, in an era of modern philanthropic giving. Using the notion of a 'discursive tradition,' I place the study of Islamic philanthropy in the debates about the role of philanthropy in culture production, higher education.

I submit that by a close critical examination of the discourses of Islamic philanthropy (I.P.) during crisis situations, we can understand the phenomenon of how these two groups seek to legitimize their work, gain followers as well as gain greater philanthropic support. I hope to show that the discourses of philanthropy have become more 'inclusive' and 'liberal', over a period of time and are influenced as much by cultural dimensions and institutional constraints – governmental as well as societal- in American society, as they are by religious practices among American Muslims. These changes in the discourse of I.P. have occurred in the context of a 'crisis' mode, with the American Muslim community responding to challenges – both external and internal. Crisis can be understood as one of the 'techniques' that have been used to frame discourses of American Islamic Philanthropy. This discourse about 'Islam' and 'Philanthropy,' are not based on any permanence of the categories of Islam or philanthropy, but have involved a constant process of interpretation and re-interpretation by several groups of people. While each of the groups has sought to position their work as addressing the needs of contemporary society, they have relied on tropes of tradition and history to legitimize their claims.

With the growing realization that critical thinking is at the heart of social change and in particular, religious education is key to creating a citizenry that is actively engaged in promoting a just society, both Islamic Society of North America (ISNA) and Zaytuna College have positioned learning and higher education, as being part of the 'responsibility' of the Muslim community and argued for greater philanthropic support. Tropes of Islamic philanthropy, classical notions of learning and the like have been used, to continually re-interpret how Islamic philanthropy should be used, for educating the future citizens of America.

I will use a Foucaldian genealogical approach to 'problematize' the discourse of IP, in conjunction with a critical perspective advocated by James Gee (2011). I contend that my approach is genealogical in that I seek to examine how and under what conditions, did the American Muslim communities decided to create understandings of religious philanthropy in ways that they did.

The ever-changing discourses of philanthropy among the two organizations I study here have been influenced by mainstream philanthropy, race, ethics, international affairs, 'crisis' and community building efforts. Primarily, my interest is to look at how crisis situations have caused a shift or discontinuity in these discourses. Foucault's advice is to look for 'ruptures' or 'discontinuities' in discourses as points that yield interesting insights into the transformation of discourses. A similar trend is evident in the discourses of philanthropy and community building among the prominent Sunni Muslim group today – Islamic Society of North America (ISNA). Foucault further reminds us that discursive practices systematically 'can define the objects of which they speak.' (1972, p.49). This paper will examine how the American Muslim community incorporated tradition, as part of defining what charity and philanthropy mean, in contemporary America, especially; when it comes to education.

WHAT IS A 'TRADITION' AND 'DISCURSIVE TRADITION'?

While tradition and virtues are considered anti-thetical to the modern way of thinking and living, scholars such as Alasdair MacIntyre have argued otherwise. In *After Virtue* (1981), MacIntyre argues that we can understand the 'dominant moral culture of advanced modernity adequately from the standpoint external to that culture.' (p.ix). This important work in moral philosophy is an interesting starting point for the discussion on the role of ethics, tradition and virtue in contemporary America. His understanding of morality is based on the premise that our contemporary utterance and practices can be understood as a 'series of fragmented survivals from an older past and that the insoluble problems which they have generated for modern theorists will remain insoluble until this is well understood.' (p.111). This means that tradition does play into our contemporary understandings of what a 'just' or 'moral' society should look like.

Before we undertake an analysis of the discourse of philanthropy among American Muslims, it is imperative to understand what a 'discursive tradition.' is Talal Asad, a scholar who has worked in the Foucaldian tradition says: "An Islamic discursive tradition is simply a tradition of Muslim discourse that addresses itself to conceptions of the Islamic past and future, with reference to a particular Islamic practice in the present. Clearly, not everything that Muslims say and do belongs to an Islamic discursive tradition. Nor is an Islamic tradition in this sense necessarily imitative of what was done in the past."(1986, p.14). By this, Asad means that the anthropological understanding of Islam should move beyond the reified notions of 'Islam' of Orientalists and that of a 'dramatic narrative' of the ethnographers, such as Clifford Geertz. The reason that the idea of tradition is important is because Muslims throughout the world still harken back to traditions, both religious and cultural in terms of their practice of religion (Pew, 2011).

My analysis of the texts, discourses of these two large groups is based on the assumption of there being a constant evolution of discourses and practices of Islam and not an 'essentialist' understanding of Islam or Muslim societies. I seek to also understand the role of tradition and reason within these discourses, and whether reason plays a public role in mediating between these discourses, as this is central to the analysis of a changing discursive tradition.

This discursive positioning of I.P. is following the argument of Talal Asad, who has called for an anthropology of Islam that treats it as a 'discursive tradition', and not an unchanging analytical concept. Asad suggests that in their representation of "Islamic tradition," Orientalists and Anthropologists have ignored the role of reasoning and argument surrounding traditional practices, he argues. It is only recently that scholars have started examining the role of tradition and traditional leaders, *Ulama*, in the process of adjudicating the process of interpreting between competing discourses and using their reason in this process (Zaman, 2002). Asad points to the distinction made by Abdallah Laroui, who has differentiated 'tradition as structure' from 'tradition as ideology'. Asad further contends that the process of winning someone over to follow your traditional process involves reasoning and not just force, and it is a part of Islamic discursive tradition. He says "Power and resistance, are thus intrinsic to the development and exercise of any traditional practice." (p.8).This follows from the fact that different styles of reasoning have followed different historical eras and each has fought its own battles, to survive. The idea that traditions are essentially homogenous is a wrong idea, he points out.

This approach of treating Islam as a practice oriented religion is crucial for my argument, as it enables us to place philanthropy in the context of how American Muslims themselves have used philanthropy for various purposes – community building, preserving their religion and culture as well as building institutions of higher education, such as Zaytuna College. By tracing the changes of these discourses genealogically, we can understand how American Muslim organizations have understood the role of philanthropy as well as their own place in the American landscape. This is not to undermine the role of theology or interpretive practices. Orthodoxy is as relevant in this process as is Orthopraxy. In the case of Islam, one can argue that one informs the other, in a dialectical process. Following Foucault's suggestion of not relying on 'cultural totalities,' of world-view, or ideal types, I have sought to work through the problem before me, using practices of philanthropy and the discourses that form them, as my starting point (Foucault, 1969).

Ghaneabassiri has argued for understanding this development in his book *A History of Islam in America* (2010), where he contends that the descendants of African slaves- who were often Muslims- had preserved the early Islamic traditions, which their forebears had practiced, in a form that had amalgamated both Islamic and non-Muslim traditions. He gives the example of *Saraka* or rice cakes given by women in Georgia as one such example. The syncretic evolution of practices and at times, paradigmatic shift in understandings of philanthropy can unpack much for us. This facet of I.P. may offer us new perspectives of looking at Islam in America too (see Table 1).

METHODS AND SAMPLING STRATEGY

I am using Discourse Analysis as a method and Qualitative research methodology as my guiding framework. As Taylor and Bogdan suggest, this refers in the broadest sense to 'research that produces descriptive data – people's own written or spoken words and observable behavior.' (1998, p.7) This means focusing on how people attach meanings to things in their lives. As my research questions revolve around how forces in mainstream American society do impacting American Muslims' understand and practice of charity and philanthropy[2], this approach seems appropriate. As Denzin and Lincoln further suggest, "Qualitative research also involves a range of empirical materials – case study, personal experience, introspection, life story, interview, cultural texts, historical and visual texts." (2008, p.2).

Table 1. The transition from traditional to a more 'discursive' formation of traditional Islamic philanthropy

Traditional Discourses of Islamic Philanthropy	Discursive Traditions of Islamic Philanthropy
1. Zakat as a religious obligation, towards other Muslims 2. Charity for local individuals and family 3. Purely religious motifs and symbolism	1. Zakat as a 'choice' 2. Global humanitarianism 3. Non-religious and cultural positioning of zakat

In this paper, I compare the changing discourse of philanthropy towards culture/ educational institutions among two institutions: Zaytuna College and the 'Cultural pluralists' represented by Islamic Society of North America (ISNA), the largest membership based group of Muslims in North America.

DATA COLLECTION METHODS

I will use a variety of resources for the project that I undertake in this paper. I will use a variety of existing primary and secondary resources that will help me map the changing discourses of philanthropy in the organizations under study. Some of the sample documents that will be helpful include:

- Historical data including speeches etc
- Websites of organizations
- Dissertations or books about the organizations and key personalities
- Biographical information about key personalities that may be relevant to my research questions

FINDINGS AND DISCUSSION

Crises are key to understanding how philanthropic discourses in the American Muslim community transformed. I argue that with each of these crises offer us what Hermann et al (2001) have called Occasions for Decision (OFD), during which, the American Muslim community responded in different ways. I will trace the changing discourses of philanthropy among the leadership of Zaytuna College and ISNA – as two paradigmatic groups, to map the genealogy of the discourse.

I will briefly describe how each event organization frames 'crisis' and the need for philanthropic support towards itself. My attempt goes beyond a purely 'dramatic narrative' of events and actors, and looks at the analytical import of what occurred. This strategy is key, if we are to avoid 'essentializing' about groups or communities, as Asad has argued (Asad, 1986). This also implies that historical and other forces acting on the events are of equal import, besides the belief system of these groups. The political economy, history of internal discourses, power relations with the government and other social groups all become important, in this perspective.

I focus on the tropes of 'Islam in Crisis' that each of these organizations have invoked, in an effort to understand how they conceptualize the need for community mobilization and greater 'education,' among American Muslims. The existing geopolitical movements in the Middle East, with the rise of ISIS, lack of democracy in the

Middle East and growing Islamophobia in Europe and the U.S., could be considered moments of 'crisis', in the Muslim world, based on the definition of crisis offered by Boin et al., (Boin, 2010). Further, these two events represent a deep involvement of American Muslims in political activism in the U.S. as Ghaneabassiri (2010) has argued. He suggests that post the Iranian Revolution, American Muslims had started to get increasingly involved in the political life in America, hoping to influence the ethical framework of American political and social life. Siddiqui (2014) argues that this was a result of the choices placed before the community, at large – whether to be isolationists or to get actively involved in the public and political life of the U.S. Most American organizations chose the latter, he contends.

Ghaneabassiri suggests that many leaders such as Abdul Rauf saw Islam as offering an ethical tradition and an alternative to the capitalist model in place. Ghaneabassiri suggests that despite calls for unity during the 1950s and 1960s, there was no great urgency to 'unite' in America, as the disunity did not threaten their existence. But these events, as we will see, challenged this assumption.

THE FIVE DISCONTINUITIES IN AMERICAN MUSLIM PHILANTHROPY

The manner in which philanthropy has been understood and practiced among American Muslims has gone through various stages of evolution. These can be considered 'discontinuities,' that emerged during each time period. These rules of formation form the 'archive,' that Foucault referred to, in the Archaeology of Knowledge (1969). The archive in this sense means the 'discursive mechanism which limit what can be said, in what form and what is counted as worth knowing and remembering.' (Mills, p.57). In the case of American Muslim communities, various factors such as slavery, changes in immigration laws, community in-fighting between various groups for domination and gradual emergence of some sense of cohesion – in terms of identity – can be counted as being part of this 'archive.'

As Boin et al.argue in their book *Crisis Management* (2005), that the task of leaders during crisis situations boils down to the following five tasks "sense making, decision making, meaning making, terminating, and learning. Their definition of crisis incorporates a fundamental challenge to the norms, values of a system/ group of people, who have been impacted by this crisis. In the case of American Muslim communities, there has been a discourse of a 'crisis,' which leaders such as Sh. Hamza Yusuf and others have alluded to, and continue to build their arguments, on this basis. But looking at the environment in the U.S., which is characterized by freedom of religion, absolute freedom of conscience, one would not see a 'crisis.' Perhaps he is referring to the lackadaisical norms of religious learning and practice in the U.S., as constituting this 'crisis,' where religion is becoming more a 'cultural' artifact, rather than something that is a lived reality.

I have outlined five major periods of discontinuities in the table below. Each one corresponds roughly to five periods that are briefly explained here:

1. **Antebellum America:** This was an era, when Islam was 'lost' in America. Ghaneabassiri in his book A History of Islam in America (2010) argues that during this phase, the predominantly Muslim slaves who were brought from West Africa could not practice their religion and were either forced to practice it in secret or give it up, altogether; adopting the faith of their masters. However, he has shown that certain practices, in particular, charitable practices survived; in a very different form.

2. **Early 20th century:** This phase saw the emergence of groups of people and communities that sought to establish themselves in the U.S. and the 'sojourner,' mindset was dropped. As Ghaneabassiri (2010) has shown, this phase was crucial for the formation of Islamic Centers, community organizations etc.

3. **The 1960s era:** This phase saw the most powerful movements among American Muslims including Nation of Islam, establishment of the Muslim Students Association etc. these came about as a reaction to various movements and ideas present at that time, including the Civil Rights movement etc.

4. **2001:** This phase, starting in 2001 was largely shaped by an assimilationist attitude, with ISNA leading the way in promoting 'cultural pluralism.' This period, one can argue, was initiated by the deep anxieties felt by American Muslim communities, in the after-math of the September 11 attacks that put Muslims front and center of the American war on terror.

5. **2014:** The gradual evolution of cultural pluralism among American Muslim groups has made it 'mainstream' and the dominant mode of organizing social and political life. This has led to calls for 'strategic' philanthropy and participation in greater civic initiatives, among American Muslim communities. This can be seen, I argue, in the growing awareness among American Muslims for issues of global importance, collaborations across faith-lines and also increasing sensitivity and incorporation of 'development' discourse in their philanthropic efforts (see Table 2).

THREE FORMULATIONS OF PHILANTHROPIC TRADITION AMONG AMERICAN MUSLIMS

It appears that tradition has been used in practice, by American Muslim groups in many different formulations. While the *Ulema* or religious leaders, following their

Table 2. Change in Dominant discourses of philanthropy among American Muslims

Antebellum America (17th and 18th century)	Early 20th century	1960s and 1990s	2001	2014
• Subaltern philanthropy	• Co-optation of dominant discourse • Subaltern philanthropy	• Establishment discourse • Anti-establishment Muslims • Cultural	• Cultural pluralism	• 'Strategic' philanthropy • Continuing Cultural Pluralism

respective legal traditions have sought to ground Islamic practices in the U.S. in their own way, the leaders of social movements, NGOs and those described above have tradition, that has been interpretive. Asifa Quraishi, a legal expert and professor at University of Wisconsin, Madison has argued that Islamic law in the U.S. has evolved in a manner, similar to that of U.S. Constitutional Law (Quraishi, 2007).

Similarly, Alasdair MacIntyre argues that tradition is always part of any 'system' of though, even if it is liberalism, which focuses its attention on critiquing tradition. MacIntyre argues in *After Virtue* that: "We are apt to be misled here by the ideological uses to which the concept of a tradition has been put by conservative political theorists. Characteristically such theorists have followed Burke in contrasting tradition with reason and the stability of tradition with conflict. Both contrasts obfuscate." (1981, P.221). He goes on to point out that all new thinking occurs in a 'tradition,' whether it is physics or medieval logic. His formulation of tradition challenges conventional understanding of the term, which is meant to be unchanging or timeless. There is very little that it timeless or eternal, MacIntyre would argue, following his logic.

Further, as MacIntyre argues, there needs to be an awareness of whether a tradition is 'alive' or 'dead' and this distinction makes all the difference. To quote him "Traditions, when vital, embody continuities of conflict. Indeed when a tradition becomes Burkean, it is always dying or dead." (p.221). By a 'Burkean' tradition, he means the formulation of a tradition which is considered unchanging or not open to critique. I contend that Islamic tradition is very much alive and thriving, with its internal tensions, arguments and often public spats –with other variations of traditions within the broad umbrella of what we know as 'Islam.'

Here are three key ways in which I argue tradition is being re-interpreted among American Muslim groups, in the realm of philanthropy. This analysis is based on an inductive reasoning of the way that both Zaytuna college establishes its discourse as well as ISNA's evolution, as an organization. Each one points to a permutation of what it means to be 'Islamically' philanthropic:

1. **Islamic philanthropy as a 'negotiated reality':** Sarah Mills points out in her book Discourse (1997) that groups of individuals can negotiate their position in society and garner power through one's 'interactional power, ' i.e., how one can negotiate one's position through the use of linguistic power and this may well be in conflict with one's ascribed status within a group (p.84). As in the case of ISNA and Zaytuna College, groups, one can see this negotiation going on. While ISNA was, in its formative years, opposed to aligning with the government policies – both domestic and foreign- it has, over the years, evolved into an organization that stands to garner greater legitimacy and philanthropic support, through aligning with the US government policies and positions, on many issues.

This is part of the 'negotiated reality,' and can be seen as emerging out of the organization's 'interactional power.'

2. **Tradition helping define what is 'Islamic':** What about current day Islamic philanthropic practices is 'Islamic?' As the ongoing debate about the 'Islamicness' of Daesh (ISIS) suggests, this is not a settled question. While a vast majority of scholars around the world have come out and denounced ISIS as nothing but an aberration and a political outcome of failed states (Iraq and Syria)[3]. One of the first points made in the letter issued by the Muslim scholars is "It is forbidden in Islam to issue fatwas without all the necessary learning requirements. Even then fatwas must follow Islamic legal theory as defined in the Classical texts," this harks back to the value of 'Islamic tradition,' in terms of defining what is 'Islamic.' On the other hand, a public intellectual and scholar such as Reza Aslan has argued that Daesh are indeed 'Islamic,' agreeing with the assessment of several journalists and writers such as Bob Woodard, whose Atlantic article went viral and sparked much debate[4]. 'A Muslim is anyone who claims he is one,' is Aslan's argument and this is also part of the Muslim tradition, as there is no orthodoxy, like the Catholic church to determine what is indeed 'Islamic,' or not. This goes against Talal Asad's formulation of a *discursive tradition*, since he suggests that 'not everything that Muslims say or do it Islamic.' How then one to determine what is is 'Islamic'?

Is charity towards Red Cross by a Muslim 'Islamic' charity, in that it fulfils the obligation of religious charity, or it is something else? What about giving money to a research initiative that is focused on Cancer Research? I contend that there are no ready-made answers to these questions. However, I would point to Islamic traditions of *ijma* or consensus and related ideas that suggest that if a group of people agree on an idea, then the decision is valid, from a normative and legal perspective. Keeping this in mind, we can argue that an action that is deemed 'Islamic' can be considered 'Islamic' if a group of people or scholars think it is so. If they agree that forms of charitable giving to an NGO counts as legitimate 'zakat,' then it becomes so.

3. **Re-interpretation of virtue ethics and challenge to the individualistic notions of morality:** One of the fundamental ways that Islamic ethics in general and philanthropic practices in particular have played out in American history have been in the realm of the conception of ethics. As MacIntyre has argued, enlightenment ideals posited a very individualistic morality for society, a notion that has informed 'liberal' traditions in the U.S. (MacIntyre, 1981). While religious morality in the U.S. has been based on communitarian and societal norms, one can argue that the individualistic morality has been ascendant and has been one of the fundamental bedrocks of the 'American way of life,' as scholars such as Robert Bellah have argued. Islamic ideals of virtue, community and solidarity, as seen through the efforts to 'reform' society or contribute to the social and communal life have been predicated in efforts to reinterpret Islamic norms in the American context.

MacIntyre's notion that morality and virtues should be located and made sense of in the community from where they originate and not in the individuals' lives is particularly helpful in the case of American Muslims.

ZAYTUNA COLLEGE'S POSITIONING OF 'CRISIS OF LEARNING' AMONG MUSLIMS

Zaytuna's founder, Sheikh Hamza Yusuf has repeatedly called on addressing the 'crisis of authority' among Muslims around the world. In particular, his insistence on addressing the knowledge gap that exists among American Muslims, who are not familiar with the basics of Islam is a motif that has led to the establishment of the institution of higher learning. As its mission is: "to educate and prepare morally committed professional, intellectual and spiritual leaders who are grounded in Islamic tradition and conversant with the cultural currents and critical ideas shaping modern society." This institution, which will offer Bachelors and higher levels of education is being positioned as the next big move, to address the 'crisis of learning' among American Muslims. The first class of graduates came out with flying colors and the accreditation that the school received is testament to the need for such institutions of higher learning, pointed out Sh. Yusuf.

Sh. Yusuf has talked about the post 9/11 crisis of identity among American Muslims as also being acute[5]. Several scholars have written thoughtfully about the attacks of September 11, 2001 and its impact on American Muslims (Ghanea-bassiri, 2010; Esposito, 2011; Safi, 2005; Ernst, 2008). While there is widespread agreement that this act, in effect brought about a great amount of Islamophobia and greater misrepresentation about Islam in the public sphere, it is not often seen as the event that also altered how Islamic philanthropy is perceived in the U.S. Post 9./11, the PATRIOT ACT was passed, which gave sweeping powers to various agencies of the U.S. to crack down on any activities that were deemed harmful to the American national interests. This included clamping down on organizations that provided 'material support' to terrorist groups or individuals, anywhere in the world. This led, these scholars suggest, to not only a curtailment of civil liberties, but also clamping down on several Muslim NGOs that functioned for several years, carrying out work both domestically and internationally (Harb & Haddad, 2014; Singer, 2008; Alterman, 2008).

While the attacks of 911 brought on a renewed interest in studying radical Islam and the dangers it posed to America, it did not 'change everything' for American Muslims, argues scholar of American Islam, Edward Curtis IV. He says "For much of the twentieth century, it was not Muslim immigrants, but rather indigenous African American Muslims who were, from the point of view of federal authorities, the public and potentially dangerous face of American Islam. The parallels between earlier and later periods of state surveillance are striking. We seem to be living in a new age of consensus in which, like the late 1940s and 1950s, a vital center has identified Islamic radicalism, and by extension Muslim American dissent, as an existential problem, a dangerous expression of extremism." Curtis is arguing for looking back at American history, particularly with the growth of the NOI and other nationalist movements that were clearly seen as a threat to American sovereignty. The incidents of 911 further compounded the discourse of 'Good Muslim, bad Muslim' say Haddad and Harb. This notion, borrowed from the famous book 'Good Muslim, Bad Muslim' by Mahmood Mamdani, argues that the 'moderate Muslims' are to be cultivated while 'extremists' are to be treated with suspicion and are a clear threat to the US and much of the Western world. What has shifted, according to Curtis is the perception of fear. In the 1940s and 1950s it was the Black Muslims who were the object of fear and surveillance and now it is the Brown Muslim, he contends. There is also a conflation of various discourses of national security, religion, secularism and Islamic norms of philanthropy, when one speaks of the tragic events of 911.

As a solution to the identity crisis that many Muslim societies are facing and also the 'crisis of knowledge,' Sh. Yusuf says "We have many economic problems and also political ones, including the ones in Ukraine. In the past, these conflicts have led to major conflagrations, such as the World Wars." He suggests that these were failures of leaders at that time in solving problems at a deeper level and our inability to 'define our terms clearly,' and as a result, we look at them superficially.

Yusuf's example of the Great Recession, as a problem of knowledge – in bailing out banks versus addressing the deep epistemic causes of this problem – to demonstrate that we do have real problems before us. "We need to understand systems at the philosophical base, there is a philosophy behind consumerism and capitalism, that needs to be addressed," he suggests.

Further, building on his tropes of a better and more philosophically sound knowledge system, he goes on to say: "Knowledge has been defined by a materialistic system that does not acknowledge other forms of knowledge. In our tradition, our epistemology is different from that of the dominant model. If we don't understand the epistemological differences, then we become victims of world-views that do not share the first principles. If we don't know what the epistemology and understand how we know 'truth,' then it is replaced by a different types of ignorance." His call, throughout, seems to be on the need to address the 'crisis' of ignorance and false knowledge that seeks war, consumerism and aggression; where there is an absolute need for peace, justice and equality.

Zaytuna's mission is to create a new discourse of the role of education in American society. It seeks to go beyond just seeking to create knowledge for the sake of creating jobs, but rather sees its agenda as 'reforming society,' as is evident from this quote "Education is a prerequisite for forging a healthy and ethical society which does not mean reproducing a distorted elitist notion, but grounding knowledge and education in a Prophetic tradition rooted in serving humanity as the door to serving the Creator. When education becomes solely about a job, a cubicle and a bottom line dollar amount, then all of us are diminished for the value of the human is measured by the material and not the spiritual or metaphysical." (Bazian, 2015, p.1). How does this education address specifically the challenges of economy and justice in a global order that is dominated by Neoliberal policies and inequalities is not completely addressed, but one can see that since they are claiming to base the organization's philosophy on Islamic ethical values, there would perhaps be an attempt to address this crucial aspect, as well.

While American Muslims were reeling from the shock of the attacks of 911 and trying to make sense of what had just occurred, this shift in the establishment discourse towards Islam did help, at least momentarily. But as we see, immediately following the passage of the PATRIOT Act and Executive Order 13224 and anti-terrorist funding guidelines from the Treasury Department, there was a strong reaction towards Muslim philanthropic sector. Zahra Jamal, in her policy report titled *Ten Years after 911* for the Washington D.C. think tank ISPU suggests that there was up to a 50 percent drop in donations to Muslim humanitarian relief organizations post 911 (Jamal, 2011). The discourse about I.P. at this time became couched in the 'war on terror' and was primarily influenced by a 'securitization discourse.' American Muslim organizations sought to distance themselves from those entities and militant ideologies that had brought about these violent acts, but the aftereffects of this violent act lingers, as the Treasury Department has come up with new guidelines for those wanting to support organizations and individuals in 'troubled spots', from an ethical or humanitarian perspective. Yusuf seems to be alluding to all of the above factors, when he speaks of the Muslim world being in a 'state of crisis,' and not being able to find its place in any society. His construction of Islam being in crisis is important, as he enjoys a wide following, around the U.S. and even globally.

ISLAMIC SOCIETY OF NORTH AMERICA'S TURN FROM PAROCHIALISM TO 'CULTURAL PLURALISM'

ISNA is the largest Muslim membership based organization in the U.S. that also enjoys wide legitimacy both within the community, as well as from the U.S. Government. As the de-facto representative of the Muslim community, the organization has carved a niche as the leading organization for creating an 'American Muslim' identity as well as educational programs – including inter-faith and related programs, contributing to its educational mission.

While ISNA and its member organizations sought to control the damage done to the image of Islam and Muslims in general, with the attacks of September 11, 2001; they also released certain fatwas (religious rulings). One such example drew parallels between the Qur'anic injunctions about the sanctity of life and how the terrorists who attacked the twin towers had violated it. This fatwa also reminded Muslims that any attack on a civilian can be considered unlawful and should not receive any support from righteous Muslims. This fatwas was signed by many prominent leaders who were part of ISNA. More than 145 Muslim organizations endorsed this fatwa.

On the other hand, the government of the U.S. sought to limit the damage to U.S. national security, through the passage of the PATRIOT ACT, many scholars and thinkers have pointed out that this had serious effects on how philanthropy towards Muslim institutions was perceived (Jamal, 2009). Shariq Siddiqui argues in his dissertation that President Obama's opening statement during his inaugural address on January 20, 2009 that the U.S. today is "nation of Christians and Muslims, Hindus and Jews" with the president of Islamic Society of North America (ISNA) Ingrid Mattson present as a significant landmark in the American Muslim community's history. Shariq contends that ISNA has had to embrace a broad identity, of being 'cultural pluralists,' as it had to gain legitimacy within the American Muslim community, which is incredibly diverse. "Because of the incredible diversity within the Muslim American community, ISNA needed to embrace a broad identity for internal legitimacy. This internal legitimacy was vital in order to counter the Islamophobia that impeded external legitimacy," he adds (p.4). This move towards embracing cultural pluralism could be seen as both a pragmatic move, as well as an effort to consciously reinterpret notions of diversity within Islam, which seek to honor diversity of opinion.

One can also see how the moves by ISNA leaders to try to win their intellectual freedom during crisis points such as the First Gulf War and subsequent incidents helped win a strong base of support. This positioning of the organization is key for understanding how ISNA navigated differences. ISNA used a combination of both religious as well as practical, organizational discourses to justify its stand, in this instance. The original positioning of ISNA in the 1950s and 60s was of an organization that was ambiguous about the concept of an 'American Muslim' identity. One can argue that it possibly did not exist, as many of the students and young professionals who were part of the Muslim Student Association (MSA) – the precursor to ISNA- were of immigrant origin and imagined going back to their home countries after their education in the U.S. was complete. Many did, however, those who stayed back and found jobs in the U.S. did not imagine living here successfully. It took several decades for an 'American Muslim consciousness' to emerge among this group and ISNA was among the first to make a progressive shift towards integration, if not assimilation into the American social fabric.

Following the successful annual convention in 1997, when more than twenty one thousand American Muslims showed up, Siddiqui says: "The fact that the organization did not represent all of the Muslim American community, particularly a large number of African-American Muslims, did not deter the leaders of ISNA to declare success." (p.135). This has been possible because of the moral and practical legitimacy that ISNA enjoys, argues Siddiqui.

CONCLUSION

I have attempted, in this short paper, to show that Islamic Philanthropy is being interpreted as a 'discursive tradition' in the U.S. by leaders of Muslim organizations, who are thus providing new interpretive models, while working in various traditional systems, that have been codified and set as benchmarks by classical Islamic scholars. These models offer new ways of making sense of zakat and sadaqa, which go beyond the traditional ways of understanding these practices and offer avenues such as humanitarian aid, community development – for the practice of zakat and sadaqa. Discourses of giving around specific crisis events, I have argued, give us clues about how this process occurs. While ISNA has veered towards 'cultural pluralism,' Zaytuna seemed to have found a more solid base in its religious roots, of basing its epistemology on classical Islamic scholarship and learning.

The central mediating factor seems to be 'reason' and the re-interpretation of religious tradition. While traditionally, there has been a tension in how much to interpret and how much to follow 'as is', the norms of I.P., there has been a constant refrain of accommodation, interpretive practices in normative Islam. While practicing Muslims follow traditional norms in giving, there seems to be a growing awareness and acceptance of the use of reasoning and a pragmatic awareness of the need for reimagining the norms of zakat in America. While not exhaustive, the discussion in this paper has touched upon some salient points that can be developed further.

I have also argued that the framing of I.P. among Muslims in America by Muslim leaders has been carried out in a pragmatic, yet 'traditional' manner, thus making sure that while traditional practices are respected, there is an awareness of the need for 'innovation' in this sector. While the organizational discourses from the Muslim NGOs have clashed or not resonated with other institutional or governmental discourses, there has often been a recourse to accommodation, innovation in methodologies or at times, radical re-thinking of the ethical norms in Islam, that would justify a certain course of action. The discourse of social justice has been a recurring one in Islamic philanthropy and one that both the groups under examination – ISNA and the Black Muslims have adopted, in varying degrees to justify their work and gain legitimacy.

By using the discourses of community development, Muslim cosmopolitanism and ethnic ties, both organizations and leaders have gained legitimacy among the grassroots American Muslim communities and channeled religious giving towards causes such as education, community development etc. As Haddad and Harb argue, "American Muslims are increasingly choosing to integrate into American society through participation in and production of American culture in both civil engagement and in new, innovative ways such as political involvement, scholarship and interfaith engagement." (2014, p. 478). While there are a tiny minority of Muslims, who are very rigid in their interpretation of how they view their theology, most major American Muslim organizations – both religious and nonreligious- are open to collaborating, incorporating and working with those with whom they do not necessarily share the same theological/ epistemic lens, when it comes to religious issues. As Siddiqui argues "Due to their incredible diversity, Muslim Americans are largely cultural pluralists. They draw from each other and our national culture to develop their religious identity and values. Religious identity does remain constant or uniform. Instead it is shaped by the interactions between the diverse groups that comprise Muslim America." (p.215). This interaction, that Siddiqui points to, is key to the development of the American Muslim identity, which is taking shape, slowly. In the competing and at times conflicting discourses of how Islam should be practiced, American Muslim organizations are not only contributing to the debate of the role of religion in America, but also defining their own place in the

American social fabric. This debate may further our understanding of how religion, religious authority and the power to shape discourses in the public sphere occurs in contemporary America.

While the American government's efforts at regulating and managing the fall out of the militant NOI were seen as a necessity by many, the current surveillance of Muslims by NYPD and other measures to curb the civil liberties of Muslim non-profit groups are seen as violating the basic rights of American Muslims (Harb & Haddad, 2014). One can see in these measures, a conflation of various discourses with that of philanthropy. These include discourses of: National security, identity, poverty and International Affairs.

It is interesting to note that the two organizations under examination in this article – Zaytuna College and ISNA responded very differently to similar situations and their internal dynamics of power were also quite distinct. Pragmatism seems to be the guiding force for most American groups in terms of reconciling their beliefs with the realities that face them. While this does not imply that they are compromising on their traditional beliefs, one must recall that Islamic norms allow for a vast range of interpretive strategies for these groups to find their path in a complex and inter-connected world. This fact has allowed for a healthy 'discursive tradition' in the field of Islamic Philanthropy to exist. The organizations in question are doing well and their missions remain relevant. All the while, their educational agenda – of being sources of learning, knowledge and organization, to be the mediators for creating an 'authentic American Islam' – have remained central to their missions.

REFERENCES

Asad, T. (1986). *The Idea of an Anthropology of Islam*. Washington, DC: Center for Contemporary Arab Studies.

Benthall, B. (2003). *The Charitable Crescent, The Politics of Aid in the Muslim World*. London: I.B. Tauris.

Benthall, B. (2008). *Returning to Religion*. London: IB Tauris.

Boin, . (2005). *Public Leadership Under Pressure*. Cambridge, MA: Cambridge University Press. doi:10.1017/CBO9780511490880

Esposito, J., & Kalin, I. (2011). *Islamophobia: The Challenges of Pluralism in the 21st Century*. New York: Oxford University Press.

Frumkin, P. (2006). *Strategic Giving: The Art and Science of Philanthropy*. Chicago: University of Chicago Press. doi:10.7208/chicago/9780226266282.001.0001

Gee, J. P. (2011). *How to do Discourse Analysis*. New York: Routledge Press.

GhaneaBassiri, K. (2010). A history of Islam in America: from the new world to the new world order. Cambridge, MA: Cambridge University Press.

Giving, U. S. A. (2013). *Annual Report on Philanthropy*. Indianapolis, IN: Lilly School of Philanthropy.

Haddad & Harb. (2014). *Making Islam an American Religion*. Religions Journal.

Hermann, M., Hermann, C., & Hagan, J. (. (2001). How Decision Units influence Foreign Policy Decisions. *International Studies Review*. doi:10.1111/1521-9488.00234

Jamal, Z. (2011). *Ten Years After 911*. Washington, DC: ISPU.

Jon, B. A., & Von Hippel, K. (2007). *Understanding Islamic Charities*. Washington, DC: CSIS Press.

Leaman, O. (1985). *An introduction to Classical Islamic Philosophy*. Cambridge, MA: Cambridge University Press.

MacIntyre, A. (1977). Epistemological Crises, Dramatic Narrative and the Philosophy of Science. *The Monist*, *60*(4), 453–472. doi:10.5840/monist197760427

Moody, M., & Payton, R. (2008). *Understanding Philanthropy: Meaning and Mission*. Indianapolis, IN: Indiana University Press.

Safi, O. (2003). *Progressive Muslims: On Justice, Gender and Pluralism*. One World Press.

Siddiqui, S. (2014). *Navigating Identity through Philanthropy: A History of ISNA*. Diss.

Sievers, B. (2011). Civil Society, Philanthropy and the Fate of the Commons. Boston: Tufts University Press.

Singer, A. (2008). Charity in Islamic Societies. Cambridge, MA: Cambridge University Press.

Wuthnow, R. (2004). *Saving America? Faith based services and the future of Civil Society*. Princeton, NJ: Princeton University Press.

Zaman, M. (2002). *The Ulama in Contemporary Islam*. Princeton, NJ: Princeton University Press.

ENDNOTES

1   Bazian, H. (2014, March 2012). An Islamic model for Sustainable Development. Retrieved from You Tube https://www.youtube.com/watch?v=FYd7tq5PEjk

2   I will use the word 'philanthropy' to refer to charity and philanthropy in Islam (zakat), henceforth. While charity refers to short-term emotion driven giving, philanthropy is considered more 'strategic' and 'scientific' in approach to solving social problems.

3   Markowe, L. (2014, Sept 24). Muslim Scholars Release Open Letter To Islamic State Meticulously Blasting Its ideology. Huffington post. Retrieved from http://www.huffingtonpost.com/2014/09/24/muslim-scholars-islamic-state_n_5878038.html

4   Kaufmann, S. (2015, April 4). Reza Aslan perfectly explains what Islamophobes are getting wrong about ISIS. Salon. Retrieved from http://www.salon.com/2015/04/06/reza_aslan_isis_is_technically_islamic_but_thats_still_no_excuse_for_islamophobia/

5   Yusuf, H. (2014, Sept 5) The Crisis of Knowledge. Retrieved from You Tube. https://www.youtube.com/watch?v=NIc-4CdIF9U

Section 3
Higher Education Fundraising and Philanthropic Support in Action

Chapter 9

Effective Approaches in Higher Education Development:
A Survey in Fundraising Best Practices

Andrew Aaron Shafer
Aquinas College, USA & North Park University, USA

ABSTRACT

Effective approaches in higher education development will look at a variety of topics ranging from corporate and foundation relations, to alumni participation, the importance of online giving, campaigns, top advancement trends in higher education, and the ever-critical cultivation of major and mega gifts. The education of a constituency about the importance of private gifts to both public and private institutions cannot be overstated as well given that tuition costs soar yet prospective students, parents, and boards continue to fight for the value proposition. After reading, reviewing, and studying this chapter, faculty, students, and professionals alike will have surveyed knowledge of effective approach in higher education development and will have a greater appreciation for the work that development staff encounter every day. The objective of this book "to explore contemporary and future philanthropy approaches and development theory in international higher education," will certainly be enhanced exponentially by the thorough and useful information presented.

DOI: 10.4018/978-1-4666-9664-8.ch009

Every year new advancement strategies and tactics are presented in books, papers, online, and at conferences around the world. Fundraise this way, engage alumni that way, marketing your mission with this twist. The reality? Advancement, and more specifically, development/fundraising at its core has not changed in hundreds of years.

This chapter will look at a variety of topics ranging from corporate and foundation relations, to alumni participation, the importance of online giving, campaigns, top advancement trends in higher education, and the ever-critical cultivation of major and mega gifts. The education of a constituency about the importance of private gifts to both public and private institutions cannot be overstated given that tuition costs soar yet prospective students, parents, and boards continue to fight for the value proposition. After reviewing, faculty, students, and professionals alike will have surveyed knowledge of effective approaches in higher education development and will have a greater appreciation for the work that development staff encounter every day.

CAPITAL VS. COMPREHENSIVE CAMPAIGNS IN MODERN FUNDRAISING

"Capital Campaign" vs. "Comprehensive Campaign". In the early days of fundraising campaigns, during the middle of the 20th century, most campaigns just focused on capital needs specific to facilities. Of course, other campaigns focused on endowment needs, scholarship, programs, or other special priorities. During the past 15 to 20 years, the approach to campaigning has expanded, and now most campaigns are comprehensive campaigns that include facilities, endowment, scholarship (in the case of higher education), programmatic, and operating support. Mega-campaigns in health care and higher education are frequently setting goals of a billion dollars or more. These mega-campaigns are almost always comprehensive campaigns that include all gifts to all areas of the organization given during the campaign period.

Comprehensive campaigns frequently raise question about how to "count" gifts but the reality is that comprehensive campaign production and results include any and every dollar raised in the organization. This can include but is not limited to cash, securities, gifts-in-kind, and estate gifts (planned giving). Major gifts, annual gifts, monthly gifts, lifetime gifts; regardless of the frequency, duration, or size of a gift it is a common misconception that one "counts" more in a comprehensive campaign than another.

The Council for the Advancement and Support of Education (CASE) publishes counting standards and below are their recommendations. These should always be referenced through CASE prior to and during any campaign as they do change periodically ('Preliminary Report of the Campaign Standards Working Group', n.d.).

CASE Recommendations

The working group makes the following recommendations specific to campaign counting and reporting (see attachment for proposed language recommendations and a comparison with current language in the third edition of the CASE Management and Reporting Standards):

- Revocable gifts may be included in campaign totals at face value if they are pledged during the campaign, documented, and as long as they are reported separately from outright gifts and irrevocable deferred gifts.
- Irrevocable deferred gifts may be included in campaign totals at face value, but both face and discounted present values should be reported.
- Conditional pledges may be included in campaign totals if there is a reasonable expectation that the conditions under which the pledge is made will be met during the campaign period and if there is appropriate documentation.
- Campaigns should be tied to the strategic goals of the institution, and for this reason the length of a campaign may vary. However, in order to maximize the commitment of volunteers, donors, staff and others, CASE recommends that a comprehensive campaign period generally not exceed eight years.
- Government funds are very important to helping institutions achieve their strategic goals, they are often secured competitively and help leverage private funds, and fundraising staffs often are integral to securing government support. However, CASE reaffirms its position that comprehensive campaigns are fundamentally philanthropic ventures designed to raise resources from the private sector. Therefore securing government funds does not fall under the definition of philanthropy as a private act. For this reason, government funds should not be included in campaign totals, but institutions should work to raise visibility and recognition for the value of government funding in accomplishing institutional goals.
- CASE should include a disclaimer to the revised campaign guidelines recognizing that within increasingly complex gift agreements, there will be situations not expressly covered in these guidelines and standards.

Although annual gifts are likely smaller in size than what many donors would consider a "lifetime gift," their frequency can at times before even more valuable than more zeroes at the end. When an annual giving solicitation is made for an organization that is currently operating within the parameters of a comprehensive campaign, the materials should be branded and consistent in look and feel with your campaign branding. The tendency here is to create something completely unique to signify that "this is our annual giving direct mail campaign – send us everything that is in your pockets, couch cushions, and car crevasses." The new challenge is to shift the thinking to be more about developing the "pipeline."

A comprehensive campaign is truly meant to be a catalyst for fundraising within any organization. Very likely, if a church group needs a new sanctuary, they will fundraise for a sanctuary and only for a sanctuary. The sanctuary will be built, the church services will continue, but needs within the organization will still be lacking. This is the value of a comprehensive campaign. Not only should the church fundraise for that new sanctuary, but it should also fundraise for ongoing needs.

The annual giving "pipeline" is critical to long term success. Without it, your major gift prospect portfolio will be weak at best; nonexistent at worse. Annual giving mailing, therefore, must speak to the necessary task of thinking about direct mail campaigns, phone-a-thons, and annual fundraising events through a whole new light. There should be a seamless transition between a prospective donor visit in Fargo on Tuesday, and a fundraising gala in Nashville on Saturday. Messaging, graphics, and branding should all be part of your story. By focusing on a more purpose driven annual gift campaign, you can start to see a significant difference in the way that your donor consider support for the organization.

Alumni participation rates are an ongoing barometer for an institution's ability to reach out to its largest and broadest affinity group, its alumni. Although it is a small factor in most ratings and rankings, that rate does tell a story. In other words, alumni participation rates are important, they are a number, but they should not be the driving factor for any campaign.

There is no single way to run a campaign. Every campaign is different and truly depends on the needs or organization. It is not uncommon to even see two campaigns in the same organization vary greatly and both be successful. The best campaigns are those that are based on a sophisticated and thoroughly developed strategic plan that outlines the funding priorities most critical at that time. We call this plan the *Comprehensive Advancement Strategic Plan* or the CASP. The CASP is any institution's ticket to fundraising freedom. The document is a working document, not one that you begrudgingly create and then shelve the next week. No, the CASP should be printed, copied, published (internally), and shared broadly within the organization. For your key volunteers you could also share the document with them to the extent that they understand the confidential nature of its content.

Complete Advancement Strategic Plan, Sample Table of Contents

1. Introduction & Mission
2. The Advancement Team
3. Goals
4. Fundraising
    a. Annual Giving
    b. Gift Societies
    c. Planned Giving
    d. Corporate & Foundation Relations
    e. International Advancement
5. Alumni Relations & Special Events
6. School and Program Efforts
7. Communications
8. Where we are. Where we need to be. How we get there.
9. Appendix A - Donor Commitment Continuum
10. Appendix B - Plan for Development with Deans & Academic Leaders
11. Appendix C - Daily Gift Processing Procedures
12. Appendix D - Advancement Strategic Plan in Previous Year
13. Appendix E - Projections for Fundraising in Current Year

The Design School at Stanford University ("d school," 2014) focuses on the concept of "design innovation." This way of working, thinking, and progressing in any industry or initiative is becoming commonplace. Design innovation simply correlates with creativity and a progressive attitude that encourages anyone to think beyond institutional history or tradition. Comprehensive campaigns are no different. Any comprehensive campaign, performed at the highest levels, should allow for design innovation to be at its forefront. This concept can relate to the internal planning phases but more importantly should be seen in the conversations with donors that every development office hopes results in mega-gifts. Any development officer or academic leader must be creative when working with constituents who are each successful in their own right and who certainly fully express their own passions as the focus of their philanthropy.

TOP ADVANCEMENT TRENDS IN 2015

In 2015, there are several trends to look for within your own organization but also within those organizations that you may serve in volunteer leadership roles, on boards, committees, or as an advisor. A few trends that will likely continue and commence include a greater emphasis on crowdfunding initiatives, enhanced corporate reorganization for philanthropy, tighter foundation restrictions and regulations, and further prioritization of pipeline development and retention through alumni participation in higher education.

CORPORATE REORGANIZATION FOR PHILANTHROPY

As corporations continue to recalibrate after the great recession, they also work to determine how best to support the world's philanthropic landscape. Most corporations want to support all types of 501(c)3 organizations for the inherent goodness that is given. However, many corporations are also interested in the tax benefits of philanthropic support as well as the recognition that frequently follows a significant gift. The more that organizations can ensure that a corporation's investment is publicly recognized (only if the corporation actually wants the public "thanks," of course), the better off the organization will be long term. This is where the cycle of donor development comes alive. Stewardship for corporations is truly a blurred line between a simple thank you and cultivation of that next gift. The upcoming decade will likely see continued reorganization in corporate philanthropy during the first half of the period followed by "settling in" that will lead to more clear-cut specifications for gift proposals.

There are many different ways which corporations may support higher education. Frequently, these organizations give through a foundation structure. These types of foundations could be endowed foundations, corporate foundations, a partnership foundation, or even a scientific foundation (Cagney and Ross, 2013).

Endowed foundations may be created by an individual or a company. Corporate foundations enjoy a flow of funding from the company to which it is linked. The lifespan of a corporate foundation is often linked to the parent company. A partnership foundation may be created by any public body and could possibly be a mix of private company funding, university funding, and even other public funding.

Corporate reorganization for philanthropic support is critical and does exhibit a huge for potential funding opportunities in organizations of all types. The internal structure of an organization's philanthropy, however, is still a corporation's leadership decision.

DONOR PIPELINE DEVELOPMENT AND RETENTION

Securing new donations and gifts is hard enough; keeping those donors engaged and giving again is even more difficult. Another trend seems to be a stronger focus on donor pipeline development and retention. Think about this, if on any given year, your organization has 500 regular donors who you can rely on making a gift, without a doubt. In addition to those 500, you have 500 new donors, but you then have attrition of 50%. At the start of the next year, you would not have gained any donors! Roger M. Craver in his new book, *Retention Fundraising; The New Arts and Science of Keeping Your Donors for Life,* has a great chapter titled "Losing Donors Through the Leaky Bucket" (Craver, 2015). Craver argues that there are three things that can happen while a donor is in your bucket, and two things that need to happen to keep the leaks to a minimum. The three things that may happen while a donor is active with your organization are that they will stay and become loyal supporters, they will leave because of a lifestyle change (move, illness, retirement, etc.), or they will switch their giving to another comparable organization (Craver, 2015). Quality and purpose driven marketing as well as the quality of experiences the donor receives immediately after the gift is made will drive what is next for that donor's relationship to your organization (Craver, 2015).

Developing a strategic retention plan for your institution and your development shop should be top of mind and an area of focus. Retention and stewardship certainly go hand in hand and as the four areas of the donor lifecycle (Engagement, Cultivation, Solicitation, Stewardship) take shape in a personalized way for you, retention will likely see a natural fit in your regular day to day business plan.

EMPHASIS ON CROWDFUNDING INITIATIVES

In 2013 alone, over $5.1B was raised through nonprofit crowdfunding programs. It is no wonder that this significant number has grown in 2014 thanks to the ongoing barometer for giving that is the internet and social media. Of the $335.17B given philanthropically in 2013, $5.1B only accounts for 1.5% of that giving yet online giving in that same period rose 13.5%. The numbers are according to both the *Blackbaud Index* and *Giving USA* data. For those that are not infatuated with facts and figures, the simple fact of the matter is that crowdfunding can be done by anyone, inexpensively, and with generally great success if marketed correctly. Go ahead, give it a shot in 2015; here are some suggestions on how you can make it happen.

Dating back to the 1700s, the roots of crowdfunding can be found among cultures and countries from across the globe. The thought of having a critical mass of people pool funds together for one common cause is quite simply logical and results in a much more expeditious turnaround for projects than other types of financing. It was not until 1997 that modern day crowdfunding really became a reality. A British rock band sought online gifts from their fans to support their reunion tour and soon-thereafter, *ArtistShare* became the first known crowdfunding platform available online ('The History of Crowdfunding', n.d.).

Joseph Hogue in his 2015 book, *Step-By-Step Crowdfunding*, suggests that there are "Six Habits of Highly Successful Crowdfunding." These six habits are broad based but applicable to any organization of any scope and size. The six habits are Personal, Comprehensive, Team Builder, Aggressive, Creative, Strategic (Hogue, 2015).

A few key steps to launch crowdfunding at your own institution are outlined below. While not difficult to understand, the steps can at times be difficult to implement. For a first time launch at any institution, of any size, encouragement to work by committee and with all arms of advancement, cannot be understated. These arms generally include advancement services, alumni relations, development, and marketing/communications.

After your committee or working group is established, the selected of a platform for your crowdfunding initiative is a good next step. For many, a regular CRM system may have the capability of fulfilling your needs for a user friendly online platform. The good news here is that by 2015, hundreds of platforms are available for use by institutions both large and small. As of this writing, there are approximately 18 platforms that most frequently are used for crowdfunding campaigns. For larger universities, it is even possible that your own IT unit may have the capacity to actually build a simple system unique to your institution, saving you from the at-times-expensive nature of processing fees for service. One thing to look for is a progress bar feature, letting your constituents know how close the particular project is getting to being fully funded.

As with any fundraising campaign or initiative, it is critical to share the impact of your priorities with prospect investors. Hogue, in his latest text, wrote that he believes the most overlooked stage in crowdfunding is the most important, the pre-launch phase (Hogue, 2015). In this planning phase, you can truly conduct a mini-feasibility study as a proof of concept before your crowdfunding even launches, potentially saving you and your institution extensive time and money in the long run.

Illustrations and examples of e-mail that were used in a recent crowdfunding campaign can be found in Figures 1 through 12 (** Emails used with permission of Aquinas College, Nashville, Tennessee).

Figure 1.

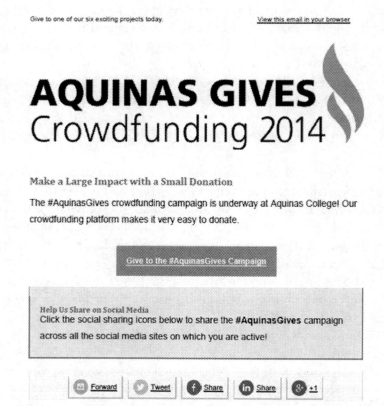

WHERE WE ARE TODAY

In today's world of constant connectivity and mobile tethering, online giving among philanthropic organizations and online investing for for-profit organizations cannot be forgotten. Having mobile friendly devices that allow donors and investors to give on the spot and in the moment is critical.

It is also important to remember that while online giving and specifically crowd-funding initiatives do increase an organizations pipeline for major gifts, only about 2% of the more than $335 billion given in 2013 was collected through the internet. Comparatively, that 2% figure illustrates a 14% growth as compared to the previous year, this is all according to the *Chronicle of Philanthropy* and the *Blackbaud Index* *(MacLaughlin, 2015)*.

Figure 2.

IMPACT ON HIGHER EDUCATION

In his recently published book, *Crowdfunding for Social Good,* Devin D. Thorpe mentions three common themes as impact is highly saught after in crowdfunding campaigns. Those three are utilizing matching grants, being creative, and spreading the word (Thorpe, 2014). Matching grants are what can incentivize someone to make a rather fast giving decision. Unlike major gift cultivation, especially in higher education, crowdfunding cultivation is fast. It may be as simple as the opening of an e-mail and click of a mouse. Knowing that if you "act now" your gift may be matched 1:1, 2:1, or even better is possibly all a donor needs to actually make the gift. Being creative, as previously discussed, is quite possible the single biggest driver for

Figure 3.

crowdfunding success. Crowdfunding is all about busting the status quo and driving dollars to new and innovative opportunities! Creativity is king here, repeating what the institution down the street or across the state did is unlikely to work for you too. Thinking about a project from a different perspective or from a brand new angle is what prospective donors are craving when making a crowdfunding decision. Finally, spreading the word is the marketing power necessary to obtaining that critical mass of large donor relationships. Social media and other digital marketing strategies and tactics, along with the occasion compliementary print advertisement, must extend far behold your typically audiences. Spreading the word to those that you may not have touched in years or taking the chance in even reaching out to new audiences with your message of growth and quick impact initiatives can also be a great way to further send your message far and wide.

Figure 4.

Study abroad opportunities today are some of the most exciting memories in a student's collegiate career. Critical to the success of Vision 2020, Truth & Charity is creating a competitive edge in higher education through a compelling study abroad program. By partnering with a property in Bracciano, Italy owned by the Dominican Sisters of St. Cecilia, the School of Business is taking students on the inaugural study abroad trip in May 2015 thanks in large part to your investment here. You are blazing a trail to this great new program at Aquinas!

Donate to Study Abroad

Muhammed Chaudhry, President and CEO of the Silicon Valley Education Foundation, learned about crowdfunding and wanted their organization to engage in this quick, typically small gifts, large impact, opportunity (Thorpe, 2013). Setting a goal of $30,000, the organization only raised $27,000 but over 220 donors contributed that sum. Chaundhry commented that through those 223 donors, they have plans in place to potentially raise over $150,000 in other major gifts through follow up and further solicitations (Thorpe, 2013). This is the truly crowdfunding impact at work. Taking the chance to use this fast fundraising approach to drive other major gift solicitation cannot be underestimated and should never be forgotten.

Many non-profit organizations are beginning to engage in fundraising activities each year. Some even limit these activities to one critical day of giving. This "one day" concept is particularly popular among institutions of higher education. Purdue University, for instance, raised over $7.5M in one day during their first *Purdue Day of Giving* in early 2014.

Figure 5.

Figure 6.

Figure 7.

Figure 8.

Figure 9.

Thanks to your generosity, these crowdfunding projects are being implemented.   <u>View this email in your browser</u>

AQUINAS GIVES
Crowdfunding 2014

Crowdfunding Projects Becoming a Reality

Your AquinasGives crowdfunding gifts in December raised over $30,000 for Aquinas College students. Read about the progress on these projects below.

Total Progress
103 %

Mannequin for the School of Nursing

"Nursing Anne," the new Manikin for the School of Nursing's Castello Center at St. Thomas West Hospital in Nashville has been purchased and placed into service thanks to generous support of crowdfunding. The Castello Center is operational this semester and is truly a unique opportunity for students to experience "on the job" type training. The Center is scheduled to be dedicated on April 13, 2015.

The more common approach, particularly in higher-ed is a set period for crowd-funding, built on a popular platform available online (dozens of options are out there for low cost based on giving percentage), and designed to be mobile and user friendly. At my current institution, we engaged in a 15 day program to really drive participation among new and existing donors. The *#aquinasgives - Crowdfunding 2014* project also shows progress in a strategic plan that has struggled to bring several

Figure 10.

Dissection Microscopes for the School of Arts & Sciences

The School of Arts & Sciences is proceeding with the ordering and purchasing of a new dissection microscope with full accessories, including an LCD viewing screen. We anticipate this microscope will be installed and functional in our biology laboratory by early summer, 2015.

Study Abroad Trip for the School of Business

The generous support of donors to crowdfunding have made it possible for several students from the School of Business to participate in the new AquinasAbroad program at our new international campus in Bracciano, Italy. The first group of students will spent the Fall 2015 semester in Bracciano and many will now be able to take advantage of less financial burden thanks to crowdfunding.

Study Carrels for Seton Lodge Residents

New study carrels for the Aquinas Residence Hall, Seton Lodge, have been purchased thanks to crowdfunding. They will be in student rooms for use when they return for the Fall 2015 semester. The carrels will be a wonderful addition to the space that is currently not inclusive of a well lit space dedicated to advance study and education.

larger projects to fruition due to poor institutional history. By creating confidence with the six aforementioned projects that were successfully funded (overall campaign ended on scheduled and at 101% of goal achieved), the institution certainly hopes that many of these larger priorities will see greater interest.

KEY TAKEAWAYS

In the case presented herein, the in-depth look at crowdfunding and one institution's successful implementation of this new fundraising strategy should serve as a reminder that although best practices are important to consider always, effective

Figure 11.

TeachLive Software for the School of Education

The TLE TeachLivE™ Lab is a mixed-reality teaching environment supporting teacher practice in classroom management, pedagogy and content. The TLE TeachLivE™ Lab, developed at the University of Central Florida, is currently being implemented across 42 campuses in the United States and growing to include multiple school districts and international partners. Each partner utilizes the TLE TeachLivE™ Lab in a unique manner depending on the needs of their students, teachers, professors, and community stakeholders. The TLE TeachLivE™ Lab provides pre-service and in-service teachers the opportunity to learn new skills and to craft their practice without placing "real" students at risk during the learning process.

Tennis Court Resurfacing to Bring Back Athletics

The resurfaced tennis courts at Aquinas College will be completed soon now that Nashville's long winter seems to be coming to a close. Of the four courts currently on campus, 3 will be resurfaced and rejuvenated while the fourth will remain as a sport court for other uses including street hockey, dodgeball, basketball, and soccer. The newly finished tennis courts will be available for the enjoyment of all students by Fall 2015.

approaches constantly shift. In 2012, the Jumpstart our Business Startups (JOBS) Act was passed in the United States Congress ("Jumpstart our Business Startups," 2012). This act, while applicable to private business, also shows that it is a best practice among any business, for profit or not, to participate in the exercise of meeting goals through many small gifts that contribute to one large goal.

Crowdfunding does take time to really do it well and correctly. Selecting a platform to use (or building one customized for your organization if you have the IT support internally), selecting projects that are likely to garner interest, and marketing the entire initiative are the three most critical pieces to these projects. If done well, organizations should see donations from many new donors who, hopefully, can become major gift prospects thanks to the process. The marketing outcomes and annual giving pipeline that results cannot be underestimated. And finally, any

Figure 12.

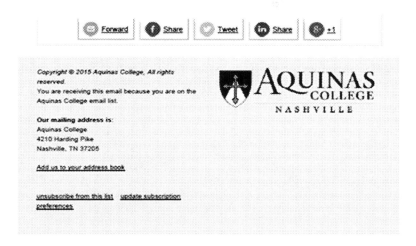

organization that is successful in these efforts must show the fruits from these labors very quickly. Stewardship after the crowdfunding campaign can make or break success in the future. In the end, however, modern day crowdfunding has a place in the strategic plan of any advancement operation no matter if you raised a few thousand dollars annually or a few billion. Please, share your successes and failures in crowdfunding with us; things that you learned and things that you wished you had done differently.

Building the pipeline of major gift prospects through a robust toolkit of direct mail, digital marketing, and leadership annual giving while renewing the institution's commitment to stewardship, and focusing on the long term growth and funding priorities; these should be the areas of focus for any institution who have a desire to practice effective approaches in higher education development.

CASE STUDY EXECUTIVE SUMMARY: *AQUINASGIVES* CROWDFUNDING CAMPAIGN

The Challenge

Creating and sustaining a reliable pipeline for major gift prospects is a concern for most nonprofits worldwide. Bold vision and big funding priorities mean that the large support is key but the smaller more frequent gifts provide sustainability. Simply put, the challenge revolves around the absolute best way to raise multiple small gifts for one small to medium sized project with a reasonably quick turnaround so that supporters can witness and be a part of the benefit of their investment. In this case, there was also a previously existing issue with the college not following through on programs and changes as it received funding. Crowdfunding campaigns were thought to offer a wonderful opportunity for short turnaround or production times in execution of the projects.

The Solution

Crowdfunding provides an excellent way to fund multiple small to medium size projects through many smaller gifts rather than a few larger major or principal gifts. We looked at Aquinas College and their efforts to engage in the first crowdfunding campaign for their institution. Six projects were put together from areas of the college across its campus.

The college quickly had to turn these projects around so that stewardship could then take place. In any campaign, but especially in crowdfunding campaigns, stewardship proved to be one of the most critical areas of focus. Without proper recognition, it appeared to be very unlikely that the majority of supporters to the *AquinasGives* campaign would consider a second or even third gift. Investing in crowdfunding appears to only work if the institution is prepared. This includes both the development office and also, in the case of academia, the academic leadership or provost's office.

Finally, this case also made a good case for support that only once a year, twice at most, can most organizations support such a crowdfunding initiative. It is definitively different than many other annual fund type programs due to the intense nature of marketing that goes into the program. The marketing and communications aspect of a campaign of this kind is the foundation for success. A strong communication plan, which was present for the *AquinasGives* example, is the only way to ensure that thorough planning takes place for promoting the mini-campaign.

The Result

Each of the six projects created for this crowdfunding campaign were listed at or below $5,000 in total dollars needed for implementation. Of the six, four ended up being full funded but even still the other two projects had enough financial support to be executed on and the overall campaign reached 103% of its stated goal.

Another stated goal of this initiative was for the organization to increase the total number of gifts and donors to the college. Real time statistics and results are available for crowdfunding since the majority of investments made will be completed online. The completion of a critical mass of new projects (six, in this case) also showed Aquinas' constituency that the college can execute on a plan and with the proper funding can create new opportunities for its faculty and students.

CASE STUDY TEACHING NOTES: *AQUINASGIVES* CROWDFUNDING CAMPAIGN

1.   Given Aquinas' issues related to follow up and follow through with the execution of projects once fundraising is completed, do you agree with the approach to begin building rapport with consituents through smaller projects generally associated with programs such as crowdfunding? Why or why not?
     a.   Student responses will vary. Being an opinion type question, this should help spur debate and lively discussion. Some may not even agree with the issue of follow through or may feel that there is not enough information to properly answer the question. This is where creative license and some assupmptions may need to be made on the part of students engaged in this study.
2.   List and discuss the CASE counting standards for development and discuss their relevance to a crowdfunding campaign.
     a.   Counting standard are always relevant to any campaign, regardless of the type, size, or scope. Crowdfunding is no different and therefore the same standards should always be applied. It would unusual for any one campaign to not follow the relevant standards in the industry.
          i.   **CASE Recommendations:** The working group makes the following recommendations specific to campaign counting and reporting (see attachment for proposed language recommendations and a comparison with current language in the third edition of the CASE Management and Reporting Standards):
          ii.   Revocable gifts may be included in campaign totals at face value if they are pledged during the campaign, documented, and as long as they are reported separately from outright gifts and irrevocable deferred gifts.
          iii.   Irrevocable deferred gifts may be included in campaign totals at face value, but both face and discounted present values should be reported.
          iv.   Conditional pledges may be included in campaign totals if there is a reasonable expectation that the conditions under which the pledge is made will be met during the campaign period and if there is appropriate documentation.

v. Campaigns should be tied to the strategic goals of the institution, and for this reason the length of a campaign may vary. However, in order to maximize the commitment of volunteers, donors, staff and others, CASE recommends that a comprehensive campaign period generally not exceed eight years.

vi. Government funds are very important to helping institutions achieve their strategic goals, they are often secured competitively and help leverage private funds, and fundraising staffs often are integral to securing government support. However, CASE reaffirms its position that comprehensive campaigns are fundamentally philanthropic ventures designed to raise resources from the private sector. Therefore securing government funds does not fall under the definition of philanthropy as a private act. For this reason, government funds should not be included in campaign totals, but institutions should work to raise visibility and recognition for the value of government funding in accomplishing institutional goals.

vii. CASE should include a disclaimer to the revised campaign guidelines recognizing that within increasingly complex gift agreements, there will be situations not expressly covered in these guidelines and standards.

3. Using the outline for the Comprehensive Advancement Strategic Plan (CASP), explain how and where an intiative such as crowdfunding would fit in to the CASP.

a. There are a few different ways in which students couple approach this question. The most likely scenario is that crowdfunding campaigns should fall under section IV of the CASP in "fundraising." Some student may argue that crowdfunding should be its own subsection with IV and some may argue that it should fall under IV – A. Annual Giving. It would also be more than appropriate for students to discuss the intense need for excellent marketing and communications plans for crowdfunding. Because of this requirement, students may also mention that crowdfunding should fall under section VII of the CASP in "Communications."

REFERENCES

Cagney, P., & Ross, B. (2013). *Global Fundraising: How the World is Changing the Rules of Philanthropy* (1st ed.). Wiley, John & Sons. doi:10.1002/9781118653753

Craver, R. (2015). *Retention fundraising: The new art and science of keeping your donors for life*. Medfield, MA: Emerson & Church.

dSchool, Institute of Design at Stanford, Home. (2014). Retrieved March 4, 2015, from http://dschool.stanford.edu/

Giving USA: The Annual Report on Philanthropy for the year 2013. (2014). Chicago: Giving USA Foundation.

Hogue, J. (2015). Step-By-Step Crowdfunding. Academic Press.

Jumpstart Our Business Startups (JOBS) Act. (2012, April 5). Retrieved May 15, 2015, from https://www.sec.gov/spotlight/jobs-act.shtml

Preliminary Report of the Campaign Standards Working Group. (n.d.). Retrieved 2 March 2015, from www.case.org/samples_research_and_tools/case_reporting_standards_and_management_guidelines/faq_rsmg/preliminary_report.html

The History of Crowdfunding. (n.d.). Retrieved 2 March 2015, from https://www.fundable.com/crowdfunding101/history-of-crowdfunding

Thorpe, D., & Sampson, R. (n.d.). *Crowdfunding for social good: Financing your mark on the world*. Academic Press.

Chapter 10

The Role of Philanthropy on the Strategic Planning Process of a Selective Liberal Arts and Science College

Wayne P. Webster
Ripon College, USA

Rick C. Jakeman
The George Washington University, USA

Susan Swayze
The George Washington University, USA

ABSTRACT

This chapter describes how constituencies of a four-year, private liberal arts and science college perceived the effect of philanthropy on the strategic planning process. Due to their reliance upon tuition revenues and private support, liberal arts and science colleges are particularly susceptible to ebbs and flows in the economy. How these institutions plan for the future and the extent to which philanthropy factors into strategic plans provides crucial information about the future of these higher education institutions (Connell, 2006). Gaining a deep understanding of how philanthropy shapes a strategic planning process and the decision-making model that was used during the process provides insight into how philanthropy, strategic planning, and decision-making models intersect to form a new decision-making model, described as feedback and revenue.

DOI: 10.4018/978-1-4666-9664-8.ch010

INTRODUCTION

Liberal arts and sciences colleges are uniquely American institutions. As highlighted, their very existence is due to the philanthropic generosity of wealthy individuals and/or religious or philosophical movements (Thelin, 2004). As private institutions, they receive little direct state or federal government support and rely predominantly on tuition revenues, endowment earnings, and philanthropic support to balance their budgets (Balderston, 1995). Philanthropic support and earnings off of endowed gifts are on a rise during a time when increasing net tuition revenue is a challenge for all but a few institutions (Rivard, 2015). In a recent article in the Chronicle of Higher Education, Ripon College Board of Trustee Chair Ron Peterson underscored the important role governing boards of private liberal arts colleges play in fiduciary oversight of their institutions by stating that they must be prepared to "contribute green paper, gray matter, and brown shoe leather (Biemiller, 2015)." By providing high-touch experiences for their students in and out of the classroom, including low student to faculty ratios, liberal arts institutions are not particularly cost-efficient (Stimpert, 2004). Due to their reliance upon private support and tuition revenues, liberal arts and sciences institutions are particularly susceptible to ebbs and flows in the economy. How these institutions plan for the future and the extent to which philanthropy factors into these plans was an important question to examine (Connell, 2006). Further, what decision-making model was used to craft these plans was worth investigating.

Providing additional research and literature on this timely topic added to the current literature and helps in the effort to give current and future private liberal arts college presidents, governing boards, and other members of the campus community, a frame of reference by which to compare and guide their actions relating to these issues. Having a sense of how a similar institution carried out a strategic planning process in the shadow of economic challenges is beneficial to liberal arts and science institutions' campus and governance board leadership. In addition, scholars and researchers in the field will find this study beneficial as it provides additional literature in these emerging subject areas. The recently announced closure and sudden reopening of Sweet Briar College, a nationally ranked liberal arts and sciences institution, due to donor intervention provides additional urgency to examine how a financial sustainability plan can be best crafted (Bidwell, 2015).

The purpose of the study was to address deficiencies in the literature by providing an in-depth view of how the constituencies of a four-year, private liberal arts and science college in the United States believed philanthropy affected a strategic planning process and how administrative decision-making models were used during this planning process. The case study, which was conducted at a singular private liberal arts and science college following a recently completed strategic planning process, answers the following research questions: (a) How did philanthropy affect planning for capital projects within a strategic plan?; (b) How did philanthropy affect the focus of current and future academic offerings of an institution? It is common for case studies to focus on one institution so that researchers can conduct an in-depth examination of the functioning of an institution.

As private institutions, private four-year liberal arts and science colleges rarely receive funding from government sources with the exception of grants for research and the indirect benefits received through government financial aid programs supporting students. As a result, these colleges primarily depend on three sources of funding which include tuition and fees, endowment earnings, and philanthropic gifts (Balderston, 1995). While private liberal arts and science colleges have become increasingly dependent on tuition, endowment earnings, and gifts to sustain and enhance their programs, leaders of those institutions will be required to focus more of their attention on financial issues (Balderston, 1995).

Colleges will strive to keep the cost of tuition and education affordable and accessible for all. Thus, they will be called upon to seek other sources of support, including philanthropic gifts (Connell, 2006). As a result, colleges will need to take philanthropic trends and outlook into account when crafting their strategic long range plans (Connell, 2006). To what extent college leadership is willing to alter their strategic plans in order to maximize philanthropic support may have implications on the mission, values, and financial outlook of their institution (Pully, 2002). Similarly, the degree to which leaders of these institutions believe philanthropy should play a role in the development of their college's strategic plans may change the influence philanthropy does or does not have over the process.

BACKGROUND

The institution which served as the site for this research has been given the pseudonym of Selective College. Selective College has the distinction of having served as a coeducational institution from its inception. Today, the college boasts an enrollment between 1,000 – 1,500 students with more than 90% living on campus. Selective College also provides an intimate learning experience with the student to faculty ratio of less than 15:1. During fiscal year 2012, Selective College, had expenses totaling nearly $50 million and a revenue stream nearly equaling that amount. Selective College is predominantly dependent upon tuition, board and fees, as well as philanthropic support for operating revenue. Members of the Selective College Board of Trustees have historically been the largest philanthropic supporters of the institution and thus have significantly impacted the college's finances and investments in facilities and programs. In recent years, the college has completed or begun two major building projects. How Selective came to the decision to significantly invest in their facilities using gifts and debt was a major focus of this study.

MAIN FOCUS OF THE CHAPTER

While there are numerous models regarding governance and decision-making processes in higher education and beyond, there are three main models that are most apt and widely-used. The collegial, political, and bureaucratic models highlight the primary spectrum of involvement in the decision-making process from one of total consensus-building to one of almost complete dictation of the goal and the path necessary to succeed (Tierney, 2008). The collegial, political, and bureaucratic models provide the three most basic approaches to decision-making and are thus most likely to be utilized due to their simplicity and common acceptance. Other models, such as cybernetic, rational, and cultural are also amongst the many decision-making theories that have been identified. Due to the intimate culture of private liberal arts and science colleges, it is assumed that a collegial and collaborative decision-making approach is most likely to be used. However, given the recent economic recession that has dramatically affected the financial state of these institutions, it is possible that other types of models may be used out of necessity to make quick and strategic decisions. Some common descriptions of these three models, as well as an analysis of each follows.

Tierney (2008) describes the collegial model as "a view of academic life that assumes a community of scholars operates around notions of respect and consensus" (p. 152). By nature, the collegial model encourages consultation and shared governance amongst all members of the respective community (Bess & Dee, 2008). Governing by consensus, as advocated by the collegial model of decision-making, has deep roots in higher education. Prior to the rise in power of college and university presidents in the 20th Century, the faculty of respective institutions served as the heart and soul of the institution both literally and figuratively. Faculty approval of operations of the university was, and remains, an important weathervane regarding the direction of the institution to both internal and external constituencies. The symbolism, which remains an important aspect of academic culture, continues to support a culture and precedence that encourages consensus-building (Tierney, 2008).

Proponents of the use of the collegial model in higher education decision-making process cite that the "loosely coupled and decentralized nature of the academy is well suited to such a framework" (Tierney, 2008, p. 152). At the core of their existence, colleges and universities encourage and reinforce the need to foster an environment of inclusion of various thoughts and ideas. To dictate policy, rather than to openly debate it, would stifle this sense of community that truly makes higher education different from any other sector. A decision that is reached by consensus, which includes numerous points of view, would seemingly produce a well-thought out outcome (Tierney, 2008). Additionally, use of the collegial model helps to create a sense of loyalty and buy-in by the participants who subsequently embrace the decision as their own (Bess & Dee, 2008). Liberal arts and science colleges, in general, embody the philosophy of the collegiality model through their embrace of a shared governance model of operation. In particular, faculty governing bodies are consistently consulted and kept apprised of fluctuating conditions at their college by the administration (Gibson, 1992).

It is not uncommon for the faculty to have final say on new initiatives involving the curriculum or in the setting of admissions standards at liberal arts and science colleges (Gibson, 1992). Beyond faculty involvement, it is also common for senior administration to regularly consult student and staff leadership, as well as representative bodies of external constituencies such as alumni and parent boards. By involving and updating various constituencies of pending actions, the senior leadership creates this sense of community that is unique to liberal arts and science colleges. It can be argued that while the collegial model creates a buy-in from members of the academic community, it also results in a decision that supports the status quo or the least objectionable option (Tierney, 2008; Bess & Dee, 2008). Detractors of the use of the collegial model further state that the common ground that participants of a consensus decision-making exercise are striving to obtain is unrealistic and never existed (Tierney, 2008).

According to Bess and Dee (2008) a culture where the political model is utilized is "identified through its reliance on negotiation and bargaining among interest groups and coalitions within the organization" (p. 377). Further, a quid pro quo is established wherein support for a particular need or initiative is rewarded by the promise of future support for another need or initiative (Bess & Dee, 2008). The political model is also identified as having a decentralized form of governance where the power shifts from group to group and the dissemination of information can be ambiguous (Bess & Dee, 2008). The political model came to light in the 1960s and 1970s and is viewed as middle ground between consensus-building and a bureaucracy (Tierney, 2008).

The political model is often utilized during employment contracts through collective bargaining and with interactions with external constituencies such as donors, community leaders of the town or city the college is located within, or with legislators (Tierney, 2008). Although political negotiating is often utilized, it can be argued that it is difficult to use as a reliable model due to the natural ebb and flow that takes place during negotiating. It incorporates aspects of the collegial and bureaucratic models, but does so inconsistently and unreliably (Tierney, 2008). The political model appears to be utilized out of necessity rather than by the desire of any parties who are involved with the negotiation.

Max Weber (1864-1920) first described the bureaucratic model as it "assumes that decisions and planning take place by way of a coordinated division of labor, a standardization of rules and regulations, and a hierarchical chain of command" (Tierney, 2008, p. 151). In a bureaucratic culture, rules such as specified roles and reinforcing reporting relationships are followed in order to ensure efficient performance (Bess & Dee, 2008). Information is also disseminated extensively and in a top-down fashion. Attempts are also made to reduce uncertainty and ambiguity for the college or university by valuing and embracing rationality in the decision-making process (Bess & Dee, 2008). According to Bess and Dee (2008, p. 547), in a bureaucratic organization there is little deviance from "organizational mandates" and the decision-making power is centralized.

Supporters of the use of a bureaucratic model in higher education claim that a more centralized and formal governance structure would result in higher quality outcomes (Tierney, 2008). They further state that with stronger presidential authority, 'antiquated' practices such as tenure could be eliminated, mediocre faculty could be dismissed, and the preservation of unproductive academic departments could be halted in order to ensure efficiency and quality (Tierney, 2008). The bureaucratic model views faculty as an asset to be managed rather than as a participatory factor in the decision-making process and that they should be utilized in a manner that most effectively advances the mission and needs of the institution (Tierney, 2008).

Robert Birnbaum (1991) suggests that the collegial, political, and bureaucratic models can live and thrive simultaneously within an organization. This system of co-existence is referred to as the cybernetic model. Senior administrators who use all three models simultaneously are better able to monitor various issues more effectively using these multiple frames of reference and leadership (Birnbaum, 1991). Thus, the three models are complementary to one another rather than being in competition (Birnbaum, 1991). The cybernetic model creates loops for negative feedback which serve as built in thermostats that alert the administration that a 'reset' is needed in a certain area of function of the institution (Birnbaum, 1991). Birnbaum (1991) argues that this model is particularly useful at an institution that has both loosely-coupled and closely-coupled organizational models.

Two other types of decision-making appear in the literature: rational decision-making and cultural decision-making. First, Weiss (1982) describes rational decision-making as one that follows as an established, or ordered, process for making a calculated decision. The model assumes that full information is available to the decision makers, and that possible consequences are rationalized before the decision is executed (Weiss, 1982). The ordered process by which decisions are made in the rational decision-making model differs from the cultural decision-making model. The cultural decision-making model encourages practitioners to "consider real or potential conflicts not in isolation but on the broad canvas of organizational life" (Tierney, 1988, p. 6). Further, the cultural model encourages leaders to "implement and evaluate everyday decisions with a keen awareness of their role in and influence upon organizational culture" (Tierney, 1988, p. 6). This model assumes that imperfect information exists for the solution and possible consequences, and the decision-making process must consider the framework of organizational culture within an institution (Tierney, 1988). Environmental elements, including the institution's mission statement, how new members are socialized, and perceived differences in leadership structures inform the decision-making process in this model (Tierney, 1998).

Although the collegial, political, and bureaucratic models best represent the range of traditional decision-making models that are utilized by college and university leadership, there are others that may be better fits for some institutions. It is possible that the studies cited for these three options were situational to specific institutions and in reality are not applicable to a broad sector of higher education. It is also possible that this research and use of these models are no longer applicable to today's world of higher education. Much has changed over the past few years in terms of financial affairs, enrollment and internal communications; therefore perhaps a new set of decision-making models would be more appropriate. In reality, it is possible that no model will fully encompass the decision-making process of any institution as these decisions are complex and have various factors impacting the process at any time. It is also unknown the degree to which philanthropy and fundraising impacts these models at an institution which routinely seeks external support. However, the researchers believe that the collegial, political, and bureaucratic models represent the best range of decision-making models for liberal arts and science colleges.

SOLUTIONS

In order to answer the research questions, 23 semi-structured interviews with key informants (e.g., the college president, faculty, staff, and governing board members) were conducted during a campus site visit on the heels of the formal approval of the strategic plan by the Board of Trustees. To supplement the interviews, a document analysis of recent press releases, news and magazine articles, and fundraising campaign materials related to the strategic planning process were also conducted as part of the study. The review of these materials provided another perspective regarding how the planning process was facilitated, what decision-making model was used to carry out this process, and the resulting reactions of internal and external constituencies to this process.

The case study revealed three major findings. The first finding confirms the role of donor and philanthropic considerations and the influence they have over the strategic planning and decision-making processes. Donor and philanthropic considerations did influence both administrative decisions (i.e., construction of new buildings, performance reporting functions) and curricular aspects of the College (i.e., interdisciplinary academic work, student research opportunities). The second finding describes the rationale for strategic planning as being more business-oriented than altruistic. Declining revenues from enrollment and lower earnings from the endowment, spurred the growth in revenue-generating staff positions to attract new forms of tuition revenue and donor support as part of the strategic plan. The final finding describes a new decision-making model that emerged during the strategic planning process at the campus. The new decision-making model was more business-minded, accelerated in time, and limited collegial decision-making. That is, consensus-seeking processes that require extended time were absent from the process. Rather, key informants described decisions that were formed by senior administrators and vetted by faculty, alumni, students, and Board members in one-time meetings. These three findings serve as a foundation for a contemporary discussion of philanthropy and administrative decision-making models and their role at liberal arts and science colleges.

Finding One: Donors and Philanthropic Considerations Do Have Influence over Administrative and Academic Processes and Decision-Making

While there did not appear to be any significant donor influence over the core academic liberal arts program and mission of the college, donor influence and philanthropic considerations did appear to influence academic and administrative decisions of Selective College. Perhaps the most obvious example of philanthropic influence over the strategic plan decision-making process, and affecting both academic and administrative processes, was the combination of business and science departments into one new physical structure. As described by many members of the campus community, merging two academic disciplines with significant facility needs into one facility not only met programmatic needs, it also multiplied the potential donor base needed to support the construction. While the idea of integrated learning between the business and science disciplines played a supporting role in the decision to build a joint facility, it is clear that financial limitations and the hope of developing a broader donor base played the leading role in the decision. This compromise of placing two disciplines into one facility made the project financially feasible and will ultimately strengthen both academic programs by placing them in a state-of-the-art facility as well as provide unique integrated learning opportunities within its walls.

A member of the administration confirmed the belief that financial and philanthropic considerations were a driving force behind the merger of business and science into one building. He said:

[We] did a little bit of looking at fundraising capacity and, and my response was, [we are] not certain that [we] can imagine getting the support to build a science building from our alumni base. I think we can get good support from our business alumni. You know my guess is that it [business department facility] is about a $6 million project and the laboratory is about a $35 million budget, and [we] think we can raise the $6 million twice but I don't think we can raise half of that, of the laboratory building. So, let's merge the two together and see if maybe for, for $35 or 40 million so we can build a combined building, and we will not break out the donors and so all our donor pool is working on the project. So it was purely pragmatic reasons driving the decision to put those departments together.

Even though the merger of the two disciplines was viewed as being a financial decision, some observers saw this merger as a way to creatively address the problem. One person said:

My impression is that between the president and some trustees, the idea was that we… could get more funding for the building if it weren't just a science building. But they needed something to attract former business alums, or alums who are doing business even if they haven't been business majors, who would donate to this project. And then one way to do that would be to fuse it and then maybe [the president] decided that 'wow, we could pitch this as we're integrating, you know, because liberal arts is all about putting different disciplines together' and so… there was a lot of faculty buy-in to that too, initially.

In addition to new capital projects, philanthropic support advanced special projects and initiatives at Selective College, including the presidential portfolio projects. Presidential portfolio projects are student and faculty initiated research and experiential learning projects. Not only do donors make these projects feasible, they can also have influence over which portfolio projects occur by funding them, or not funding them. Further, the recent addition of a new campus chaplain was donor-driven. The new position was purportedly pushed and funded by a donor, the idea of creating a strong tie to the church associated with the founding of Selective College was proposed as a way to broaden the tent of prospective donors.

Finally, philanthropic considerations influenced administrative decisions of Selective College. In order to show return on investment to its governing board and select donors, Selective College implemented an administrative function to measure outcomes of various aspects of its operations. This including the push for academic and co-curricular program heads to demonstrate quantitative evidence that their program is making the desired effect on students as well as the campus and local community. Feeling forced to demonstrate return on investment and to focus on the bottom line, in order to receive funds to maintain or expand their operations, can result in programs focusing less on providing learning opportunities and experiences and more on proving their relevance and defending their place on campus. One campus member said:

I think one of the changes we've had with our strategic plan is a real focus on measurement and milestones to identify progress…and a commitment to that. As a result of that we also had a donor, I believe, who had some specific requirements in terms of performance and allocation on a gift. And I think that was a further support that we were directionally sound.

The issues facing Selective College, and the way that institution tackled those challenges, can likely be found at dozens of other similarly situated liberal arts colleges across the country (Jaschik, 2010). Increasing philanthropic support is a common strategy to budgetary challenges, particularly when there is not a strong sense that the price tag can be increased to maximize net tuition revenue (Kiley, 2012). The leadership of liberal arts and science colleges, that are primarily tuition dependent, understand that the survival and success of their institution depends on its ability to gain ground thanks to donor support. As alluded to by Cook (1997), there are few measurements of performance more important than how effective a president, and their administration, is in raising philanthropic support and managing donor expectations. It is possible that the need to show solid performance in fundraising efforts, in order to help secure the legacy of the current administration and show positive movement forward, has opened the door for more donor influence and input at liberal arts and sciences colleges.

The finding that philanthropy does not influence decisions surrounding the core curriculum of Selective College is comforting to those who believe that the curriculum of a college is the foundation upon which it exists and is, thus, beyond influence. By not allowing philanthropy or tuition revenues to dictate the core of the academic program, Selective College did not find itself chasing fads, such as allied health programs, and instead invested in its liberal arts and sciences academic core. Others may argue that by not broadening the core curriculum, and finding ways to further maximize tuition revenues or leverage philanthropic dollars, leaves the college with few opportunities to be nimble and inventive. In addition, with an increased focus on post-graduate outcomes, prospective students and their families may feel that an inability to review the curriculum to make it more contemporary may mean that institution's degree has less value in today's job market. While the liberal arts and sciences mission of Selective College was not changed by considerations focused on maximizing revenue, many academic and administrative decisions of the college were susceptible to this influence.

Finding Two: Business Oriented Rationale for Undertaking Strategic Planning Process by Reacting to External Influences

An important outcome of this study was gaining an insight into why Selective College undertook a strategic planning process when it did and what was the expected outcome of this process. The evidence gained from the various sources of data makes it clear that the overall goal for completing the planning process was to create a plan for the college to follow over the next five years. In many ways, the need for a solid plan was a needed response to the recent economic depression that had reduced Selective College's endowments, as well as estimated family contributions towards tuition and fees. Selective College, in response to what was occurring in the external market, revised its business model in order to maximize short-term revenues. One individual reflected on the impetus for undertaking the strategic planning process when he stated:

[W]e got really serious about business planning right after the economic down turn. Right so the economic down turn came late in what 2008, early 2009? You get the idea. So the summer of 2009 we had a task force get together and we said... let's presume this sticks around a while. We cobbled together the budget for next year. You know we said 'gee, maybe we're going to have to not make payments to [employee retirement funds],' well that didn't have to happen. But you know it was a possibility. We had a whole series of contingencies some of which we had to exercise some of them we didn't. And we said alright instead of, instead of doing this ad hoc here, let's come up with a long term plan.

As Balderston (1995) notes, institutions have become increasingly dependent on tuition revenues, endowment earnings, and fundraising activities to remain viable. Creating a plan to maximize these revenue streams, in response to external market forces, was important for the future vitality of Selective College. Reacting to external market forces by focusing on short and long term plans to increase revenues is a change of mindset for higher education institutions where change occurs much more deliberately. A new plan was also important in identifying, and subsequently, creating ways to improve the programs and facilities to attract higher quality students as well as those who can pay more for their education. One person said:

We sort of had an unspoken strategic plan before we got our written one and that was to get the campus into a position where students wanted to come and live comfortably and engage in student life and you can see...a quick visit to the campus shows you all the recent dormitories and that sorority house that we've built and things we've done there including the stadium, the [athletic] center to do that was never really a part of a written strategic plan like the one we have now.

A faculty member agreed that new facilities attract more high-caliber students. She said:

One of the reasons that [the sciences], don't have...large enrollment majors is their facilities are out of date and it's hard for them to attract students ... and obviously new facilities ... has the potential to attract more and better students. So, [business department] was put there because it was growing and big and the other set of departments [sciences] were put there because they were small and needed to grow.

A solid plan for the immediate future provides Selective College with a vision that it can now take to its donor-base in order to begin the process of fundraising for these needs.

The negative influence of the recent economic depression on colleges and university balance sheets forced institutions to retrench and rethink how they operate (Jaschik, 2010). Private liberal arts and sciences colleges like Selective College were particularly susceptible given its modest endowment, its regional draw for students, and the modest estimated financial contribution of its average student. As Hammond (1984) cited, economic depressions often have crippling effects on the enrollment and budget scenarios for small liberal arts college. This is particularly relevant when considering that most small liberal arts colleges gain 75% of their revenue from tuition and fees (McPherson & Schapiro, 1999). While Selective seemingly rode out the recession better than many institutions, creating a plan to strengthen its finances and prioritize its spending was important in order to be better prepared for future economic downturns.

Creating the Draw for Prospective Students

Part of preparing for a stronger financial future for Selective College included the creation of unique programs and upgrades to key facilities that will attract not only more students, but more academically strong students. Selective College assumed that a percentage of higher achieving students would come from wealthier socio-economic backgrounds, which would enable them to pay more for an education that they assess as being higher in quality. Part of increasing that perceived quality includes creating programs, such as the integration between science and business, which provides unique learning opportunities with a nod towards the future. One person said:

You know, these small schools…are very enrollment driven so, if we had to put our weight on one over the other, I think [the assumption that Selective College] needs to be attractive to science majors was very important to us. Your science majors are your more high-end ACT kid typically. They have maybe a little higher propensity to persist … But then I and you know we can't discount our facility, our science facility was really worn out… not cutting edge in any way. [T]he building is also a difficult one to maintain and it was, it's just time and all of our competitors have a new science facility.

The strategic plan capitalized on the broadly held belief that families with means will pay more for what they perceive as having added value. A danger exists here in that Selective College cannot unilaterally pull out of the arms race with other colleges and universities who are trying to attract this student profile. However, there is no evidence that Selective seriously entertained the idea of eliminating, reducing, or consolidating existing programs and operations in order to reduce costs. A critical review of existing operations may have led to cost savings that could have been reinvested into the program, in addition to proposed investments funded by new philanthropic gifts or increased enrollment revenues.

Importance of a Strategic Plan in Attracting Philanthropic Support

Finally, having a solid plan for the future is important for stakeholders, particularly for donors and prospective donors. Not only does it provide donors with a sense of where the college is heading, it also provides a vision that can inspire them. A strategic plan can become a reality with the assistance and generosity of donors. It is also clear that people want to support successful, innovative, and impactful organizations. Having a plan for the future not only shows steadiness and strength, it also reaffirms the college's current and future sense of purpose and mission. As stated by Kotler and Murphy (1981), conducting a strategic planning process shows willingness by institutional leadership to examine the greater higher education environment and position their college in a way to be successful moving forward. As evidenced at Selective College, and referred to in the literature, strategic plans often provide the basis for subsequent fundraising initiatives. By having a clear, concise, measurable, and endorsed plan for the future, the various constituencies can work together to provide the appropriate resources towards programs, facilities, and personnel that will make the vision of the plan a reality.

Finding Three: An Emerging Decision-Making Model Focused on Feedback and Revenue

Over the course of this study, it was apparent that the decision-making model used during the strategic planning process at Selective College was not purely collegial, nor political, nor bureaucratic in nature. There was little evidence given by participants or in official documents of negotiation or quid pro quo as Bess and Dee (2008) suggests should be found in instances of political decision-making. There was also a lack of a formal rigid structure in the process that Tierney (2008) describes as being core to a bureaucratic exercise. Bess and Dee (2008) describe a pure collegial decision-making model as encouraging consultation and shared governance amongst all members of the campus community. The process was also not purely collegial in that it was not an example of governance by consensus. Contrary to the scenario that Gibson (1992) describes, the faculty of Selective College did not have final say over which new initiatives were to be included or excluded.

One person expressed concerns that the lack of a strategic planning and governance committee resulted in less faculty input and control of the process. She stated:

I think the lack of continuity has made us more defuse. I will say that from our administrator's point of view that might be a better thing. Because what is does is it allows them [the administration] to control the conversation. … If the faculty feel like… governance is ours, which we do, then one of the things on this campus is that administrators have to be in sync with the faculty. And, if there is a diffusion of these sort of duties and conversations, it allows the administration to come in with the final word and say, 'well this is what I'm hearing.' Because we are not actually talking to one another… so when [the president] says this [strategic plan] was generated by a faculty discussion and discussion with the trustees, that's absolutely true. And he was in on, or the dean was in on, most of those conversations in various ways. … What most of us would want is a real Quaker model of going to the meeting house and just talk and get consensus. You know it didn't happen that way.

Another individual countered this idea. He indicated that the creation of a planning and governance committee would have been good for enhancing internal communication, but it likely would not have altered the outcomes of the process. He stated:

I will probably always wonder if we should have...after two or three years we could have created something that we called the strategic planning committee. And it could have held hearings and...I don't know that they would have gotten different or more input. Maybe they wouldn't even have got as much input as we did by doing things very...loosely, very organically with lots of different groups that were never called strategic planning committees. But at least the perception would have been 'oh yes, that's the damage, I got to say my piece about the strategic plan.' I think that there was so much discussion going on in so many different venues that, and also informally, that collectively there was far more information that went into the plan than if we...had been structured.

While various college constituents were given the opportunity for input, the final outcomes were not the product of a collegial Quaker-style town hall process where the pathway chosen was that of least resistance. Based on participant feedback and other data uncovered by the researcher, a new feedback and revenue-focused model was used during this process. One individual described the process as top down and not faculty-based, indicating:

[W]ho determines our priorities? Some of those probably come from trustees. Trustees talk to the president. The president talking to the business office, talking to development office... And then, feedback or input comes from the faculty and sometimes they ask for that and maybe...suggest directions that trustees and administration can go, but more often, and maybe this is just a bias from a faculty perspective, it seems to come from the top down rather than the bottom up.

A faculty member agreed. He described the process as being one where there were many opportunities for input, but that the end result, was driven from the top down. He said:

I think there were a number of...times when this information was...discussed. ... [B]ut for me it was, it was almost more about 'okay here's what we're going to do, kids.' And less about 'what do you want to do, kids?' So [the] number and kind of opportunities [for input and feedback were] certainly sufficient. I don't think anybody is, is going to...quibble or question...what the guiding principles are. I don't think…anybody particularly wants to fight about those but, but I think in some cases a view might be that this came more from the top down rather than from the bottom up and…that just may be the way things are.

Whether it was due to the economic pressures felt by Selective College during the recent recession, or the increasing professionalization of higher education administration, the new decision-making form that emerged met the need to make quick and decisive decisions. This evidence suggests that the traditional collegial, bureaucratic, and political models may be out of date and not useful for contemporary decision-making in higher education when considering the recent economic recession.

The decision-making model that emerged from the data has similarities to the cybernetic model championed by Birnbaum (1991) in that systems for input were put into place during the planning process at Selective College. However, given the size and culture of liberal arts and science colleges, as is the case at Selective College, employing different decision-making styles for various situations is not likely to be well received in a tightly-coupled organization. One person addressed what she saw as a possible change in decision-making practices in high education. She stated:

This college is more democratically run than the one I came from. Not to say the one I came from was total oligarchy or something but just that there was a continuum. But, I actually wonder if even this institution is moved to be…slightly less democratic. Every body has to have a say and everything to…get your voice heard but then…the appointed people make decisions, I think probably it's moved over in that direction. I think it is [because] these are different times. … looking back now, I see it was just a wonderful time. The stock market was going up and everything was great, and seemed like a real…stable and…enriching place. The pile seemed to be getting bigger and now I think we're all… struggling and that is different.

Another individual agreed, indicating a change in the planning processes conducted in higher education. He stated:

I sort of grew up and then began teaching in an era where when we talk about strategic planning the faculty thought, whether rightly or wrongly, that it should have a major role in the planning and implementation of any plan. I mean the world has changed and so you know in the last 35 years I think, and I don't mean this as a negative comment, but I think a lot of…college and university administration has become both more professional and perhaps more corporate. So I suspect that for many of us who sort of long for the good old days, if they were the good old days, that we're not going to have that kind of direct input into the process. So, at some level, those folks who were basically…making the final decisions may in fact tell us what's going on and you know give us some idea and…some input into that process. So, I think a lot of us then would like to say 'well I think building A should be a higher priority than building B or I think we should do this instead of that'. I'm not sure in 2012 that's really going to be realistic for many colleges and universities as they move forward.

While there may be healthy competition between individuals and departments, there is not a strong basis for competition for substantial resources as might be found between Schools of a large loosely-coupled university. Thus, using various decision-making styles to accommodate different individuals or departments would not be an effective model in a lean administrative structure. In addition, with a small hierarchy, the need for 'thermostats' to alert the administration about departments or individuals losing focus or underperforming seems unnecessary (Birnbaum, 1991). The feedback and revenue model is a better fit for institutions like Selective College, which is a tightly-coupled organization that works to provide an quality product using limited resources. While feedback was accepted and encouraged, decisions were ultimately vetted based on their ability to enhance the finances of the college. One person summarized the process as a work in progress, yet representative of difficult decision-making processes at private liberal arts colleges. He stated:

I generally think the communication at the college, and I think this is typical of a lot of colleges,…takes place in pockets. Sometimes communication is inaccurate in those pockets. I don't think we've done a good enough job quite frankly of assembling the right people together with the president and maybe with [the board of trustees], with other people so they at least hear from us. … We could have done a better job of that. I think we did a good job trying to engage the faculty and certainly some outside constituents as we developed the plan. I mean, could we have done more? Sure. But I think that we probably didn't have to do as much because we felt the faculty was really aligned on this integrated learning [concept] since it came from them. … I think there's always 20% in any organization that says … 'I don't want to change.' … I think, overall, we did a good job. Could we have done better? Yes.

The rational and cultural decision-making models do not appear to be an exact model for the recently completed strategic planning process at Selective College. The boundedness construct of the rational model was not met as it was not clear who was charged with making final decisions, and within what timeline, with no formal committee in place. Further, the perceived significance construct was not met as there was no evidence of policy changes that carry consequences with them as an outcome of the planning process. While the focus on offering opportunities for feedback was in deference to the traditional collegial culture of Selective College, the planning process at Selective did not examine or address all of the issues at the core of the cultural decision-making model. While the liberal arts and sciences mission was reinforced during the process, other broad areas of focus in the cultural model, such as environment, socialization, and what is expected of institutional leadership, were not addressed.

The feedback and revenue model for decision-making allows for input from the broader community including faculty, staff, and alumni via formal and informal venues. Whether it be through representative committee structures where faculty and staff leaders funnel input to the senior leadership and the board, or through participation during question and answer sessions in scheduled town hall meetings, opportunities for input were given. However, unlike the pure collegial decision-making models, that input could be used or disregarded. As Tierney (2008) describes, collegial decision-making is truly present when "a community of scholars operates around notions of respect and consensus" (p. 152). Ultimately, the senior administration and the board of trustees made the final decisions about the future of the college and the best path to take in order to reach the desired outcomes. As a result, while opportunities for collegial input were granted and encouraged, the ultimate decisions were made by the senior administration and the governing board.

In addition to feedback, this new decision-making model stressed the use of opportunities to maximize revenue through tuition, fees, and philanthropy. While feedback from faculty, staff, and other constituencies was encouraged during this process, the ultimate scale by which various proposals were measured by was whether or not these initiatives would help to generate additional revenues for Selective College. Recommended outcomes of this planning process validate this observation via investments in facilities, personnel, and programs to attract and retain more students and higher quality students. One person stated:

We have a beefed up ... the student support services program. [They] have really upped the ante on what they're trying to do. ... We got lots of new ways of tracking some of the students who are under achieving on the student support services side. There are tutoring services being offered for the students who simply need more help.

In addition, creating a vision for the future that includes opportunities for donors to realize immediate measurable results encourages philanthropic investment into the organization. According to a staff member, investments in personnel in the college's development operations have been deliberate. She stated:

On the budgeting side I know that we also did do some budgeting to make sure we had enough staff within the development office. That office started out five or six years ago with a very skeleton group. So one of the key things that they did early

245

on was realize that if we are going to be in the next five, six years at that point in time, embarking on a capital campaign that we'd know we'd be embarking on... we have to get that staff in, established, settled. We've got to give them information they need. We've got to give them the research they need. We got to give them the tools and they've got to be ready, they've got to get ready to run.

A significant outcome of a strategic planning process is gaining a perspective of how an institution is viewed in the marketplace (Stevens, Loudon, Oosting, Migliore, & Hunt, 2013). Having external input from stakeholders and others regarding the strengths, weaknesses, opportunities, and threats that most accurately describe an institution is a valuable outcome of this process (Stevens et al., 2013). As was the case with Selective College, providing formal venues for feedback from external constituencies, whether it be through alumni representation in the process or by facilitating external listening and feedback sessions, adds an important element to the discussion. The opportunity for feedback from key external stakeholders will likely continue as the college may undertake a feasibility study prior to launching a fundraising campaign focused on the outcomes of the strategic planning process.

During the course of a feasibility study, key donors and prospective donors will be given the opportunity to share their reactions and interest in various aspects of the college's strategic plan. Feasibility studies are considered as being a best practice for institutions who are preparing to launch fundraising campaigns (Mai, 1987). It is during this exercise that it is determined which aspirations for the college have support amongst the donor base, thus it should be included in a subsequent campaign, and which may need to be addressed using other resources (Mai, 1987). While the strategic plan may be complete, which aspects of it can be funded through philanthropic support is often decided based on feedback from key external stakeholders. An additional factor in the success of a potential campaign, which can be assessed during a feasibility study, is whether or not the institution has the donor base, the culture of philanthropy, a mature fundraising organization (Pierpoint & Wilkerson, 1998).

In reality, higher education administration has become far more professional and organized in recent decades (Balderston, 1995). Fewer faculty members and deans are finding their way to the presidency and into other senior administrative positions (Cook, 1997). Thus, an increasing number of staff members end up spending their entire careers as professional higher education administrators having limited classroom experience, research expertise, or having served on faculty committees. Not having experience collaborating on various topics with their peers as a member of the faculty, administrators do not have first-hand experience using collegial decision-making models in a professional setting. Instead, they are serving in positions in fundraising, admissions, marketing, and finance, where decisions often need to be made quickly in order to mitigate risk or maximize opportunities. The feedback and revenue model of decision-making has similarities to how businesses and corporations function, where key administrators are entrusted and expected to make decisions.

While the use of this new form of decision-making leads to a decreased sense of shared governance and ownership from various constituencies, it does allow the institution to be quickly decisive and responsive to changes in the external environment. In the case of Selective College, which was not financially strapped, nor flush, being able to create a plan to increase the quality and quantity of students was important. Similarly, by having a vision ready to reveal to donors was important and allowed the college to take advantage of opportunities to gain financial support. Given the recent shifts in the higher education landscape, it is likely that traditional decision-making models will need to be modified as institutions grapple with decisions in the future. For private liberal arts colleges like Selective College, the emerging feedback and revenue decision-making model allowed for broad input but attempts to mitigate errors by leaving ultimate decision-making authority with senior administrators and the governing board.

RECOMMENDATIONS

Findings of the study led to four primary actionable recommendations for college and university leadership engaged in a strategic planning process. The first recommendation is that a strategic planning exercise is valuable in garnering philanthropic support. The second recommendation focuses on the importance of selecting a decision-making model that is right for the institution and the current state of the institution. More affluent colleges and universities might opt to employ a collegial decision-making model with an extended time frame. Other institutions, like Selective College, may need to use a different model, such as the feedback and revenue model, to create an expeditious yet comprehensive future institutional plan.

A third recommendation suggests that investments in revenue generating positions in admissions, development, and marketing are key to the financial success of institutions. However, college and university leadership must keep in mind that the ultimate measure of success is the quality of instruction by faculty and staff in and out of the classroom. Investments in revenue generating positions should not be made in lieu of investments in the faculty. Fourth, campus leadership must be cognizant of the importance of philanthropy. Few private institutions would have been founded, or continue to exist, without donor support. Public institutions seem to be increasingly reliant upon philanthropy given a continued decrease in state support

(Casteen, 2011). The pursuit of philanthropic support should not come at the loss of institutional mission and values. Finally, while new investments in programming and operations are necessary to maintain quality measures, new expenditures should be balanced with cost-cutting or cost-sharing efforts when appropriate.

Recommendation One: Strategic Plans Play an Important Role in Garnering Philanthropic Support

While the process of how a strategic planning exercise is carried out can be debated, the outcome of this process provides numerous benefits to institutions. Utilization of a strategic planning process results in a comprehensive business and operational plan which is helpful with setting fundraising priorities, prioritizing investments in programs and personnel, and budget modeling. Carrying out a planning process every five to seven years maintains communication among campus stakeholders on the institutional priorities, while allowing for flexibility due to changes in the economic and educational climate. While world and campus events can make aspects of a planning process seemingly void within a matter of a few years, having an agreed upon set of priorities by which all decisions can be measured provides campus stakeholders with a sense of direction. A strategic plan does not limit an institution from making a nimble and unforeseen move, but it engages college and university leadership to weigh that decision against previously established goals.

An established "checks and balances" protocol between the goals of a strategic plan and the temptation of pursuing previously unforeseen philanthropic development opportunities provides various constituencies with a sense of confidence about the direction of the institution. Included amongst those constituencies are faculty, staff, students, friends, alumni, and foundations who are current or potential donors to the institution. The strategic plan gives donors a feeling of whether their investment in that institution is wise and provides context for the investment. The strategic plan also helps the institution by creating a menu of priorities to be used in a proactive way with donors and preempts them from creating ways to give that may not fit with the mission and values and long-term priorities of the college.

Recommendation Two: Decision-Making Models Used during a Planning Process Must Fit the Culture and State of the Institution

A critical component of the strategic planning process, and whether it will be successful in galvanizing faculty, staff, administration, and alumni towards reaching goals, is how decisions are made regarding what is included in the plan. The decision-making model used during a planning process provides opportunities for engagement for various constituencies, but it also influences the pace by which decisions are made, and the culture of decision-making for campus decisions. The model utilized in various planning processes must match the culture and needs of the institution as determined by its current state and the perceived significance of the decision. For some colleges and universities, a prolonged collegial decision-making process may be feasible and necessary, while other institutions may need to make quick and more bureaucratic-like decisions in order to respond to current or imminent threats or opportunities.

In the case of Selective College, a decision-making model emerged somewhere in the spectrum between the collegial and bureaucratic decision-making models. The feedback and revenue model allowed and created formal and informal venues for constituent input and feedback on an accelerated timeline. Central to the model, senior administration and trustees made the final decisions with revenue generation being the primary filter by which decisions were made. While full-faculty and staff support is sacrificed in decision-making, it allows institutions to be nimble by entrusting a leadership group to make final and, if need be, expeditious decisions. This model assumes a high level of confidence or trust in the campus leadership; mistrust and poor leadership will alienate the strategic plan from the campus community. Senior leaders using this model should assume their employment condition depends on the success of these decisions.

Colleges and universities that are either relatively affluent or cash strapped are more likely to benefit from using decision-making models, respectively, that are angled towards the collegial and bureaucratic ends of the spectrum. An affluent institution that is stable and can utilize a planning process to dream about program innovations without concern for how much or little revenue will be generated from them, or how long the process will take, has the luxury of carrying out a prolonged and diligent collegial process. An institution in the midst of a true crisis, financial or otherwise, needs to retrench immediately and is likely to benefit from the ability provided by a more bureaucratic model to be quick and decisive using a limited group of decision-makers. Either of these scenarios runs the risk of making an institution either inhibited in its ability to be nimble or of alienating constituencies not involved in the decision-making process. It is also likely that the traditional decision-making models (e.g., collegial, political, and bureaucratic) are outdated and that new models, including feedback and revenue, are necessary to match the complex internal and external environments of institutions. Ultimately, a planning process must use a decision-making model that is appropriate for the state of the college and is cognizant of the culture of that institution.

Recommendation Three: Institutional Leadership Must Embrace Donors and Philanthropy, but Not Lose Sight of Mission and Values

Donors have a key role to play in the life of liberal arts and science colleges, and an important role in promotion of institutions of higher education. Many institutions, particularly those that are private, rely on sustained support of alumni and friends through their philanthropy. In this era of reduced support from legislatures for state colleges and universities, public higher education has also ramped up their efforts in the race for philanthropic investment. Given this established trend, the role of donors and their philanthropic support for higher education is likely remain vital in the coming decades.

While donors are necessary to help fund the mission of colleges and universities, their gifts should help support these institutions and not unduly dictate their directions. Presidents and governing boards should focus on philanthropy and embrace donors, and avoid burdensome conditional gift commitments. It is important to remember that philanthropic gifts should enhance and improve the life of a college, not force it to alter its mission or values in order to meet a donor's wishes or demands. While it is important for colleges and universities to embrace the role of philanthropy in the history and culture of an institution, they should also avoid undue influences.

In order to protect against undue donor influences, the leadership of college and universities should work with their governing boards to develop and regularly review institutional gifts acceptance policies. These documents should clearly outline under what conditions certain gifts will be accepted and outline unacceptable gift conditions. Having a board-endorsed document provides the development staff and the president with guidelines by which to act in the best interest of the institution. A gift acceptance policy will help to ensure that donors act in support of the mission and values rather than using philanthropy as a way to alter them. Such a policy helps respect the role of philanthropy in the life of a college but provides donors with clear boundaries regarding what they receive in exchange for their gifts.

Recommendation Four: New Investments Should Be Balanced with Eliminations, Reductions, and Consolidations of Existing Services

While Selective College identified various areas of new investments, including facilities, personnel, and programs, there was no evidence that the elimination, reduction or consolidation of existing facilities, personnel, or programs. The need to remain competitive among peer institutions overshadowed the need to periodically and systematically examining the return on the investment of various programs or operations. Spending without committed resources is not a sustainable business model. The economics of small, moderately endowed, liberal arts and science colleges suggest that all aspects of the institution must be running at their fullest potential in order for the institution to be successful, viable, and demonstrate good stewardship of its resources.

One area for potential review is the scope of academic programs offered by colleges and universities. A large portfolio of basic and specialized academic offerings can lead to academic departments comprised of 1-2 faculty members enrolling 5-10 students. A balance between small and large departments with emphasize on creating cross-disciplinary courses and experiences for students also create opportunities to share budget, personnel, clerical support, and other resources. Another cost-sharing solutions may include joint faculty and staff appointments between program, joint ventures with regional peer institutions, and strong articulation agreements with pipeline colleges and universities.

On the administrative side, a number of possible solutions exist to free up existing resources to be invested in new endeavors. Using existing regional associations to share costs such as health care insurance, information technology and software purchases, and specialized facility maintenance positions, such as electricians, could provide cost savings. While additional 'feet on the street' are always welcomed in the development and admissions efforts, making sure that databases are being effectively used and that procedures exist to effectively use new human resources is important. Further, a review of whether an investment of $20,000 in digital marketing would produce more applicants than a $40,000 salaried admissions counselor should be considered. Investments in systems that maximize efficiencies may produce the desired results with less cost than new personnel. Whether it is in the academic or administrative side of the house, ensuring that existing expenditures are necessary and are producing the desired results is important and should be completed before new and additional investments are made.

FUTURE RESEARCH DIRECTIONS

The case study analysis of the strategic planning process at Selective College found that philanthropy influenced the development of administrative and academic goals. Further, the decision making process that created the strategic plan was revenue and feedback-focused and controlled by key administrative leaders. While specific to Selective College, the researchers assert the findings are useful to other liberal arts and science colleges that are engaging in a strategic planning process, especially in the context of an economic recession. The discussion of findings provides in-depth analysis and illustrative quotes to highlight how philanthropy influenced in the strategic planning process to inform future research among liberal arts and science colleges.

Future research to expand the knowledge of how philanthropy influences the strategic planning and administrative decision-making models should include other types of colleges and universities. Inclusion of public 4-year universities, research-intensive universities, and technical and community colleges would provide new perspectives on the existing literature. Further, placing financial resources and stress of colleges of universities as a construct for greater consideration, future research might understand if this matters in the strategic planning process. Finally, a longitudinal study to follow the outcomes of the strategic planning process and its influence on the comprehensive fundraising initiatives would better understand the relationship between these two areas. A longitudinal analysis would also illustrate how changes within the decision-making model and leadership affect the strategic planning process.

CONCLUSION

This case study of the strategic planning process at Selective College provides a unique perspective regarding how philanthropy and administrative decision-making models contribute to this dynamic and multi-faceted process. There was evidence that philanthropic support, and the desire for it, influenced facilities and peripheral academic and co-curricular initiatives. Further, the need to increase philanthropic support was matched by the need to increase net tuition, room and board, and fees from prospective students. The urgent need to increase revenue resulted in a strategic planning process that was not conducted in a fully collegial manner. Instead, feedback was sought and given, but all decisions were vetted by the administration and governing board in an effort to increase revenues.

The strategic planning process of a financially-concerned institution that strove to fully recover from a tremendous economic recession resulted in the emergence of a new decision-making model, the feedback and revenue model. It is likely that similar institutions will need to create new models, such as the feedback and revenue model, in order to withstand the new economic higher education climate. Seeking feedback from various constituencies as an institution makes financial decisions is a strategy that many higher education administrators and governing boards will look to in coming years.

REFERENCES

Balderston, F. E. (1995). *Managing today's university: Strategies for viability, change, and excellence* (2nd ed.). San Francisco, CA: Jossey-Bass.

Bess, J. L., & Dee, J. R. (2008). *Understanding college and university organization: Theories for effective policy and practice* (1st ed.). Sterling, VA: Stylus.

Bidwell, A. (2015, March 3). Two private liberal arts colleges will shut down. *U.S. News & World Report (Online)*. Retrieved at http://www.usnews.com/news/articles/2015/03/03/declining-enrollments-financial-pressure-force-two-liberal-arts-colleges-to-close

Biemiller, L. (2015, May 8). Trustees feel pressure from Sweet Briar's demise. *The Chronicle of Higher Education, 61*(34), A.12. Retrieved from: http://chronicle.com/article/Sweet-Briar-s-Demise-Puts/229877/

Birnbaum, R. (1991). *How colleges work: The cybernetics of academic organization and leadership*. San Francisco, CA: Jossey-Bass.

Casteen, J. (2011, May-June). Financial self-sufficiency and the public university. *Trusteeship Magazine, 19*(3). Retrieved from http://agb.org/trusteeship/2011/may-june/financial-self-sufficiency-and-the-public-university

Connell, C. (2006). Worlds Connect in Waterville. *International Educator, 15*(3), 56-63. Retrieved from http://www.questia.com/PM.qst?a=O&d=5045010008#

Cook, B. W. (1997, January – February). Fundraising and the college presidency in an era of uncertainty: From 1975 to the present. *The Journal of Higher Education, 68*(1), 53–86. doi:10.2307/2959936

Davis, K. (1968). Evolving models of organizational behavior. *Academy of Management Journal (Pre-1986), 11*(1), 27. Retrieved from http://search.proquest.com/docview/229589718?accountid=11243

Gibson, G. W. (1992). *Good start: A guide for new faculty in liberal arts colleges* (1st ed.). Bolton, MA: Anker.

Hammond, M. F. (1984, May – June). Survival of small private colleges: Three case studies. *The Journal of Higher Education, 55*(3), 360–388. doi:10.2307/1981889

Jaschik, S. (2010, Oct. 15). Liberal arts, post-recession. *Inside Higher Ed (Online)*. Retrieved from https://www.insidehighered.com/news/2010/10/15/augustana

Kiley, K. (2012, Nov. 19). Liberal arts colleges rethink their messaging in the face of criticism. *Inside Higher Ed (Online)*. Retrieved from: http://www.insidehighered. com///11/19/arts-colleges-rethink-their-messaging-face-criticism

Kotler, P., & Murphy, P. E. (1981, September – October). Strategic planning for higher education. *The Journal of Higher Education*, *52*(5), 470–489. doi:10.2307/1981836

Mai, C. F. (1987). The feasibility study: Essential for a successful campaign. *Fund Raising Management*, *18*(10), 84. Retrieved from http://search.proquest.com/docv iew/195938458?accountid=11243 PMID:10284866

McPherson, M. S., & Schapiro, M. O. (1999, Winter). The future economic challenges for the liberal arts colleges. *Daedalus*, *128*(1), 47–75. Retrieved from http:// www.jstor.org/stable/20027538 PMID:11645881

Pierpont, R., & Wilkerson, G. S. (1998). Campaign goals: Taking aim at a moving target. *New directions for Philanthropic Fundraising*, *1998*(21), 61-80.

Pulley, J. L. (2002, November). Occidental denies quid pro quo on gift. *The Chronicle of Higher Education*, *49*(12), A.33. Retrieved from http://proxygw.wrlc. org/login?url=http://search.ebscohost.com/login.aspx?direct=true&db=aph&AN =2608146&site=ehost-live

Rivard, R. (2015, January 29). Market up, spending up. *Inside Higher Ed (Online)*. Retrieved from: https://www.insidehighered.com/news/2015/01/29/endowment-funds-grew-donors-and-investments-came-through

Stevens, R. E., Loudon, D. L., Oosting, K. W., Migliore, R. H., & Hunt, C. M. (2013). *Strategic planning for private higher education*. Routledge.

Stimpert, J. (2004, July). Turbulent times: Four issues facing liberal arts colleges. *Change*, *36*(4), 42-49. Retrieved from http://proxygw.wrlc.org/login?url=http:// search.ebscohost.com/ login.aspx?direct=true&db=aph&AN=13866921&site=e host-live

Thelin, J. R. (2004). *A history of American higher education*. Baltimore, MD: The Johns Hopkins University Press.

Tierney, W. G. (1988, January – February). Organizational culture in higher education: Defining the essentials. *The Journal of Higher Education*, *59*(1), 2–21. doi:10.2307/1981868

Tierney, W. G. (2008). *The impact of culture on organizational decision making: Theory and practice in higher education* (1st ed.). Sterling, VA: Stylus.

Weiss, C. H. (1982, November – December). Policy research in the context of diffuse decision making. *The Journal of Higher Education*, *53*(6), 619–639. doi:10.2307/1981522

KEY TERMS AND DEFINITIONS

Administrators: Individuals who have some influence over institutional policy and how support of the institution is utilized and distributed.

Bureaucratic Model: "Assumes that decisions and planning take place by way of a coordinated division of labor, a standardization of rules and regulations, and a hierarchical chain of command" (Tierney, 2008, p. 151).

Campaign: A set period of time during which a set amount of money is raised for specifically mentioned projects and endeavors.

Capital Projects: The renovation of an existing facility or the construction of a new facility, including major changes or additions to the landscape of an institution.

Charitable Donations: Financial support of a non-profit organization or mission including, but not limited to, colleges, churches, hospitals, and youth programs.

Collegial Decision-Making Model: Calls for "decision making by consensus" (Baldridge, Curtis, Ecker, & Riley, 1977, p. 134) and allows for the full participation of the institution's constituencies.

Development Officers: Individuals who have the responsibility of advocating the institution's mission, values, and long-range plans in order to solicit philanthropic support for the institution.

Donor Incentives: A donor's reasons for giving.

Endowment: A corpus of funds which are restricted to support particular aspects of the institution including scholarships, professorships, lectureships, and the general operation of the college.

Institutional Mission: The direction, goals, and objectives for the institution.

Institutional Values: The common ethics, morals, principles, and standards an institution adheres to and embraces.

Philanthropists: Individuals who donate their time, money, and/or resources to support a non-profit cause or organization.

Philanthropy: The act of financially supporting a non-profit institution or mission.

Political Decision-Making Model: According to Bess and Dee (2008) a culture where the political model is utilized is "identified through its reliance on negotiation and bargaining among interest groups and coalitions within the organization" (p. 377).

Chapter 11

The Role of Corporate and Foundation Relations Development Officers (CFRs)

Morgan R. Clevenger
Wilkes University, USA

Cynthia J. MacGregor
Missouri State University, USA

ABSTRACT

Corporate and foundation relations development officers (CFRs) play a vital role in philanthropy and resource development within higher education. Specifically, these leaders focus time building relationships with individuals who represent corporations and foundations that are able contribute to the needs and programs of an academic institution (Clevenger, 2014; Hunt, 2012; Sanzone, 2000; Saul, 2011; Walton & Gasman, 2008). CFRs must be intimately familiar with their own institution, organizational priorities, and key leaders to be able to create and orchestrate touch-points, engagement and volunteer opportunities, and mutually beneficial inter-organizational partnerships. CFRs manage a complex intersection of internal constituents' programs and interests while simultaneously trying to meet aggressive signature philanthropic platforms for companies or foundation programmatic initiatives.

DOI: 10.4018/978-1-4666-9664-8.ch011

Copyright ©2016, IGI Global. Copying or distributing in print or electronic forms without written permission of IGI Global is prohibited.

INTRODUCTION

Organizations do not operate in a vacuum. Organizations must interact with their external environment through other organizations in inter-organizational relationships while contending with various environmental factors, such as politics, social constraints, and economies (Clevenger, 2014; DeMillo, 2011; Rhodes, 2001). As higher education continues to face resource challenges, academic institutions have purposely engendered a variety of funding partners including corporations and foundations (Clevenger, 2014; Cohen, 2010). These significant organizational partners are forced to justify funding and engagement with academic institutions. "In an environment of receding economies, deregulation, global competition, ever-changing tax codes, and increased financial accountability, corporate philanthropy to academia has been in transition for an ad hoc activity to a long-term business strategy" (Abbot et al., 2011, p. 2). Foundations, and even governments, have also organized to be more strategic and long-term oriented to create win-win relationships to benefit the organizations and society.

Higher education fundraising professionals and management typically follow the Association of Fundraising Professionals' (AFP) formula for justifying and defining causes and include items such as "mission, vision, history, statement of community problem, goals of the campaign, objectives to meet these goals, programs and services, staffing, governance, facility needs, endowment, budget for the campaign, statement of needs, gift range chart, and named-giving opportunities" (Saul, 2011, p. 167). However, leaders of corporations and foundations also want to understand the intended impact a higher education institution and/or its programs and services make, the strategies to support those programmatic intents, and a detailed explanation of all metrics for performance, which may need to include proof of a successful track record (Clevenger, 2014; Saul).

While many examples of best practices originate from a corporate interface, these concepts are applicable to any external funding partner including foundations, governments, and special interest organizations willing to partner and engage on key initiatives. Academic institutions' corporate and foundation relations development officers (CFRs) are specialists in creating win-win relationships to mutually benefit two or more organizations simultaneously. These individuals' roles have evolved during the past 50 years. Larger academic organizations often have teams managing various intersects with corporations, foundations, and other partnering entities.

Managing these complex inter-organizational relationships has become a special concern for CFR officers. "Inter-organizational relationships are subject to inherent development dynamics" (Ebers, 1999, p. 31). Ebers' (1999) explanation of these four dynamics includes "[1] the parties' motives...[2] the pre-conditions and

contingencies of forming inter-organizational relationships...[3] the content and...
[4] the outcomes" (p. 31). Beyond these dynamics, organizations continue to learn
how to act and to react with other organizations (Clevenger, 2014; Ebers; Meyer &
Rowan, 1977; Morgan, 2006; Pfeffer & Salancik, 2003). "Many dynamics may be
planned, negotiated, and controlled" (Clevenger, pp. 464-465). Morgan (2006) said,
"organizations must develop cultures that support change and risk taking" (p. 91).

Because so many stakeholders are involved, organizational politics and communications are vital to trafficking CFR functions (Clevenger, 2014). On the higher
education side, senior leaders, fundraisers, deans, researchers, program directors,
and faculty manage their respective functions to support an institution's mission.
On the corporate side, senior leaders, researchers, public relations and community
champions, and program managers also desire various relationships to support their
goals. Foundations, too, often have programmatic emphases.

The three processes to operationalize and track organizational learning and
respective inter-organizational engagement include understanding, re-evaluation,
and adjustment (Clevenger; Ebers, 1999; Ring & Van de Ven, 1994). Ebers (1999)
indicated,

*In the course of an ongoing inter-organizational relationship, the parties may for
instance learn more about the environmental challenges and opportunities that
affect the contents and outcomes of their relationship; they may learn more about
one another, for example, about their goals, capabilities, or trustworthiness; and
they may learn how they could perhaps better design their relationship in order to
achieve desired outcomes. (p. 38)*

Ebers (1999) said these dynamics push inter-organizational relationships "to evolve
over time" (p. 38). This key point is of particular interest to CFRs, who ultimately
often represent all interests for a college or university to negotiate resources and
employee engagement.

Ebers (1999) denoted that a wide range of variables and changes in the environment
of organizations (i.e, the academic institution, a corporation, and/or a foundation)
effects how organizations interact with one another. Examples may include having
a change in an administrative leader or other key personnel, changes in priorities
or emphasis, reductions or increases in funding, or lack of outcomes. These factors
touch on a wide array of political, economic, social, and organizational dynamics.
Aldrich (1979) indicated three sources of an organization's ability to interact with
other organizations include leadership, other organizations' behaviors, and social
and cultural forces. The latter two are external while most scholars contend that
leadership is internal (Aldrich, 1979; Bolman & Deal, 2008; Carroll & Buchholtz,

2015). These varied sources create a constant flux of variables for CFRs to manage to foster strong, inter-organizational relationships and engagement of key decision makers to generate win-win outcomes.

BACKGROUND

To understand the complexities facing CFR officers, it is important to review the environment they function within and how it has evolved over the past century. Higher education and other organizations function within different cultures with different standard operating procedures and timeline expectations for turnaround (Clevenger, 2014). A review of the complexity of inter-organizational relationships gives depth to understanding the broad and deep challenges facing organizations and the CFRs who manage their interface. Higher education has evolved with varying ways to manage resource development and to engage other organizations such as corporations and foundations. Additionally, corporations and foundations have evolved during this same time frame to manage how and why they engage with other organizations, such as colleges and universities. Other third-party organizations exist to ensure social, political, economic, and environmental success is attended to by higher education.

Inter-Organizational Relationships

CFR officers often have a more complex development role because they interface with other organizations made up of many individuals who represent a corporation or foundation and their respective goals. Ideally, having a single point of contact narrows communications and expectations management; however, real-world inter-organizational relationships can include multiple individuals with differing expectations and demands.

Inter-organizational interaction occurs external to each organization in the *open systems* concept (Cropper, Ebers, Huxham, & Ring, 2008; Katz & Kahn, 2005; Morgan, 2006; Shafritz, Ott, & Jang, 2005; Thompson, 2005). However, organizations' internal systems highly influence the functionality of organizations and how they interact with other organizations and their environments (Bolman & Deal, 2008; Carroll & Buchholtz, 2015; Clevenger, 2014; Morgan, 2006; Shafritz et al., 2005). Internal systems include: *structure*, which may vary depending on size of the institution and type of industry for businesses, and includes policies; *human resources* roles of leadership, all levels of management, and employee volunteerism; *politics* made up of networks of individuals, subgroups, and relations; and *organizational culture*—communicated as mission, vision, and values, but also deeper historic roots and behaviors (Bolman & Deal, 2008; Herman, 2008; Morgan, 2006; Saiia, 2001).

"An organization's goals and values may be shared by other organizations" (Ashforth & Mael, 1989, p. 23). "A good relationship, however, does not happen by itself. ... Each party involved must actively participate in building a good relationship" (Cummings, 1991, p. 301). Relationships between higher education and organizations such as corporations and foundations should have compatible agendas (Andresen, 2006; Clevenger, 2014; Crutchfield & Grant, 2008). To build a relationship or foster a partnership between a higher education institution and a corporation or foundation, the onus begins with the higher education side to develop and foster the relationship (Clevenger, 2014; Tromble, 1998).

Assessing organizational compatibility is an important first step (Clevenger, 2014; Fischer, 2000). "Organizations should perform due diligence on potential corporate [or foundation] partners, doing as much research as they can to make sure their motives, goals, and integrity are aligned, rather than rushing in when a company [or foundation] dangles a grant [or other resource]" (Crutchfield & Grant, 2008, p. 76). Second, after determining a common agenda—which may have multiple initiatives, interests, or programs—each organization must weigh the pros and cons of being associated. Such inter-organizational relationships require "mutual understanding and shared values" (Fischer, 2000, p. 190). Third, after mutually compatible goals are established, a plan—typically managed by CFRs—is put in place to help the relationship to stay on track.

Ring and Van de Ven (1994) identified three key processes to implement successful inter-organizational relationships: negotiations to identify needs and outline expectations, commitments to solidify and formalize intentions, and execution of commitments. Additionally, Andresen (2006) said,

No partnership is perfect. The bottom line is to go into the partnership with eyes open, more positives than negatives in regard to fit and benefits, and a plan for compensating for weaknesses within the alliance. Inevitably, the benefits that partners receive will change, and one partner may perceive diminishing value. (p. 105)

Finally, attention must be constantly given to the inter-organizational relationships to continue on-going activities (Clevenger, 2014).

Partnerships with like-minded organizations are valuable because they are often able to reach audiences or to advance common causes through wider communications, increased marketing channels, additional distribution systems, a myriad of political connections, and the resources of more experts to create win-win propositions over time to achieve success (Andresen, 2006; Clevenger, 2014; Eddy, 2010).

"Direct relationships exist between business and academic institutions to the benefit of both…[and]…both parties…maintain separate identities…[yet]…often complementary missions" (Elliott, 2006, p. 59).

Higher Education

An early study by Smith (1968) identified why higher education rationalized seeking corporate engagement. Traditionally, private institutions sought private support from alumni, alumnae, and community partners (including corporations, foundations, and governments); whereas public institutions were funded by the state and federal governments. Because of tough economic times and growth of programs and educational accessibility, most higher education institutions sought to diversify funding. Thus, private academic institutions pursued governmental support as public institutions' enrollments swelled, and public universities better organized their own private foundations to seek alumni and alumnae giving as well as corporate support (Smith, 1968). "The distinction between public and private universities is close to meaningless today" (Litan & Mitchell, 2011, p. 142). Buchanan's (1991) observation still holds true today:

As higher education attempts to carry out its mission of education, research and service with reduced fiscal resources from the state and federal levels, revenue from the private sector has become increasingly important…. Cooperation between business and education is a necessity due to the interrelationships existing between these segments of society. (p. 1)

Another historic perspective is the development of the field of institutional advancement and the role of CFRs. Jacobson (1978) defined *institutional advancement* as "primarily responsible for maintaining and improving the relationship of an institution of higher education with society and selected publics in a way that most effectively contributes to the achievement of the institution's purposes" (p. 2). *Institutional advancement* was birthed in Greenbrier County, West Virginia in 1958 through a grant from the Ford Foundation. The attendees of a 3-day conference included a range of stakeholders such as higher education presidents, college and university trustees, fundraisers, public relations organizations, and business and industry executives. The goal was to determine how to coordinate efforts within higher education institutions to include external relations of fundraising, government relations, marketing, public relations, and alumni and alumnae relations. Collectively, these and other external relations were classified as *institutional advancement* (Elliott, 2006; Worth, 2002).

Coordination of fundraising efforts insured against single fundraising projects conflicting or threatening the overall success of a college or university's efforts (Clevenger, 2014; Pollard, 1958; Worth, 2002). In 1974, the American Alumni Council and the American College Public Relations Associations merged to create the Council for Advancement and Support of Education (CASE). CASE lends support for philanthropic and other resource development trainings and best practice sharing including alumni and alumnae programming, corporate and foundation relations, and marketing professionals. CASE provides various affinity groups for professionals, including corporate and foundation relations.

More recently the Network of Academic Corporate Relations Officers (NACRO) formed in 2007, to promote university relations with corporate interests "because of the lack of corporate expertise available by CASE" (M. Thomas, personal communication, February 2, 2012). NACRO's goal is to assist CFRs and other higher administration liaisons to develop strategies and maximize the relationships between higher education and industry and to develop metrics and reporting methodologies (Abbott et al., 2011; Cleland et al., 2012). NACRO members *are typically* from research-based, four-year universities (NACRO, 2015). NACRO provides several benefits to corporate-higher (or business-industry) education networks, including (but not limited to): student and professional placement, faculty and center expertise, fellowships, university-industrial research, consulting, university event participation, continuing and executive education, rental of equipment and facilities, economic development, technology transfer, and good will (Abbott et al., 2011; Castillo et al., 2015; Cleland et al., 2012; Johnson, 2007a, 2008).

CFR officers have constant pressure to negotiate and execute on major initiatives with corporations and foundations. Rhodes (2001) identified several factors in the rising cost of higher education that create major financial challenges for colleges and universities and the need for significant funds from partners. Such challenges include technology expenses and the costs related to implementation; the processing of labor-intensity to educate students, which comes with a price tag of highly educated and credentialed professionals' costs; initiating new programs to meet current world demands; and, in many instances, the opportunity costs of inclusivity for providing the means for all people to have access to higher education. Colleges and universities seek to deliver high-impact, quality education as well as partner with appropriate other organizations providing mutually beneficial ventures and funding and impact into the community—locally, statewide, regionally, nationally, and internationally, which serves the greater public (Abbott et al., 2011; Clevenger, 2014; Fischer, 2000; Pollard, 1958).

Operating an educational organization is expensive, and the education industry is broad. For example, in the U.S., "according to the Education Industry Association, education is rapidly becoming a $1 trillion industry, representing 10 percent of America's GNP and second only in size to the health care industry. Education companies alone generate more than $80 billion in annual revenues" (Saul, 2011, p. 14). Resource challenges continue to force higher education to diversify funding and to partner with corporations, foundations, and other organizations (Carroll & Buchholtz, 2015; Clevenger, 2014; Elliott, 2006; Gould, 2003; Hearn, 2003; Pfeffer & Salancik, 2003; Pollack, 1998; Sanzone, 2000; Saul, 2011). CFR officers must keenly plan and execute rich engagement with these organizations (Abbott et al., 2011; Brock, 2007; Castillo et al., 2015; Cleland et al., 2012; Clevenger, 2014; Fulton & Blau, 2005; Saul, 2011).

The process of building a relationship with a donor (whether an individual, a corporation, or a foundation) from a college or university's perspective is *cultivation* (Sheldon, 2000). To attract corporate or foundation attention, support, and engagement, colleges and universities identify ways to engage with them through various opportunities such as boards, special events, and programs of interest (Clevenger, 2014; Sheldon, 2000). "How long donors stay involved and how long they keep giving is related directly to the time and effort given to support the ongoing relationship" (Greenfield, 2008, p. 20). The key, however, is to realize that individual staffs turn over; it is organizations that remain (Greenfield). "It is important, then, for strong inter-organizational relationships to be constructed" (Clevenger, 2014, p. 98). Higher education has much to offer corporations, foundations, and other community organizations including: skills and abilities of students and graduates for enriching the community while gaining real-world experience, research laboratories and other resources to advance ideas, and mutually beneficial ventures that could serve the greater public (Abbott et al., 2011; Castillo et al., 2015; Cleland et al., 2012; Clevenger, 2014; Fischer, 2000; Pollard, 1958).

Corporations

A business or corporate organization is a profit-seeking entity (Acar, Aupperle, & Lowry, 2001; Jacoby, 1973), which has registered with a state government to become a legal entity (Ringleb, Meiners, & Edwards, 1997). Traditionally, corporate or business entities belong to shareholders of some type, whether private or public, whose interests are primarily financial (Acar et al., 2001; Berle & Means, 1968; Carroll & Buchholtz, 2015).

Through the late 1980s "many companies provided significant gifts and in-kind donations in support of research, scholarships, and student activities in ad hoc, nonstrategic ways" (Cleland et al., 2011, p. 2). Today, companies want to function as partners, engage employees at all levels, communicate their giving and programmatic initiatives, and measure the impact and outcomes of their activities (COP, 2007;

Clevenger, 2014). Companies use a variety of factors to determine which colleges or universities to partner with such as competency, a successful track record, a potential to improve return on investment (ROI), and intangibles such as good relationship management (Clevenger; Philip, 2012). Companies want to take responsibility and contribute positively as good corporate citizens. The World Economic Forum (2002) universally defines *corporate citizenship* as:

The contribution a company makes to society through its core business activities, its social investment and philanthropy programmes, and its engagement in public policy. The manner in which a company manages its economic, social and environmental relationships, as well as those with different stakeholders, in particular shareholders, employees, customers, business partners, governments and communities determines its impact. (p. 1)

Companies engage as corporate citizens for a wide range of reasons. Corporate "citizenship activities therefore encompass corporate investments of time and money in pro bono work, philanthropy, support for community education and health, and protection of the environment" (Gardberg & Fombrun, 2006, p. 329). Corporations of all sizes generally have the same goals of fulfilling their duties, such as helping communities, recruiting students, networking with faculty, leveraging resources, developing new technologies, continuing education, leadership development, and building brand reputation (BBIC, 2002; Carey, 2012; Clevenger; Hoerr, Kucic, Wagener, & Nolan, 2010; Philip; Rubenstein, 2004). Note, however, that truly philanthropic resources are far and few between today. Business are more strategic in how and why they give and entangle themselves with academic institutions.

While Philip (2012) advocated a decentralized approach and said that companies often want a "decentralized approach" because "every business and division manages its own relationships" (p. 6), Clevenger's (2014) dissertation interviews with executives highlighted that they desired the centralized model "to better allocate resources, focus on the inter-organizational relationship even with a myriad of complex relationships at various levels, and to centralize reporting and accountability" (p. 419). McGowan (2012) supported a "holistic model" emphasizing a relationship's focus and institutional coordination in a "strategic relationship" (p. 5). However, McGowan noted that "one model does not fit all" (p. 7) because each relationship depends on the focus, the institution's staff size, and availability of college or university resources that corporations are interested in tapping. Carey (2012) indicated a single "point of contact in corporate [and foundation] relations can be [a] very helpful shortcut to contacting the right person in the right department at the [college or] university" (p. 7). Brennan (2000) promoted cross-education among schools, colleges, and resource departments on campus. "Basically, all individuals within a university with information or a need to engage with a corporation meet to strategize and build a comprehensive picture and relationship regarding that company" (Clevenger, p. 419). Saul (2011) observed the following:

Over the last five years, something extraordinary has taken place: the market has begun to place an economic value on social outcomes [including education]. Indeed, social impact has become a valuable economic commodity: people are willing to pay for it, sacrifice for it, invest in it, and work for it. This phenomenon extends well beyond do-gooders and environmentalists to include mainstream consumers, investors, corporations, employees, and governments. Corporations alone are spending billions on environmental sustainability, social responsibility, and philanthropy. Consumers are spending more for goods and services related to health, the environment, social justice, and sustainable living. Governments are spending more than ever on education and health care. (p. 5)

Quality ideas, faculty, and programs are what matter most. Strategically matching "social, community, and public needs can create immense benefits for all parties" (Benioff & Adler, 2007, p. xv). McGowan (2012) believed corporations have a plethora of options to partner with academic institutions. Companies tend to want streamlined interactions, well-defined goals and expectations, mutually beneficial projects, and timeline responses to inquiries and reporting. These clear expectations help to create the most effective frameworks for higher education institutions, and particularly for CFRs.

Corporate support usually comes in one of the three major methods: direct giving (i.e. cash), in-kind donations or services, or programmatic funding through related corporate foundations (Giving USA Foundation, 2015; Rose, 2011). However, no matter which of the three methods are involved, benefits are typically expected, identified, and monitored (Clevenger, 2014; Tromble, 1998). Today "corporations no longer consider themselves 'donors' to academia; they consider themselves 'investors'" (Abbott et al., 2011, p.1). Total contributions from all philanthropic sources in 2014 was $358.38 billion with 15% focused on education; corporations continue to provide roughly 5% of all philanthropic funds, which is $17.919 billion (Giving USA Foundation). While corporate giving has fluctuated since the two recent recessions, there is a current increase in giving.

Organizations Supporting Corporate-Higher Education Relationship

Concern for academic-industry relationships is emphasized by four third-party organizations in the United States: the Business-Higher Education Forum (BHEF), the Committee to Encourage Corporate Philanthropy (CECP), the Government-University-Industry Research Roundtable (GUIRR), and University-Industry Demonstration Project (UIDP). These entities provide leadership and support for these inter-organizational collaborations.

The BHEF is comprised of college and university administrators and business and industry leaders dedicated to current world solutions for education and workforce training and development (BHEF, 2015). BHEF promotes the United States' global competitiveness through support of science, technology, engineering, and math (aka STEM) as well as college- and work-readiness programming. CECP includes a diverse range of corporate leaders, nonprofit partners, the media, the independent sector, and government institutions (Benioff & Adler, 2007). CECP creates a venue for corporate chief executive officers' (CEOs) concerns and initiatives to be heard, to promote discipline in corporate philanthropy, and to set standards and best practices for philanthropy and other resource measurement.

Created in 1984, GUIRR serves as a forum to address scientific training, globalization, and the impact of governmental regulations and policies (Fox, 2006). Formed in 2006, the UIDP fosters a stronger relationship between universities and companies—of all sectors—to focus on contracting, intellectual property policy, and technology transfer practices. (UIDP, 2015). Previously UIDP had been the University-Industry Partnership (or IDP) formed in 2003. The group has yielded policies and best practices relating to intellectual property and other legal frameworks that perpetuate university-industry relationships.

Foundations

A foundation "is a separate legal entity organized under state law either as a nonprofit or as a charitable trust" (Edie, 1991, p. 205). "Foundations operate like corporations and individuals in their social exchange behavior. Foundation grants are provided to nonprofit agencies in exchange for activities that satisfy the interests of founders, trustees, and managers" (Mixer, 1993, p. 83). The Foundation Center in New York was founded in 1956 and is the leading source of information on foundations in the United States and is growing globally connecting 450 information networks (Foundation Center, 2015). Foundations have their own boards and staff. From a legal perspective in the U.S., foundations are required to distribute a minimum of 5% of interest income annually (COP, 2007; Sheldon, 2000). During high economic times, foundations may give more; however, the 5% minimum insures stability in the long-term even when economic times are challenging, such as the two recessions already experienced in the 21st Century. In 2012, there were "86,192 foundations" in the United States "with $715-billion in assets and $52 billion in giving" (Foundation

Center, 2014, p. 2). Education continues to be a significant benefactor (Foundation Center, 2014). Total contributions from all philanthropic sources in 2014 was $358.38 billion; foundations provided roughly 15% of all philanthropic funds, which is $53.757 billion (Giving USA Foundation, 2015). With a more steady economy, foundations can continue to give more, which is the current trend.

Foundations usually have established guidelines, timelines, expectations for performance, and processes (Ciconte & Jacob, 2009; Tromble, 1998). The size of the foundation (i.e., financial status and amount of staff) makes a difference in its formality or informality with processes, timelines, and requirements. "Small foundations more closely resemble individual donors. Large foundations…see themselves as innovators, agents of change on a large scale, the Research and Development branch of society" (Locke, 1996, p. 21). Although it is possible to build relationships between CFRs and appropriate foundation officers, it is necessary to identify relevant areas of interest to pursue (Clevenger, 2014; Tromble, 1998). Corporate foundations "require tangible evidence of impact, progress, return on dollars invested" (Locke, 1996, p. 20). Effective foundations "nimbly address systematic problems… take stock of what's being learned and share this information with others, engage stakeholders…and collaborate with other funders" (McCray, 2012, p. 1). Traditionally, foundations perform evaluations retrospectively for internal consumption, while today both formative and summative evaluations are conducted "to assess the effectiveness of their programming and to increase organizational learning" (Fulton & Blau, 2005, p. 29). McIlnay (1998) explained that foundations had a confounding history in the 20th Century from their inception through a myriad of political and economic forces that have challenged and enhanced their abilities to function. In the most recent decades, greater competition exists for their resources.

Corporate foundations are a formalized type of nonprofit organizations created by parent corporations as independent entities for programmatic and charitable purposes. These foundations are used to direct corporate funds for program-specific interests and programs for nonprofits (including higher education) and are heavily influenced by the corporations' goals and values—maintaining close ties and alignment. Funding is given in the form of foundation grants (Ciconte & Jacob, 2009; Mixer, 1993; Sheldon, 2000; Walton & Gasman, 2008; Worth, 2002). Corporate foundation creation surged in the 1950s. In the 1960s and 1970s corporations truly became corporate citizens with the goal of helping society-at-large in a variety of areas. Additionally, "corporations discovered the power of doing good" (Ciconte & Jacob, 2009, p. 178). "Corporate foundations, however, can be considered direct agents of their sponsoring firms" (Mixer, 1993, p. 83). Typically, motivation for corporate philanthropy includes "response to community obligations" or "large, visible signature programs that tackle critical issues" (Lim, 2010, p. 4). An attractive feature of a corporate foundation is its ability to serve as a holding tank (or reserve) for funds…not to cut back on its normal level of charitable support during less-profitable years for the corporation (Edie, 1991).

Eighty-one percent of U.S. companies have established a corporate foundation (Rose, 2011). Fulton and Blau (2005) reported that foundations

…are experimenting with ways to put more of their endowments to philanthropic use: through socially responsible investing, ensuring that funders aren't investing in businesses antithetical to their missions; through shareholder activism that allows foundations to advocate for changes in corporate policy; and through 'program related investments' (PRIs) and loans from the corpus in ventures with a social benefit that may generate enough cash to repay the investment. (p. 25)

Corporate foundations come in a wide range of sizes and vary greatly in governance and management philosophies. Pinney (2012) said,

In some cases, corporate foundations are managed almost autonomously from the company and its broader corporate citizenship strategy. In other, the corporate foundation and its philanthropy are directly integrated and managed as part of corporate citizenship, which in turn is integrated with business strategy. Some foundations are led and staffed from outside the company by individuals with nonprofit or academic backgrounds but little or no experience in business. Others are led from within the company by those with strong business backgrounds but limited experience working outside that realm. Given this broad mix, it is unsurprising to see a range of opinions on the role and value of corporate foundations. (p. 10)

Corporate foundations need "to align and engage their efforts more closely with business" goals (Pinney, 2012, p. 4). Corporate foundations are also challenged to increase communications, to integrate with business activities, to measure outcomes, to collaborate strategically and intensively, and to use activities as competitive advantages. Corporate foundations are "an important instrument for value creation" (Pinney, p. 7). As governments have failed to meet needs and as society has increased demands, corporations, corporate foundations, and other foundations are turned to for resources and delivery systems (Pinney). "Corporate foundations and giving programs are well situated to exemplify philanthropy as an innovative investment in society" (Pinney, p. 18). McIlnay (1998) believed that foundations have a variety of roles to play including citizen, activist, and partner.

CORPORATE AND FOUNDATION RELATIONS DEVELOPMENT OFFICER: MAESTRO, PUPPET MASTER, OR MENACE?

Determining how to manage the organizational expectations of corporations, foundations, and other funding organizations involves several factors: the type and size of academic institution and the organization of its resource development functions, the size and goals of the external funding partner and the goals of the college or university, the persona and experience of the fundraiser or CFR and their funding organizations' counterpart, and both organizations' capacity to manage these complex relationships (Clevenger, 2014).

Fundraising functions range from small, traditional offices to larger organizations with either decentralized or centralized models (Johnson, 2008; McCoy, 2011). Larger organizations tend to have more staff and have specialists able to give full-time attention to corporate and foundation relations. And yet even larger organizations separate out corporate fundraising as corporate relations officer (or CRO) and foundation relations as grants officer or foundation relations officer (FRO).

The role of CFRs has evolved over time. An early facet was merely identification of organizational partners, solicitation, and stewardship of funds—just as processes for individual donors. However, corporations and foundations are much more complex and involve multiple people, various programs, and more volatile resources. Regardless of title, these CFRs must have a toolbox filled with an eclectic range of expertise to be effective in dealing with organizations: relationship emphasis, knowledge, ability to create value propositions, political savvy, excellent communications, ethical integrity, professionalism, stewardship, powerful influence, nimbleness, and patience.

While modern fundraising and resource strategies may include value-driven ROI propositions for corporations and foundations, there is not a total erosion of philanthropic efforts. Rather, as Saul (2011) promoted, there is a "renaissance" (p. 177) of thinking and new processes are being used to navigate the complexities of many funders' goals. Corporations and foundations—along with academic institutions—desire to improve social and environmental conditions through a wide range of social, medical, educational, scientific, environmental, artistic, and technological programs and initiatives.

Types of Development Programs

There are three primary development and CFR relations models found to be operating in higher education: philanthropic, centralized, or decentralized (Johnson, 2008). Additionally, a fourth model could be a hybrid of the others, depending on the size of the higher education institution and its approach (McCoy, 2011).

The philanthropic model is the traditional approach and focuses on matching corporate direct engagement and foundations with programming in a college or university; measurement is based on financial support. The decentralized model allows each academic institution—or college or school at a university—to build appropriate relationships with companies and foundations; measurement is based on each unit's objectives. The centralized, industrial-focused model coordinates institution-wide efforts to maximize interfacing with corporations and foundations under CFRs; measurement is based on a number of factors. The approach depends on the size of institution and the number of stakeholders potentially involved. However, regardless of size of institution, many corporations and foundations desire a single point of contact—or CFR—to interface, traffic, track, and manage relationships. Jacobson (1978) indicated a centralized program

...establishes working relationships with business in interests and university activities; solicits gift support from business and industry in a systematic manner; [and] provides a centralized office for assistance, guidance, and coordination of all matters as needed involving contact between corporations and university programs. (p. 22)

A central contact increases efficiencies and conserves resources (Castillo et al., 2015). In 2008, 42% of universities operated within the philanthropic model; 33%, in the decentralized model; and 25%, in the centralized, industrial-focused model (Johnson, 2008).

The decentralized system seems to be more cost effective but uncoordinated and potentially duplicating and counter-productive to higher education efforts (Johnson, 2007b). The centralized, industrial-model and the philanthropic model are more costly to operate and labor intensive but typically better organized as a key gatekeeper to manage the inter-organizational relationships and represent the academic institutions in maximizing networks and publicity (Clevenger, 2014; Johnson, 2007b; Pollack, 1998). However, the total impact of relationships is difficult to measure given the large number of intangibles involved (Johnson, 2007a).

Collaborations on campuses have been encouraged in recent years (Burson, 2009). Previously, the traditional approach yielded non-central efforts, silo creation, duplication of efforts, and individualistic interactions. The integrated approach for collaboration has created coordination, central relationship contact for a designated corporation, communication, concerted institutional representation, shared learning, and increased performance.

The Role of Corporate and Foundation Relation (CFR) Development Officers

The new era of resource development in the 21st Century requires higher education administrators, CFRs, and other fundraisers to not only create a case for support and engagement but to rethink the value propositions for corporations and other partners (Brock, 2007; Clevenger, 2014; Fulton & Blau, 2005; Saul, 2011). Brock (2007) and Saul (2011) both indicated that understanding other organizations' values and needs; speaking their language; creating solutions for business problems, opportunities, and needs; and assuring efficiency and effectiveness catapult relationship success.

Brock (2007) said, "Understand important trends and directions driving the industry. Understand their key measures of success. Try to anticipate the problems, challenges, and opportunities they face" (p. 2). Corporations and other partners are operating in a more and more complex environment with multiple needs and goals. Quantifying impact is the key for higher education and other organizations to engage in today's complex resource environment (Brock; Clevenger, 2014; Fulton & Blau, 2005; Saul, 2011). A main concern is determining the right opportunities for partnership (Hunt, 2012).

Ideally, a higher education institution should provide a centralized system to best coordinate and to maximize engagement with corporations and foundations (Clevenger, 2014).

CFRs spend time managing expectations, providing ongoing communications, and finding ways to keep organizations engaged (Clevenger; Hunt, 2012). The role of CFRs has expanded and continues to be more complex to manage and steward expectations and deliverables on behalf of an academic institution through multiple inter-organizational relationships. These relationships cover hundreds of initiatives and programs. The pressure on CFRs continues to increase as demands for additional resources and opportunities increases driving higher education to diversify funding streams and grow exponentially.

The Corporate and Foundation Relation Development Officers' Toolbox

Higher education leadership needs to create navigable, friendly systems to aid representatives with corporations and foundations in navigating working relationships with colleges and universities (Clevenger, 2014; Pollack, 1998; Sanzone, 2000). "Higher education and corporations have differing goals and objectives and different approaches to inter-organizational relationships" (Clevenger, p. 415). Additionally, higher education institutions need to think more like corporations or foundations think, to deeply understand their own resource capacities that support and help to define their value propositions, to seek appropriate funding or program partners, to create common dialogue and ongoing communication, and to embrace a transparent and accountable mind-set to measure and report activities and outcomes (Clevenger, 2014; Saul, 2011).

CFR leaders must have a toolbox filled with expertise to be effective in dealing with organizations: relationship emphasis, knowledge, ability to create value propositions, political savvy, excellent communications, ethical integrity, professionalism, stewardship, powerful influence, nimbleness, and patience. This particular set of tools provides CFRs the ability to represent their academic institution's interest while balancing the demands and expectations from corporations and foundations.

- **Relationship Emphasis:** The main function of CFRs is building relationships. Such a collaborative capacity "uses empathy and interpersonal understanding to build mutually beneficial relationships and connect and engage diverse groups of people" (Pinney & Kinnicutt, 2010, p. 19). "Key supports to develop and sustain strategic partnerships include strong relationships nurtured over time, trust, frequent and open communication, shared values and vision, and a common understanding of what it means to be involved in the partnership" (Eddy, 2010, p. xi). Motivations for the relationships between higher education and corporations and foundations include both intrinsic and extrinsic dynamics. When both parties have established intrinsic motivation, partnerships are likely to develop and be long lasting. Extrinsic motivation for resources or a network is also important; however, if either party in the relationship is forced on the other, is hindered or limited, or emphasizes short-term performance from pressures, then ill-fitting relationships ensue (Eddy, 2010). While resources may be at stake, the greatest benefit of mutual relationships is the social capital or long-term social benefit to society (Clevenger, 2014; Eddy, 2010; Fulton & Blau, 2005; Saul, 2011).
- **Knowledge:** CFRs need to be internally networked in their academic institution to be apprised of programs, initiatives, and research by maintaining relationships and up-to-date information with key internal stakeholders (Clevenger, 2014; Kinnicutt & Pinney, 2010; Pinney & Kinnicutt, 2010). This information may be stored in a database system as well as monitored on the college or university's website and/or provide via internal list serves. CFRs must also know where to get information and how to interface with internal stakeholders and external organizations to help develop mutual metrics for monitoring partnerships.
- **Ability to Create Value Propositions:** From knowledge and information about their institution's purposes and goals of programs, initiatives, and research, CFRs are able to create opportunities for corporate and foundation

relations representatives through proposals to offer win-win opportunities, thus offering value to funding partners. The process is iterative and flexible to meet each funding partner's goals or needs (Castillo et al., 2015).

- **Political Savvy:** A myriad of political and cultural issues face both higher education and funding organizations in managed relationships, such as formal authority, rules, regulations, decision making, control of boundaries, technology, interpersonal alliances, network capacities, control by counter organizations, management control, and other unknown variables (Bolman & Deal, 2008; Herman, 2008; Morgan, 2006; Saiia, 2001). Seven key variables for CFRs to manage include: (1) conflict vs. trust, (2) individual motivations vs. relationships, (3) institutional loyalty vs. shared values, (4) changed objectives vs. open communication, (5) lack of resources vs. organizational resources, (6) shift of key players vs. a strong champion, and (7) individual focus vs. partnership focus (Eddy, 2010). Each "of these items must continually be monitored and balanced to foster and to maintain positive, productive partnerships" (Clevenger, 2014, p. 108).

- **Excellent Communications:** CFRs raise both internal and external awareness (Pinney & Kinnicutt, 2010). CFRs can aid external partners in understanding and demystifying how to navigate a college or university (Castillo et al., 2015). CFRs track milestones and agreements as well as provide detailed reports including both qualitative and quantitative metrics to provide both parties with appropriate information for monitoring progress and outcomes (Castillo et al., 2015; Pinney & Kinnicutt, 2010). Likewise, CFRs then learn of corporate and foundation's likes, dislikes, and future plans to convey back to their academic institution.

- **Ethics:** The Golden Rule—do unto others as you would have them do unto you—is the most practical tool for behavioral ethics (Carroll & Buchholtz, 2015). Evans (2000) said,

It is always valuable to try to determine the conventions and standards that have been followed in the profession over the years. ...By raising ethical questions and by dealing with ethical matters in conferences and in literature, the development profession can help to sensitize individual practitioners. (pp. 365-366)

A host of other ethical tests are helpful such as common sense, comfort with making something public, and the *Big Four* (Carroll & Buchholtz). The Big Four includes greed, speed, laziness, and haziness. Any of these unethical actions lead to major issues quickly in CFR. Caboni's (2010) research yielded six concerns in fundraising ethics: commission-based compensation, dishonest solicitation, donor manipulation, exaggeration of professional experience, and institutional mission abandonment, and unreasonable enforcement of pledges. All of these issues are also contrary to ethical integrity.

- **Professionalism:** The most important professional consideration for CFRs is a comfort level with ambiguity. Dynamics are constantly changing within a college or university, the economy, organizational goals of corporations and foundation, and key contacts within any organization (Clevenger, 2014). All of these factors create chaotic, ever-changing demands pushing CFRs to adjust and to respond accordingly.
- **Stewardship:** An ongoing process is providing appropriate thanks, accolades, recognition, praise, and touch points to keep organizations engaged; this process is *stewardship* (Bunce & Leggett, 1994; Castillo et al., 2015; Clevenger, 2014; Sheldon, 2000). These processes must be meaningful to the respective donor organizations. "The institution must prove its ability to consistently use and manage gifts and other corporate revenue responsibly" (Sanzone, 2000, p. 324).
- **Powerful Influence:** CFRs use "organizational awareness and interpersonal communication skills to influence others" (Pinney & Kinnicutt, 2010, p. 21). Additionally, it takes friends and allies to achieve goals (Bolman & Deal, 2008). Identifying key stakeholders, planning relationship steps, assessing timelines, and negotiating contribute to developing and managing influence.
- **Nimbleness:** While organizations may take the time to create strategies and goals and approve funding, they often demand quick responses to ideas, concerns, or questions. CFRs must be nimble to organize and respond to inquiries, provide key content, navigate internal liaisons with programs and departments, have a keen knowledge of fundraising materials and value propositions, and understand whom to get information from on short notice (Castillo et al., 2015; DeYoung, 2014; McCray, 2012).
- **Patience:** Fundraising is part art and part science (Garecht, 2015). A basic concept for all fundraisers is patience: realizing building relationships takes time (Burnson, 2009; Ciconte & Jacob, 2009; Clevenger, 2014; Garecht). Dealing with corporations and foundations means those organizations are internally processing decisions for funding relating to opportunities; the more people involved, the longer the process.

SOLUTIONS AND RECOMMENDATIONS FOR MANAGING CORPORATE AND FOUNDATION RELATIONS

Higher education must offer a cafeteria plan of opportunities (Clevenger, 2014). Pollack (1998) said, "the more areas of involvement, the stronger the partnership" (p. 16). "Key supports to develop and sustain strategic partnerships include strong relationships nurtured over time, trust, frequent and open communication, shared values and vision, and a common understanding of what it means to be involved in the partnership" (Eddy, 2010, p. xi). Main concerns for higher education tend to focus on the need for viable resources to operate and grow, enriching student experiences, and creating real-world solutions (Clevenger). Corporations' main needs from academic institutions include availability of an educated and equipped workforce, ability to contribute back to society as corporate citizens, to foster brand development, and collaborating to conduct research, while foundations look to the academy to partner on issues or initiatives (Clevenger).

Managing the process with so many complexities of multiple internal stake-holders, aggressive and demanding funding partners, and administrative functions such as taxes, legal protocols, and reporting require much planning, tracking, and follow-up. Several emerging best practices have come from across the nation through academicians, fundraising practitioners, and liaisons from funding agencies through NACRO, which have created three white papers with models to address the inner-workings of inter-organizational behavior, complex web of activities, and depth of stakeholder management techniques.

Emphasis on Fundraising via Inter-Organizational Relationships

Organizations invariably must interact with one another, particularly if it is purposeful to devise mutually beneficial ventures (Clevenger, 2014; Pfeffer & Salancik, 2003; Shafritz et al., 2005). Organizations must approach inter-organizational relationships with ethical frameworks and processes as a basis (Clevenger, 2014). Higher education institutions have to place inter-organizational relationships for fundraising and philanthropy as a central priority (Bornstein, 2003, 2011; Clevenger, 2014).

Brock (2007), Clevenger (2014), Sanzone (2000), and Saul (2011) all indicated that understanding the other organization's values and needs; speaking their language; creating solutions for business problems, opportunities, and needs; and assuring efficiency and effectiveness catapult relationship success. Ring and Van de Ven (1994) identified three key processes for successful inter-organizational relationships: negotiations to identify needs and expectations, commitments to solidify and formalize intentions, and execution of commitments.

Partnerships with organizations "are interactive, ongoing, dynamic relationships that evolve and change over time" (Sanzone, 2000, p. 322). Successful inter-organizational relationships have four main concerns: organizations have had to develop strategic advantages, to provide cooperative advantages, the ability to respond to complexity, and to navigate scrutiny to build success (Fulton & Blau, 2005). Each organization must have its own agendas established to investigate potential mutual interests with other organizations or be totally open to wanting new opportunities (Clevenger, 2014). "Once mutually compatible goals are established, the relationship works through a plan to help stay on track" (Clevenger, 2014, p. 91). Saul (2011) said organizations seek reciprocity and ROI that includes performance as well as transparency and reporting.

Focusing on Key Areas of Interest for Higher Education

Higher education has its own agenda for desiring to engage with corporations and foundations. Colleges and universities are committed to forming partnerships and networks with the business community and foundations are integral components to help fulfill their mission (Clevenger, 2014; Gould, 2003). The goal of engaging corporations and foundations is to develop tailored partnerships where CFRs work closely with companies and foundations to identify value-added opportunities for deep relationship. Businesses and other organizations are given access to the intellectual assets in a higher education setting that will help to benefit society as a whole. Such attention improves the quantity and quality of organizational relationships to benefit the entire college or university while building value for corporations and foundations.

Engaging corporate and foundation partners begins with a needs assessment then internal planning and matching of college or university priorities. Major needs for higher education today include "viable resources, student enrichment, and real-world connectivity" (Clevenger, 2014, p. 268). *Viable resources* is the primary motive for a higher education institution to accept corporate citizenship engagement and financial support from companies as well as foundation partners and includes funding for students, endowments, sponsorships, sponsored research, in-kind gifts, building funds, and vendor relationships (Clevenger; Eddy, 2010; Fischer, 2000; Gould, 2003; Rhodes, 2001; Rose, 2011).

A main emphasis of today's higher education experience is "to provide real-world experiences for students to apply what they are learning in the classroom and to understand how their discipline or field of study fits into today's complex society" (Clevenger, 2014, p. 285). External partners—particularly corporations—provide a range of *student enrichment* opportunities, which is the second major motive for a higher education institution and includes scholarships, programs, in-class projects, idea generation, competitions, and internships"(Clevenger, p. 278). Corporations and other organizations "can provide students opportunities to take what they are learning in the classroom and apply it to the real world as well as learning how their expertise situates itself in today's society" (Clevenger, p. 279). Examples include providing real world issues or projects for in-class synthesis, idea generation to create new businesses or solutions for solving real-world issues by applying knowledge and skills, various competitions with rewards, and career development opportunities such as internships.

Higher education "is greatly aware of its role in society and exists to serve its students, the local community, the state, the region, the United States, and the world" (Clevenger, 2014, p. 286). Academic institutions collaborate with governments, corporations, foundations, and other organizations to contribute solutions to real-world problems through connectivity in various capacities (Clevenger; Pollack, 1998; Sanzone, 2000; Saul, 2011; Siegel, 2012). *Real-world connectivity* includes social connectivity, economic connectivity, cultural connectivity, environmental connectivity, and sustainability (Clevenger).

Focusing on Key Areas of Interest for Corporations and Foundations

Current trends in why corporations and foundations engage in relationships with higher education include workforce development, community enrichment, brand development, and research (Clevenger, 2014). These areas often overlap and are concerned with promoting causes, discoveries, and investing in social capital. As one might anticipate, society looks to higher education for answers, creativity, and employable individuals. Additionally, corporations and foundations in the 21st Century have begun to focus on long-term impact and sustainability. With that consideration in mind—and tough economic times the past dozen years—funding and philanthropy opportunities have been steam lined by organizations to a single signature program or initiative, or certainly fewer but stronger relationships instead of trying to fund all considerations in smaller, less significant ways.

In order to compete in today's economy, the value of a higher education has never been greater. A major output of higher education is to provide a highly skilled and educated workforce to society. Workforce development is the top reason entities engage with higher education. *Workforce development* includes internships, graduate recruitment, training and development, executive leadership, and specialist consultation (Clevenger, 2014).

Community enrichment highlights community commitment and motives for inter-organizational engagement as well as summarizes five major areas of importance for corporations, foundations, and other organizations and causes to engage with academic institutions as sub-themes including community development, economic development, employment, higher education resources, and environmental protection (Clevenger, 2014).

Corporations and foundations need a range of marketing mediums to support brand development to create and maintain a positive public image. *Brand recognition* is provided in name or logo repetition through advertising, promotions, and sponsorships (Clevenger, 2014).

A main emphasis for higher education—particularly universities—is research. *Research* arrangements between a college or university and a corporation or other partner may take on various forms such as collaborative partnerships, sponsored research, or industry sustainability research solutions (Clevenger, 2014). Collaborations include a wide array of partners—such as multiple colleges and universities, corporations and foundations, and governments—rallying around a major cause or concern such as medical research or a scientific discovery (Clevenger). Sponsored research entails potential future co-ownership of intellectual property or patents. "Industry sustainability research solutions may enable an entire industry to improve for better efficiencies to maximize scarce resources, increase longevity of product usefulness, or create improved processes or operations such as technology-related equipment" (Clevenger, 2014, p. 321). Research agreements and academic sponsorship guidelines outline roles and responsibilities of all parties (Clevenger).

Managing the Process

While many best practices have been found, large teams of academicians and practitioners associated with NACRO have spent recent years developing processes to facilitate and provide the latest tools, ideas, and content to appropriately manage higher education and external partnerships. While these ideas primarily focus on corporations, they are likely replicable in working with foundations, corporate foundations, government agencies, and other organizations. Five key emphases for CFRs, which may be adapted and implemented to fit the academic institution, include providing (1) institutional support, (2) mutual benefits, (3) one-stop shopping, (4) integrated research development, and (5) campus coordination (Abbott et al., 2011; Cleland et al., 2012). Institutional support is important, so all administration and programs are invested in the importance of corporate and foundation relations including adequate staffing, research, and internal funding to execute on agreed-upon programming. Obviously, only those relationships with mutual benefit are entered into to maximize the academic institution's goals while meeting those of external partners. A central point of contact—the CFR—allows for streamlined interactions as a one-stop shop. Integrated research development is often tough, but it pushes an academic institution to set its priorities for research, development, and technology transfer, including needed staffing and equipment. Finally, campus coordination is made easier through only key liaisons to minimize confusion and duplication of efforts. The campus coordination interfaces with the CFR as the single-point-of-contact with each corporation or foundation.

Several models provide frameworks to understand CFR functions. The first is the Partnership Continuum by Wayne C. Johnson, former vice president of HP University Relations (Johnson, 2003). NACRO constituents have crafted four important visuals emphasizing partnerships: the Corporate Engagement Process (Cleland et al., 2012), the Metrics Pyramid (Cleland et al., 2012), the Corporate Relationship Continuum (Cleland et al., 2012), and the Center Development Cycle (Castillo et al., 2015).

The HP Relationship Continuum (Figure 1) provides a y-axis of "Levels of Engagement" and x-axis ranging from "Traditional Engagement to Holistic Engagement" (Abbott et al., 2011, p. 3). Five seemingly sequential stages of organizational partnerships include awareness, involvement, support, sponsorship, and strategic partnership (Abbott et al., 2011).

The Corporate Engagement Process (Figure 2) is a sophisticated flow diagram to elaborate on seven major steps (Cleland et al., 2012, p. 4) to matriculate partners, including: creating access, building awareness of academic programs and offerings,

Figure 1. The partnership continuum (Johnson, 2003)

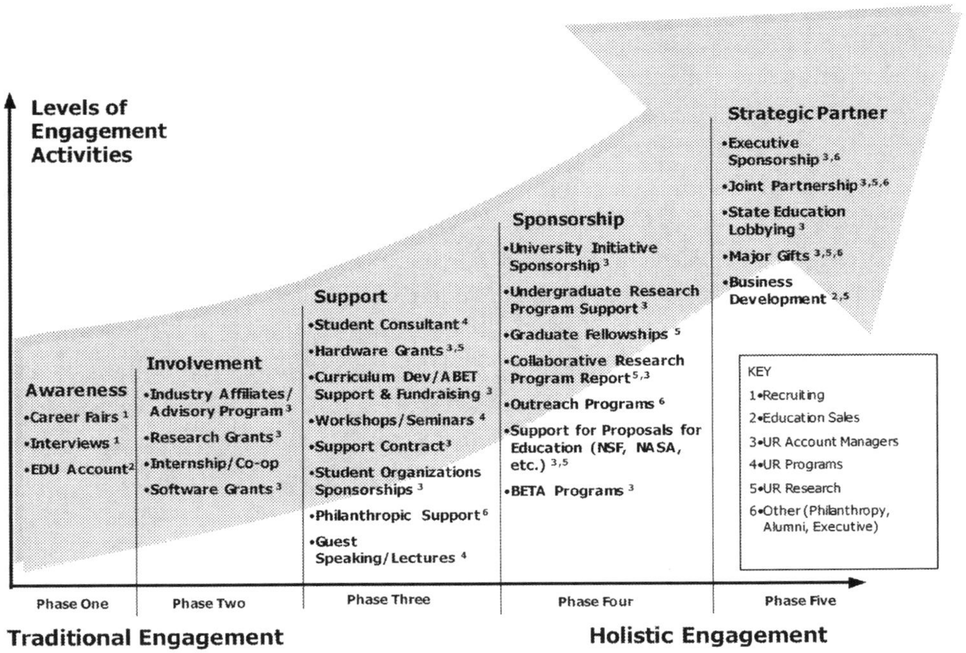

Figure 2. The corporate engagement process (Cleland et al., 2012)
This process was designed by a team from the Network of Academic Corporate Relations Officers (NACRO) team including: Todd A. Cleland, University of Washington; Beth Colledge, Penn State University; Mona Ellerbrock, University of California, Davis; Kathy Lynch, Boston University; Don McGowen, Tufts University; Sacha Patera, Northwestern University; Jennifer Schwartz, University of Maryland; and Jon See, Purdue University).

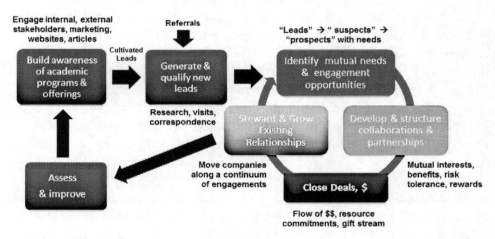

generating potential partnership leads, defining official mutual needs and creating engagement opportunities with external partners, developing supportive structure for managing collaborations and partnerships, executing a legal memorandum and financial commitment, and implementing and monitoring each initiative including the stewardship component.

As with other fundraising schema, NACRO constituents created The Metrics Pyramid (Figure 3) to illustrate work expectations and roles and responsibilities (Cleland et al., 2012). Three pyramid sections from the bottom up include development staff or CFRs, internal organizational liaisons and peers, and the senior leadership on top. CFRs have the broadest responsibility, then organizational peers. Senior administrators play a key role, but spend a somewhat lesser amount of time.

The Corporate Relationship Continuum in Figure 4 (Cleland et al., 2012) provides a y-axis of "Levels of Engagement" and x-axis ranging from "Traditional Engagement" to "Partnership" (Cleland et al., 2012, p. 11). Five seemingly sequential stages of organizational partnerships include "Single Point of Engagement," "Managed Relationship," "Tailored Relationship," "Broad Based Engagement," and "Strategic Partner" (Cleland et al, 2012, p. 11).

Most recently, NACRO has determined that best practices for CFRs' functionality is to focus on five types of opportunities: (1) philanthropic donations for a specific program, (2) higher education-initiated ventures typically based on faculty

Figure 3. The metrics pyramid (Cleland et al., 2012)
This pyramid was designed by a team from the Network of Academic Corporate Relations Officers (NACRO) team including: Todd A. Cleland, University of Washington; Beth Colledge, Penn State University; Mona Ellerbrock, University of California, Davis; Kathy Lynch, Boston University; Don McGowen, Tufts University; Sacha Patera, Northwestern University; Jennifer Schwartz, University of Maryland; and Jon See, Purdue University).

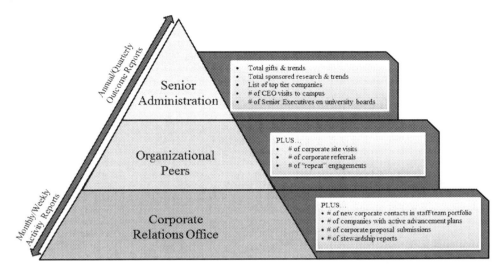

objectives, (3) awards tied to government opportunities where the academy and corporate partners are needed, (4) economic development needs, typically workforce oriented, and (5) industry-driven opportunities and initiatives that often have deliverables as outcomes (Castillo et al., 2015). Additionally, NACRO has best defined the process stages for CFRs to facilitate and foster the process of relationships: (1) engage key stakeholders, (2) define expectations that build and implement partnerships, (3) launch and monitor relationships, (4) maintain support systems for ongoing engagement including stewardship, and (5) periodically evaluate and make adjustments or improvements (Castillo et al., 2015) (see Figure 5).

Key Takeaways for Implementation

CFRs and their respective institutions must understand the complexities and resource investment to successfully interact with corporations and foundations. A key priority is making sure the academic institution has set internal goals and priorities. Higher education has much to offer other organizations and society, so it must understand and package those offerings to create mutually beneficial inter-organizational relationships. The onus is on the higher education side to initiate activities, monitor and track progress, and report back on programs.

The Role of Corporate and Foundation Relations Development Officers (CFRs)

Figure 4. The corporate relationship continuum (Cleland et al., 2012)

This continuum was designed by a team from the Network of Academic Corporate Relations Officers (NACRO) team including: Todd A. Cleland, University of Washington; Beth Colledge, Penn State University; Mona Ellerbrock, University of California, Davis; Kathy Lynch, Boston University; Don McGowen, Tufts University; Sacha Patera, Northwestern University; Jennifer Schwartz, University of Maryland; and Jon See, Purdue University).

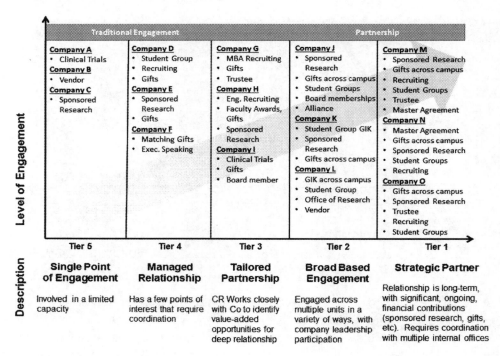

Corporate resources tend to be more volatile as they are directly tied to corporations' annual profitability. Foundation resources tend to be more stable as foundations are legally required to give away a minimum of 5% interest income annually. While individual giving is a larger overall corpus of dollars, society and higher education institutions pay more notice to corporate and foundation giving as they are often larger single amounts, have programmatic focus, and maintain higher profiles.

On-going inter-organizational relationships involve a variety of stages that must be proactively managed by CFRs. Effective CFRs—regardless of title—must have a toolbox filled with an eclectic range of expertise to be effective in dealing with funding organizations: a relationship emphasis, knowledge of their own institution, an ability to create value propositions, political savvy, excellent communications, ethical integrity, professionalism, stewardship, powerful influence, nimbleness, and patience. An on-going process of analysis by CFRs understands motives, preconditions and contingencies of maintaining strong inter-organizational relationships,

Figure 5. Center development cycle (Castillo et al., 2015)
This cycle was designed by a team from the Network of Academic Corporate Relations Officers (NA-CRO) team including: Brent Burns, Michigan Technological University; R. D. Castillo, University of Arizona; Beth Colledge, Penn State University; Mona Ellerbrock, University of California, Davis; Victor Haroldson, University of California, Davis; Cody Noghera, University of California San Diego; Anne O'Donnell, University of California San Diego; Sacha Patera, Northwestern University; Jon See, Purdue University; and Olof Westerstahl, University of Illinois at Urbana-Champaign).

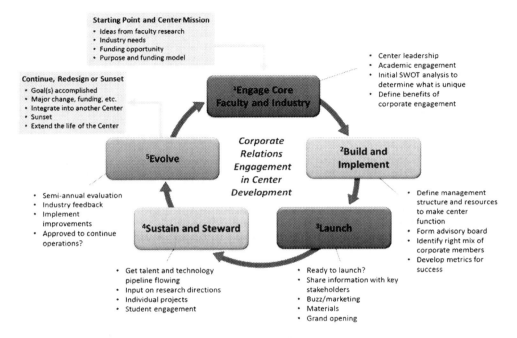

understanding the depth and content of each program, and aiding in the measurement and reporting of the outcomes. Beyond these dynamics, organizations continue to learn how to act and to react with other organizations to create win-win outcomes (Clevenger, 2014; Ebers, 1999; Meyer & Rowan, 1977; Morgan, 2006; Pfeffer & Salancik, 2003).

Utilizing the toolbox and successfully navigating these complex inter-organizational relationships would allow a CFR to be a maestro. Juggling the multiple priorities with too much force, lack of knowledge, unprofessional manipulation, or improper timing would yield a CFR trying to control and force issues, which creates a one-sided puppet master mentality. A CFR would likely be a menace if behaving unethically, ignoring key internal or external priorities, or asking more of external funding relationships than stewarding the process.

FUTURE RESEARCH DIRECTIONS

Additional research on higher education's inter-organizational relationships would provide more and diverse types of best practices regarding sizes of CFR functions and development offices, operational systems in fundraising offices, and a deeper understanding of expectations of CFRs. As colleges and university adopt models provided by NACRO, tracking of performance and utilization would be helpful to continue to influence realities faced by CFRs. Metrics developed by NACRO need to be reported on by higher education institutions adopting and implementing measures; those reports need to be aggregated, and implications can be assessed as influenced by practice and adjustment. Past research by AFP and CASE could be replicated to see how corporate and foundation relations have changed in the most recent century.

CONCLUSION

Corporations and foundations engage with an academic institution because of the various and quality opportunities, an array of academic resources, access to human capital, compatible relationships with an amiable mindset toward community, forward-thinking nature, and attention to inter-organizational relationships. Academic institutions offering many opportunities create a greater likelihood for corporations and foundations to find multiple areas of mutual interest.

Organizations needing resources should "Understand important trends and directions driving the industry. Understand their key measures of success. Try to anticipate the problems, challenges, and opportunities they face" (Brock, 2007, p. 2). Corporations, foundations, and other organizations are operating in a continually more complex environment facing multiple and complex needs and goals. Additionally, quantifying impact is the key for higher education and nonprofits to engage in today's complex resource environment (Brock; Clevenger, 2014; Fulton & Blau, 2005; Saul, 2011). On the higher education side, while many variables may be tracked, dollars are the primary monitoring measurement for corporate and foundation engagement (Hartford, 2000). However, colleges and universities typically measure "success by student achievement, faculty research and scholarship, alumni accomplishments, and contributions to society" (Clevenger, 2014, p. 415). The ultimate goal is developing strong relationships for long-term mutual benefit and productivity (Bruch & Walter, 2005; Carroll & Buchholtz, 2015; Clevenger; Eddy, 2010; Siegel, 2012).

REFERENCES

Abbot, E., Borchert, A., Dwyer, M., Fuller, C., Gibbs, G., Hanifan, M., …Zeller, K. (2011). *Five elements of a successful twenty-first century university corporate relations program.* White Paper, Network of Academic Corporate Relations Officers Benchmarking Committee, August 2, 2011. Retrieved from http://www.nacroonline.org/ assets/docs/essential%20elements_white_paper_final.pdf

Acar, W., Aupperle, K. E., & Lowry, R. M. (2001). An empirical exploration of measures of social responsibility across the spectrum of organization types. *The International Journal of Organizational Analysis, 9*(1), 26–57. doi:10.1108/eb028927

Aldrich, H. E. (1979). *Organizations and environments.* Englewood Cliffs, NJ: Prentice-Hall.

Andresen, K. (2006). *Robin Hood marketing: Stealing corporate savvy to sell just causes.* San Francisco, CA: Wiley & Sons.

Ashforth, B. E., & Mael, F. (1989). Social identity theory and the organization. *Academy of Management Review, 14*(1), 20–39.

Benioff, M., & Adler, C. (2007). *The business of changing the world: Twenty great leaders on strategic corporate philanthropy.* New York, NY: McGraw-Hill.

Berle, A. A., & Means, G. C. (1968). *The modern corporation and private property.* New York, NY: Harcourt Brace and World.

Bolman, L. G., & Deal, T. D. (2008). *Reframing organizations: Artistry, choice, and leadership* (4th ed.). San Francisco, CA: Wiley.

Bornstein, R. (2003). *Legitimacy in the academic presidency: From entrance to exit.* Washington, DC: Roman & Littlefield Publishers.

Bornstein, R. (2011). *Fundraising advice for college and university presidents: An insider's guide.* Washington, DC: AGB Press.

Brennan, M. J. (2000). Strategic corporate alliances: The importance of internal institutional collaborations. In M. K. Murphy's (Ed.), Corporate and foundation support: Strategies for funding education in the 21st century (pp. 51-54). New York, NY: Case.

Brock, D. (2007, July 5). Focus on a customer's need to buy, not on your need to sell. *EyesOnSales.* Retrieved from http://www.eyesonsales.com/content/article/focus_on_a_customers_need_to_buy_not_your_need_to_sell

Bruch, H., & Walter, F. (2005). The keys to rethinking corporate philanthropy. *MIT Sloan Management Review*, *47*(1), 48–55.

Buchanan, P. W. (1991). *Variables influencing corporate giving to higher education in Michigan.* (Unpublished doctoral dissertation). The University of Michigan, Ann Arbor, MI.

Building Business Investment in Community (BBIC). (2002). *The business of giving back: 2002 survey of business and community giving.* Retrieved from http://www.mnchamber.com/foundation/2002_Summary_Report.pdf

Bunce, R. L., & Leggett, S. F. (1994). *Dollars for excellence: Raising private money for private schools and public schools.* London: Precept Pr.

Burson, E. N. (2009, August 13-14). *Management of the long-term relationship.* Presentation at the NACRO Annual Meeting, Seattle, WA. Retrieved from http://www.nacroonline.org/conference-presentations

Business-Higher Education Forum (BHEF). (2015). Retrieved from http://www.bhef.com/about

Caboni, T. C. (2010). The normative structure of college and university fundraising behaviors. *The Journal of Higher Education*, *81*(3), 339–365. doi:10.1353/jhe.0.0094

Carey, K. (2012). *Partnering with universities NACRO 2012: Managing different drivers of corporate funding–research funding, branding/marketing, and recruiting.* Presentation at the NACRO Conference, Evanston, IL. Retrieved from http://www.nacroonline.org/conference-presentations

Carroll, A. B., & Buchholtz, A. K. (2015). *Business & society: Ethics and stakeholder management.* Stamford, CT: Cengage Learning.

Castillo, R. D., Colledge, B., Ellerbrock, M., Haroldsen, V., Noghera, C., Patera, S., & See, J. (2015). *Engagement of academic corporate relations officers in university-industry centers of research excellence.* White Paper, Network of Academic Corporate Relations Officers Benchmarking Committee, July 15, 2015. Retrieved from http://www.nacroonline.org/assets/docs/Benchmarking/nacro%20center%20development%20paper-full.pdf

Ciconte, B. L., & Jacob, J. G. (2009). *Fundraising basics: A complete guide* (3rd ed.). Sudbury, MA: Jones and Bartlett.

Cleland, T. A., Colledge, B., Ellerbrock, M., Lynch, K., McGowan, D., Patera, S., . . . See, J. (2012). *Metrics for a successful twenty-first century academic corporate relations program.* White Paper, Network of Academic Corporate Relations Officers Benchmarking Committee, Retrieved from http://www.nacroonline.org/ assets/ metrics%20whitepaper%202012%20final.pdf

Clevenger, M. R. (2014). *An organizational analysis of the inter-organizational relationships between a public American higher education university and six United States corporate supporters: An instrumental, ethnographic case study using Cone's corporate citizenship spectrum.* (Unpublished doctoral dissertation). University of Missouri-Columbia, Columbia, MO.

Cohen, A. M. (2010). *The shaping of American higher education: Emergency and growth of the contemporary system* (2nd ed.). San Francisco, CA: Jossey-Bass.

Council for the Advancement and Support of Education (CASE). (2015). Retrieved from http://www.case.org

Cropper, S., Ebers, M., Huxham, C., & Ring, P. S. (Eds.). (2008). *The Oxford handbook of inter-organizational relations.* New York, NY: Oxford University Press. doi:10.1093/oxfordhb/9780199282944.001.0001

Crutchfield, L. R., & Grant, H. M. (2008). *Forces for good: The six practices of high-impact nonprofits.* San Francisco, CA: Jossey-Bass.

Cummings, D. L. (1991). Building relationships with grantseekers. In J. P. Shannon (Ed.), *The corporate contributions handbook: Devoting private means to public needs* (pp. 299–309). San Francisco, CA: Jossey Bass.

DeMillo, R. A. (2011). *Abelard to Apple: The fate of American colleges and universities.* Cambridge, MA: MIT.

DeYoung, B. (2014, July 14). *Be nimble: The third tip in assessing your fundraising strategies.* Retrieved from http://www.jenzabar.com/blog/fundraising-strategies-nimble/

Ebers, M. (1999). The dynamics of inter-organizational relationships. *Sociology of Organizations, 16,* 31–56.

Eddy, P. L. (2010). *Partnerships and collaborations in higher education. ASHE Higher Education Report, 36(2).* San Francisco, CA: Wiley.

Elliott, D. (2006). *The kindness of strangers: Philanthropy and higher education.* New York, NY: Rowman & Littlefield Publishers.

Evans, G. A. (2000). Ethical issues in fund raising. In P. Buchanan (Ed.), *Handbook of institutional advancement* (3rd ed.; pp. 363–366). Washington, DC: CASE.

Fischer, M. (2000). *Ethical decision making in fund raising.* New York, NY: Wiley.

Foundation Center. (2014). *Key facts on U.S. foundations, 2014 edition.* Retrieved from http://foundationcenter.org/gainknowledge/research/keyfacts2014/pdfs/Key_Facts_on_US_Foundations_2014.pdf

Foundation Center. (2015). *About foundation center.* Retrieved from http://foundationcenter.org/about/

Fox, M. A. (2006). Universities, businesses and public authorities—and the inclusive development of society. In L. E. Weber & J. J. Duderstadt (Eds.), *Universities and business: Partnering for the knowledge society* (pp. 187–199). London: Economica Ltd.

Fulton, K., & Blau, A. (2005). *Looking out for the future: An orientation for twenty-first century philanthropists.* Cambridge, MA: The Monitor Group.

Gardberg, N. A., & Fombrun, C. J. (2006). Corporate citizenship: Creating intangible assets across institutional environments. *Academy of Management Review, 31*(2), 329–346. doi:10.5465/AMR.2006.20208684

Garecht, J. (2015). Major donor fundraising 101. *The Fundraising Authority.* Retrieved from http://www.thefundraisingauthority.com/individual-fundraising/major-donor-fundraising-101/

Giving U. S. A. Foundation. (2015). Giving USA 2015: The annual report on philanthropy for the year 2014. Chicago, IL: Giving USA Foundation.

Gould, E. (2003). *The university in a corporate culture.* New Haven, CT: Yale University Press.

Greenfield, J. M. (2008). Rights of donors. In J. G. Pettey (Ed.), *Ethical fundraising: A guide for nonprofit boards and fundraisers* (pp. 19–36). Hoboken, NJ: Wiley.

Hearn, J. C. (2003). *Diversifying campus revenue streams: Opportunities and risks.* Washington, DC: American Council on Education.

Herman, R. D. (2008). Regulation in the nonprofit sector: Symbolic politics and the social construction of accountability. In J. G. Pettey (Ed.), *Ethical fundraising: A guide for nonprofit boards and fundraisers* (pp. 235–245). Hoboken, NJ: Wiley.

Hoerr, T., Kucic, B., Wagener, A., & Nolan, M. (2010, August 11). *Small and medium-sized businesses: Finding mutual value.* Presentation at the 2010 NACRO Annual Conference, Urbana-Champaign, IL. Retrieved from http://www.nacroonline.org/conference-presentations

Hunt, P. C. (2012). *Development for academic leaders: A practical guide for fund-raising success.* San Francisco, CA: Jossey-Bass.

Jacobson, H. K. (Ed.). (1978). *Evaluating advancement programs: New directions for institutional advancement.* San Francisco, CA: Jossey-Bass.

Johnson, J. (2007a, August 16). *Making the connection: Metrics of success.* Presentation at the NACRO Annual Meeting, Minneapolis, MN. Retrieved from http://www.nacroonline.org/conference-presentations

Johnson, J. (2007b, August 16). *Making the connection: University-Industry relations and corporate relations models.* Presentation at the NACRO Annual Meeting, Minneapolis, MN. Retrieved from http://www.nacroonline.org/conference-presentations

Johnson, J. (2008, April 14-15). *Survey tools and implications: Measuring impact.* Presentation at the NACRO Annual Meeting, Atlanta, GA. Retrieved from http://www.nacroonline.org/conference-presentations

Johnson, W. C. (2003). University relations: The HP model. *Industry and Higher Education, 17*(6), 391–395. doi:10.5367/000000003322776280

Katz, D., & Kahn, R. L. (2005). Organizations and the system concept. In J. Shafritz, J. Ott, & Y. Jang (Eds.), *Classics of organization theory* (6th ed.; pp. 480–490). Boston, MA: Thomson Wadsworth.

Kinnicutt, S., & Pinney, C. (2010). Getting to the roots of success: The leadership competencies that grow corporate citizenship pros. *The Corporate Citizen, 4,* 26–30.

Lim, T. L. (2010). *Measuring the value of corporate philanthropy: Social impact, business benefits, and investor returns.* New York: Committee Encouraging Corporate Philanthropy.

Litan, R. E., & Mitchell, L. (2011). Should universities be agents of economic development? In C. J. Schramm (Ed.), *The future of the research university: Meeting the global challenges of the 21st century* (pp. 123–146). Kansas City, MO: The Ewing Marion Kauffman Foundation.

Locke, E. H. (1996, Fall). The foundations of a relationship. *Advancing Philanthropy,* 20-23.

McCoy, C. (2011). *Toward an understanding of causes and identified types of university-industry relations in U.S. public research universities.* (Unpublished master's thesis). Oklahoma State University, Oklahoma City, OK.

McCray, J. (2012). *Is grantmaking getting smarter? A national study of philanthropic practice.* Washington, DC: Grantmakers for Effective Organizations.

McGowan, D. (2012, August 1). *Academic corporate relations: Contact sport, slow waltz, or both?* Presentation at the NACRO Conference, Evanston, IL. Retrieved from http://www.nacroonline.org/conference-presentations

McIlnay, D. P. (1998). *How foundations work: What grantseekers need to know about the many faces of foundations.* San Francisco, CA: Jossey-Bass.

Meyer, J. W., & Rowan, B. (1977). Institutionalized organizations: Formal structure as myth and ceremony. *American Journal of Sociology, 83*(2), 340–363. doi:10.1086/226550

Mixer, J. R. (1993). *Principles of professional fundraising: Useful foundations for successful practice.* San Francisco, CA: Jossey-Bass.

Morgan, G. (2006). *Images of organization.* Thousand Oaks, CA: Sage.

Network of Academic Corporate Relations Officers (NACRO). (2015). Retrieved from http://www.nacroonline.org

Pfeffer, J., & Salancik, G. R. (2003). *The external control of organizations: A resource dependence perspective.* Stanford, CA: Stanford University Press.

Philip, C. S. (2012, August 1-3). *Corning and university technology collaborations.* Presentation at the NACRO Conference, Evanston, IL. Retrieved from http://www.nacroonline.org/conference-presentations

Pinney, C. (2012). *Increasing impact, enhancing value: A practitioner's guide to leading corporate philanthropy.* Council on Foundations. Retrieved from http://www.cof.org/sites/default/files/documents/files/CorporateGuide.pdf

Pinney, C., & Kinnicutt, S. (2010). *Leadership competencies for community involvement: Getting to the roots of success.* Boston: The Boston College Center for Corporate Citizenship.

Pollack, R. H. (1998). Give and take: Create a mutually beneficial relationship to bring corporate support to your campus. *Currents, 24*(2), 16–22.

Pollard, J. A. (1958). *Fund-raising for higher education.* New York, NY: Harper & Brothers, Publishers.

Rhodes, F. H. T. (2001). *The creation of the future: The role of the American university*. Ithaca, NY: Cornell University.

Ring, P. S., & Van de Ven, A. H. (1994). Developmental processes of cooperative interorganizational relationships. *Academy of Management Review, 19*(1), 90–118.

Ringleb, A. H., Meiners, R. E., & Edwards, F. L. (1997). *Managing in the legal environment* (3rd ed.). St. Paul, MN: West Publishing Company.

Rose, A. P. (2011). *Giving by the numbers 2011*. New York, NY: Committee Encouraging Corporate Philanthropy.

Rubenstein, D. (2004). *The good corporate citizen: A practical guide*. Hoboken, NJ: Wiley.

Saiia, D. H. (2001). Philanthropy and corporate citizenship: Strategic philanthropy is good corporate citizenship. *Journal of Corporate Citizenship, 2*(2), 57–74. doi:10.9774/GLEAF.4700.2001.su.00009

Sanzone, C. S. (2000). Securing corporate support: The business of corporate relations. In P. Buchanan (Ed.), Handbook of institutional advancement (vol. 3, pp. 321-324). Washington, DC: CASE.

Saul, J. (2011). *The end of fundraising: Raise more money selling your impact*. San Francisco, CA: Jossey-Bass.

Shafritz, J. M., Ott, J. S., & Jang, Y. S. (2005). *Classics of organization theory* (6th ed.). Boston: Thomson Wadsworth.

Sheldon, K. S. (2000). *Successful corporate fundraising: Effective strategies for today's nonprofits*. New York, NY: Wiley & Sons.

Siegel, D. (2012). Beyond the academic-corporate divide. *Academe, 98*(1), 29–31.

Smith, P. R. G. (1968). *The history of corporate financial assistance to member institutions of the associated colleges of Indiana 1948-1967*. (Unpublished doctoral dissertation). University of Notre Dame, Notre Dame, IN.

The Center on Philanthropy at Indiana University (COP). (2007). *Corporate philanthropy: The age of integration*. Indianapolis, IN: Indiana University. Retrieved from http://www.philanthropy.iupui.edu/files/research/corporate_giving_-_july_2007.pdf

Thompson, J. D. (2005). Organizations in action. In J. Shafritz, J. Ott, & Y. Jang (Eds.), *Classics of organization theory* (6th ed.; pp. 491–504). Boston, MA: Thomson Wadsworth.

Tromble, W. W. (1998). Corporate and foundation relations. In W. W. Tromble (Ed.), *Excellence in advancement: Applications for higher education and nonprofit organizations* (pp. 93–118). Gaithersburg, MD: Aspen Publishers.

University-Industry Demonstration Project (UIDP). (2015). Retrieved from http://sites.nationalacademies.org/pga/uidp/index.htm

Walton, A., & Gasman, M. (Eds.). (2008). *Philanthropy, volunteerism, and fundraising*. Upper Saddle River, NJ: Pearson.

World Economic Forum. (2002). *Global corporate citizenship initiative: The leadership challenge for CEOs and boards*. Retrieved from http://www.weforum.org/pdf/GCCI/GCCI_CEO_Questionnaire.pdf

Worth, M. J. (2002). *New strategies for educational fund-raising*. Portland, OR: Book News.

KEY TERMS AND DEFINITIONS

Corporate-Foundation Relations (CFR): CFR is the term used in higher education referring to both the office(s) and staff members who interface with and have responsibility for managing and orchestrating corporate and foundation relations.

Corporation: A corporation is a for-profit entity that may be publicly or privately held. In this context, business or company is synonymous with corporation.

Cultivation: Cultivation is the process university representatives use to interest corporations in engaging with an institution and its programs (Sheldon, 2000).

Engagement: Is the process of both parties—a college or university and each corporation or foundation—in a relationship taking reciprocal active interest in each other at various levels through shared goals, communication, volunteerism, and/or resource dependence.

Foundation: A foundation is a not-for-profit entity or non-governmental organization established to manage resources for the benefit of society.

Grant: Grants are a traditional type of financial support funded by foundations. An organization submits an application as part of a competitive review process.

In-Kind Support/Gift-in-Kind: Non-cash support with value (like services) is provided by some corporations to nonprofit organizations (e.g., printing, accounting, legal, technology), loaned staff or executives for special purposes, facility usage, equipment, or goods and products. Such donations are usually tax-deductible for the corporation.

Partner: A partner is a mutually-connected entity aligned with common goals.

Programmatic Initiative: Foundations and sometimes corporations desire to focus on a specific program or research project and consider it their programmatic initiative.

ROI: Return on investment, or ROI, is the measure of the efficiency or impact of an organization or program.

Signature Platform: Corporations often focus on a single cause or initiative and label it as a national platform or signature platform that they wish to own and promote.

Sponsor: A sponsor funds an opportunity and expects brand or logo recognition or other outcomes.

Stewardship: Stewardship is the process of thanking and recognizing a corporation for its support through relationship and communication by providing thank-you letters, reports, press releases, awards, public recognition, or named recognition on plaques.

Chapter 12
Alumni Giving and Social Exchange:
A Study of Alumni Giving Behavior

Lauren E. B. Dodge
University of Illinois, USA

ABSTRACT

Fundraising efforts at institutions of higher education continue to be a top priority, especially as funding from state governments decline. Public institutions have been looking to private institutions, as they are believed to have been leading the way in cultivating alumni donations since their inception. Higher education institutions must understand what determines the greatest alumni giving if the field is to improve their fundraising efforts, and student and alumni engagement is a key indicator of philanthropic gifts. A survey was administered to gather important insight into the giving behavior of alumni of an engineering department at a large research university located in the Midwestern area of the United States. The purpose of this survey is to understand the correlation between alumni giving and engagement while a student and as alumni.

INTRODUCTION

Fundraising efforts at institutions of higher education continue to be a top priority, especially as funding from state governments decline. Public institutions have been looking to private institutions, as they are believed to have been leading the way in cultivating alumni donations since their inception. Higher education institutions

DOI: 10.4018/978-1-4666-9664-8.ch012

must understand what determines the greatest alumni giving if the field is to improve their fundraising efforts; student and alumni engagement is a key indicator of philanthropic gifts.

The purpose of this survey is to understand the correlation between alumni giving and engagement while a student and as alumni. The results of this survey will guide future efforts to cultivate alumni and students, and may further contribute to the body of literature on alumni giving and university advancement.

The results of this study will not be generalizable to all departments within higher education institutions or to all alumni of departments in higher education, but these results will provide an important insight into the giving behavior of alumni of an engineering department at a large research university located in the Midwestern area of the United States, and may be used to inform future fundraising policy and initiatives. The results of this study may also provide information to other small, sciences-based, undergraduate and graduate degree granting departments and institutions of higher education regarding alumni attitudes about giving and philanthropic behavior, and may encourage these other comparable departments to implement a similar study. Information on alumni philanthropic behavior is important for institutions of higher education to continue to implement successful fundraising policy and initiatives, and for professionals working in the field to better engage with prospective donors.

BACKGROUND

Historical Overview

The history of philanthropy in the United States follows a winding and varied path to the current structure. There are diverging and converging routes, multiple organizations and individuals involved, and a plethora of purposes and interests at stake. The following overview illustrates many of the key players, paths, and interests that shaped the American system of education through philanthropic means and brings us to the present.

Early American philanthropy began in the colonies and was characterized by the wishes to teach religion, the arts, and useful sciences, and to instruct youth in the colonies so that they would be fit for employment with the church and government. Gifts were generally unrestricted, but the ones that were restricted were focused on the needs of the school: buildings, staffing, scholarships, and libraries. Early institutions were thought of as being essential to the process of bringing civilization and Christianity to the wilderness and also a means to train leaders. The goal was to create the same type of higher education as existed in England. *Having* a college was key; questions of how or what were not a main concern to early philanthropists.

This early philanthropy laid the precedent for philanthropy's later role in shaping higher education—it did not immediately open doors to new groups or welcome new philosophies, but it did build buildings, fill the libraries, and support students and professors.

A college founding boom occurred in the colonies in between 1693 and 1770, due to religious differences, rivalries among the colonies, and willingness of philanthropists to back new ventures. This pioneering attitude endowed the beginning of the American system of higher education with diffusion and diversity (Curti & Nash, 1965).

During the American Revolution, money from England was no longer available to the colonies and the classical curriculum began to be swayed by the needs, influence, and money of science and industry. Also this period marked the beginning of professional schools, women's colleges, and manual labor colleges; philanthropy initiated new ideas, as well as kept old colleges alive (Sears, 1922).

Between the American Revolution and the Civil War, the number of colleges increased from nine to 173 as part of the process of expansion in the American frontier. However, continuing funding was an issue and the newly established frontier institutions struggled to survive. Thus, the Society for the Promotion of Collegiate and Theological Education at the West was formed to raise funds. Each member institution could send an agent to the East, and territories were organized by the board to maximize effectiveness. The society helped to keep the college boom in check, rather than promote it, by being selective about the colleges they chose to assist (Curti & Nash, 1965).

During this period of college growth, Americans desired that higher education serve a purpose of practical training, as well as a classical education. The forces of philanthropy guided institutions to establish more scientific, technological and commercial instruction. A new elite class emerged during the nineteenth century – that of entrepreneurs, financiers, and industrialists, displacing the former classically trained gentlemen. Men of business became the major benefactors of practical higher education for the emerging needs of business. Interestingly, most were not college graduates, but wanted higher education to prepare American youth by reorienting higher education towards utility. Notable education philanthropists included manufacturer Joseph Wharton – Wharton School of Business at Penn, John D. Rockefeller – University of Chicago, Sylvanus Thayer – Thayer Scholl of Civil Engineering at Dartmouth, Abiel Chandler – Chandler School of Science and the Arts at Dartmouth, Abbott Lawrence – Lawrence Scientific School at Harvard (Sears, 1922).

The government was also an agent of growth in practical education through the passing of the Morrill Act of 1862 – "an act donating Public Lands to the Several States and Territories which may provide College for the Benefit of Agriculture and

Mechanic Arts" (Morrill Act, 1862). With the Morrill Act, the State did most of the pioneering during this time period, whereas in pre-Civil War days, the church led the way in founding institutions. Personal and religious philanthropy were almost entirely responsible for colleges for women, minorities, and theological schools, and contributed a significant amount to medical, and law schools; whereas private enterprise and the State were almost entirely responsible for schools of dentistry, pharmacy, and technical schools (Curti & Nash, 1965).

Organized alumni giving grew in popularity in the mid-1900s and gave institutions a stable income flow. Larger gifts provided buildings, scholarships, and professorships, and often came from class gifts, and alumni reunion/anniversary gifts. Alumni associations, fundraising campaigns, and the use of professional fundraisers all grew in popularity during this time. After WWII, alumni support exploded- in part because of the higher income of college and university graduates, and partly because of tax benefits (Curti & Nash, 1965).

Giving to Alma Mater

The following section will examine various studies on giving motivation and donative behaviors in regards to higher education philanthropy. Clotfelter (2001) examined giving trends in two generations of alumni from selective private institutions. The researcher found that alumni giving is extremely concentrated, with over half of all donations being given by just 1% of alumni. Furthermore, Clotfelter concluded that the two main determinants of giving are income, and satisfaction with their student experience and with the current direction of the institution.

Terry and Macy (2007) analyzed the determinants of alumni giving rates with a focus on financial, institutional, and demographic variables, using a cross-sectional data set collected by usnews.com from 200 colleges and universities. Analysis was performed using two empirical models highlighting statistical significance. Results indicated that the main determinants of alumni giving are institutional acceptance rate, amount of average student debt, percent of students receiving Pell grants, cost of room and board, value of the institution's endowment, public versus private institutions, percent of full-time students, and percent of female students. The researchers noted that a negative impact associated with average student debt could be due to the government's policies that students should bear more of the costs of their education creating the resulting higher debt loads. Higher debt could also diminish any sense of obligation to donate to an alma mater after graduation, and reinforces the transactional ideology that is growing among students (Terry & Macy, 2007).

Daugherty (2012) presents the question of how rising student loan debt could affect alumni giving in both the short and long term. The author discusses the ways that advancement professionals can address the challenge of connecting with young alumni that are "hobbled by debt." Millennial students increasingly view their college experience as more transactional than transformational, and advancement professionals cannot solely rely on alumni's feelings of pride towards their alma mater. Daugherty explores the ideas that alumni annoyance with debt affects their willingness to give, and that high levels of debt inhibit giving in a real way as well. The author also states that millennial students currently donate and raise money for non-profits, and higher education must compete with more emotional, "heart-tugging" causes.

Jendreck and Lynch (2012), present the idea that the reality of climbing student debt burdens severely threaten the generosity of future alumni. The researchers wanted to understand how student debt influences future giving as alumni, and presented a new twist on prior studies: "Previous research found a negative correlation between student loans and alumni giving. However, our research provides a new look at this relationship. We suspect that it is not the simple fact of having a student loan that produces a reluctance to contribute to one's alma mater but the assumption of responsibility for that debt that matters" (Jendreck & Lynch, 2012). The results of this study confirmed past research, in that alumni with loans are less likely to give than those alumni who had no financial aid at all. The researchers found these results from surveying a public, medium-sized, mid-western university's 1999-2000 and 2004-2005 graduating classes. This study provided new evidence regarding the link between alums with loans and their donative behavior: alumni giving is highly impacted by who pays back the loans. The researchers believed that prior research assumed that graduates pay off their own loans; in this study they asked graduates how they were paying off loan debt, and found that graduates who had help paying off loans were four times as likely to donate as those who had no help. Thus, the factor influencing donative behavior is not simply the presence of loans, but whether the graduate received help in paying off those loans.

Along these lines, Marr, et al. (2005), cite the fact that alumni provided over $6.8 billion in donations to institutions of higher education in 2000-2001 in juxtaposition with the ideas that colleges and universities have also begun relying more and more heavily on financial aid as a tool to manage enrollment and maximize institutional revenues, and that government support has also fallen in recent years. Additionally, student aid and debt levels have risen, but have been mainly in the form of loans, not grants. In this study, the researchers look at financial aid decisions in relation to alumni giving. "Are young alumni less likely to donate to their alma mater if they have already 'just sent them a check'? Alternatively, do young graduates view financial aid, including loans, as an enabling opportunity, without which they might not have been able to earn a degree at all?" (Marr, et al., 2005). The researchers analyzed a data set gathered from students receiving bachelor's degrees from Vanderbilt University between May 1988 and May 1990. The results of the analysis indicate that loans, whether large or small tend to decrease giving, while grants, regardless of size, increase giving. The authors suggest that discrete changes in financial aid packages could greatly change future giving by alumni – for example, the addition of a small grant to a package that already includes loans could make the institution more revenue in the end. "…a loss in future contributions increases the cost of loans. Conversely, an increase in future contributions lowers the cost of grants" (Marr, et al, 2005)

Monks' Tobit maximum likelihood estimation analysis of a year 2000 survey of a graduating class of 1989 at a set of private, highly selective colleges and universities found several interesting results: First, one consistent result across all analyses was the link between income and alumni contributions. "An increase in individual income of $10,000 raises the expected contribution by approximately 2%. Similarly, an increase in household income of $10,000 raises the expected contribution by approximately 9%" (Monks, 2003). The results also supported the notion that financial aid recipients are more likely to contribute as alumni, however this result changes when the financial aid is in the form of loans. Grant and scholarship recipients show the higher expectation of contributions, while loan recipients report lower levels of alumni giving. Another key indicator of expected giving is satisfaction with one's undergraduate experience. "In an attempt to target alumni/a who are more likely to make more generous donations, institutions could identify those students upon graduation for whom the past four (or more) year met or exceeded expectations" (Monks, 2003).

Gaier (2005) surveyed 4,000 alumni from a large Midwestern university using portions of the Comprehensive Alumni Assessment Survey: Four Year Institution, which is created by CASE: the Council for the Advancement and Support of Education. The researcher used the logistic regression model to analyze the following relationships: the relationship between alumni involvement and satisfaction with their student academic experience, the relationship between alumni involvement and demographic and extracurricular variables, the relationship between alumni involvement and graduation year, and a qualitative analysis of themes. Results from this analysis showed that as alumni satisfaction with their undergraduate experience increased, so did the odds of alumni giving and alumni participation.

Theoretical Framework

Many people make decisions to put their money into various investments depending on expectations of the monetary return or payback they will receive. Correspondingly, according to Social Exchange Theory, people "make decisions about and engage in behaviors we expect to be rewarding" (Stafford, 2008). However, Social Exchange is a voluntary exchange relying on trust and goodwill, and not on legal obligations such as in an economic exchange like investing. Unlike a purely eco-nomic exchange, social exchange does not require set specifications of timeframe or monetary amounts, but generally leaves rewards and costs open. Furthermore, social exchange rarely involves explicit bargaining (Stafford, 2008). Social Exchange theory maintains that the exchange occurs only when both parties in the exchange obtain attractive rewards (Sun, et. al., 2007). Furthermore, a reward may not be obvious to the observer, but is obvious to the giver (Halfpenny, 1999). Radcliffe, 2011, expands on this definition by stating that social exchange theory suggests that an individual's decision to give is not pure altruism, but part of an exchange cycle. The donor makes a gift and in return receives benefits such as positive feelings, connection, access, and even influence. Social exchange theory focuses on the hu-man interaction during the social exchange, in the case of philanthropy during the act of gift making and receiving (Radcliffe 2011) (see Figure 1).

The researcher's hypothesis is that Social Exchange Theory will be the most prevalent theory to emerge from the survey data results. Due to the literature and studies reviewed here, it is believed that alumni largely give based on social exchange --giving based on a benefit received, such as influence, legacy, or increased engage-ment, or based on a benefit they have already received and are "giving back." The literature review sections on historical fundraising and its effects on American education show that many philanthropists gave in order to receive a benefit of influ-ence over societal issues., Furthermore, the researchers that discussed student debt and alumni giving, Terry and Macy, 2007, Clotfelter, 2001, Monks, 2003, Marr, 2005 and Daugherty (2012), indicated that alumni with debt or responsibility for debt felt less likely to give to the institution because they were not receiving a ben-efit, but the opposite, which would indicate a mentality of social exchange. Clotfel-ter, (2001) and Gaier, (2005) found that satisfaction with their student experience was an indicator of alumni giving, which also demonstrates a mindset of social exchange.

Finally, in the author's work as a fundraiser in higher education advancement, the idea of social exchange is frequently encountered as the key to development

Figure 1.

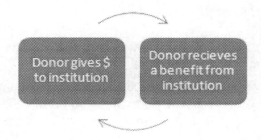

work. Anecdotally, fundraisers working personally with donors in higher education advancement rely on the concept of social exchange as part of a donor's relationship with their alma mater. It is part of the fundraiser's job to make sure the donor is having a positive giving experience and receiving a return on their philanthropic investment, whether that be in the form of positive feelings such as being thanked or meeting a recipient of their gift, or making sure a donor is receiving recognition, tax benefits, or invitations to events. Experience working within the realm of social exchange in practice is the major reason to test this theory.

MAIN FOCUS OF THE CHAPTER

Research Questions

Much data exists on the topic of giving behavior, and many surveys have been done at various institutions of higher education on the topics of alumni giving behavior, including Wastyn (2009), Terry & Macy (2007), and Clotfelter (2001). However, the specific population is a unique population and has not yet been studied in prior literature. Furthermore, the department wished to know several key data points that are not able to be learned in any other way except to create a specific survey for their alumni, thus creating a unique opportunity to conduct this research study.

A survey was created for this research project in an effort to answer the following overarching research question and sub questions:

What factors relate to alumni donating money to the department?

Subquestions:

1. How does age or degree year affect giving behavior?
2. How does the presence of student loans affect giving to the department?
3. How do perceptions of monetary need affect alumni giving to the department?
4. Do alumni donate to the department based on the idea of social exchange theory, i.e. giving in exchange for something they received?
   a. How does engagement as a student, for example, positive experiences with a professor, affect alumni giving?
   b. How do feelings of perceived value, for example, gaining more value than cost, or a positive impact on career affect alumni giving?

Method

Because the department wanted to understand the specific experience of department alumni, a survey was created as a means to directly query alumni regarding their attitudes in the area of alumni outreach and development efforts in the department. The researcher worked with the department head and one alumni volunteer to create the survey instrument, and chose to include open-ended questions and Likert scale questions, to allow alumni to provide richer detail in their responses. The survey was administered using an online survey program called WebTools.

Three survey questions allowed for respondents to provide open-ended, qualitative responses. These data were coded into categories which had emerged from the data itself. Creswell (2003) emphasizes the need for categories to be developed from the data rather than coding the data based on preconceived ideas from the researcher. Descriptive statistics, cross tabulation in Excel, and t-tests were used to examine the data. Validity of the data is also key, and has been verified in this study through three of the eight strategies Creswell (2003) delineates when discussing validity and checking accuracy: triangulation of data, clarification of researcher bias, and spending a prolonged time in the field. The quantitative and qualitative data collected in this survey has been triangulated by examining the two data types against each other to ensure correspondence. To clarify possible researcher bias and to address time in the field, the researcher discloses having spent over two years in the field, both studying and participating as a development professional, and has an in-depth familiarity with the terminology and phenomenon being studied. Explanation of researcher bias will be presented under the Biases section.

Development of Survey Instrument

The questions within the survey were initially developed to not only address the research questions of this project, but also to address informational needs of the academic department's development program. The first question involves acquiring informed consent from the participants and explains the purpose of the survey. Questions 2-5 ask about demographic data, such as the year of graduation, type of degree, and state of residence. Questions 6-8 ask the participants about their general donative behavior, while questions 9-11, 13, and 21-22 ask about the participants' donative behavior to the university and to the department. Question 12 asks for opinions about whether the university needs donations, which addresses research question 4. Questions 14 and 15 address research question 4a and 4b, by asking about the idea of impact and student engagement by department faculty and staff. Questions 16 and 17 ask about interest in alumni events. Question 18 inquires about the presence of student loan debt, which addresses research question 2. Question 19 addresses research question 4b by asking about the idea of value in regards to tuition paid to attend. Question 20 asks about whether respondents receive departmental communications, and whether they would like to.

Sampling

Because this survey only involves alumni of the specific department involved, the respondent pool was limited to living alumni of this department with active email addresses, as the survey was sent via email. This limited the pool of 4,582 living alumni to 2,179 alumni with active email addresses. All alumni received the same email inviting the alumni to take the survey and providing a link to take the survey. The email list was created and the email was sent by an administrative assistant, so no access to alumni names or emails was accessible to the researcher. The survey was open for 4 weeks, where 192 alumni responded and completed the survey, resulting in a response rate of 8.8%.

Significance

The results of this survey are significant because they will help inform future development efforts in this specific department and university. Although the results of this survey are not generalizable to all departments or universities, the results may also prove helpful to other entities in maximizing their development efforts, particularly with constituents both in a program or department and alumni of that program or department. Further significance on a societal level is that information learned from this survey could help inform the higher education and development community regarding alumni perspectives on development and giving at a university and department level, which could help to shape future directions and practices on alumni outreach and development.

Ethical Considerations

This study and the survey instrument were evaluated and approved by the Institutional Review Board at the researcher's home university. Informed consent, an evaluation of risks and benefits to participants, and confidentiality were all issues that were considered in the distribution of this study

- **Informed Consent:** Potential survey participants were provided with an informed consent statement as the first question of the survey, and could select the "Submit" option in order to affirm that they were 18 or older and wished to participate in the survey. Potential participants were also informed that they could print that page of the survey if they would like to keep a copy for their records.

- **Risks and Benefits:** Participation in this study subjected the survey respondents to no known risks. Benefits for the survey participants included more awareness of the department's alumni outreach efforts and an option to help shape future student and alumni interactions with the department. A benefit to both participants and the department was the idea that participants may be reminded of development efforts and become more involved, and be also be reminded or become aware that they can give monetarily to the department.
- **Confidentiality:** Ensuring the privacy of survey respondents was taken very seriously and appropriate measures were taken. Initial email participation invitations were sent on behalf of the researcher through an email service, and an email list of alumni was requested and delivered to this service through the researcher's assistant—no email addresses were obtained as a result of completing the survey. WebTools was the survey program used to administer and collect data from the survey, and only assigns a unique identifier to survey respondents when it delivers the data in Excel, in the form of a unique row.

Biases

This study was guided and created by a department alumni volunteer, the head of the department, and myself, a doctoral student and development director for the department, in an effort to understand the giving behavior and mindset of our alumni, and to rate the effectiveness of current development and outreach efforts. I present this as a possible bias, in that our initial goal for this survey was not solely intended to serve research purposes, but to gather information to improve the future development activities of the department.

I have worked as a development director for the department for over two years. My work as a development director involves visiting with alumni of the department in an effort to further our alumni engagement and fundraising goals. My background in advancement may also be a bias in analyzing the data collected from this survey, as my professional preference is that the survey answers be favorable towards the department and indicate a desire to give. As such, my interpretation of the data may show a possible influence towards positive answers and giving behavior.

Limitations

This survey had a response rate of 8.8%, based on the number of alumni with active email addresses, and is a small percentage representative of the total population of 4,582 at 4.2%. This response rate is significantly lower than the other response rates (20%-40%) of surveys on alumni giving included in the literature review. Generalizations based on the responses of this small sample cannot be assumed to be completely representative of every member of the population. Because the survey was administered online, via email, any of the population that does not use email was excluded. Furthermore, this survey was only administered one time, at one department, in one university. Researchers conducting surveys in similar populations at other institutions may gather very similar or dissimilar results to this survey.

Creating subgroups based on graduation year and type of degree may also have limitations; graduation year may not be completely representative of a person's age, as students enter degree programs at many ages. Graduation year or decade may also encompass a general, societal attitude or trend towards philanthropy and education during that time particular year or decade period.

Finally, how a respondent may interpret a survey question can pose a limitation to a survey study. Measures were taken to test the survey questions for clarity and understanding, but even testing cannot ensure that the wording of a survey question is clear to all respondents.

Data and Results

Descriptive statistics and cross tabulation were used to examine the research questions. This chapter begins with summary statistics of the sample and then will continue with analysis of each research question.

Description of Sample

The total number of survey respondents was 192, out of a possible 2,179 unique email addresses to which the survey link was sent. Out of the 2,179, 722 alumni opened the email, and 192 responded to the survey. Typical demographic questions were not asked of the respondents, but were instead asked to identify their current state of residence, degree earned and year of highest degree, employment status, and whether or not they are currently carrying or paying off student loan debt. The highest numbers of alumni responding to the survey are currently located in Illinois at 29% ($n=55$), then following are 14% ($n=27$) in Texas, and 8% ($n=15$) in California. This is similarly consistent with the current population as these three states include the highest concentrations of department alumni overall, with Illinois containing 64% of living alumni, and both Texas and California containing 12% each of total living alumni. A large majority 75% (n=144) of the respondents graduated from this department with only Bachelor of Science degrees, and the second largest group were the respondents that earned a Master of Science degree and a Doctor of Philosophy degree 16% (*n*=30). Employment status showed that 70% of the respondents (*n*=135) were working full time at the time of the survey, followed by 19% (*n*=37) in the retired category. Finally, the majority of respondents were not currently carrying or paying off student loan debt at 87% (*n*=167). This could be due to the fact that the majority (65%) of respondents had graduated with a B.S., M.S., or Ph.D. before 2000, and either did not accrue large amounts of debt, or have had significant time to pay off the debt. See Tables 1 and 2.

Table 1. Description of Survey Respondents: employment status, degree type, year of degree

Employment Status	% of Total Responses	*n*
Working full time	70%	135
Working part time	5%	10
With a job, but not at work because of temporary illness, strike	0%	0
Unemployed, looking for work	1%	2
Retired	19%	37
In school	2%	4
Not employed, not looking	2%	3
Other	1%	1
Degree Year		
2000-2014	34%	65
1980-1999	33%	64
1960-1979	27%	52
1940-1959	5%	9
inconclusive response	1%	2
Degree Type		
Bachelor of Science only	73%	138
Master of Science only	2%	4
Doctor of Philosophy only	6%	12
B.S. and M.S.	1%	2
M.S. and Ph.D.	16%	30
B.S. and Ph.D.	2%	3
all three	1%	2

Table 2. Description of Survey Respondents: In which state do you currently reside?

	% of Total Responses	n
Arizona	1%	1
California	8%	15
Colorado	2%	4
Connecticut	2%	3
Delaware	1%	1
Florida	2%	3
Georgia	2%	3
Iowa	1%	1
Illinois	29%	55
Indiana	2%	4
Kentucky	2%	4
Louisiana	2%	4
Massachusetts	3%	5
Maryland	1%	2
Michigan	3%	5
Missouri	4%	7
New York	2%	4
North Carolina	2%	3
New Jersey	1%	1
New Mexico	2%	3
Ohio	4%	7
Oklahoma	2%	3
Oregon	1%	1
Pennsylvania	3%	5
Rhode Island	1%	1
South Carolina	1%	1
Tennessee	1%	1
Texas	14%	27
Virginia	2%	4
Vermont	1%	2
Washington	1%	2
Wisconsin	2%	4
Other:	3%	6

Analysis of Research Questions

Overarching research question: What factors relate to alumni of the department donating money to the department? To understand what factors compel alumni to give to this department, a total of 22 questions relating to this subject were asked, and many of the survey questions map to the research subquestions in an attempt to answer the overarching question stated above. Several components are encompassed by this question, which include the following factors: year of graduation, presence of student debt, perceived need of department, and social exchange theory which includes the notion of paying back something owed or receiving a benefit for giving. However, several questions were also asked in the survey that endeavored to set a baseline of the sample's donative or giving behavior – are these respondents philanthropically inclined? And to what causes to they give?

Giving Behavior

To understand the overall giving behavior of this sample of alumni responding to the survey, analysis was first performed on survey questions 6, 7, and 8, as they directly pertain to giving behavior. Survey question 6, which pertains to overall charitable giving behavior, appears in the following table. Responses to this question show that of this sample, at least 94% have donated money to an organization or fund at some time in their life, and 85% have donated money to an organization or fund within the last year. This data supports the notion that this sample has potential to be charitable. See Table 3.

Questions 7 and 8 dig further into the notion of this sample's donative behavior. Question 7 paints a picture of the types of causes that benefit from this sample's donations. The open-ended responses were coded into the following categories that emerged from the data: *Religious/Faith-based, Social/Humanitarian, Educational*

Table 3. Summary of Responses: When was the last time you donated money to any organization or fund?

	% of Total Responses	n
This year	65%	125
Last year	20%	39
2-5 years ago	5%	10
More than 5 years ago	4%	7
Never	6%	11
Total Responses:	100%	192

(which includes giving to Illinois), *Environmental/Animal Welfare, Medical Research/ Hospitals, Political,* and *Arts/Cultural.* Educational organizations benefit the most from this group, but that may be a limitation of this survey, in that those that already donate to this department or to the university may be most likely to respond to the survey. The type of cause that benefits most highly from this sample's donations are Social and Humanitarian causes. 40% of respondents listed organizations such as the United Way, food pantries, and the Salvation Army as humanitarian organizations to which they donated. Next, 28% of respondents shared that they gave to religious organizations and the majority simply answered "church," or "my church" as their response. After that, 24% of respondents noted that they donate to medical research organizations such as the American Cancer Society, American Red Cross, and local hospital foundations. Finally, 19% of respondents noted donating to Arts and Cultural organizations, 11% noted donating to Environmental and Animal Welfare organizations, and 5% shared that they donated to various political organizations. See Table 4.

Question 8 probes further into this sample's donative behavior to learn what compels the respondents to donate to the causes they listed in Question 7. These open-ended responses were coded into the following categories: *Belief in Cause/ Mission, Perceived Need/Philanthropy, Received a Benefit/Giving Back, Loyalty, Belief that the Organization is Well Managed, Were asked by Friends/Relatives, Were asked,* and *Current financial status makes them able to give.* A belief in an organization's mission encompassed the highest number of responses—48% of the sample made statements such as, "My belief in their respective missions," "A cause I feel strongly about," and "They are causes that are important to me and my fam-

Table 4. Summary of Responses: In the last five years, which organizations or funds have received monetary donations from you?

Qualitative Codes	% of Total Responses	N
Religious/Faith-based	28%	54
Social/Humanitarian	40%	76
Educational (including IL)	49%	94
Environmental/Animal Welfare	11%	21
Medical Research/Hospitals	24%	46
Political	5%	9
Arts/Cultural	19%	36

ily." A feeling that the organization or cause is needy or a desire to give charitably was the second most noted reason that respondents gave. 23% of the respondents noted that they had a "desire to help those in need," or that they wanted to "help those less fortunate," and finally that "public education [is] underfunded in my view."

19% of the sample noted that they gave because they received a benefit or because they wanted to give back. Several sub-categories emerged from this section, including intangibles related to education: "I appreciate the value of the education I received…, " tangible benefits related to the University: "better basketball seats,", general tangible benefits: "tax write-offs,", and response to financial aid: "I received an excellent education and financial aid and I want to give some back." "Interestingly, 17% of the sample replied that they gave because of loyalty to the institution, with responses such as "They are my alma mater," and simply "loyalty." I differentiate loyalty giving from other types of giving, because loyalty giving does not indicate any sort of benefit received, it is simply a personal affectionate feeling that causes a donation. Other notable, but negligible, responses included the notions that the organization and funds are well managed, that they were asked by friends or relatives or that they were asked at all, and finally that their current financial status makes them able to give. Some examples include, "…non-profit organizations with a history of high percentage of donations going to people in need (low percentage to management, administration, and fundraising)," "they have low overhead costs," "to help friends with fundraising efforts," "frequent emails requesting donations," and "may begin donating money to alma maters now that I am in a full time position." See Table 5.

Table 5. Summary of Responses: What compels you to donate money to any above-mentioned organizations or funds?

Qualitative Codes	% of Total Responses	N
Belief in Cause/Mission	48%	93
Perceived Need/Philanthropy	23%	45
Received a Benefit/Giving Back	19%	36
Loyalty	17%	32
Belief that Organization is Well Managed	4%	7
Were asked by Friends/Relatives	6%	12
Were asked	1%	2
Current financial status makes them able to give	2%	4

Giving at the University

Next, the question of whether this sample has given to the university is examined. Responses to this question establish that a majority of this sample, 65%, has given money to the university at some point in their life. See Table 6

The respondents also report those units to which they have given in Table 7. 49% have given to the department at some point. This establishes that roughly half of this sample has donated to the department in the past, but of all who have given charitably to any organization or fund, 94%, chose to give to the department. See Table 7.

Question 8 asks respondents to give open-ended responses on the main reasons why they do or do not donate money to the university. The data groupings in Table 8 emerged from the qualitative data and were coded into their respective groups. Overall, the largest amount of alumni (29%) identified the reason of giving back or receiving a benefit as their motive for giving to the university. Statements such as the following were made on this code: "Giving back what I was given," "I want to return the support I received as a research/teaching assistant," "Giving back to the organization that aided in my development and helped our family attain the lifestyle we have," and "The university was generous in supporting my graduate education."

Table 6. Summary of Responses: Have you ever donated money to the University?

	% of Total Responses	***n***
Yes	65%	125
No	34%	66
Total Responses:	99%	191

Table 7. Summary of Responses: Which University of Illinois units, if any, have received any monetary donations from you?

	% of Total Responses	***n***
College of Liberal Arts & Sciences	21%	40
Lincoln Hall Fund for Scholarships	2%	3
Chemical & Biomolecular Engineering	49%	94
I-Fund (Athletics)	4%	7
None	34%	65
Other	20%	38
Total Responses:	130%	247

Table 8. Summary of Responses: What are the main reasons why you do or do not donate money to the University of Illinois?

Qualitative Codes	% of Total Responses	N
Giving back or receiving a benefit	29%	55
Insufficient funds (subset - recent grad, low impact)	16%	31
Believe in the mission	15%	29
Negative opinions	13%	24
Other giving priorities	5%	9
Loyalty	4%	8
No reason	4%	7
Need	3%	6
No interest	3%	6
No Need	3%	5
Philanthropy	3%	5
Asked/Not asked	2%	4
Don't know where/how it will be spent	2%	3
Don't know how to donate	1%	2

Two noteworthy subsets emerged from the next code – 16% of respondents noted that they did not give because of insufficient funds. Out of these 31 respondents, 11 gave responses simply noting that they didn't have the funds to give, i.e. "Budget is limited," or "I can't afford it." However, two further subsets emerged, that of not giving due to because they are still paying off student loans/they are a recent graduate, or not giving because they don't think it is enough to make an impact. 13 of the 31 respondents made statements that indicated they did not donate because they are either paying off students loans, or because they are a recent graduate: "Haven't yet, I will in the future, just graduate," Am freshly out of school and am looking to donate once I get my career advanced and have more to offer," "fresh graduate," and "still have outstanding debts that need to be paid off first" were some of the statements made. Finally, 7 of the 31 respondents indicated that they do not give because it will not make an impact. Several respondents made statements such as, "don't think my donation will make any difference," "I can't afford to donate enough to get a building named after me," "I would like to, but when I do I would like it to be a significant amount," and finally, "I don't think it will make a real impact. I don't know what the money will go toward." This final statement is also related to a previously mentioned notion that donors would like to know where their money is going/how it will be spent.

15% of respondents noted that they gave because of a belief in the mission and wanting to support this cause, with many statements offered such as "feel that [the department] does important work," and "because I respect the university mission and want to support the university." Next, 13% of respondents indicated that they do not give or no longer give because of some negative opinion about the university. The largest subset (10 of 24) of negative opinions involved tuition – that it was too high or had increased too much since they were a student, or that they felt they had already paid, so they didn't feel a need to donate. Examples include, "the exponential increase in tuition is not something I support," "I paid to go there and the current students pay quite a bit," and "The cost of my education was so exorbitant that I feel revulsion at the idea of donating." The statements regarding having already paid for something and need feeling compelled to donate reflect the above-mentioned notion of a university education no longer being seen as transformational, but now being viewed as much more transactional as cost goes up. Other negative opinions varied widely, and included family members not being accepted to the university, having a poor experience as a minority student at the university, or not being invited to give a seminar.

Finally, the rest of the qualitative statements made were widely segmented into reasons for giving such as loyalty, need, and pure philanthropy, and reasons for not giving including having other giving priorities, no interest or no reason, donations were not needed, they were not asked to give, not knowing how the money will be spent, or not knowing how to donate (see Table 8).

In summary, examination of the above responses to survey questions 6, 7, 8, 9, 10, and 11 establish a baseline for this sample's current donative behavior, including overall donative behavior, and donative behavior towards the university, and to the department. The following statistics emerged to describe this sample: 94% have donated funds to an organization or cause in their lifetime, with 85% donating in the past year. The top three types of causes to which this sample donates are: Educational (49%), Social/Humanitarian (40%), and Religious/Faith-based (28%). The top three reasons that responses donate to the causes listed include: Belief in Cause/Mission (48%), Perceived Need/Philanthropy (23%), Received a Benefit/Giving Back (19%). 65% of the sample reported having donated funds to the university at some time in their life, and 49% reported having donated funds to the department. The top reasons reported as to why respondents donate or do not donate funds to the department include: Giving Back or Receiving a Benefit (29%), Insufficient funds (16%) and Belief in the Mission (15%).

Research Subquestion 1: How Does Age or Degree Year affect Giving Behavior?

Table 9 illustrates three findings involving the notion of how age or year of graduation affects giving behavior to the department. First, the second column

Table 9. Donative vs. department giving by graduation year

	% of total responses	Total alumni	# that give to department	% that give to dept	# that are donative	% that are donative	% of those who are donative that gave to department
2000-2014	34%	65	6	9%	54	83%	11%
1980-1999	33%	64	40	63%	64	100%	63%
1960-1979	27%	52	40	77%	52	100%	77%
1940-1959	5%	9	8	89%	9	100%	89%
Inconclusive response	1%	2	0	0	2	100%	0%
Total Responses:	100%	192	94 total	49%	181 total	94%	

shows the breakdown of alumni respondents by graduation year, with the majority of respondents having graduated between 2000-2014. The third column shows the breakdown of respondents that reported giving to the department, broken down by graduation year. This demonstrates that as graduation year goes back in time, the percentage of those giving increases. A limitation to this finding may be that it becomes easier to have a higher percentage of giving participation as alumni report older graduation dates, because there are simply fewer respondents. The fourth column shows the breakdown by graduation year of those that reported any donative behavior –demonstrating that only those graduating between 2000-2014 do not have 100% giving behavior. Finally, the fifth column shows the percentages of those that gave to the department out of those that reported being donative.

Discussion of research subquestion 1 (How does age or degree year affect giving behavior?). Overall, the first finding from this table is that as degree year gets older, giving participation increases. The second finding is that only those graduating between 2000-2014 did not have 100% of the group reporting donative behavior. The third and most major finding is that as degree year gets older, those that are donative report higher giving participation rate to the department. This is noteworthy because this finding mirrors findings in the literature that suggest that millennials do not see their alma maters as donation-worthy, and may view their educational experience as more transactional than transformational (Daugherty, 2012). This finding shows that this group (2000-2014) is not donating to the department because of lack of funds; 83% of this group reports having donated to some organization or cause at some time in their life. However, only 11% has reported giving to the department.

These data show that age or degree year does have an effect on giving behavior in general, and also has an even bigger effect on giving to the department. As Table 9 shows, as age or degree year increases, giving increases, both to the department, and in general.

Research subquestion 2: How does the presence of student loans affect giving to the department? Survey question 18 directly pertains to this research question, and shows that the majority (87%) of this sample is not currently carrying or paying off student loan debt (see Table 10).

Next, the responses to survey question 18 were cross tabulated with giving to the department. Out of the 167 respondents that noted they had no current student loan debt, 92 respondents or 56% stated that they had given funds to the department. Out of those 25 respondents that reported carrying or still paying off student debt, only 2 respondents or 8% noted that they had given to the department. A limitation here could be related to age or graduation year instead of only correlating to debt. It is possible that alumni who more recently graduated are likely to have student debt, which could also be a factor in department giving, and vice versa (see Table 11).

Discussion of research subquestion 2 (How does the presence of student loans affect giving to the department?). The above data show that the presence of student debt indicates less of a likelihood of department giving, while the absence of student debt indicates more of a likeliness to donate to the department. Some of the quali-

Table 10. Summary of Responses: Are you currently carrying or paying off student loan debt?

	% of Total Responses	**N**
Yes	13%	25
No	87%	167
Total Responses:	100%	192

Table 11. Those that gave to the department by presence or absence of student loan debt

Presence of Debt	**% of Total Responses**	**n**	**# That Gave to department**	**% That Gave to Department**
Yes	13%	25	2	8%
No	87%	167	92	56%

tative responses, regarding tuition and loans, to survey question 11 speak to this point: "Right now I am paying back student loan debt and trying to get more financially stable."

Research subquestion 3: How do perceptions of monetary need affect alumni giving to the department? Survey question 12 provides evidence to support the notion that 44% of alumni respondents think of the university as a charitable organization or at least think that it needs funds from alumni donations; 49% stated that the university needs donation somewhat, but only 6% of this sample felt that the university does not need donations from alumni.

Table 13 cross tabulates the perception of need by respondents with whether they give donations to the department. Of the 85 respondents that said the university needs money a great deal, 60, or 71% donated funds to the department. 95 respondents said that the university needs donations somewhat, and 31 respondents (33%) donated funds to the department. Finally, 18% of those that said the university does not need donations, or 2 out of 11, gave donations to the department. One limitation of this cross tabulation is that respondents stated their opinions of giving to the *university* in survey question 12, whereas the responses are cross tabulated with giving to the *department*. This was done this way for consistency as the other cross tabulations use department giving.

Discussion of research subquestion 3 (How do perceptions of monetary need affect alumni giving to the department?) The data displayed in Tables 12 and 13

Table 12. Summary of Responses: In your opinion, how much does the university need donations from alumni?

	% of Total Responses	n
Needs a great deal	44%	85
Needs somewhat	49%	95
Does not need	6%	11
Total Responses:	99%	191

Table 13. Department giving by perceived need

	% of Total Responses	n	# That Donated to Department	% That Donated to Department
Needs a great deal	44%	85	60	71%
Needs somewhat	49%	95	31	33%
Does not need	6%	11	2	18%

show that perceptions of monetary need do affect alumni giving. As the perception of need increases, department giving also increases: 71% of those that felt there was a great deal of need donated funds to the department, while 33% of those that felt there was somewhat need donated, and finally, only 18% of those that felt there was no need donated to the department.

Research subquestion 4: Do alumni donate to the department based on the idea of social exchange theory, i.e. giving in exchange for something they received? This question is divided into two subquestions in order to be able to address two notions of gaining value: that of positive interaction with a faculty or staff member, and that of impact on career versus how much was spent, or a high return on an investment.

Research subquestion 4a: How does engagement as a student, for example, positive experiences with a professor, affect alumni giving? Survey question 14 directly maps to the research question in that a close relationship with a professor or staff member could indicate a positive experience in the department. 7% of the sample reported an extremely close relationship with a professor or staff member, 33%, the largest amount of responses, reported a moderately close relationship, and 24% stated their relationships were not at all close (see Table 14).

Table 15 displays the data by cross tabulating giving to the department by feelings of closeness with a professor or staff member. Of the 13 respondents that reported an extremely close relationship, 11 of them (85%) reported giving to the department.

Discussion of research subquestion 4a (How does engagement as a student, for example, positive experiences with a professor, affect alumni giving?) Table 15

Table 14. Summary of Responses: During your time at the university, which of the following best describes your relationship with at least one or more professors or staff members in the department?

	% of Total Responses	*n*
Extremely close	7%	13
Very close	16%	31
Moderately close	33%	63
Slightly close	20%	38
Not at all close	24%	47
Total Responses:	100%	192

Table 15. Department giving by feelings of closeness

	% of Total Responses	*n*	# That Donated to Department	%That Donated to Department
Extremely close	7%	13	11	85%
Very close	16%	31	17	55%
Moderately close	33%	63	33	52%
Slightly close	20%	38	16	42%
Not at all close	24%	47	17	36%

demonstrates that respondents that reported higher feelings of closeness with a faculty or staff member also reported higher rates of giving to the department. This shows a correlation between student engagement with the department and higher participation in giving to the department.

Research subquestion 4b: How do feelings of perceived value, for example, gaining more value than cost, or a positive impact on career affect alumni giving? Survey questions 15 and 19 address this research question. Responses to question 15 (Table 17) show that 71% of the respondents believe that their time at the university had a High Positive impact on their life and career, and responses to question 19 (Table 16) support the notion that respondents perceive that they received much more value from their education than the cost that they paid to attend.

Table 18 demonstrates that respondents felt they received much more value than the cost they paid in tuition, or a high return on investment, donated in a higher percentage (63%) than those felt they received somewhat more value than cost, the same value as cost, or less value than cost.

Table 16. Summary of Responses: Please rate your perceived value of your education compared to the tuition you paid to attend

	% of Total Responses	*n*
Much more value than cost	68%	131
Somewhat more value than cost	15%	29
About the same	11%	21
Somewhat less value than cost	3%	6
Much less value than cost	1%	2
Total Responses:	98%	189

Table 17. Summary of Responses: Select the level of impact you believe your time at the university has had on your life and career

	% of Total Responses	***n***
High positive	71%	136
Moderate high	25%	50
Little/no impact	2%	3
Moderate negative	2%	3
High negative	0%	0
Total Responses:	100%	192

Table 18. Department giving by perceived value of degree

	% of Total Responses	***n***	**# That Donated to Department**	**% That Donated to Department**
Much more value than cost	68%	131	82	63%
Somewhat more value than cost	15%	29	8	28%
About the same	11%	21	2	10%
Somewhat less value than cost	3%	6	0	0%
Much less value than cost	1%	2	0	0%

Table 19 also shows that respondents who felt that their degree had a high positive or moderately high positive impact on their career donated more money to the department than those that felt their degree had little to no impact or a negative impact on their career. In fact, those that felt anything but positive impact gave zero percent to the department.

Discussion of research subquestion 4b (How do feelings of perceived value, for example, gaining more value than cost, or a positive impact on career affect

Table 19. Department giving by impact on life/career

	% of Total Responses	***n***	**# That Donated to Department**	**% That Donated to Department**
High positive	71%	136	74	54%
Moderate high	26%	50	20	40%
Little/no impact	2%	3	0	0
Moderate negative	2%	3	0	0
High negative	0%	0	0	0

alumni giving?) Tables 18 and 19 demonstrate that feelings of perceived value do have an effect on alumni giving, in that the higher value received or the higher a positive impact exists, alumni giving rates increase.

Discussion of research subquestion 4 (Do alumni donate to the department based on the idea of social exchange theory, i.e. giving in exchange for something they received?) Based on findings from subquestions 4a and 4b, alumni giving does relate to giving to the department when benefits are present, such as a positive impact on career, positive interactions with faculty or staff, or gaining a higher value from their degree than it cost to attend. In each of these examples, respondents reported higher giving rates as benefits increased, and lower or no giving as benefits decreased, demonstrating a mindset of social exchange.

FUTURE RESEARCH DIRECTIONS

Much research has been done on donative behaviors and the psychology of giving. However, the topic of loyalty giving is an area that may be helpful to all implicated parties in order to further understand and harness this type of giving and these donors. Furthermore, as student debt continues to be an issue, more research on its effect on academic philanthropy will be necessary in order to keep up with possible changes in the donative behavior of alumni. Finally, future research could be done on the phenomenon demonstrated in this study of younger donors giving funds to social issues, but not to higher education. If academic institutions are to continue to rely on funding from personal donations, further work and research are needed to stay relevant to future generations' donative interests.

CONCLUSION

Discussion of overarching research question (What factors relate to alumni of the department donating money to the department?). Results of the survey encompass many factors that relate to the giving behavior of the alumni of the department. Responses to the survey revealed that the year of graduation from the department, which could be an indicator of age, have a connection to giving, in that as alumni get older the presence of giving generally increases. This could be due to several factors, including the idea that tuition was less costly for older alumni, older alumni generally have more disposable income, or perhaps that older alumni have different values than those of younger alumni. The presence of student loans also has a correlation to diminishing giving: alumni that report currently carrying student loans also report lower rates of giving (Terry & Macy, 2007, Daugherty, 2012, Jendreck

& Lynch, 2012, Marr, et. al., 2005). A limitation to this finding is that having loans could also be an indicator of age, so these results could be due to age as well as the presence or absence of loans.

The perception of need is also an indicator that alumni are more willing to give; giving rates increased as alumni reported feeling that the university needed money. Finally, the theory of social exchange did appear to relate to alumni giving to the department. The responses to the survey question *"What compels you to donate money..."* exemplify the attitudes conveyed in the survey. The notion of social exchange is illustrated by the following statements: "Giving back to the organization that aided in my development and helped our family attain the lifestyle we have," "to give back to those that helped me," and "benefitted from the degree." However, two other sizeable categories also emerged that indicate responses not explained by social exchange. In Public Good theory, the collective interest of donors and donees is the main tenet, and donors give in order to further the public good of society or an organization that contributes to the public good. Public good theory is demonstrated by statements made in response to this question: "to help those less fortunate," and "giving to charity." Organizational Identity Theory maintains that individuals that belong to an organization share in the success and the failure of the organization, and therefore donate in order to contribute to success. This theory could be relevant to those alumni who are interested in the "success" of their alma mater especially in more visible circumstances as rankings or athletics wins. Organizational identity theory is present in the following statements: "they are my alma mater," and simply, "loyalty."

Implications

- **Alumni:** Implications from this study that are relevant to alumni of higher education institutions include the notions of how institutions can cultivate alumni to be future donors while they are students by educating students to be philanthropically aware of the funding model of the institutions, and how institutions can demonstrate social value to both students and alumni that are philanthropically inclined towards social issues. Because of alumni interest in management of funds, institutions could share financial data in the form of annual reports.
- **Administrators/Academic Institutions:** Academic institutions could encourage future alumni giving by making sure to demonstrate value and return on investment to current students. Demonstrating value may be more difficult as tuition rises however; as today's students may feel that their educational experience was more transactional than transformational.

- **Fundraisers:** Implications for fundraisers are a further understanding of how donors to institutions of higher education think about donations, especially by age group. As fundraisers approach potential donors, awareness of possible mindset will be key, as shown by the difference in age group regarding to what type of cause donors donate.

REFERENCES

Clotfelter, C. T. (2001). Who are the alumni donors? Giving by two generations of alumni from selective colleges. *Nonprofit Management & Leadership, 12*(2), 119–138. doi:10.1002/nml.12201

Creswell, J. (2003). *Research Design: Qualitative, quantitative, and mixed methods approaches*. Thousand Oaks, CA: Sage Publications.

Curti, M., & Nash, R. (1965). *Philanthropy in the shaping of American higher education*. Rutgers University Press.

Daugherty, B. (2012, September). Debt threat: The scale of student loan obligations undermines alumni giving. *Currents*, 41-43.

Gaier, S. (2005). Alumni Satisfaction with Their Undergraduate Academic Experience and the Impact on Alumni Giving and Participation. *International Journal of Educational Advancement, 5*(4), 279–288. doi:10.1057/palgrave.ijea.2140220

Halfpenny, P. (1999). Economic and Sociological Theories of Individual Charitable Giving: Complimentary or Contradictory? *Voluntas: International Journal of Voluntary and Nonprofit Organizations, 10*(3), 197–215. doi:10.1023/A:1021200916487

Jendreck, M., & Lynch, J. (2012). Student loans and alumni giving: Who repays the loan? *International Journal of Educational Advancement, 11*(1).

Marr, K. A., Mullin, C. H., & Siegfried, J. J. (2005). Undergraduate financial aid and subsequent alumni giving behavior. *The Quarterly Review of Economics and Finance, 45*(1), 123–143. doi:10.1016/j.qref.2003.08.005

McDearmon, J. T. (2010). What's in it for me: A qualitative look into the mindset of young alumni non-donors. *International Journal of Educational Advancement, 10*(1), 33–47. doi:10.1057/ijea.2010.3

Monks, J. (2003). Patterns of giving to one's alma mater among young graduates from selective institutions. *Economics of Education Review, 22*(2), 121–130. doi:10.1016/S0272-7757(02)00036-5

Morrill Act of 1862. (n.d.). Retrieved May 20, 2015, from http://www.ourdocuments.gov/doc.php?flash=true&doc=33

Radcliffe, S. (2011). *A study of alumni engagement and its relationship to giving behaviors.* Retrieved May 20, 2015, from http://digitalcommons.bucknell.edu/masters_theses/2/

Sears, J. B. (1922). *Philanthropy in the history of American higher education.* Washington, DC: Government Printing Office.

Stafford, L. (2008). Social Exchange Theories. In L. A. Baxter (Ed.), *Engaging theories in interpersonal communication: Multiple perspectives* (pp. 377–389). Thousand Oaks, CA: Sage Publications. doi:10.4135/9781483329529.n28

Sun, X., Hoffman, S., & Grady, M. (2007). A multivariate causal model of alumni giving: Implications for alumni fundraisers. *International Journal of Educational Advancement*, 7(4), 307–332. doi:10.1057/palgrave.ijea.2150073

Terry, N., & Macy, A. (2007). Determinants of alumni giving rates. *Journal of Economics & Economic Education Research*, 8(3), 3–17.

Wastyn, M. L. (2009). Why alumni don't give: A qualitative study of what motivates non-donors to higher education. *International Journal of Educational Advancement*, 9(2), 96–108. doi:10.1057/ijea.2009.31

Compilation of References

1994 Statement quoting in part, American Association of University Professors , 1966 Statement on Professional Ethics, at ¶ 3. (n.d.). Available at http://www.aaup.org/AAUP/pubsres/policydocs/contents/statementonprofessionalethics.htm?PF=1

2007 Census of Agriculture, United States Summary and State Data. (2007). *Summary of Farm by Typology: 2007*. Retrieved from http://www.agcensus.usda.gov/Publications/2007/Full_Report/usv1.pdf

Abbot, E., Borchert, A., Dwyer, M., Fuller, C., Gibbs, G., Hanifan, M., ...Zeller, K. (2011). *Five elements of a successful twenty-first century university corporate relations program*. White Paper, Network of Academic Corporate Relations Officers Benchmarking Committee, August 2, 2011. Retrieved from http://www.nacroonline.org/ assets/docs/essential%20elements_white_paper_final.pdf

Abi-Mershed, O. (2010). *Trajectories of education in the Arab world: Legacies and challenges*. New York, NY: Routledge.

Abu Dhabi Ports. (2015). *Kizad*. Retrieved from http://www.adports.ae/en/article/industrial-zone/kizad-1.html

Acar, W., Aupperle, K. E., & Lowry, R. M. (2001). An empirical exploration of measures of social responsibility across the spectrum of organization types. *The International Journal of Organizational Analysis*, *9*(1), 26–57. doi:10.1108/eb028927

Ag Leader Insights. (2014, Spring). *Mapping New Classroom Opportunities; Rewarding careers in precision agriculture*. Author.

Aiken, M., & Hage, J. (1968). Organizational interdependence and intra-organizational structure. *American Sociological Review*, *33*(6), 912–930. doi:10.2307/2092683

Ajayi Ade, J. F., & Goma Lameck, K. (1996). The African Experience with Higher Education. Accra: The Association of African Universities.

Al-Asaly, S. (2003). *Political reform and economic institutional building: A case study of budgetary institutional reform in Yemen*. Presented at the ERF 10th Annual Conference, Marrakech, Morocco.

Compilation of References

Aldrich, H. E. (1979). *Organizations and environments*. Englewood Cliffs, NJ: Prentice-Hall.

Al-Lamki, S. M. (2002). Higher education in the Sultanate of Oman: The challenge of access, equity and privatization. *Journal of Higher Education Policy and Management*, 24(1), 75–86. doi:10.1080/13600800220130770

Allen, G. (2014, May 23). Koch Foundation Criticized Again For Influencing Florida State. *NPR*. Retrieved from http://www.npr.org/2014/05/23/315080575/koch-foundation-criticized-again-for-influencing-florida-state

Allison, G. T. (1971). *Essence of decision: Explaining the Cuban missile crisis*. Boston, MA: Little Brown.

Alnaqbi, W. (2011). *The relationship between human resource practices and employee retention in public organisations: An exploratory study conducted in the United Arab Emirates*. Perth: Edith Cowan University.

Alpay, S. (2003). *Economic development, openness to trade and environmental sustainability in the MENA countries*. Presented at the ERF 10th Annual Conference, Marrakech, Morocco.

Alpen Capital. (2014a). *GCC education industry*. Retrieved from http://www.alpencapital.com/downloads/GCC_Education_Industry_Report_July_2014.pdf

Alpen Capital. (2014b). *GCC Education sector undergoing an exciting phase of growth, says Alpen Capital's latest report*. Retrieved from http://www.alpencapital.com/news/2014-July-2.html

Alphin, H. C. Jr. (2014). Global accreditation for a knowledge-oriented community: Foundational change breeds global access to educational and economic opportunity. In *Handbook of Research on Transnational Higher Education* (Vol. 1, pp. 303–328). Hershey, PA: IGI Global. doi:10.4018/978-1-4666-4458-8.ch016

ALS Association. (2014). *The ALS ice bucket challenge*. Retrieved from http://www.alsa.org/fight-als/ice-bucket-challenge.html

Altbach, P. G. (1998). *Comparative higher education: Knowledge, the university, and development*. Westport, CT: Ablex Publishing.

Altbach, P. G. (2002). Knowledge and education as international commodities: The collapse of the common good. *Industry and Higher Education*, 28, 2–5.

Altbach, P. G. (2007). Peripheries and centres: Research universities in developing countries. *Higher Education Management and Policy*, 19(2), 111–134. doi:10.1787/hemp-v19-art13-en

AMA. (2011). *Management Centre Europe to open Middle East office in Abu Dhabi*. Retrieved from http://www.amanet.org/news/5201.aspx

American Association of Community Colleges. (2000). *Community Colleges Past to Present (Based on material from National Profile of Community Colleges: Trends & Statistics, Phillippe & Patton, 2000)*. Retrieved from http://www.aacc.nche.edu/AboutCC/history/Pages/pasttopresent.aspx

American Association of University Professors (AAUP). (1915, December). Declaration of Principles on Academic Freedom and Academic Tenure. *AAUP Bulletin; Quarterly Publication of the American Association of University Professors, 1*(Part 1).

American Association of University Professors. (1966). *Statement on government of colleges and universities*. Retrieved September 2002 from http://www.aaup.org/statements/Redbook/Govern.htm

American Association of University Professors. (2006). Statement of Principles on Academic Freedom and Tenure. In *AAUP Policy* (10th ed.; pp, 3-11). Available at http://www.aaup.org/AAUP/pubsres/policydocs/contents/1940statement.htm

Amutabi, M. N. (2013). *The NGO Factor in Africa: The Case of Arrested Development in Kenya*. London: Taylor and Francis.

Andreoni, J. (1988). Privately provided public goods in a large economy: The limits of altruism. *Journal of Public Economics, 35*(1), 57–73. doi:10.1016/0047-2727(88)90061-8

Andresen, K. (2006). *Robin Hood marketing: Stealing corporate savvy to sell just causes*. San Francisco, CA: Wiley & Sons.

ANQAHE. (2015). *History*. Retrieved from http://www.anqahe.org/index.php/about/history

Arnove, R. F. (1980). *Philanthropy and Cultural Imperialism: The Foundations at Home and Abroad*. Boston, MA: G.K. Hall.

Arulampalam, W., & Stoneman, P. (1995). An investigation into the givings by large corporate donors to UK charities, 1979-86. *Applied Economics, 27*(10), 935–945. doi:10.1080/00036849500000073

Asad, T. (1986). *The Idea of an Anthropology of Islam*. Washington, DC: Center for Contemporary Arab Studies.

ASHE. (2012). Philanthropy, volunteerism & fundraising in higher education (ASHE Reader Series). New York City, NY: Pearson Custom Publishing.

Ashford, E. (2015, January 5). *Fundraising is all about cultivating relationships*. Retrieved from http://www.ccdaily.com/Pages/Funding/Fundraising-is-all-about-cultivating-relationships.aspx

Ashforth, B. E., & Mael, F. (1989). Social identity theory and the organization. *Academy of Management Review, 14*(1), 20–39.

Association for the Study of Higher Education. (2011). ASHE Higher Education Report. *Special Issue: Philanthropy and Fundraising in American Higher Education, 37*. doi:10.1002/aehe.3702

Association of Fundraising Professionals. (2003). *The Fundraising Dictionary Online*. Retrieved from http://www.afpnet.org/ResourceCenter/ArticleDetail.cfm?ItemNumber=3380

Association of Fundraising Professionals. (2009). *About National Philanthropy Day*. Retrieved from http://www.afpnet.org/content.cfm?ItemNumber=4033

Compilation of References

Austin, J. B. (2011, July 12). *Purdue fundraising shows growth*. Purdue University News Service. Retrieved from http://www.purdue.edu/newsroom/general/2011/110712CalvertYearend.html

Avolio, B. J., Walumbwa, F. O., & Weber, T. J. (2009). Leadership: Current theories, research, and future directions. *Annual Review of Psychology*, *60*(1), 421–429. doi:10.1146/annurev.psych.60.110707.163621 PMID:18651820

Backer, L. (2013, January 29). *Monitoring University Governance*. Retrieved May 26, 2015, from http://lcbpsusenate.blogspot.com/2013/01/statement-of-senate-chair-made-at.html

Backer, L. C. (2010, September 17). *Law at the End of the Day: The University and the Panopticon: Naturalizing "New" Governance Forms for Behavior Control Beyond Law*. Retrieved from http://lcbackerblog.blogspot.com/2010/09/university-and-panopticon-naturalizing.html

Backer, L. C. (2012a, May 4). *Monitoring University Governance*. Retrieved June 9, 2015. Available http://lcbpsusenate.blogspot.com/2012/05/on-institutional-role-of-faculty-senate.html

Backer, L. C. (2012b, May 9). *Monitoring University Governance*. Retrieved June 9, 2015. Available http://lcbpsusenate.blogspot.com/2012/05/on-institutional-roel-of-faculty-senate.html

Backer, L. C. (2015, May 1). *Monitoring University Governance*. Retrieved June 8, 2015. Available http://lcbpsusenate.blogspot.com/2015/05/power-and-control-through-prism-of.html

Bailey, T., & Kienzal, G. (1999). *What Can We Learn About Postsecondary Vocational Education From Existing Data?*. Retrieved from http://ccrc.tc.columbia.edu/media/k2/attachments/vocational-education-existing-data.pdf

Balderston, F. E. (1995). *Managing today's university: Strategies for viability, change, and excellence* (2nd ed.). San Francisco, CA: Jossey-Bass.

Barnes, N. G., & Lescault, A. M. (2013). *College presidents out-blog and out-tweet corporate CEO's as higher ed delves deeper into social media to recruit students*. Center for Marketing Research. University of Massachusetts Dartmouth. Retrieved from http://www.umassd.edu/cmr/socialmediaresearch/

Barrow, C. W. (1990). *Universities and the capitalist state: Corporate liberalism and the reconstruction of American*. Academic Press.

Bastedo, M. N. (2012). *The organization of higher education: Managing colleges for a new era*. Baltimore, MD: John Hopkins University Press.

Bauer, D. (1993). *The fund-raising primer*. New York, NY: Scholastic Inc.

Becker, G. (1974). A theory of social interactions. *Journal of Political Economy*, *82*(6), 1063–1094. doi:10.1086/260265

Bellamy, R., & Miller, K. (2014, May 14). My View: FSU learns from Koch association. *Tallahassee Democrat*. Retrieved March 3, 2015, from http://www.tallahassee.com/story/opinion/columnists/2014/05/14/view-fsu-learns-koch-association/9097603/

Bender, T. (1997). Politics, intellect, and the US university, 1945-1995. *Daedalus, 126,* 1–38.

Beney, A. (2010, December 16). Giving cause for hope. *Times Higher Education.* Retrieved from https://www.timeshighereducation.com/features/giving-cause-for-hope/414584.article

Benioff, M., & Adler, C. (2007). *The business of changing the world: Twenty great leaders on strategic corporate philanthropy.* New York, NY: McGraw-Hill.

Benson, V., & Morgan, S. (2014). *Cutting-Edge Technologies and Social Media Use in Higher Education* (pp. 1–436). Hershey, PA: IGI Global; doi:10.4018/978-1-4666-5174-6

Benthall, B. (2003). *The Charitable Crescent, The Politics of Aid in the Muslim World.* London: I.B. Tauris.

Benthall, B. (2008). *Returning to Religion.* London: IB Tauris.

Berle, A. A., & Means, G. C. (1968). *The modern corporation and private property.* New York, NY: Harcourt Brace and World.

Berman Edward H. (1971). American Influence on African Education: The Role of the Phelps-Stokes Fund's Education Commissions. *Comparative Education Review, 15*(2), 132-145.

Berman Edward, H. (1983). *The Ideology of Philanthropy. The Influence of the Carnegie, Ford, and Rockefeller Foundations on American Foreign Policy.* Albany, NY: SUNY Press.

Bernstein, A. R. (2013). *Funding the future: Philanthropy's influence on American higher education.* New York City, NY: R&L Education.

Bernstein, A. R. (2013). *Funding the Future: Philanthropy's Influence on American Higher Education.* Lanham, MD: Rowman & Littlefield.

Bess, J. L., & Dee, J. R. (2008). *Understanding college and university organization: Theories for effective policy and practice* (1st ed.). Sterling, VA: Stylus.

Bidwell, A. (2015, March 3). Two private liberal arts colleges will shut down. *U.S. News & World Report (Online).* Retrieved at http://www.usnews.com/news/articles/2015/03/03/declining-enrollments-financial-pressure-force-two-liberal-arts-colleges-to-close

Biemiller, L. (2015, May 8). Trustees feel pressure from Sweet Briar's demise. *The Chronicle of Higher Education, 61*(34), A.12. Retrieved from: http://chronicle.com/article/Sweet-Briar-s-Demise-Puts/229877/

Birnbaum, R. (1988). *How colleges work: The cybernetics of academic organization and leadership.* San Francisco, CA: Jossey-Bass.

Birnbaum, R. (1991). *Faculty in governance: The role of senates and joint committees in academic decision making.* San Francisco: Jossey-Bass.

Birnbaum, R. (2000). *Management fads in higher education: Where they come from, what they do, why they fail.* San Francisco: Jossey-Bass.

Compilation of References

Blackmur, D. (2008). A critical analysis of the INQAAHE Guidelines of Good Practice for higher education quality assurance agencies. *Higher Education*, *56*(6), 723–734. doi:10.1007/s10734-008-9120-x

Blake, R., & Moulton, J. S. (1985). *Managerial grid III*. Houston, TX: Gulf.

Bloland, H. G. (2002). No longer emerging, fundraising is a profession. *The CASE International Journal of Education Advancement*, *3*(1), 7–21.

Boin, . (2005). *Public Leadership Under Pressure*. Cambridge, MA: Cambridge University Press. doi:10.1017/CBO9780511490880

Bolman, L. G., & Deal, T. D. (2008). *Reframing organizations: Artistry, choice, and leadership* (4th ed.). San Francisco, CA: Wiley.

Bongila, J.-P. K. (2002). *Funding Strategies for Institutional Advancement of Private Universities in the United States: Applications for Afro-Congolese Universities*. Retrieved from dissertation.com

Booz Allen Hamilton. (2013). *Booz Allen Hamilton to support business and economic growth in the Kingdom of Saudi Arabia*. Retrieved from http://www.boozallen.com/media-center/press-releases/2013/02/booz-allen-to-support-economic-growth-in-saudi-arabia

Bornstein, R. (2003). *Legitimacy in the academic presidency: From entrance to exit*. Washington, DC: Roman & Littlefield Publishers.

Bornstein, R. (2011). *Fundraising advice for college and university presidents: An insider's guide*. Washington, DC: AGB Press.

Bouoiyour, J. (2003). *The determining factors of foreign direct investment in Morocco*. Presented at the ERF 10th Annual Conference, Marrakech, Morocco.

Boverini, L. (2006). When venture philanthropy rocks the ivory tower. *International Journal of Educational Advancement*, *6*(2), 84–106. doi:10.1057/palgrave.ijea.2150011

Brahim, M., & Rachdi, H. (2014). Foreign direct investment, institutions and economic growth: Evidence from the MENA region. *Journal of Reviews on Global Economics*, *3*, 328–339. doi:10.6000/1929-7092.2014.03.24

Bremmer, R. (1988). *American philanthropy*. Chicago, IL: The University of Chicago Press.

Brennan, M. J. (2000). Strategic corporate alliances: The importance of internal institutional collaborations. In M. K. Murphy's (Ed.), Corporate and foundation support: Strategies for funding education in the 21st century (pp. 51-54). New York, NY: Case.

Brison, J. D. (2005). *Rockefeller, Carnegie, and Canada: American Philanthropy and the Arts and Letters in Canada*. Montreal: McGill-Queen's University Press.

Brittingham, B. E., & Pezzullo, T. R. (1990). *The campus green: Fund raising in higher education*. Washington, D.C.: ERIC Clearinghouse on Higher Education.

Brock, D. (2007, July 5). Focus on a customer's need to buy, not on your need to sell. *EyesOnSales*. Retrieved from http://www.eyesonsales.com/content/article/ focus_on_a_customers_need_to_buy_not_your_need_to_sell/

Brock, D. (2007, July 5). Focus on a customer's need to buy, not on your need to sell. *EyesOnSales*. Retrieved from http://www.eyesonsales.com/content/article/focus_on_a_customers_need_to_buy_not_your_need_to_sell

Brubacher, J. S., & Rudy, W. (1997). *Higher education in transition: A history of American colleges and universities* (4th ed.). New Brunswick, NJ: Transaction Publishers.

Bruch, H., & Walter, F. (2005). The keys to rethinking corporate philanthropy. *MIT Sloan Management Review*, *47*(1), 48–55.

Buchanan, P. W. (1991). *Variables influencing corporate giving to higher education in Michigan.* (Unpublished doctoral dissertation). The University of Michigan, Ann Arbor, MI.

Building Business Investment in Community (BBIC). (2002). *The business of giving back: 2002 survey of business and community giving.* Retrieved from http://www.mnchamber.com/foundation/2002_Summary_Report.pdf

Bullock, M. B. (1980). *An American Transplant: The Rockefeller Foundation and Peking Union Medical College.* Berkeley, CA: University of California Press.

Bunce, R. L., & Leggett, S. F. (1994). *Dollars for excellence: Raising private money for private schools and public schools.* London: Precept Pr.

Burden-Leahy, S. M. (2009). Globalisation and education in the postcolonial world: The conundrum of the higher education system of the United Arab Emirates. *Comparative Education*, *45*(4), 525–544. doi:10.1080/03050060903391578

Bureau of Labor Statistics. (2015). *North Dakota*. Retrieved from http://www.bls.gov/regions/midwest/north_dakota.htm)

Burns, J. M. (1978). *Leadership*. New York: Harper Collins.

Burson, E. N. (2009, August 13-14). *Management of the long-term relationship*. Presentation at the NACRO Annual Meeting, Seattle, WA. Retrieved from http://www.nacroonline.org/conference-presentations

Burt, C. D. (2012). The importance of trust to the funding of humanitarian work. Humanitarian work psychology. In S. C. Carr, M. MacLachlan, & A. Furnham (Eds.), *Humanitarian Work Psychology* (pp. 317–331). Basingstoke, UK: Palgrave Macmillan.

Business-Higher Education Forum (BHEF). (2015). Retrieved from http://www.bhef.com/about

Caboni, T. C. (2012). Toward professionalization: Fundraising norms and their implications for practice. In *Found in ASHE, Philanthropy, volunteerism & fundraising in higher education* (pp. 725–746). New York City, NY: Pearson Learning Solutions.

Compilation of References

Caboni, T. C., & Proper, E. (2007). Dissertations related to fundraising and their implications for higher education research.Louisville, KY: Association for the Study of Higher Education (ASHE) *Annual Conference.*

Caboni, T. C.Timothy C. Caboni. (2010). The normative structure of college and university fundraising. *The Journal of Higher Education, 81*(3), 339–365. doi:10.1353/jhe.0.0094

Cagney, P., & Ross, B. (2013). *Global Fundraising: How the World is Changing the Rules of Philanthropy* (1st ed.). Wiley, John & Sons. doi:10.1002/9781118653753

Callahan, D. (1999). *1 billion for ideas: Conservative think tanks in the 1990s.* Washington, DC: National Committee for Responsive Philanthropy.

Carbone, R. F. (1986). *An agenda for research on fund raising.* College Park, MD: Clearinghouse for Research on Fund Raising.

Carey, K. (2012). *Partnering with universities NACRO 2012: Managing different drivers of corporate funding–research funding, branding/marketing, and recruiting.* Presentation at the NACRO Conference, Evanston, IL. Retrieved from http://www.nacroonline.org/conference-presentations

Carole, M.-B. (2006). *Philanthropie et Grandes Universités Privées Américaines: Pouvoir et Réseaux d'influence.* Bordeaux: Presses Universitaires de Bordeaux.

Carroll, A. B., & Buchholtz, A. K. (2015). *Business & society: Ethics and stakeholder management* (7th ed.). Mason, OH: Thomson South-Western.

Carson, J. B., Tesluk, P. E., & Marrone, J. A. (2007). Shared leadership in teams: An investigation of antecedent conditions and performance. *Academy of Management Journal, 50*(5), 1217–1234. doi:10.2307/20159921

Cash, S. B. (2005). Private voluntary support to public universities in the late nineteenth century. *International Journal of Educational Advancement, 5*(4), 343–358. doi:10.1057/palgrave.ijea.2140225

Casteen, J. (2011, May-June). Financial self-sufficiency and the public university. *Trusteeship Magazine, 19*(3). Retrieved from http://agb.org/trusteeship/2011/mayjune/financial-self-sufficiency-and-the-public-university

Castillo, R. D., Colledge, B., Ellerbrock, M., Haroldsen, V., Noghera, C., Patera, S., & See, J. (2015). *Engagement of academic corporate relations officers in university-industry centers of research excellence.* White Paper, Network of Academic Corporate Relations Officers Benchmarking Committee, July 15, 2015. Retrieved from http://www.nacroonline.org/assets/docs/Benchmarking/nacro%20center%20development%20paper-full.pdf

Castillo, M., Petrie, R., & Wardell, C. (2014). Fundraising through online social networks: A field experiment on peer-to-peer solicitation. *Journal of Public Economics, 114*, 29–35. doi:10.1016/j.jpubeco.2014.01.002

Chandler, J. (2011, July 18). FSU Faculty Approves Koch Deal, With Caveats. *WCTV.tv*. Retrieved March 3, 2015, from http://www.wctv.tv/news/floridanews/headlines/UPDATE_FSU_Faculty_Senate_Releases_Review_of_Koch_Deal.html

Cheit, E. F., & Lobman, T. E. (1979). *Foundations and higher education: Grant making from golden years through steady state*. Berkeley, CA: Carnegie Council on Policy Studies in Higher Education.

Cheng, K.-M. (2011). Fund-raising as institutional advancement. In P. G. Altbach (Ed.), *Leadership for world-class universities: Challenges for developing countries* (pp. 159–175). New York, NY: Routledge.

Cheslock, J. J., & Gianneschi, M. (2008). Replacing State Appropriations with Alternative Revenue Sources: The Case of Voluntary Support. *The Journal of Higher Education*, 79(2), 208–229. doi:10.1353/jhe.2008.0012

Cheslock, J., & Gianneschi, M. (2008). Replacing state appropriations with alternative revenue sources: The case of voluntary support. *The Journal of Higher Education*, 79(2), 208–229.

Choudaha, R., & Chang, L. (2012). *Trends in international student mobility*. World Education Services. Retrieved from http://www.uis.unesco.org/Library/Documents/research-trends-international-student-mobility-education-2012-en.pdf

Ciconte, B. L., & Jacob, J. G. (2009). *Fundraising basics: A complete guide* (3rd ed.). Sudbury, MA: Jones and Bartlett.

Claire, G. (2003). *The Greater Good: How Philanthropy Drives The American Economy and Can Save Capitalism*. New York, NY: Times Books.

Clawson, P. (2009). *Demography in the Middle East: Population growth slowing, women's situation unresolved*. The Washington Institute. Retrieved from http://www.washingtoninstitute.org/policy-analysis/view/demography-in-the-middle-east-population-growth-slowing-womens-situation-un

Cleland, T. A., Colledge, B., Ellerbrock, M., Lynch, K., McGowan, D., Patera, S., . . . See, J. (2012). *Metrics for a successful twenty-first century academic corporate relations program*. White Paper, Network of Academic Corporate Relations Officers Benchmarking Committee, August 2, 2012. Retrieved from http://www.nacroonline.org/assets/metrics%20whitepaper%20 2012%20final.pdf

Cleland, T. A., Colledge, B., Ellerbrock, M., Lynch, K., McGowan, D., Patera, S., . . . See, J. (2012). *Metrics for a successful twenty-first century academic corporate relations program*. White Paper, Network of Academic Corporate Relations Officers Benchmarking Committee, Retrieved from http://www.nacroonline.org/ assets/metrics%20whitepaper%202012%20final.pdf

Clevenger, M. R. (2014). *An organizational analysis of the inter-organizational relationships between a public American higher education university and six United States corporate supporters: An instrumental, ethnographic case study using Cone's corporate citizenship spectrum* (Unpublished doctoral dissertation). University of Missouri-Columbia, Columbia, MO.

Compilation of References

Clevenger, M. R. (2014). *An organizational analysis of the inter-organizational relationships between a public American higher education university and six United States corporate supporters: An instrumental, ethnographic case study using Cone's corporate citizenship spectrum.* (Unpublished doctoral dissertation). University of Missouri-Columbia, Columbia, MO.

Cloete, Bailey, Pillay, Bunting, & Maassen. (2011). *Universities and Economic Development in Africa.* Wynberg: CHET.

Clotfelter, C. T. (2001). Who are the alumni donors? Giving by two generations of alumni from selective colleges. *Nonprofit Management & Leadership, 12*(2), 119–138. doi:10.1002/nml.12201

Clotfelter, C. T. (2007). Patron or bully? the role of foundations in higher education. In R. Bacchetti & T. Ehrlich (Eds.), *Reconnecting education and foundations* (pp. 213–248). San Francisco, CA: Jossey-Bass.

Cohen, A. M. (2010). *The shaping of American higher education: Emergency and growth of the contemporary system* (2nd ed.). San Francisco, CA: Jossey-Bass Publishers.

Cohen, M. D., & Sproull, L. S. (Eds.). (1996). *Organizational learning.* Thousand Oaks, CA: Sage.

Cohen, M. L., & Khan, E. (2013). Scientific engagement defining gaps and creating opportunities for cooperative research and global security in the broader Middle East and North Africa (BMENA) region. In K. M. Berger (Ed.), *Future Opportunities for Bioengagement in the MENA Region.* Washington, DC: AAAS.

Cohen, M., March, J. G., & Olsen, J. P. (1972). A garbage can model of organizational choice. *Administrative Science Quarterly, 17*(1), 1–25. doi:10.2307/2392088

Collins, R. (1979). *The credential society: An historical sociology of education and stratification.* New York City, NY: Academic Press.

Community College Daily- American Association of Community Colleges. (2014, November 20). *Signs of hope for state funding.* Retrieved http://www.ccdaily.com/Pages/Campus-Issues/Signs-of-hope-for-state-funding.aspx

Connell, C. (2006). Worlds Connect in Waterville. *International Educator, 15*(3), 56-63. Retrieved from http://www.questia.com/PM.qst?a=O&d=5045010008#

ConSCU. (2014). *BOR awarded $500,000 Kresge Foundation Grant.* Retrieved from: http://www.ct.edu/newsroom/bor_awarded_500000_kresge_foundation_grant

Cook, W. B. (1997). Fundraising and the college presidency in an era of uncertainty: From 1975 to the present. *The Journal of Higher Education, 68*(1), 53–86. doi:10.2307/2959936

Cook, W. B., & Lasher, W. F. (1996). Toward a theory of fund raising in higher education. *The Review of Higher Education, 20*(1), 33–51. doi:10.1353/rhe.1996.0002

Corbin, J., & Strauss, A. (2008). *Basics of qualitative research: Techniques and procedures for developing grounded theory* (3rd ed.). Thousand Oaks, CA: SAGE Publications.

Council for Aid to Education. (2015, January 28). *Colleges and Universities Raise $37.45 Billion in 2014*. New York, NY: Author.

Council for the Advancement and Support of Education (CASE). (2015). Retrieved from http://www.case.org

Council on Foreign Relations. (2014). *Egypt info service: The Egyptian Women and Economy*. Retrieved from http://www.cfr.org/world/egypt-info-service-egyptian-women-economy/p24141

Covington, S. (1997). *Moving a public policy agenda: The strategic philanthropy of conservative foundations*. Washington, DC: National Committee for Responsive Philanthropy.

Craver, R. (2015). *Retention fundraising: The new art and science of keeping your donors for life*. Medfield, MA: Emerson & Church.

Creswell, J. (2003). *Research Design: Qualitative, quantitative, and mixed methods approaches*. Thousand Oaks, CA: Sage Publications.

Cropper, S., Ebers, M., Huxham, C., & Ring, P. S. (Eds.). (2008). *The Oxford handbook of inter-organizational relations*. New York, NY: Oxford University Press. doi:10.1093/oxford-hb/9780199282944.001.0001

Crutchfield, L. R., & Grant, H. M. (2008). *Forces for good: The six practices of high-impact nonprofits*. San Francisco, CA: Jossey-Bass.

Cummings, D. L. (1991). Building relationships with grantseekers. In J. P. Shannon (Ed.), *The corporate contributions handbook: Devoting private means to public needs* (pp. 299–309). San Francisco, CA: Jossey Bass.

Curti, M. E. (1958). The history of American philanthropy as a field of research. *The American Historical Review, 62*(2), 352–363. doi:10.2307/1845188

Curti, M., & Nash, R. (1965). *Philanthropy in the shaping of American higher education*. Rutgers University Press.

Cutlip, S. M. (1990). *Fund raising in the United States: Its role in America's philanthropy*. New Brunswick, NJ: Transaction Publishers.

Cutlip, S. M. (1990). *Fundraising in the United States (Its role in America's philanthropy)*. New York, NY: Transaction Publishers.

Daniels, A. (2015, February 19). Mega-Gifts on the Rise at Colleges, Study Says. *The Chronical of Philanthropy*. Retrieved from https://philanthropy.com/article/Mega-Gifts-on-the-Rise-at/227955

Darrat, A. F., & Al-Shamsi, F. S. (2003). *On the path to integration in the Gulf region: Are the Gulf economies sufficiently compatible?*. Presented at the ERF 10th Annual Conference, Marrakech, Morocco.

Daude, C., & Stein, E. (2007). The quality of institutions and foreign direct investment. *Economics and Politics, 19*(3), 317–344. doi:10.1111/j.1468-0343.2007.00318.x

334

Compilation of References

Daugherty, B. (2012, September). Debt threat: The scale of student loan obligations undermines alumni giving. *Currents*, 41-43.

Davis, K. (1968). Evolving models of organizational behavior. *Academy of Management Journal (Pre-1986), 11*(1), 27. Retrieved from http://search.proquest.com/docview/229589718?accoun tid=11243

Davis, C. H. F. III, Deil-Amen, R., Rios-Aguilar, C., & Canche, M. S. G. (2012). *Social Media in Higher Education: A Literature Review and Research Directions.* The Center for the Study of Higher Education at the University of Arizona and Claremont Graduate University.

Day, D. L. (1998). *The effective advancement professional: Management principles and practices.* Gaithersburg, MD: Aspen Publishing.

DeAngelo, L., & Cohen, A. (2000). *Privatization: The challenge ahead for public higher education.* Washington, DC: U.S. Department of Education.

Dee, J. R. (2014). *Organization, administration, and leadership: Addressing the relevance gap in higher education research.* Washington, DC: American Education Research Association (AERA) Division J Blog. Retrieved from: http://aeradivisionj.blogspot.com/2014/07/organization-administration-and.html

DeMillo, R. A. (2011). *Abelard to Apple: The fate of American colleges and universities.* Cambridge, MA: MIT.

Devils Lake North Dakota. (2015). *Visitor Guide,* 1-20.

DeYoung, B. (2014, July 14). *Be nimble: The third tip in assessing your fundraising strategies.* Retrieved from http://www.jenzabar.com/blog/fundraising-strategies-nimble/

Di Maggio, P. (1983). Review: A Jaundiced View of Philanthropy. Philanthropy and Cultural Imperialism: The Foundations at Home and Abroad by Robert F. Arnove. *Comparative Education Review, 27*(3), 442–445. doi:10.1086/446388

Dill, D., & Helm, K. (1988). Faculty participation in strategic policy making. In Higher Education: Handbook of Theory and Research (vol. 4, pp. 319-355). New York: Agathon Press.

DiMaggio, P. J., & Powell, W. W. (1983). The iron cage revisited. Institutional isomorphism and collective rationality in organizational fields. *American Sociological Review, 48*(2), 147–160. doi:10.2307/2095101

DiMaggio, P. J., & Powell, W. W. (1991). *The new institutionalism in organizational analysis.* Chicago, IL: University of Chicago Press.

DiMaggio, P. J., & Powell, W. W. (2012). *The iron cage revisited. Institutional isomorphism and collective rationality in organizational fields (revised). In Philanthropy, volunteerism & fundraising in higher education (ASHE Reader)* (pp. 100–140). New York, NY: Pearson Learning Solutions.

Drezner, N. (2006). Recessions and Tax-Cuts: Economic Cycles' Impact on Individual Giving,Philanthropy, and Higher Education. *International Journal of Educational Advancement, 6*(4), 289–305. doi:10.1057/palgrave.ijea.2150036

Drezner, N. D. (2011). *Philanthropy and fundraising in American higher education. ASHE Higher Education Report, 37(2)*. San Francisco, CA: Wiley.

Drezner, N. D. (2011). *Philanthropy and fundraising in American higher education*. Hoboken, NJ: Wiley.

Drezner, N. D. (2011). Special issue: Philantropy and fundraising in American higher education. *ASHE Higher Education Report, 37*(2), 1–155.

Drezner, N. D. (2011). The Influence of Philanthropy on American Higher Education. *ASHE Higher Education Report, 37*(2), 17–26.

Drezner, N. D. (2013). *Expanding the donor base in higher education: Engaging non-traditional donors*. New York, NY: Routledge.

Drezner, N. D., & Huehls, F. (2014). *Core concepts in higher education: Fundraising and institutional advancement: Theory, practice, and new paradigms*. Florence, KY: Routledge.

Drezner, N. D., & Huehls, F. (2014). *Philanthropy and fundraising in higher education: Theory, practice, and new paradigms*. New York, NY: Taylor & Francis Group.

Drezner, N. D., & Huels, F. (2014). *Fundraising and institutional advancement: Theory, practice, and new paradigms*. New York, NY: Routledge.

dSchool, Institute of Design at Stanford, Home. (2014). Retrieved March 4, 2015, from http://dschool.stanford.edu/

Duggan, M., Ellison, N. B., Lampe, C., Lehnart, A., & Madden, M. (2015). *Social Media Update 2014*. Washington, DC: Pew Research Center Internet, Science & Tech. Retrieved from http://www.pewinternet.org/2015/01/09/social-media-update-2014/

Duncan, B. (1999). Modeling charitable contributions of time and money. *Journal of Public Economics, 72*(2), 213–242. doi:10.1016/S0047-2727(98)00097-8

Duncan, B. (2004). A theory of impact philanthropy. *Journal of Public Economics, 88*(9-10), 2159–2180. doi:10.1016/S0047-2727(03)00037-9

Ealy, L. T. (2012). Investing in the ideas of liberty: Reflections on the philanthropic enterprise in higher education. *Independent Review, 17*(2), 177–191.

Ebers, M. (1999). The dynamics of inter-organizational relationships. *Sociology of Organizations, 16*, 31–56.

Eckert, G., & Pollack, R. (2000, September). Sowing the seeds of philanthropy. *CASE Currents, 26*(7), 46–49.

Compilation of References

Eddy, P. L. (2010). *Partnerships and collaborations in higher education. ASHE Higher Education Report, 36(2).* San Francisco, CA: Wiley.

Edwards, K. (2004). The university in Europe and the US. In R. King (Ed.), *The University in the Global Age* (pp. 27–44). Houndmills, UK: Palgrave Macmillan.

Eid, F., & Paua, F. (2002). *Foreign direct investment in the Arab World: The changing investment landscape* (Working Paper Series). Beirut: School of Business, The American University.

Elhiraika, A. M. (2007). Explaining growth in an oil dependent economy: The case of the United Arab Emirates. In J. B. Nugent & M. H. Pesaran (Eds.), *Explaining Growth in the Middle East.* Oxford, UK: Elsevier.

Elliott, D. (2006). *The kindness of strangers: Philanthropy and higher education.* New York, NY: Rowman & Littlefield Publishers.

Emirates Competitiveness Council. (2011). *Policy in action: The UAE in the global knowledge economy: Fast-forwarding the nation.* Retrieved from http://www.ecc.ae/docs/default-source/ecclibrary/ecc_policy_in_action_issue_01_knowledge_economy_jan_2011_english.pdf?sfvrsn=0

Eric, A. (1964). *African Universities and Western Tradition.* Cambridge, MA: Harvard University Press.

Esposito, J., & Kalin, I. (2011). *Islamophobia: The Challenges of Pluralism in the 21st Century.* New York: Oxford University Press.

Essex, G. L., & Ansbach, C. (1993, June). Fund raising in a changing economy: Notes for presidents and trustees. *Foundation Development Abstracts, 3*(2), 2-4.

Evans, G. A. (2000). Ethical issues in fund raising. In P. Buchanan (Ed.), *Handbook of institutional advancement* (3rd ed.; pp. 363–366). Washington, DC: CASE.

Fain, P. (2014, August 7). Linking Business and Budgets. *Inside HigherEd.* Retrieved from https://www.insidehighered.com/news/2014/08/07/new-workforce-fund-louisiana-ties-money-jobs-and-private-donations

Fearn, H. (2010). *Fundraisers recommended to tap Eastern promises of financial aid.* Times Higher Education. Retrieved from http://www.timeshighereducation.co.uk/news/fundraisers-recommended-to-tap-eastern-promises-of-financial-aid/413396.article

Finkin, M., & Post, R. (2009). *For the common good: Principles of American academic freedom.* New Haven, CT: Yale University Press.

Fischer, M. (2000). *Ethical decision making in fund raising.* New York, NY: Wiley.

Flaherty, C. (2014, June 25). Not Interested in Koch Money. *Inside Higher Ed.* Retrieved March 3, 2015, from https://www.insidehighered.com/news/2014/06/25/professor-says-brooklyn-college-missed-chance-get-millions-koch-foundation

Flanagan, J. (2002). *Successful fundraising: A complete handbook for volunteers and professionals*. New York, NY: McGraw-Hill.

Fleishman, J. (2007). *The Foundation: A Great American Secret; How Private Wealth Is Changing The World*. New York, NY: Public Affairs.

Forcier, F. M. (2011, September/October). Innovation Through Collaboration: New Pathways to Success. *Association of Governing Boards of Universities & Colleges, 5*(19). Retrieved from http://agb.org/trusteeship/2011/9/innovation-through-collaboration-new-pathways-success

Foundation Center. (2014). *Foundation Yearbook*. New York, NY: The Center.

Foundation Center. (2014). *Key facts on U.S. foundations, 2014 edition*. Retrieved from http://foundationcenter.org/gainknowledge/research/keyfacts2014/pdfs/ Key_Facts_on_US_Foundations_2014.pdf

Foundation Center. (2015). *About foundation center*. Retrieved from http://foundationcenter.org/about/

Fox, M. A. (2006). Universities, businesses and public authorities—and the inclusive development of society. In L. E. Weber & J. J. Duderstadt (Eds.), *Universities and business: Partnering for the knowledge society* (pp. 187–199). London: Economica Ltd.

Frank, D. A. (1980). The Carnegie Philanthropy and Private Corporate Influence on Higher Education. In Philanthropy and Cultural Imperialism: The Foundations at Home and Abroad. Boston, MA: G.K. Hall.

Freeman, H. L. (1991). Corporate strategic philanthropy: A million here, a million there, it can add up to real corporate choices. In *Vital Speeches of the Day* (pp. 246-250). Salt Lake City, UT: Academic Press.

Frumkin, P. (2006). *Strategic Giving: The Art and Science of Philanthropy*. Chicago: University of Chicago Press. doi:10.7208/chicago/9780226266282.001.0001

Fulton, K., & Blau, A. (2005). *Looking out for the future: An orientation for twenty-first century philanthropists*. Cambridge, MA: The Monitor Group.

Gaier, S. (2005). Alumni Satisfaction with Their Undergraduate Academic Experience and the Impact on Alumni Giving and Participation. *International Journal of Educational Advancement, 5*(4), 279–288. doi:10.1057/palgrave.ijea.2140220

Gardberg, N. A., & Fombrun, C. J. (2006). Corporate citizenship: Creating intangible assets across institutional environments. *Academy of Management Review, 31*(2), 329–346. doi:10.5465/AMR.2006.20208684

Garecht, J. (2015). Major donor fundraising 101. *The Fundraising Authority.* Retrieved from http://www.thefundraisingauthority.com/individual-fundraising/major-donor-fundraising-101/

Compilation of References

Garvin, C. C. Jr. (1975). *Corporate philanthropy: The third aspect of social responsibility.* New York, NY: Council for Financial Aid to Education.

Garvin, D. A. (1980). *The economics of university behavior.* New York: Academic Press.

Gee, J. P. (2011). *How to do Discourse Analysis.* New York: Routledge Press.

Geiger, R. L. (1993). *To advance knowledge: The growth of American research universities, 1900-1940.* Oxford, UK: Oxford University Press.

George, B. (2004). *Authentic leadership: Rediscovering the secrets to creating lasting value.* San Francisco, CA: Jossey Bass.

George, B., Mariama, A., & Paul, E. (2004). *African Universities, the Private Sector and Civil Society, Forging Partnerships for Development.* Accra: African Regional Council of the International Association of University Presidents.

GhaneaBassiri, K. (2010). A history of Islam in America: from the new world to the new world order. Cambridge, MA: Cambridge University Press.

Gibson, G. W. (1992). *Good start: A guide for new faculty in liberal arts colleges* (1st ed.). Bolton, MA: Anker.

Gill, J. (2008). *Oiling the learning machine.* Times Higher Education. Retrieved from http://www.timeshighereducation.co.uk/403223.article

Gilpin, R. (2001). *Global political economy: Understanding the international economic order.* Princeton, NJ: Princeton University Press.

Giroux, H. A. (2014). *Neoliberalism's war on higher education.* New York: NY Haymarket Books.

Giving U. S. A. Foundation. (2015). Giving USA 2015: The annual report on philanthropy for the year 2014. Chicago, IL: Giving USA Foundation.

Giving USA: The Annual Report on Philanthropy for the year 2013. (2014). Chicago: Giving USA Foundation.

Giving, U. S. A. (2013). *Annual Report on Philanthropy.* Indianapolis, IN: Lilly School of Philanthropy.

Glier, J. (2004, May 13). *Higher education leadership and fundraising.* Remarks to the Council for Industry and Higher Education. CIHE Council meeting, London, England.

Godwin, S. M. (2006). Globalization, education and Emiratisation: A study of the United Arab Emirates. *The Electronic Journal of Information Systems in Developing Countries, 27*(1), 1–14.

Gold, M. (2014, January 5). *Inside the Koch-backed political network, an operation designed to shield donors.* Retrieved June 10, 2015, from http://www.washingtonpost.com/politics/koch-backed-political-network-built-to-shield-donors-raised-400-million-in-2012-elections/2014/01/05/9e7cfd9a-719b-11e3-9389-09ef9944065e_story.html

Gose, B. (2013). *Strategic philanthropy comes to higher education.* The Chronicle of Higher Education. Retrieved from http://chronicle.com/article/Strategic-Philanthropy-Comes/140299/

Gose, B. (2013). Strategic philanthropy comes to higher education. *The Chronicle of Higher Education, 19*(July). Retrieved from http://chronicle.com/article/Strategic-Philanthropy-Comes/140299

Gould, E. (2003). *The university in a corporate culture.* New Haven, CT: Yale University Press.

Gouldner, A. W. (1954). *Patterns of industrial bureaucracy.* New York, NY: Free Press.

Greene, R. (2011). *LightSquared Wireless Broadband – A Detriment to rural America?* Retrieved from http://precisionpays.com

Greenfield, J. M. (2008). Rights of donors. In J. G. Pettey (Ed.), *Ethical fundraising: A guide for nonprofit boards and fundraisers* (pp. 19–36). Hoboken, NJ: Wiley.

Grossman, A., Letts, C. W., & Ryan, W. (1997). Virtuous capital: What foundations can learn from venture capitalists. *Harvard Business Review, 75*(2), 36–50. PMID:10165448

Gumport, P. (2000). Academic Restructuring: Organizational Change and Institutional Imperative. *Higher Education,* (39), 67-91.

Gumport, P. J. (2000). Academic restructuring: Organizational change and institutional imperatives. *Higher Education, 39*(1), 67–91. doi:10.1023/A:1003859026301

Guo, C., & Saxton, G. D. (2014). Tweeting social change: How social media are changing nonprofit advocacy. *Nonprofit and Voluntary Sector Quarterly, 43*(1), 57–79. doi:10.1177/0899764012471585

Haddad & Harb. (2014). *Making Islam an American Religion.* Religions Journal.

Haddad, M. M., & Hakim, S. R. (2003). *Did September 11 alter the sovereign risk in MENA? An empirical investigation.* Presented at the ERF 10th Annual Conference, Marrakech, Morocco.

Halfpenny, P. (1999). Economic and Sociological Theories of Individual Charitable Giving: Complimentary or Contradictory? *Voluntas: International Journal of Voluntary and Nonprofit Organizations, 10*(3), 197–215. doi:10.1023/A:1021200916487

Hall, C., & Thomas, S. (2012, April). *Advocacy philanthropy and the public policy agenda: The role of modern foundations in American higher education.* Paper presented at the American Education Research Association, Vancouver, BC.

Hall, M. S. (1991). Linking corporate culture and corporate philanthropy. In J. P. Shannon (Ed.), *The corporate contributions handbook: Devoting private means to public needs* (pp. 105–118). San Francisco, CA: Jossey Bass.

Hall, P. D. (1992). Teaching and research on philanthropy, voluntarism, and non-profit organizations: A case study of academic innovation. *Teachers College Record, 93*(3), 403–436.

Hammack, D. C., & Anheier, H. K. (2013). *A Versatile American Institution: The Changing Ideals and Realities of Philanthropic Foundations.* Washington, DC: Brookings Institution Press.

Compilation of References

Hammond, M. F. (1984, May – June). Survival of small private colleges: Three case studies. *The Journal of Higher Education*, *55*(3), 360–388. doi:10.2307/1981889

Hanafu, S., & Tiltnes, A. A. (2008). The employability of Palestinian professionals in Lebanon: Constraints and transgression. *Knowledge, Work and Society*, *5*(1), 1–15.

Handley, A., & Chapman, C. C. (2011). *Content Rules: How to Create Killer Blogs, Webinars, (and More) that Engage Customers and Ignite Your Business.* Hoboken, NJ: John Wiley & Sons, Inc.

Hannan, M. T., & Freeman, J. (1977). The population ecology of organizations. *American Journal of Sociology*, *83*(5), 929–984. doi:10.1086/226424

Hannan, M. T., & Freeman, J. (1984). Structural inertia and organizational change. *American Sociological Review*, *49*(2), 149–164. doi:10.2307/2095567

Harbaugh, W. T. (1998). What do donations buy? A model of philanthropy based on prestige and warm glow. *Journal of Public Economics*, *67*(2), 269–284. doi:10.1016/S0047-2727(97)00062-5

Hardy, D. E., & Katsinas, S. G. (2007). Classifying Community Colleges: How Rural Community Colleges Fit. *New Directions for Community Colleges*, *13*(137), 5–17. doi:10.1002/cc.265

Harvard University. (2015). *Social media.* Retrieved from http://www.harvard.edu/social-media

Hearn, J. C. (2003). *Diversifying campus revenue streams: Opportunities and risks.* Washington, DC: American Council on Education.

Held, D., McGrew, A., Goldblatt, D., & Perraton, J. (1999). *Global transformations: Politics, economics and culture.* Stanford, CA: Stanford University Press.

Hendrickson, R. M., Lane, J. E., Harris, J. T., & Dorman, R. H. (2012). *Academic leadership and governance of higher education: A guide for trustees, leaders and aspiring leaders of two- and four-year institutions.* New York, NY: Stylus Publishing.

Hermann, M., Hermann, C., & Hagan, J. (. (2001). How Decision Units influence Foreign Policy Decisions. *International Studies Review.* doi:10.1111/1521-9488.00234

Herman, R. D. (2008). Regulation in the nonprofit sector: Symbolic politics and the social construction of accountability. In J. G. Pettey (Ed.), *Ethical fundraising: A guide for nonprofit boards and fundraisers* (pp. 235–245). Hoboken, NJ: Wiley.

Hertog, S. (2013). *The private sector and reform in the Gulf Cooperation Council (No. 30).* London: London School of Economics and Political Science.

Hodson, J. B. (2010). Leading the way: The role of presidents and academic deans in fundraising. In J. B. Hodson & B. W. Speck's (Eds.), Perspectives on fund raising: New directions for higher education, number 149 (pp. 39-49). San Francisco, CA: Jossey-Bass.

Hoerr, T., Kucic, B., Wagener, A., & Nolan, M. (2010, August 11). *Small and medium-sized businesses: Finding mutual value.* Presentation at the 2010 NACRO Annual Conference, Urbana-Champaign, IL. Retrieved from http://www.nacroonline.org/conference-presentations

Hogue, J. (2015). Step-By-Step Crowdfunding. Academic Press.

Hollis Ernerst, V. (1938). *Philanthropic Foundations and Higher Education*. New York, NY: Columbia University Press.

Horsley, S. (2006). *Wal-Mart's hypocrisy: A free enterprise 'success' story that's not so free*. United for a Fair Economy. Retrieved September 20, 2006, from http://www.faireconomy.org

Hossler, D. (2004). Refinancing Public Universities: Student enrollments, incentive-based budgeting, and incremental revenue. In E. P. S. John & M. D. Parsons (Eds.), *Public Funding of Higher Education: Changing Contexts and New Rationales* (pp. 145–163). Baltimore, MD: Johns Hopkins Press.

Hoy, K. H., & Miskel, C. G. (2008). *Educational administration: Theory, research and practice*. New York, NY: Allyn and Bacon.

Hundley, K. (2011, May 9). Billionaire's role in hiring decisions at Florida State University raises questions. *Tampa Bay Times*. Retrieved March 3, 2015, from http://www.tampabay.com/news/business/billionaires-role-in-hiring-decisions-at-florida-state-university-raises/1168680

Hunt, P. C. (2012). *Development for academic leaders: A practical guide for fundraising success*. San Francisco, CA: Jossey-Bass.

Hutcheson, P. A. (2000). *A professional professoriate: Unionization, bureaucratization, and the AAUP*. Nashville, TN: Vanderbilt University Press.

ICEF. (2014). *Summing up international student mobility in 2014*. ICEF Monitor. Retrieved from http://monitor.icef.com/2014/02/summing-up-international-student-mobility-in-2014/

Inderjeet. (2002). American Foundations and the Development of International Knowledge Networks. *Global Networks, 2*(1), 13–30.

INQAAHE. (2013). *Constitution*. Retrieved from http://www.inqaahe.org/main/about-inqaahe/constitution/constitution-html

INQAAHE. (2015). *INQAAHE 2015*. Retrieved from http://www.acbsp.org/page/inqaahe2015

International Labour Organization. (2011). *A skilled workforce for strong, sustainable and balanced growth: A G20 training strategy*. Geneva: International Labout Office.

Jacobson, H. K. (1990). Research on institutional advancement: A review of progress and a guide to literature. *The Review of Higher Education, 13*(4), 433–488.

Jacobson, H. K. (Ed.). (1978). *Evaluating advancement programs: New directions for institutional advancement*. San Francisco, CA: Jossey-Bass.

Jamal, Z. (2011). *Ten Years After 911*. Washington, DC: ISPU.

Jaschik, S. (2010, Oct. 15). Liberal arts, post-recession. *Inside Higher Ed (Online)*. Retrieved from https://www.insidehighered.com/news/2010/10/15/augustana

Compilation of References

Jaumont, F. (2014). *Strategic Philanthropy, Organizational Legitimacy, and the Development of Higher Education in Africa: The Partnership for Higher Education in Africa (2000-2010).* (Ph.D. dissertation). New York University.

Jeffrey, P., & Gerald, S. (2003). *The External Control of Organizations. A Resource Dependence Perspective.* Stanford, CA: Stanford University Press.

Jendreck, M., & Lynch, J. (2012). Student loans and alumni giving: Who repays the loan? *International Journal of Educational Advancement, 11*(1).

Johnson Grossnickle and Associates. (2013). *Million dollar ready assessing the institutional factors that lead to transformational gifts.* Indianapolis, IN: Indiana University-Purdue University Indianapolis (IUPUI) Lilly Family School of Philanthropy. Retrieved from http://www.philanthropy.iupui.edu/files/research/million_dollar_ready_executive_summary_booklet_low_res.pdf

Johnson, J. (2007a, August 16). *Making the connection: Metrics of success.* Presentation at the NACRO Annual Meeting, Minneapolis, MN. Retrieved from http://www.nacroonline.org/conference-presentations

Johnson, J. (2007b, August 16). *Making the connection: University-Industry relations and corporate relations models.* Presentation at the NACRO Annual Meeting, Minneapolis, MN. Retrieved from http://www.nacroonline.org/conference-presentations

Johnson, J. (2008, April 14-15). *Survey tools and implications: Measuring impact.* Presentation at the NACRO Annual Meeting, Atlanta, GA. Retrieved from http://www.nacroonline.org/conference-presentations

Johnson, W. C. (2003). University relations: The HP model. *Industry and Higher Education, 17*(6), 391–395. doi:10.5367/000000003322776280

Johnstone, D. B. (1998). *The financing and management of higher education: A status report on worldwide reforms.* The World Bank.

Jon, B. A., & Von Hippel, K. (2007). *Understanding Islamic Charities.* Washington, DC: CSIS Press.

Joseph, K. (2008). *Philanthropists & Foundation Globalization.* New Brunswick, NJ: Transaction Pub.

Jumpstart Our Business Startups (JOBS) Act. (2012, April 5). Retrieved May 15, 2015, from https://www.sec.gov/spotlight/jobs-act.shtml

Kapur, D., & Crowley, M. (2008). *Beyond the ABCs: Higher education and developing countries* (No. Working Paper Number 139). Washington, DC: Center for Global Development.

Katsinas, S. G., Tollefson, T. A., & Reamey, B. A. (2008). *Funding Issues in U.S. Community Colleges: Findings from a 2007 Survey of the National State Directors of Community Colleges.* Retrieved from http://www.aacc.nche.edu/Publications/Reports/Documents/fundingissues.pdf

Katz, S. N. (2012, March 25). Beware Big Donors. *The Chronicle of Higher Education*. Retrieved from http://chronicle.com/article/Big-Philanthropys-Role-in/131275/

Katz, D., & Kahn, R. L. (2005). Organizations and the system concept. In J. Shafritz, J. Ott, & Y. Jang (Eds.), *Classics of organization theory* (6th ed.; pp. 480–490). Boston, MA: Thomson Wadsworth.

Katz, M. (1975). *Class, bureaucracy, and schools: The illusion of educational change in America*. New York, NY: Praeger.

Kaufman, B. (2004). Juggling act: Today's college or university president must be a champion fundraiser and a strong internal leader. *University Business*, *7*(7), 50–52.

KAUST. (2015). *Our vision at KAUST*. Retrieved from http://www.kaust.edu.sa/vision.html

Keidan, C. (2014, October 23). Why philanthropy merits scholarly study. *Times Higher Education*. Retrieved October 20, 2014 from: http://www.timeshighereducation.co.uk/features/why-philanthropy-merits-scholarly-study/2016437.fullarticle

Keidan, C., Jung, T., & Pharoah, C. (2014). *Philanthropy education in the UK and continental Europe: Current provision, perceptions and opportunities*. London, UK: Centre for Charitable Giving and Philanthropy.

Kelly, K. S. (1991). *Fundraising and public relations: A critical analysis*. Hillsdale, NJ: Lawrence Erlbaum Associates.

Kelly, K. S. (2002). The state of fundraising theory and research. In *New strategies for educational fundraising* (pp. 39–55). New York, NY: Rowman & Littlefield Publishers.

Kerr, C. (2001). *The uses of the university*. Cambridge, MA: Harvard University Press.

Kezar, A. (2011). Understanding and facilitating Organizational change in the 21st century: Recent research and conceptualizations. *ASHE-ERIC Higher Education Report*, *28*.

Khaleej Times. (2014). *Dubai Investments signs deal with University of Balamand*. Retrieved from http://www.khaleejtimes.com/biz/inside.asp?xfile=/data/uaebusiness/2014/November/uaebusiness_November329.xml&section=uaebusiness

KHDA. (2013). *The higher education landscape in Dubai 2012*. Dubai: Knowledge and Human Development Authority.

Kiley, K. (2012, Nov. 19). Liberal arts colleges rethink their messaging in the face of criticism. *Inside Higher Ed (Online)*. Retrieved from: http://www.insidehighered.com///11/19/arts-colleges-rethink-their-messaging-face-criticism

Kinnicutt, S., & Pinney, C. (2010). Getting to the roots of success: The leadership competencies that grow corporate citizenship pros. *The Corporate Citizen*, *4*, 26–30.

Compilation of References

Kinnison, W. A., & Ferin, M. J. (1989). The three-party relationship. In J. W. Pocock (Ed.), *Fundraising Leadership: A Guide for Colleges and University Boards* (pp. 57–61). Washington, DC: Association of Governing Boards of Universities and Colleges.

Knight, J. (2008). The internationalization of higher education: Complexities and realities. In D. Teferra & J. Knight (Eds.), *Higher Education in Africa: The International Dimension.* Chestnut Hill, MA: Boston College Center for International Higher Education.

Kotler, P., & Murphy, P. E. (1981, September – October). Strategic planning for higher education. *The Journal of Higher Education, 52*(5), 470–489. doi:10.2307/1981836

Krotseng, M. V. & Ruch, C. (2013). *Promoting and Sustaining Change Through Collaboration and Consortia.* American Association of State Colleges and Universities.

Kuemmerle, W. (1999). The drivers of foreign direct investment into research and development: An empirical investigation. *Journal of International Business Studies, 30*(1), 1–24. doi:10.1057/palgrave.jibs.8490058

Lagemann, E. C. (2002). Toward a fourth philanthropic response: American philanthropy and its public. In *The perfect gift: The philanthropic imagination in poetry and prose* (p. 103). Bloomington, IN: Indiana University Press.

Larson, M. S. (1977). *The rise of professionalism.* Berkeley, CA: University of California Press.

Lavrusik, V. (2009, July 23). 10 Ways Universities are Engaging Alumni using Social Media. *Mashable.* Retrieved from http://mashable.com/2009/07/23/alumni-social-media/

Leaman, O. (1985). *An introduction to Classical Islamic Philosophy.* Cambridge, MA: Cambridge University Press.

Leslie, L. L., & Ramey, G. (1988). Donor Behavior and Voluntary Support for Higher Education Institutions. *The Journal of Higher Education, 59*(2), 117–132. doi:10.2307/1981689

Let's Get Ready. (2014). *Let's get ready to launch college success program.* Retrieved from: http://letsgetready.org/index.asp?page=17&press=139

Leukemia & Lymphoma Society. (n.d.). *Team in Training.* Retrieved from http://www.teamin-training.org/ March 14, 2015.

Levinthal, D. (2014). Inside the Koch brothers' campus crusade. Washington, DC: The Center for Public Integrity.

Levinthal, D. (2014, September 12). *Koch foundation proposal to college: Teach our curriculum, get millions.* Retrieved March 3, 2015, from http://www.publicintegrity.org/2014/09/12/15495/koch-foundation-proposal-college-teach-our-curriculum-get-millions

Levy, B. R. (2012). *Defining your leadership role in promoting ethical practice.* Presentation at the Association of Fundraising Professionals' 49th AFP International Conference on Fundraising, Vancouver, BC. Retrieved from http://conference.afpnet.org/

Lewis, G., et al. (2010). Accomplishments of the Partnership for Higher Education in Africa, 2000–2010. New York, NY: New York University.

Lilly Family School of Philanthropy. (2014, Dec. 3). *Significant growth in online giving seen on #GivingTuesday 2014, initial data from major donation processing platforms show*. Retrieved from http://www.philanthropy.iupui.edu/news/article/significant-growth-in-online-giving-seen-on-givingtuesday-2014-initial-data-from-major-donation-processing-platforms-show

Lim, T. L. (2010). *Measuring the value of corporate philanthropy: Social impact, business benefits, and investor returns*. New York: Committee Encouraging Corporate Philanthropy.

Lindahl, W. E. (2010). *Principles of Fundraising: Theory and Practice*. Sudbury, MA: Jones and Bartlett.

Linvill, D. L., McGee, S. E., & Hicks, L. K. (2012). Colleges' and universities'' use of Twitter: A content analysis. *Public Relations Review*, *38*(4), 636–638. doi:10.1016/j.pubrev.2012.05.010

Litan, R. E., & Mitchell, L. (2011). Should universities be agents of economic development? In C. J. Schramm (Ed.), *The future of the research university: Meeting the global challenges of the 21st century* (pp. 123–146). Kansas City, MO: The Ewing Marion Kauffman Foundation.

Locke, E. H. (1996, Fall). The foundations of a relationship. *Advancing Philanthropy,* 20-23.

Longfield, C. (2014). *The Blackbaud Index for Higher Education: Higher Education Fundraising Performance in 2013*. Blackbaud.

Lovejoy, K., Waters, R. D., & Saxton, G. D. (2012). Engaging stakeholders through Twitter: How nonprofit organizations are getting more out of 140 characters or less. *Public Relations Review*, *38*(2), 313–318. doi:10.1016/j.pubrev.2012.01.005

Lublin, J. S. (2011, December 3). Transparency Pays Off In 360-Degree Performance Reviews. *WSJ*. Retrieved from http://online.wsj.com/article/SB10001424052970203501304577086592075136080.html

Luomi, M. (2009). Abu-DFhabi's alternative-energy initiatives: Seizing climate-change opportunities. *Middle East Policy*, *16*(4), 102–117. doi:10.1111/j.1475-4967.2009.00418.x

Lynch, K. (2006). Neo-liberalism and marketization: The implications for higher education. *European Educational Research Journal*, *5*(1), 1–17. doi:10.2304/eerj.2006.5.1.1

M+R. (2014). *2014 M+R Benchmarks*. Available from http://www.mrbenchmarks.com

MacAllister, J. A. (1991). Why give? Notes to a new CEO. In J. P. Shannon (Ed.), *The corporate contributions handbook: Devoting private means to public needs* (pp. 121–125). San Francisco, CA: Jossey Bass.

MacIntyre, A. (1977). Epistemological Crises, Dramatic Narrative and the Philosophy of Science. *The Monist*, *60*(4), 453–472. doi:10.5840/monist197760427

Compilation of References

MacLaughlen, S. (2014). *Charitable Giving Report: How Nonprofit Fundraising Performed in 2013*. Blackbaud.

Mahani, S., & Milki, A. (2011). Internationalization of higher education: A reflection on success and failures among foreign universities in the United Arab Emirates. *Journal of International Education Research*, *7*(3), 1–8.

Mahmood & Mamadou (Eds.). (1994). *Academic Freedom in Africa*. Dakar: CODESRIA.

Mai, C. F. (1987). The feasibility study: Essential for a successful campaign. *Fund Raising Management*, *18*(10), 84. Retrieved from http://search.proquest.com/docview/195938458?accountid=11243 PMID:10284866

Mangan, K. (2015). *UAE incident raises questions for colleges that open campuses in restrictive countries*. The Chronicle of Higher Education. Retrieved from http://chronicle.com/article/UAE-Incident-Raises/228565/

Mangan, K. (2013). How Gates shapes state higher-education policy. *The Chronicle of Higher Education*, *19*(July). Retrieved from http://chronicle.com/article/How-Gates-Shapes-State/140303

March, J. G., & Cohen, M. (1974). *Leadership and ambiguity: The American college president*. New York, NY: McGraw-Hill.

March, J. G., Schulz, M., & Zhou, X. (2000). *The dynamics of rules: Change in written organizational codes*. Palo Alto, CA: Stanford University Press.

March, J. G., & Simon, H. A. (1958). *Organizations*. New York, NY: Wiley.

Marginson, S., & van der Wende, M. (2006). *Globalisation and higher education*. OECD. Retrieved from http://www.oecd.org/edu/research/37552729.pdf

Mark, D. (2002). *American Foundations: An Investigative History*. Cambridge, MA: MIT Press.

Marr, K. A., Mullin, C. H., & Siegfried, J. J. (2005). Undergraduate financial aid and subsequent alumni giving behavior. *The Quarterly Review of Economics and Finance*, *45*(1), 123–143. doi:10.1016/j.qref.2003.08.005

Martínez Alemán, A. M., & Wartman, K. L. (2009). *Online Social Networking on Campus: Understanding What Matters in Student Culture*. New York, NY: Routledge.

Maslen, G. (2012). *Worldwide student numbers forecast to double by 2025*. University World News. Retrieved from http://www.universityworldnews.com/article.php?story=20120216105739999

Maxwell, M. M. (2003). Individuals as donors. In E. R. Tempel (Ed.), *Hank Rosso's Achieving Excellence in Fund Raising* (pp. 161–176). San Francisco, CA: John Wiley & Sons.

McAlexander, J. H., & Koenig, H. F. (2012). Building communities of philanthropy in higher education: Contextual influences. *International Journal of Nonprofit and Voluntary Sector Marketing*, *17*(2), 122–131. doi:10.1002/nvsm.1415

McCoy, C. (2011). *Toward an understanding of causes and identified types of university-industry relations in U.S. public research universities.* (Unpublished master's thesis). Oklahoma State University, Oklahoma City, OK.

McCray, J. (2012). *Is grantmaking getting smarter? A national study of philanthropic practice.* Washington, DC: Grantmakers for Effective Organizations.

McDearmon, J. T. (2010). What's in it for me: A qualitative look into the mindset of young alumni non-donors. *International Journal of Educational Advancement, 10*(1), 33–47. doi:10.1057/ijea.2010.3

McGowan, D. (2012, August 1). *Academic corporate relations: Contact sport, slow waltz, or both?* Presentation at the NACRO Conference, Evanston, IL. Retrieved from http://www.nacroonline.org/conference-presentations

McIlnay, D. P. (1998). *How foundations work: What grantseekers need to know about the many faces of foundations.* San Francisco, CA: Jossey-Bass.

McKeown, M. P. (1996). State Funding Formulas: Promise Fulfilled? In D. S. Honeyman, J. L. Wattenbarger, & K. C. Westbrook (Eds.), *A Struggle to Survive: Funding Higher Education in the Next Century* (pp. 49–85). Thousand Oaks, CA: Corwin Press.

McLean, M. (2010). Citizens for an unknown future: Developing generic skills and capabilities in the Gulf context. *Learning and Teaching in Higher Education: Gulf Perspectives, 7*(2), 9–30.

McPherson, M. S., & Schapiro, M. O. (1999, Winter). The future economic challenges for the liberal arts colleges. *Daedalus, 128*(1), 47–75. Retrieved from http://www.jstor.org/stable/20027538 PMID:11645881

Mellahi, K., Guermat, C., Frynas, G., & Al Bortamani, H. (2003). *Motives for foreign direct investment in Gulf coopoeration countries: The case of Oman.* Presented at the ERF 10th Annual Conference, Marrakech, Morocco.

Merle, C., & Roderick, N. (1965). *Philanthropy in the Shaping of American Higher Education.* New Brunswick, NJ: Rutgers University Press.

Meyer, H., & Rowan, B. (1978). The structure of educational organizations. In M. Meyer (Ed.), Environments and organizations, (pp. 78-109). San Francisco, CA: Jossey Bass.

Meyer, J. W., & Scott, W. R. (1977). Institutionalized organizations: Formal structure as myth and ceremony. *American Journal of Sociology, 83*(2), 340–363. doi:10.1086/226550

Meyer, J. W., & Scott, W. R. (1983). *Organizational environments: Ritual and rationality.* Beverly Hills, CA: Sage Publications.

Michael, A. O. (2007). *Higher Education in Postcolonial Africa: Paradigms of Development, Decline, and Dilemmas.* Trenton, NJ: Africa World Press.

Compilation of References

Michael T. Miller, Faculty Governance Units and Their Leaders: A National Profile, The NEA 2002 Almanac of Higher Education 51, 52 . (2002). Available http://www.nea.org/assets/img/PubAlmanac/ALM_02_07.pdf

Miller, M. T. (1991). *The college president's role in fund raising.* (Unpublished thesis). University of Nebraska-Lincoln, Lincoln, NE.

Miller, K., & Bellamy, R. (2012). Fine Print, Restrictive Grants, and Academic Freedom. *Academe, 98*(3).

Miller-Millesen, J. L. (2003). Understanding the behavior of nonprofit boards of directors: A theory-based approach. *Nonprofit and Voluntary Sector Quarterly, 32*(4), 521–547. doi:10.1177/0899764003257463

Milliron, M. D., De los Santos, G. E., & Browning, B. (2003). Feels like the third wave: The rise of fundraising in the community college. *New Directions for Community Colleges, 2003*(124), 81–93. doi:10.1002/cc.137

Mina, W. (2014). United Arab Emirates FDI outlook. *World Economy, 37*(12), 1716–1730. doi:10.1111/twec.12169

Minor, J. T. (2003). Assessing the senate: Critical issues considered. *The American Behavioral Scientist, 46*(7), 960–977. doi:10.1177/0002764202250122

Minor, J. T. (2004). Understanding faculty senates: Moving from mystery to models. *Review of Higher Education, 27*(3), 343–363. doi:10.1353/rhe.2004.0004

Mittal, A. ((2006). Turning the tide: Challenging the Right on campus. Oakland, CA: The Institute for Democratic Education/Speak Out and The Oakland Institute.

Mixer, J. R. (1993). *Principles of professional fundraising: Useful foundations for successful practice.* San Francisco, CA: Jossey-Bass.

Moghadam, V. M. (2003). *Modernizing women: Gender and social change in the Middle East* (2nd ed.). Boulder, CO: Lynne Rienne Publishers, Inc.

Monks, J. (2003). Patterns of giving to one's alma mater among young graduates from selective institutions. *Economics of Education Review, 22*(2), 121–130. doi:10.1016/S0272-7757(02)00036-5

Moody, M., & Payton, R. (2008). *Understanding Philanthropy: Meaning and Mission.* Indianapolis, IN: Indiana University Press.

Morgan, G. (2006). *Images of organization.* Thousand Oaks, CA: Sage.

Morrill Act of 1862. (n.d.). Retrieved May 20, 2015, from http://www.ourdocuments.gov/doc.php?flash=true&doc=33

Mortenson, T. (2004, January). State Tax Fund Appropriations for Higher Education FY1961 to FY2004). *Postsecondary Education Opportunity* (no. 139). Oskalossa, IA: Mortenson Research Seminar on Public Policy Analysis of Opportunity for Post-Secondary Education. Retrieved from http://www.postsecondary.org/last12/139TAXFY04.pdf

Mulhere, K. (2014, November 4). Students want Koch, corporate influence off campus. *Inside-HigherEd*. Retrieved from https://www.insidehighered.com/news/2014/11/04/students-want-koch-corporate-influence-campus

Murphy, R. D., Jr., & Salehi-Isfahani, D. (2003). *Labor market flexibility and investment in human capital*. Presented at the ERF 10th Annual Conference, Marrakech, Morocco.

Murphy, J. (1976). *Carnegie Corporation and Africa, 1953-1973*. New York, NY: Teachers College Press.

Murphy, M. (2010). *An Energized Future*. Delta Sky Magazine.

Network of Academic Corporate Relations Officers (NACRO). (2015). Retrieved from http://www.nacroonline.org

North Dakota Implement Dealers Association. (2010) *Economic Impact of North Dakota's Retail Farm Equipment Dealers*. Paper presented at the North Dakota Implemented Dealers Association, Bismarck, ND.

Norton, M. (2009). *The worldwide fundraiser's handbook: A resource for mobilisation guide for NHOS and community organisations*. London: Directory of Social Change.

Nour, S. S. O. M. (2014). *Overview of knowledge transfer in MENA countries - The case of Egypt (No. #2014-017)*. Maastricht, The Netherlands: United Nations University.

O'Meara, K. (2007). Striving for what? Exploring the pursuit of prestige. Higher Education: Handbook of Theory and Research, 22, 121–179.

OECD. (2012). *OECD Week 2012*. Retrieved from http://www.oecd.org/social/family/50423364.pdf

Ogden, T. N., & Starita, L. (2009). *Social Networking and Mid-size Non-profits: What's the Use?* Philanthropy Action.

Onyeiwu, S. (2003). *Analysis of FDI flows to developing countries: Is the MENA region different?*. Presented at the ERF 10th Annual Conference, Marrakech, Morocco.

Onyeiwu, S. (2000). Foreign direct investment, capital outlflows, and economic development in the Arab World. *Journal of Development and Economic Policies*, 2(2), 27–57.

Oplatka, I., & Hemsley-Brown, J. (2010). The globalization and marketization of higher education: Some insights from the standpoint of institutional theory. In F. Maringe & N. Foskett (Eds.), *Globalization and Internationalization in Higher Education* (pp. 65–80). New York, NY: Continuum International Publishing Group.

350

Compilation of References

Orr, D. W. (1999). Education for globalization (modern Western education system). *The Ecologist, 29*(3), 166.

Osei-Kofi, N. (2010). Coercion, possibility, or context? questioning the role of private foundations in american higher education. *Discourse (Abingdon), 31*(1), 17–28. doi:10.1080/01596300903465393

Paradise, A. (2015). *Results from the 2014 CASE Survey of Community College Foundations* [White paper]. Retrieved May 19, 2015, Council for Advancement and Support of Education: http://www.case.org/Documents/WhitePapers/CCF_Survey2014.pdf

Parker, S. (2010). *Lessons from a Ten-Year Funder Collaborative. A Case Study of the Partnership for Higher Education in Africa.* Clear Thinking Communication.

Paschyn, C. M. (2013). *Women in the Gulf: Better educated but less employed.* Al-Fanar Media. Retrieved from http://www.al-fanarmedia.org/2013/10/women-in-the-gulf-better-educated-but-less-employed/

Pătruţ, B., Pătruţ, M., & Cmeciu, C. (2013). *Social Media and the New Academic Environment: Pedagogical Challenges* (pp. 1–511). Hershey, PA: IGI Global; doi:10.4018/978-1-4666-2851-9

Pătruţ, M., & Pătruţ, B. (2013). *Social Media in Higher Education: Teaching in Web 2.0* (pp. 1–474). Hershey, PA: IGI Global; doi:10.4018/978-1-4666-2970-7

Payton, R. L. (1988). *Philanthropy: Voluntary action for the public good.* New York, NY: American Council on Education/Macmillan Series on Higher Edu.

Perry, M., Field, K., & Supiano, B. (2013). The Gates effect. *The Chronicle of Higher Education, 19*(July). Retrieved from http://chronicle.com/article/The-Gates-Effect/140323

Pfeffer, J. (1972). Size and composition of corporate board of directors. *Administrative Science Quarterly, 21*, 218–228. doi:10.2307/2393956

Pfeffer, J. (1987). A resource dependence perspective on interorganizational relations. In M. S. Mizruchi & M. Schwartz (Eds.), *Intercorporate relations: The structural analysis of Business* (pp. 22–55). Cambridge, UK: Cambridge University Press.

Pfeffer, J., & Salancik, G. R. (1978). *The external control of organizations: A resource dependence perspective.* New York, NY: Harper & Row.

Philip, C. S. (2012, August 1-3). *Corning and university technology collaborations.* Presentation at the NACRO Conference, Evanston, IL. Retrieved from http://www.nacroonline.org/conference-presentations

Pierpont, R., & Wilkerson, G. S. (1998). Campaign goals: Taking aim at a moving target. *New directions for Philanthropic Fundraising, 1998*(21), 61-80.

Pinney, C. (2012). *Increasing impact, enhancing value: A practitioner's guide to leading corporate philanthropy.* Council on Foundations. Retrieved from http://www.cof.org/sites/default/files/documents/files/CorporateGuide.pdf

Pinney, C., & Kinnicutt, S. (2010). *Leadership competencies for community involvement: Getting to the roots of success*. Boston, MA: The Boston College Center for Corporate Citizenship.

Pollack, R. H. (1998). Give and take: Create a mutually beneficial relationship to bring corporate support to your campus. *Currents, 24*(2), 16–22.

Pollard, J. A. (1958). *Fund-raising for higher education*. New York, NY: Harper & Brothers, Publishers.

Powell, W., & DiMaggio, P. (1991). *The New Institutionalism in Organizational Analysis*. Chicago, IL: Univ. of Chicago Press.

Preliminary Report of the Campaign Standards Working Group. (n.d.). Retrieved 2 March 2015, from www.case.org/samples_research_and_tools/case_reporting_standards_and_management_guidelines/faq_rsmg/preliminary_report.html

Prewitt, K., Mattei, D., Steven, H., & Stefan, T. (Eds.). (2006). *The Legitimacy of Philanthropic Foundations: United States and European Perspectives*. New York, NY: Russell Sage Foundation Publications.

Prince, R. A., & File, K. M. (2001). *The seven faces of philanthropy: A new approach to cultivating donors*. San Francisco, CA: Jossey-Bass.

Proper, E., & Caboni, T. C. (2014). *Institutional advancement: What we know*. New York, NY: Palgrave Macmillan. doi:10.1057/9781137374288

Pulley, J. L. (2002, November). Occidental denies quid pro quo on gift. *The Chronicle of Higher Education, 49*(12), A.33. Retrieved fromhttp://proxygw.wrlc.org/login?url=http://search.ebscohost.com/login.aspx?direct=true&db=aph&AN=2608146&site=ehost-live

Quinterno, J., & Orozco, V. (2012). *The great cost shift: How higher education cuts undermine the future middle class*. New York, NY: Demos.

RacesOnline.com. (n.d.). *True Blue 5K*. Retrieved from http://trueblue5k.racesonline.com/ on March 14, 2015.

Radcliffe, S. (2011). *A study of alumni engagement and its relationship to giving behaviors*. Retrieved May 20, 2015, from http://digitalcommons.bucknell.edu/masters_theses/2/

Raines, J. P., & Leathers, C. G. (2003). *The economic institutions of higher education: Economic theories of university behavior*. Cheltenham, UK: E. Elgar.

Rasmussen, D. (2011, May 6). Opinion Columnist. *Florida Today*. Retrieved from http://www.floridatoday.com/article/CD/20110508/OPINION05/105080315/David-Rasmussen-Philanthropy-academic-freedom-can-co-exist?odyssey=mod_sectionstories

Rasmussen, D. W. (2011, May 8). David Rasmussen: Philanthropy, academic freedom can co-exist. *Tallahassee Democrat*.

Compilation of References

Raven, J. (2011). Emiratizing the education sector in the UAE: Contextualization and challenges. *Education. Business and Society: Contemporary Middle Eastern Issues*, 4(2), 134–141. doi:10.1108/17537981111143864

Ray, B. (2007). Reconnecting Education & Foundations, Turning Good Intentions into Educational Capital. Stanford, CA: Carnegie Foundation for the Advancement of Teaching.

Ray, B. (2008, January 1). Florida State receives major gifts for studies in free enterprise, ethics. *Florida State University News*. Retrieved March 3, 2015, from https://fsu.edu/news/2008/11/10/bbt.gift/

RCSI. (n.d.). *RCSI Bahrain*. Retrieved from https://www.rcsi.ie/rcsi_bahrain

Reichart, J. (1999). *Corporate ethics and environmental values: Issues, perceptions, and the logic of stakeholder action.* (Unpublished dissertation). University of Virginia, Richmond, VA.

Reuben, R. (2008). *The use of social media in higher education for marketing and communications: A guide for professionals in higher education.* Academic Press.

Reuters. (2014). *Dubai Investments plans investments in education, healthcare.* Gulf Business. Retrieved from http://gulfbusiness.com/2014/10/dubai-investments-plans-investments-education-healthcare/

Rhodes, F. H. T. (2001). *The creation of the future: The role of the American university.* Ithaca, NY: Cornell University.

Riesman, D. (1956). *Constraint and variety in American education.* Lincoln, NE: University of Nebraska Press.

Ringleb, A. H., Meiners, R. E., & Edwards, F. L. (1997). *Managing in the legal environment* (3rd ed.). St. Paul, MN: West Publishing Company.

Ring, P. S., & Van de Ven, A. H. (1994). Developmental processes of cooperative interorganizational relationships. *Academy of Management Review*, 19(1), 90–118.

Risa, L. (2007). Faculty in the Corporate University: Professional Identity, Law and Collective Action, 16 Cornell J. L. & Pub. *Pol'y*, 263, 306–310.

Rivard, R. (2015, January 29). Market up, spending up. *Inside Higher Ed (Online).* Retrieved from: https://www.insidehighered.com/news/2015/01/29/endowment-funds-grew-donors-and-investments-came-through

Robbins, S., & Stylianou, A. C. (2003). Global corporate web sites: An empirical investigation of content and design. *Information & Management*, 40(3), 205–212. doi:10.1016/S0378-7206(02)00002-2

Roelofs, J. (2003). *Foundations and public policy: The mask of pluralism.* Albany, NY: State University of New York Press.

Roelofs, J. (2007). Foundations and Collaboration. *Critical Sociology*, *33*(3), 479–504. doi:10.1163/156916307X188997

Romano, J. (2014, April 19). Column: Some fear Charles Koch's influence damages FSU's integrity. *Tampa Bay Times*. Retrieved from http://www.tampabay.com/news/education/college/some-fear-charles-kochs-influence-damages-fsu-integrity/2175919

Romano, J. C., Gallagher, G., & Shugart, S. C. (2010). More than an Open Door: Deploying Philanthropy to Student Access and Success in American Community Colleges. *New Directions for Student Services*, *2010*(130), 55–70. doi:10.1002/ss.360

Rose, A. P. (2011). *Giving by the numbers 2011*. New York, NY: Committee Encouraging Corporate Philanthropy.

Rosenbaum, T. E. (1989). *Rockefeller Philanthropies in Revolutionary Russia*. Rockefeller Archive Center Newsletter.

Rossi, P. H., Lipsey, M. W., & Freeman, H. E. (2004). *Evaluation: A systematic approach* (7th ed.). Thousand Oaks, CA: Sage.

Rowland, A. W. (1983). Research in institutional advancement: A selected, annotated compendium of doctoral dissertations. Washington, DC: Council for the Advancement and Support of Education (CASE).

Rowland, A. W. (1986). *Handbook of institutional advancement: A modern guide to executive management, institutional relations, fundraising, alumni administration, government relations, publications, periodicals, and enrollment management*. San Francisco, CA: Jossey Bass.

Rubenstein, D. (2004). *The good corporate citizen: A practical guide*. Hoboken, NJ: Wiley.

Rupp, R. (2009). Higher education in the Middle East: Opportunities and challenges for U.S. universities and Middle East partners. *Global Media Journal*, *8*(14).

Safi, O. (2003). *Progressive Muslims: On Justice, Gender and Pluralism*. One World Press.

Saiia, D. H. (2001). Philanthropy and corporate citizenship: Strategic philanthropy is good corporate citizenship. *Journal of Corporate Citizenship*, *2*(2), 57–74. doi:10.9774/GLEAF.4700.2001.su.00009

Salama, S. (2013). *Emiratisation quotas won't work, warns academic*. Gulf News. Retrieved from http://gulfnews.com/business/sectors/employment/emiratisation-quotas-won-t-work-warns-academic-1.1262779

Sanzone, C. S. (2000). Securing corporate support: The business of corporate relations. In P. Buchanan (Ed.), Handbook of institutional advancement (vol. 3, pp. 321-324). Washington, DC: CASE.

Compilation of References

Sanzone, C. S. (2000). Securing corporate support: The business of corporate relations. In P. Buchanan (Ed.), *Handbook of Institutional Advancement* (3rd ed.; pp. 321–324). Washington, DC: CASE.

Saul, J. (2011). *The end of fundraising: Raise more money selling your impact.* San Francisco, CA: Jossey-Bass.

Sawahel, W. (2015a). *More cross-border campuses in the Arab states.* University World News. Retrieved from http://www.universityworldnews.com/article.php?story=20150320011437374

Sawahel, W. (2015b). *Universities urged to develop links with industry.* University World News. Retrieved from http://www.universityworldnews.com/article.php?story=20150326160428148

Saxton, G. D., & Guo, C. (2014). Online stakeholder targeting and the acquisition of social media capital. *International Journal of Nonprofit and Voluntary Sector Marketing*, *19*(4), 286–300. doi:10.1002/nvsm.1504

Saxton, G., & Wang, L. (2013). The social network effect: The determinants of giving through social media. *Nonprofit and Voluntary Sector Quarterly*, *43*(5), 850–868. doi:10.1177/0899764013485159

Schaefer, G., & Hersey, L. N. (2015forthcoming). Enhancing Organizational Capacity and Strategic Planning Through the Use of Social Media. In H. Asencio & R. Sun (Eds.), *Cases on Strategic Social Media Utilization.* Hershey, PA: IGI Global.

Schein, E. H. (1985). *Organizational culture and leadership.* San Francisco, CA: Jossey-Bass.

Schervish, P. G., & Havens, J. J. (1998). Embarking on a republic of benevolence: New survey findings on charitable giving. *Nonprofit and Voluntary Sector Quarterly*, *27*(2), 237–242. doi:10.1177/0899764098272007

Schofer, E., & Meyer, J. W. (2005). The worldwide expansion of higher education in the twentieth century. *American Sociological Review*, *70*(6), 898–920. doi:10.1177/000312240507000602

Schulman, D. (2014). *Sons of Wichita: How the Koch brothers became America's most powerful and private dynasty.* Academic Press.

Schultz, T. P. (1997). Asssessing the productive benefits of nutrition and health: An integrated human capital approach. *Journal of Econometrics*, *77*(1), 141–158. doi:10.1016/S0304-4076(96)01810-6

Scott, W. R. (1987). *Organizations: Rational, natural and open systems.* Hoboken, NJ: Prentice-Hall, Inc.

Scott, W. R. (1995). Introduction: Institutional theory and organization. In W. R. Scott & S. Christnesne (Eds.), *The Institutional Construction of Organizations.* Thousand Oaks, CA: Sage.

Scott, W. R. (2001). *Institutions and organizations.* Thousand Oaks, CA: Sage.

Sears, J. B. (1922). *Philanthropy in the history of American higher education.* Washington, DC: Government Printing Office.

Sears, J. B. (1990). *Philanthropy in the History of American Higher Education*. New Brunswick, NJ: Transaction Publishers.

Shafritz, J. M., Ott, J. S., & Jang, Y. S. (2005). *Classics of organization theory* (6th ed.). Boston, MA: Thomson Wadsworth.

Sheldon, K. S. (2000). *Successful corporate fundraising: Effective strategies for today's non-profits*. New York, NY: Wiley & Sons.

Shimoni, B. (2008). *The new philanthropy in Israel: Ethnography of major donors (No. Article 2)*. Jerusalem: The Hebrew University of Jerusalem.

Shirazi, F., Gholami, R., & Higon, D. A. (2009). The impact of information and communication technology (ICT), education and regulation on economic freedom in Islamic Middle Eastern countries. *Information & Management, 46*(8), 436–433. doi:10.1016/j.im.2009.08.003

Shuaa Capital. (2008). *Vision 2008: UAE equity markets*. Retrieved from http://www.arabruleo-flaw.org/compendium/Files/UAE/104.pdf

Siddiqui, S. (2014). *Navigating Identity through Philanthropy: A History of ISNA*. Diss.

Siegel, D. (2007). Constructive engagement with the corporation. *Academe, 93*(6), 52–55.

Siegel, D. (2008). Framing involvement: Rationale construction in an inter-organizational collaboration. *Journal of Further and Higher Education, 32*(3), 221–240. doi:10.1080/03098770802220413

Siegel, D. (2012). Beyond the academic-corporate divide. *Academe, 98*(1), 29–31.

Sievers, B. (2011). Civil Society, Philanthropy and the Fate of the Commons. Boston: Tufts University Press.

Signs of Hope for State Funding. (2014, November 20). *Community College Daily-American Association of Community College*. Retrieved from http://www.ccdaily.com/Pages/Campus-Issues/Signs-of-hope-for-state-funding.aspx

Silverman, F. (2004). *Collegiality and service for tenure and beyond acquiring a reputation as a team player*. Westport, CT: Praeger.

Singer, A. (2008). Charity in Islamic Societies. Cambridge, MA: Cambridge University Press.

Sirsly, C.-A. T. (2009). 75 years of lessons learned: Chief executive officer values and corporate social responsibility. *Journal of Management, 15*(1), 78–94.

Slinker, J. M. (1988). *The role of college or university presidents in institutional advancement*. (Unpublished doctoral dissertation). Northern Arizona University, Flagstaff, AZ.

Slover-Linett, C., & Stoner, M. (2012). *Social media and Advancement: Insights from Three Years of Data*. The Council for Advancement and Support of Education.

Compilation of References

Smith, P. R. G. (1968). *The history of corporate financial assistance to member institutions of the associated colleges of Indiana 1948-1967.* (Unpublished doctoral dissertation). University of Notre Dame, Notre Dame, IN.

Smith, A. (2012). *Real time charitable giving.* Washington, DC: Pew Internet & American Life Project.

Soma, H., & Darwin, S. (2005). *Globalization, Philanthropy & Civil Society.* New York, NY: Springer.

Speck, B. W. (2010). The Growing Role of Private Giving in Financing the Modern University. *New Directions for Higher Education,* 8–16.

Sperling, J. M., Marcati, C., & Rennie, M. (2014). *GCC women in leadership: From the first to the norm.* McKinsey & Company.

Sporn, B. (1999). *Adaptive university structures: An analysis of adaptation to socioeconomic environments of U.S. and European higher education.* London, UK: Jessica Kingsley.

Stafford, L. (2008). Social Exchange Theories. In L. A. Baxter (Ed.), *Engaging theories in interpersonal communication: Multiple perspectives* (pp. 377–389). Thousand Oaks, CA: Sage Publications. doi:10.4135/9781483329529.n28

Steck, H. (2003). Corporatization of the University: Seeking Conceptual Clarity. *The Annals of the American Academy of Political and Social Science, 585*(1), 66–83. doi:10.1177/0002716202238567

Steer, L., Ghanem, H., & Jalbout, M. (2014). *Arab youth: Missing educational foundations for a productive life?* Washington, DC: Center for Universal Education at Brookings.

Stevens, R. E., Loudon, D. L., Oosting, K. W., Migliore, R. H., & Hunt, C. M. (2013). *Strategic planning for private higher education.* Routledge.

Stimpert, J. (2004, July). Turbulent times: Four issues facing liberal arts colleges. *Change, 36*(4), 42-49. Retrieved from http://proxygw.wrlc.org/login?url=http://search.ebscohost.com/login.asp x?direct=true&db=aph&AN=13866921&site=ehost-live

Strauss, L. (2001, December). *Trends in Community College Financing: Challenges of the Past, Present, and Future.* Retrieved from ERIC database. (ED467983)

Strauss, V. (2014, March 28). *The Koch brothers' influence on college campus is spreading.* Retrieved June 10, 2015, from http://www.washingtonpost.com/blogs/answer-sheet/wp/2014/03/28/the-koch-brothers-influence-on-college-campus-is-spreading/

StudentAdvisor.com. (n.d.). *Top 100 social media colleges.* Retrieved from http://www.studentadvisor.com/top-100-social-media-colleges

Sturgis, R. (2006). Presidential leadership in institutional advancement: From the perspective of the president and the vice president of institutional advancement. *International Journal of Higher Educational Advancement, 6*(3), 221–231. doi:10.1057/palgrave.ijea.2150019

Suchman, M. C. (1995). Managing legitimacy: Strategic and institutional approaches. *Academy of Management Review*, *20*, 571–610.

Sulek, M. (2010). On the Classical Meaning of Philanthôpía. *Nonprofit and Voluntary Sector Quarterly*, *39*(3), 385–408. doi:10.1177/0899764009333050

Sun, X., Hoffman, S., & Grady, M. (2007). A multivariate causal model of alumni giving: Implications for alumni fundraisers. *International Journal of Educational Advancement*, *7*(4), 307–332. doi:10.1057/palgrave.ijea.2150073

Tamuno, C. (1986). *The Roles of the Rockefeller Foundation, Ford Foundation and Carnegie Corporation in the Development of the University of Ibadan 1962-1978*. (Ph.D. dissertation). The University of Pittsburgh.

Tarawneh, E. (2011). Assessing and understanding quality in the Arab region. In T. Townsend & J. MacBeath (Eds.), *International Handbook of Leadership for Learning* (Vol. 2, pp. 1107–1124). New York: Springer. doi:10.1007/978-94-007-1350-5_60

Teferra, D. (2008). The internationalization of dimensions of higher education in Africa: Status, challenges and prospects. In D. Teferra & J. Knight (Eds.), *Higher Education in Africa: The International Dimension*. Chestnut Hill, MA: Boston College Center for International Higher Education.

Tempel, E. R., Seiler, T. L., & Adrich, E. E. (2010). *Achieving excellence in fundraising*. San Francisco, CA: Jossey-Bass.

Terlaak, A. (2007). Order without law? The role of certified management standards in shaping socially desired firm behaviors. *Academy of Management Review*, *32*(3), 968–985. doi:10.5465/AMR.2007.25275685

Terry, N., & Macy, A. (2007). Determinants of alumni giving rates. *Journal of Economics & Economic Education Research*, *8*(3), 3–17.

Texas Christian University. (2014). *#TCUGivesDay*. Retrieved from http://tcugivesday.tcu.edu/

Thacker, S., & Cuadra, E. (2014). *The road traveled: Dubai's journey towards improving private education*. Washington, DC: The World Bank.

The American University in Cairo. (2012a). *AUC holds second annual conference on Arab giving and civic participation*. Retrieved from http://www.aucegypt.edu/news/Pages/NewsRelease.aspx?rid=294

The American University in Cairo. (2012b). *The chronicles 2012*. Cairo: The American University in Cairo. Retrieved from http://www.aucegypt.edu/research/ebhrc/publications/Documents/Chronicles2012/2012_chronicles_final-version.pdf

The Center on Philanthropy at Indiana University (COP). (2007). *Corporate philanthropy: The age of integration*. Indianapolis, IN: Indiana University. Retrieved from http://www.philanthropy.iupui.edu/ files/research/corporate_giving_-_july_2007.pdf

Compilation of References

The Cultural Division of the Embassy of the United Arab Emirates. (2011). *Education in UAE: K-12 education.* Retrieved from http://uaecd.org/k-12-education

The History of Crowdfunding. (n.d.). Retrieved 2 March 2015, from https://www.fundable.com/crowdfunding101/history-of-crowdfunding

The National. (2013). *Room to improve private universities in the UAE.* Retrieved from http://www.thenational.ae/thenationalconversation/editorial/room-to-improve-private-universities-in-the-uae

The World Bank. (1999). *Education in the Middle East and North Africa: A strategy towards learning for development.* Human Development Network.

The World Bank. (2015). *Middle East and North Africa.* Retrieved from http://www.worldbank.org/en/region/mena

Thelin, J. (2011). *A History of American Higher Education.* Baltimore, MD: The Johns Hopkins Press.

Thelin, J. R. (2004). *A history of American higher education.* Baltimore, MD: The Johns Hopkins University Press.

Thelin, J. R., & Trollinger, R. W. (2013). *Philanthropy and American Higher Education.* New York, NY: Palgrave Macmillan.

Thelin, J. R., & Trollinger, R. W. (2014). *Philanthropy and American higher education.* New York, NY: Palgrave Macmillan. doi:10.1057/9781137318589

Thompson, J. D. (1967). *Organizations in action.* New York, NY: McGraw-Hill.

Thompson, J. D. (2005). Organizations in action. In J. Shafritz, J. Ott, & Y. Jang (Eds.), *Classics of organization theory* (6th ed.; pp. 491–504). Boston, MA: Thomson Wadsworth.

Thorpe, D., & Sampson, R. (n.d.). *Crowdfunding for social good: Financing your mark on the world.* Academic Press.

Tierney, W. G. (1988, January – February). Organizational culture in higher education: Defining the essentials. *The Journal of Higher Education, 59*(1), 2–21. doi:10.2307/1981868

Tierney, W. G. (2008). *The impact of culture on organizational decision making: Theory and practice in higher education* (1st ed.). Sterling, VA: Stylus.

Tilak, J. B. G. (2005). *Private higher education: Philanthropy to profits.* Barcelona: Global University Network for Innovation and Palgrave Macmillan.

Tiyambe, Z. P., & Olukoshi, A. (2004). *African Universities in the Twenty-First Century* (Vol. 2). Dakar: Council for the Development of Social Science Research in Africa.

Tolbert, P. S. (1985). Institutional environments and resource dependence: Sources of administrative structure in institutions of higher education. *Administrative Science Quarterly, 30*(1), 1–13. doi:10.2307/2392808

Tolbert, P. S., & Hall, R. H. (2008). *Organizations: Structures, processes and outcomes*. New York, NY: Pearson.

Tournès, L. (2002). La diplomatie culturelle de la fondation Ford, Vingtième Siècle. *Revue d'histoire*, *4*(76), 65–77.

Trenwith, C. (2013). *Emiratisation failing to cut UAE jobless rate - Al Mulla*. ArabianBusiness. com. Retrieved from http://www.arabianbusiness.com/emiratisation-failing-cut-uae-jobless-rate-al-mulla-526191.html

Tromble, W. W. (1998). Corporate and foundation relations. In W. W. Tromble (Ed.), *Excellence in advancement: Applications for higher education and nonprofit organizations* (pp. 93–118). Gaithersburg, MD: Aspen Publishers.

Tromble, W. W. (1998). *Excellence in advancement: Applications for higher education and nonprofit organizations*. Gaithersburg, MD: Aspen Publishing.

Twale, D. J., & Luca, B. M. (2008). *Faculty incivility: The rise of the academic bully culture and what to do about it*. San Francisco, CA: Jossey-Bass.

U.S. Department of Education. (2012). *National Center for Education Statistics, Education Directory, Colleges and Universities, 1949-50 through 1965-66; Higher Education General Information Survey (HEGIS), "Institutional Characteristics of Colleges and Universities" surveys, 1966-67 through 1985-86; Integrated Postsecondary Education Data System (IPEDS), "Institutional Characteristics Survey"(IPEDS-IC:86-99); and IPEDS Fall 2000 through Fall 2011, Institutional Characteristics component*. Retrieved from http://nces.ed.gov/programs/digest/d12/tables/dt12_306.asp

UNESCO. (2010). *Towards an Arab higher education space: International challenges and societal responsibilities* (B. Lamine, Ed.). Cairo: UNESCO.

UNICEF. (2013). *At a glance: State of Palestine*. Retrieved from http://www.unicef.org/infoby-country/oPt_statistics.html

United States Department of Labor. (2010). *Trade Adjustment Assistance Community College Career Training Program Summary*. Retrieved from http://www.doleta.gov/taaccct/

University of Memphis Alumni Association. (2014). *Young Alumni*. Retrieved from http://memphis.edu/alumni/youngalumni/index.php# on

University-Industry Demonstration Project (UIDP). (2015). Retrieved from http://sites.nationalacademies.org/pga/uidp/index.htm

Varghese, N. V. (2009). *Globalization, economic crisis and national strategies for higher education development*. Paris: International Institute for Educational Planning.

Villalonga, B., & McGahan, A. M. (2005). The choice among acquisitions, alliances, and divestitures. *Strategic Management Journal*, *26*(13), 1183–1208. doi:10.1002/smj.493

Compilation of References

Walton, A., & Gasman, M. (Eds.). (2008). *Philanthropy, volunteerism, and fundraising*. Upper Saddle River, NJ: Pearson.

Wam. (2014). *UAE more attractive for higher education institutions than China, Singapore*. Emirates 24|7. Retrieved from http://www.emirates247.com/uae-more-attractive-for-higher-education-institutions-than-china-singapore-2014-09-19-1.563512

Wastyn, M. L. (2009). Why alumni don't give: A qualitative study of what motivates non-donors to higher education. *International Journal of Educational Advancement*, 9(2), 96–108. doi:10.1057/ijea.2009.31

Waters, R. D., Burnett, E., Lamm, A., & Lucas, J. (2009). Engaging stakeholders through social networking: How nonprofit organizations are using Facebook. *Public Relations Review*, 35(2), 102–106. doi:10.1016/j.pubrev.2009.01.006

Weerts, D. J., & Ronca, J. M. (2006, November/December). Examining Differences in State Support for Higher Education: A Comparative Study of State Appropriations for Research I Universities. *The Journal of Higher Education*, 77(6), 935–967. doi:10.1353/jhe.2006.0054

Weick, K. E. (1976). Educational organizations as loosely coupled systems. *Administrative Science Quarterly*, 21(1), 1–19. doi:10.2307/2391875

Weidner, D. J. (2008). Fundraising tips for deans with intermediate development programs. *University of Toledo Law Review. University of Toledo. College of Law*, 39(2), 393–398.

Weinstein, S. (2009). *The complete guide to fundraising management*. San Francisco, CA: Wiley. doi:10 1002/9781118387061

Weiss, C. H. (1982, November – December). Policy research in the context of diffuse decision making. *The Journal of Higher Education*, 53(6), 619–639. doi:10.2307/1981522

Weitz, E., & Shenhav, Y. (2000). A longitudinal analysis of technical and organizational uncertainty in management theory. *Organization Studies*, 21(1), 243–265. doi:10.1177/0170840600211005

Whitaker, B. (1974). *The Philanthropoids. Foundations and Society*. New York, NY: Morrow.

Wilen-Daugenti, T. (2009). *Edu: Technology and learning environments in higher education*. New York, NY: Peter Lang Publishing, Inc.

Wilkens, K. (2011). *Higher education reform in the Arab world*. Washington, DC: Saban Center at Brookings.

World Economic Forum. (2002). *Global corporate citizenship initiative: The leadership challenge for CEOs and boards*. Retrieved from http://www.weforum.org/pdf/GCCI/GCCI_CEO_Questionnaire.pdf

Worth, M. J. (1993). Educational fundraising: Principles and practice. Washington, DC: American Council on Education (ACE).

Worth, M. J. (2002). *New strategies for educational fundraising*. New York, NY: Rowman & Littlefield Publishers.

Worth, M. J. (2002). *New strategies for educational fund-raising*. Portland, OR: Book News.

Worth, M. J., & Smith, N. J. (1993). Raising Funds for Community Colleges. In M. J. Worth (Ed.), *Educational Fund Raising: Principles and Practice* (pp. 347–356). Phoenix, AZ: American Council on Education and the Oryx Press.

Wuthnow, R. (2004). *Saving America? Faith based services and the future of Civil Society*. Princeton, NJ: Princeton University Press.

Wymer, W., & Grau, S. L. (2011). *Connected Causes: Online Marketing Strategies for Nonprofit Organization*. Chicago: Lyceum Books, Inc.

Yale University & Columbia University. (2005). *2005 Environmental Sustainability Index: Benchmarking national environmental stewardship*. Yale Center for Environmental Law and Policy; Center for International Earth Science Information Network at Columbia University.

Yesufu, T. M. (Ed.). (1970s). *Creating the African University: Emerging Issues of the*. Ibadan: Oxford University Press.

Yin, R. K. (2008). *Case study research: Design and methods* (4th ed.). London, UK: Sage Publications.

Youn, T. I. K., & Murphy, P. B. (1997). *Organizational studies in higher education*. New York, NY: Garland Publishing, Inc.

Youn, T. I. K., & Price, T. M.Ted I. K. Youn; Tanya M. Price. (2009). Learning from the experience of others: The evolution of faculty tenure and promotion rules in comprehensive institutions. *The Journal of Higher Education, 80*(2), 204–237. doi:10.1353/jhe.0.0041

Yukl, G. A. (2012). *Leadership in organizations*. New York, NY: Prentice Hall.

Zaman, M. (2002). *The Ulama in Contemporary Islam*. Princeton, NJ: Princeton University Press.

Zawya. (2015). *UAE*. Retrieved from https://www.zawya.com/middle-east/countries/uae/

Zayed University. (2013). *Zayed University self-study report*. Retrieved from http://www.zu.ac.ae/main/files/contents/assessment_resource/Accreditation/MSCHE_Self-Study_2013.pdf

Zinser, R. (2003, Winter). Evaluation of a Community College Technical Program by Local Industry. *Journal of Industrial Teacher Education, 40*, 1–8. Retrieved from http://scholar.lib.vt.edu/ejournals/JITE/v40n2/zinser.html

Zunz, O. (2014). *Philanthropy in America: A history*. Princeton, NJ: Princeton University Press. doi:10.1515/9781400850242

About the Contributors

Henry C. Alphin Jr., MBA, MS, has been a part of the Drexel University community for over 12 years. Currently, he is an Administrator / Business Analyst in Drexel's Office of Information Resources and Technology (IRT), a Research Affiliate of Drexel University, and a member of the International Virtual Environments Research Group (iVERG). Mr. Alphin's academic research focuses on the intersection of philosophy, economics, and higher education. Mr. Alphin holds a Bachelor of Science in Economics from Drexel's Bennett S. LeBow College of Business, a Master of Science in Higher Education (MSHE) Research and Administration from Drexel's School of Education, and a Master of Business Administration (MBA) from the triple accredited (including AACSB) program at the Warwick Business School of Warwick University.

Jennie Lavine is currently a Business Lecturer at a Higher Education College in Abu Dhabi. She has a Bachelor of Science (Hons) in Finance, an MBA from Warwick University in the UK and is currently pursuing a PhD at Hull University in the UK. Jennie's research interests include Higher Education alongside Culture and Organizational Behavior in an international setting.

Stormy Stark is a doctoral candidate at Penn State University with a research focus on rural education in the mountain communities of Virginia. She holds a Masters degree in Higher Education Administration from Drexel University. Stormy has over 15 years of experience in the higher education sector and has spent a significant portion of her career in the classroom. In addition to her rural research Stormy is passionate about finding positive, equitable, and ethical ways to deploy technology in the education sector and exploring ethical ways to approach the school violence problems in the United States.

Adam Hocker is a doctoral candidate at The Pennsylvania State University in Educational Leadership. Adam holds a Masters' Degree in Curriculum and Instruction from Bloomsburg University in Pennsylvania where he also earned a Bachelor's of Arts degree in History and a minor in Political Science. Prior to attending Penn State, Adam taught in a private high school in Camp Hill, Pennsylvania for four years. Adam is also academically interested in technology leadership, leadership decision making, and ethics in leadership.

* * *

Larry Catá Backer was educted at Columbia University School of Law (JD 1982), Harvard University, JF Kennedy School of Government (MPP 1979) and Brandeis University (BA summa cum laude with honors in history 1977). Currently he is Professor of Law at Pennsylvania State University, Dickinson School of Law (since 2000). Formerly he was Professor of Law and Executive Director at the Comparative and International Law Center at University of Tulsa College of Law (1991-2000). He has also held a visiting appointment at University of California Hastings College of the Law (1998), as well as teaching at various Law Schools in Europe and Latin America. Professor Larry Backer researches globalization, especially as it relates to the emergence of ways of understanding constitutional and enterprise law. His most recent work touches on the regulation of multinational corporations, sovereign wealth funds, transnational constitutionalism, and the convergence of public and private law. He researches issues of governments as private actors in global markets, the development of law and social norm systems to regulate business and human rights.

Roy Y. Chan is a Ph.D. candidate in the Department of Educational Leadership and Policy Studies at Indiana University Bloomington, School of Education with a doctoral minor in Philanthropic Studies at Indiana University-Purdue University Indianapolis, Lilly Family School of Philanthropy. Roy holds a Master of Arts (M.A.) degree in Higher Education Administration from Boston College and a Master of Education (M.Ed.) degree in Higher Education Policy from the University of Hong Kong. His current research interest focuses on the economic and non-economic benefits of a bachelor's degree, the globalization and internationalization of higher education, and the role of philanthropy and fundraising in shaping U.S. public higher education. Roy is co-author of the book, Higher Education: A Worldwide Inventory of Research Centers, Academic Programs, Journals and Publications, 2014. Outside of academia, Roy serves as Director of the University of Hong Kong (HKU) Alumni Association of New England (HKUAANE), and is an active member of CASE, Philanthropy Roundtable, and the Chancellor's Club at the University of California, Irvine.

Morgan Clevenger, having worked more than two decades in fundraising and philanthropy in higher education, understands the importance of all facets in a

364

development office, quality programs, academic standards and teaching method-ologies, networking, and research. He has held various fundraising, administra-tive, teaching, and marketing positions, and is currently an Assistant Professor of Entrepreneurship at Wilkes University, and was nominated as Outstanding New Faculty in 2015. He researchers, writes, and presents widely on issues of corporate citizenship, philanthropy, higher education, nonprofit management, ethics, and en-trepreneurship. He attained a BS in journalism in 1991 and an MBA in 1996, both from West Virginia University. He achieved Certified Fundraising Executive (CFRE) status in 1997 recognizing his tenure, success, and professionalism in fundraising, marketing, and public relations. In 2014 he completed an EdD from the University of Missouri-Columbia, and his dissertation—*An Organizational Analysis of the Inter-organizational Relationships Between A Public American Higher Education University and Six United States Corporate Supporter: An Instrumental, Ethnographic Case Study Using Cone's Corporate Citizenship Spectrum*—was nominated for 10 awards across multiple disciplines.

Lauren E. B. Dodge is a Ph.D. candidate in Higher Education Administration in the department of Education Policy, Organization, and Leadership at the University of Illinois at Urbana-Champaign. Her research interests are in philanthropic behavior and fundraiser performance and evaluation. She is a strategic, thoughtful, outcomes-focused leader with training in information science and program evaluation.

Nabih Haddad is a current doctoral student in the Higher, Adult, and Lifelong Education (HALE) program at Michigan State University's College of Education. His research relates to governance and policy, globalization of higher education, and philanthropy and higher education. Nabih holds a bachelor's degree in Political Science, with a minor in Psychology from Wayne state University. He earned his master's degree in International Affairs from the School of International Affairs at The Pennsylvania State University.

Leigh Hersey joined the faculty of the Division of Public and Nonprofit Admin-istration in August 2009.She brings more than a dozen years of nonprofit fundraising experience, including four years with Arizona State University. In her last fundrais-ing position, she initiated the Twitter account that celebrated the organization's 10 year anniversary. She continues building on her experience through her research on philanthropy. In addition to working there, Dr. Hersey received her PhD in Public Administration from Arizona State University with a graduate certificate in Nonprofit Leadership & Management. Her fundraising experience provides the foundation for her continuing research in philanthropy.

Rick Jakeman's research and scholarly interests focus on college student experiences, including graduate student socialization and undergraduate student alcohol and other drug use. Specifically, his research focuses on socialization of graduate students while in academic environments, including elasticity of peer relationships, student perceptions of diversity and inclusion in the curriculum, and implications for faculty practice. He also studies undergraduate student experiences in campus parties and drinking, problem behaviors with alcohol and other drugs, and peer intervention and training as an institutional policy response. He has authored articles for the Journal of Student Affairs Research and Practice, Journal of Continuing Higher Education, Inside Higher Ed, and Online Classroom. Dr. Jakeman has seven years of professional experience in the field of student affairs, having worked in the fields of leadership development, service learning, academic advising, and residence life.

Fabrice Jaumont serves as Program Officer for the FACE Foundation in New York, and as Education Attaché for the Embassy of France to the United States. With a Ph.D. in International Education from New York University's Steinhardt School of Education, Culture and Human Development, his research finds itself at the intersection of comparative and international education, international development, cultural diplomacy, and philanthropy. His doctoral research focused on the role of U.S. private foundations in the development of higher education in Africa. His primary area of research is international development education; he came to it and continues to complement his work with his extensive expertise in heritage language education, community development, and access to knowledge for all. His involvement with various linguistic communities in North America and Europe has led him to publish several articles and book chapters on the topics of language maintenance and education development at all levels.

Sabith Khan is a Ph.D Candidate at Virginia Tech researching American Muslim philanthropy.

Cynthia J. MacGregor, EdD, is a professor in the Counseling, Leadership, and Special Education department at Missouri State University and serves as the site coordinator for the regional portion of a statewide EdD program in educational leadership offered through the University of Missouri. She earned Bachelor of Science and Master's degrees in psychology from Central Missouri State University, and her doctorate in educational leadership from the University of Missouri. Her professional employment has included Drury University, Burrell Mental Health Center, Missouri State University, and the University of Missouri in a variety of faculty, mental health, and student support roles. Her background in psychology and adult education brings a non-native perspective to the challenges of PK-20 education. Her unique vantage point, combined with her pragmatic worldview, allows her to see vexing problems within education and propose novel and systemic solutions.

Cathleen Ruch, Ed.D., is currently on staff at Lake Region State College-Dakota Precision Ag Center, as the Grants and Operations Administrator. She comes with experience with grants and administration at the System level, where she was the Grant Developer at the North Dakota University System.

Andrew Shafer brings diversity from the field into this publication with experience in non-profit management and higher education advancement. Starting his career with the Juvenile Diabetes Research Foundation, Shafer then moved into work in higher education. His positions have been at the University of Tennessee, Knoxville and at Purdue University in both Alumni Relations and Development. Currently, he serves as Vice President for Advancement at Aquinas College in Nashville, TN. In his current role, Shafer is re-building the institution's entire advancement operation to include alumni relations, development, advancement services, marketing, and communications. Putting this expertise together into a package that can be meaningful and helpful to students of all backgrounds is his passion. Impacting the power of philanthropy is his goal. Shafer also serves as Adjunct Faculty with The School of Professional Studies and The Heyman Center for Philanthropy at New York University and for the School of Business and Nonprofit Management at North Park University, Chicago. Shafer earned both his Bachelor of Arts in Communications and his Masters in Public Administration from the University of Tennessee, Knoxville.

Wayne Webster currently serves as Vice President for Development and Alumni Relations at the University of Northern Colorado. Prior to this appointment, he was Vice President for Advancement at Ripon College during a five-year $68 Million campaign. He previously served as the Director of Major Gifts and Interim Director of Planned Giving at Gettysburg College in Gettysburg, PA. Prior to his tenure at Gettysburg, Wayne worked in the development office at Doane College in Crete, NE. Wayne earned a Doctor of Education degree at The George Washington University in Washington, DC. He has a Bachelor of Arts degree in public administration and political science as well as a Master of Arts degree in management, both from Doane College. He also earned a Certificate in Fund Raising Management at The Center on Philanthropy at Indiana University. Wayne has also contributed to five articles in Successful Fund Raising and The Major Gift Report publications and recently served on the faculty of a CASE conference focused on successful campaigns. He has also presented at CASE District II and District V conferences.

Index

Become an IRMA Member

Members of the **Information Resources Management Association (IRMA)** understand the importance of community within their field of study. The Information Resources Management Association is an ideal venue through which professionals, students, and academicians can convene and share the latest industry innovations and scholarly research that is changing the field of information science and technology. Become a member today and enjoy the benefits of membership as well as the opportunity to collaborate and network with fellow experts in the field.

IRMA Membership Benefits:

- **One FREE Journal Subscription**
- **30% Off Additional Journal Subscriptions**
- **20% Off Book Purchases**
- Updates on the latest events and research on Information Resources Management through the IRMA-L listserv.
- Updates on new open access and downloadable content added to Research IRM.
- A copy of the Information Technology Management Newsletter twice a year.
- A certificate of membership.

IRMA Membership $195

Scan code to visit irma-international.org and begin by selecting your free journal subscription.

Membership is good for one full year.

Printed in the United States
By Bookmasters